Anglo-Irish Identities, 1571–1845

Anglo-Irish Identities, 1571–1845

Edited by
David A. Valone
and Jill Marie Bradbury

Lewisburg
Bucknell University Press

Associated University Presses
2010 Eastpark Boulevard
Cranbury, NJ 08512

The paper used in this publication meets the requirements of the American National Standard for Permanence of Paper for Printed Library Materials Z39.48–1984.

Library of Congress Cataloging-in-Publication Data

Anglo-Irish identities 1571/1845 / edited by David A. Valone and Jill Marie Bradbury.
p. cm.
This book originated from a NEH Summer Seminar hosted by the University of Notre Dame in the summer of 2003. Includes bibliographical references and index.
ISBN 978-0-8387-5713-0 (alk. paper)
1. National characteristics, Irish. 2. British—Ireland—History. 3. Ireland—Civilization. 4. Group identity—Great Britain. I. Valone, David A. II. Bradbury, Jill Marie, 1971- III. University of Notre Dame. IV. Title.

DA925.A55 2008
305.821'04150903—dc22
2008001996

PRINTED IN THE UNITED STATES OF AMERICA

Contents

Acknowledgments

In the course of a collaborative effort such as this, many debts are incurred both great and small. This book originated from a NEH Summer Seminar hosted by the University of Notre Dame in the summer of 2003. Chris Fox, the Director of the Keough-Naughton Institute for Irish Studies at Notre Dame, deserves credit for assembling a diverse and congenial group of scholars for that seminar, and also for being a gracious host. He also lined up an impressive list of lecturers who enriched our experience, including Claire Connolly, Ciaran Brady, Peter McQuillan, Carol Fabricant, James G. Buickerood, Joseph McMinn, Jim Smyth, and Margaret Ann Doody. The staff of the Hesburgh Library and particularly the Department of Rare Books and Manuscripts at Notre Dame provided outstanding service to all of the members of the seminar throughout our stay. We also would like to acknowledge all the members of the original seminar for their insights during the seminar: Eric Binnie, John Wrynn, Aimable Twagilimana, Chris Nagle, Virginia La Grand, Jack Healy, Evan Davis, Margaret Mc Peake, Terry J. Campbell, David H. Radcliffe, Jim Persoon, Julie M. Dugger, Mary O'Connor, Jill Bradbury, and David Valone. We would particularly like to single out Julie Dugger and Mary O'Connor; although their contributions to the seminar are not visible in this book, they greatly enriched both the social and intellectual experience during our time in South Bend. Their greater presence in this volume is sorely missed.

Editorial and administrative support was provided at Quinnipiac University by Betsy Delaney, Roberta Manganella, Rosa Nieves, Chelsea LaManna, and Emily Weed. Kathy Cooke provided much needed moral support and guidance throughout the entire process. Greg Clingham at Bucknell University Press showed unfailing interest in the project even as it stretched out over several years, and an anonymous reviewer provided detailed and insightful criticisms on each essay. The staff at Associated University Presses provided excellent service in moving the book through the final publication process.

For financial support of this venture, we would like to thank the National Endowment for the Humanities and the College of Liberal Arts at Quinnipiac University. For permission to cite material from their holdings, we would like to thank the Board of Trinity College Library. Selections from the John Herschel letters are reproduced by kind permission of the President and Council of the Royal Society of London.

Anglo-Irish Identities, 1571–1845

Introduction

Jill Marie Bradbury and David A. Valone

THE 1800 ACT OF UNION CREATED THE GEOPOLITICAL ENTITY OF THE United Kingdom of Great Britain and Ireland, but its social and cultural formation began centuries earlier and continued long after. As historians associated with the "New British History" have shown, the construction of Britain was preceded by long and complex negotiations between England, Ireland, Scotland, and, to a lesser extent, Wales. Intense struggles occurred at political, social, and cultural levels as different groups sought to define their place in a rapidly changing power structure. In Ireland, the process was complicated by the existence of the Anglo-Irish, a large population who viewed themselves primarily as English, but wrestled with its legal, economic, and social subordination to England. *Anglo-Irish Identities, 1571–1845* explores how the shifting relations between England and Ireland, and between the social subsets within Ireland, shaped the self-conceptions of this populace.

While the English presence in Ireland dates to the twelfth century, Anglicization was essentially contained to the area around Dublin until the seventeenth century. Outside of the Pale, the traditional politics and culture of the *tuath* continued to dominate Irish society. It was only after the rebellions and routs of the Gaelic lords, culminating in Hugh O'Neill's defeat at Kinsale in 1601 and the Flight of the Earls in 1607, that the English in Ireland began to control the realm in significant ways. The next two centuries brought political and social domination by the Anglo-Irish until the Act of Union initiated the demise of "Ascendancy" power by demolishing the established structures of Irish governance. The failure of the Union to unify the disparate groups of Irish society gave further impetus to separatist organizations, leading to the development of nationalist movements and identities by the mid-nineteenth century. But during the roughly two and a half centuries from the Flight of the Earls in 1607 to emergence of the Young Irelanders, questions of *Anglo*-Irish identity dominated public discourse. Who exactly were the Anglo-Irish? What was their relation to the English? To the Gaelic natives and culture? How were internal differences of religion, class, ethnicity, nationality, and residency to be aligned?

The formation of British identity in the seventeenth and eighteenth centuries has been the subject of considerable scholarship since the studies of J. G. A. Pocock and Benedict Anderson. But Ireland, by and large, has been a secondary concern in this work. Indeed, Linda Colley's *Britons: Forging the Nation 1707–1837* goes so far as to exclude Ireland from her purview, citing its ambiguous position within the political model of composite monarchy that guides her project. In other studies, Anglo-Irish identity is seen as part of a larger picture of which Scotland, Wales, and the North American colonies are also important components.[1] Among the several excellent works devoted to the topic of Ireland's position within the nascent British empire, religion and politics have dominated the discussion. Thus while S. J. Connolly's *Religion, Law, and Power: the Making of Protestant Ireland* comprehensively surveys the terrain of the seventeenth- and eighteenth-century society, his analysis is primarily concerned with political and ecclesiastical tensions and affiliations within the Protestant community.[2] Other studies of the Anglo-Irish constituency have also focused on the interaction of religious identity and political affiliation.[3] These factors are of undeniable importance in the seventeenth and eighteenth centuries, but the emphasis of recent scholarship on them has led to the neglect of other influences. *Anglo-Irish Identities, 1571–1845* seeks to correct this imbalance by integrating social, cultural, economic, and literary topics into the discussion.

For newcomers to the field, what seems to be a straightforward set of identifications rapidly collapses. "Anglo-Irish" refers variously to Irish literature written in English and to people of English descent living in Ireland. The term is of modern vintage; in the seventeenth and eighteenth century, the Anglo-Irish most commonly styled themselves "the English in Ireland." Outside of Ireland, though, they were simply "the Irish" regardless of descent. In the late eighteenth century, "Protestant Ascendancy" came into use and gradually supplanted earlier designations.[4] As a number of scholars have shown, "Anglo-Irish" is a categorization that subsumes ethnic, religious, and social complexities dating back to the twelfth-century conquest of Ireland.[5] While Anglo-Irish society was diverse to begin with, intermarriage, child-rearing practices, economic relations, religious conversion, sectarian dissension, and political exigency further undermined clear distinctions between its component groups. Moreover, the social ranks were more flexible and permeable than in other European societies,[6] with the result that self-definition and self-representation were protean and strategic, even opportunistic. As Colin Kidd has remarked, "identities were often appropriated, one group stealing the ethnic clothes of another" to endow ideological claims with historical authority.[7] To examine Anglo-Irish identity is, then, to consider the multitude of ways in which individuals and blocs of select individuals aligned with or opposed themselves to other groups in the face of changing social, political, and cultural conditions.

Of the myriad social factors shaping the self-perceptions of the Anglo-Irish, religion was undoubtedly one of the most important and intricate, and much scholarship has focused on explicating its complexities. Throughout the history of Christianity in Ireland, the mantle of religion has draped somewhat awkwardly over the cultural and political body of the island. The Christianization of pagan Ireland was relatively rapid and complete, but the resulting Gaelic style of Christianity never fully meshed with the Catholic Church at Rome. Consequently, the Norman assault on Ireland in the twelfth century was sanctioned by the Roman pontiff on religious grounds. This invasion resulted in Ireland becoming a lordship of the English crown and began the process of English settlement. The Old English were the descendants of these settlers, but over the next several centuries they largely assimilated into native Irish society and culture.[8] This "Hibernicization" was viewed negatively by the English, especially after these Old English failed to follow the crown into the Church of England. As part of Henry VIII's drive to reassert English control during the 1530s, Protestant English began settling in Ireland.[9] The seventeenth century saw a rapid increase in the "New English" population in Ireland, from less than 2 percent in 1600 to 27 percent in the early 1700s.[10] But affiliations among the Protestant settler population were complicated by the extensive migration of Scottish Presbyterians into Ulster.[11] As Nicholas Canny suggests, English officials were quick to exploit the threat posed to the Established Church of Ireland by the Scots, which led to decreasing toleration of dissent.[12] In addition to sectarian challenges, internal division beset denominational identity. In the early modern era, Catholicism in Ireland was riven by Franciscan and Jesuit influences while, as Tony Claydon and Ian McBride suggest, "the protestant community's sense of the true church as something mystical rather than human, its appeal to foreigners; its easy adoption of the divisive rhetoric of anti-popery in internal disputes; and its suspicion of attempts to impose conformity as popish persecution" complicated the unifying thrust of Protestantism in the eighteenth century.[13] Claydon and McBride's comments were made with Britain in mind, but can be said to apply to Ireland as well. Religious affiliation shaped Anglo-Irish national identity in important, but not unilateral ways.

Sectarian and denominational differences frequently took on political and ethnic overtones. Identity was a card that both the Old and New English played in obtaining power and favor from the English government. Prior to the English civil wars, the Old English frequently represented themselves as true subjects faithful to the Tudor and Stuart lines and accused the more recent settlers of profiting from plantations at the expense of the Crown. The New English countered these claims in part by painting the Old English as opportunists "who gave lip service to English law, cynically exploiting it to strengthen their already excessive authority over their traditional followers."[14] Writers such as Edmund Spenser exploited the commonality of religion between the Old English and the Gaelic Irish to link Catholicism and barbarism, tainting the Old English claims of loyalty. Tensions between the two groups were exacerbated by the patronage of monarchs from Elizabeth I on, who granted favors to shore up their position in England and abroad. Charles I, in particular, manipulated the political aspects of religious conflict between Old and New English settlers to his benefit when he offered Catholics the "Graces" in exchange for a large subsidy to fund the war with Spain.[15]

The conflicts between Catholic and Protestant came to a crisis during the struggle between crown and parliament in England. In 1641, the Gaelic Irish gentry of Ulster instigated an attack on Protestant settlers in the region. Modern estimates put the death toll at two thousand to four thousand, but contemporaries believed as many as ten thousand Protestants were killed during the initial attack.[16] The uprising soon spread beyond Ulster, uniting Old English and Gaelic Irish in support of a Catholic monarchy and pitting both against the Protestant New English and Scots Dissenters. In 1642, clergy and leaders of the revolt met to formalize their alliance as the Confederate Catholics and to draft a call for religious freedom, restoration and preservation of land titles, and loyalty to the king. The Confederate Catholics sought to unify the disparate components of their alliance under the banner "*pro Deo, pro rege, pro patria Hibernia unanmimis*."[17] The imprisonment and execution of Charles I reunited Catholics and Protestants behind the Marquis of Ormond in support of the monarch, but the royalist front was eventually defeated by Oliver Cromwell's army in 1649. With Cromwell, power was firmly restored to the Protestants. Partly in response to demands for retribution for the 1641 massacre, the interregnum parliament enacted legislation removing native Irish and Old English rebels to the western province of Connaught.

These sanctions led to an almost complete dispossession of the Catholic population. Ownership of land dropped from an estimated 59 percent in 1641 to under 10 percent in 1660, although the 1662 Act of Settlement allowed many to reclaim their holdings by demonstrating that they had not participated in the rebellion, bringing the percentage of land owned by Catholics to around 20 percent by 1688.[18] Despite this reversal, many innocent Catholics were swept up in the wave of reprisals and faced with the impossible choice of exile, transplantation, or menial service on their former estates. The final blow to Catholic hopes for dominance in social, economic, and political power came in 1690, when William defeated James II at the Battle of the Boyne.[19] The end of the seventeenth century saw a dramatic intensification of anti-Catholic legislation. Beginning in 1695, a series of acts were passed that sought to limit the concessions made by the Treaty of Limerick.[20] The popery laws, as these acts became known, severely restricted both Catholics and dissenters in many areas including access to education and professional opportunities, ownership and lease of land, and inheritances. The laws also provided for "discovery," by which Protestants could claim Catholic property if any of it was managed or disposed of in violation of the penal laws.

The extent to which the penal laws worsened the socioeconomic situation of Catholics has been a subject of much debate. To take one example, historical records suggest that discovery resulted in a further dispossession of Catholic landowners. But as Kevin Whelan and others have shown, the legal process was just as likely to be used to evade the penal laws. Similarly, strategic conversions produced a "convert interest in parliament which was sympathetic to Catholic claims."[21] But though modern historians disagree about the impact of the Ascendancy on the various classes of Catholic society, one indisputable effect was to sharpen resentment of persecution and animosity toward the ruling minority. Catholics from all socioeconomic levels were united in a political and legal, as well as religious identity. When the laws began to be repealed in the 1770s and 1780s, such associations fractured once again as landowners saw the advantages of aligning with a government that was recognizing Catholic property rights.[22]

Throughout Irish history, religion and politics have been intertwined to such an extent that it is difficult to separate their contributions to Anglo-Irish identities. As such, political considerations have received equal focus as ecclesiastical influences in recent scholarship. Contention over specific policies pursued in Ireland by the English government distinctly marked the self-perceptions of the Anglo-Irish. During the seventeenth and eighteenth centuries, debates about the constitutional relationship between

England and Ireland alienated many from a larger sense of English or British identity. After Henry II's arrival in 1171, Ireland became a lordship of the English crown. A lord deputy, appointed by the king, governed the country along with the Irish Parliament. From its first meeting in 1274, the Irish Parliament grew in power until, in 1460, it pronounced Ireland "corporate of itself." As a result, a number of reforms were instituted by the crown and the Irish lord deputies, such as Poynings' Law, the establishment of a privy council, and other measures designed to exert more control over the governance of Ireland. After his 'reconquest' in the 1530s, Henry VIII pushed major constitutional change through the Irish Parliament by having himself declared king of Ireland in 1541. The 1689 Bill of Rights reaffirmed Ireland's subordinate legal status by declaring William and Mary the sovereign rulers of Great Britain and Ireland.

Parliamentary redefinition of Ireland's status had long-lasting repercussions for how the Irish viewed themselves in relation to the English. Prior to the sixteenth century, the Old English assumed a degree of autonomy from England. While professing their loyalty to the crown, they made recourse to constitutional arguments to represent themselves as independent of outside control whenever English legislation threatened their economic interests. In the seventeenth century, Catholics such as Patrick Darcy and Hugh O'Reilly used constitutional issues to encourage an early form of nationalism. O'Reilly's *Ireland's Case Briefly Stated* argued that Irish people from all ethnic and religious background shared a history of oppression by the English.[23] This argument was overshadowed by William Molyneux's *The Case of Ireland's Being Bound by Acts of Parliament in England Stated*, which articulated a Protestant version of constitutional nationalism. Drawing on earlier works, Molyneux integrated natural rights philosophy and ancient constitutionalism with the commonwealth tradition to argue that Ireland was a sister kingdom, rather than a subordinate colony. The publication of Molyneux's treatise, along with similar claims for parliamentary autonomy by William King, archbishop of Dublin, provoked disdain and ire from the English. From their point of view, the Irish Parliament had ratified its subordinate status to English government in 1541 and 1689, and had accepted the authority and intervention of the English Parliament on numerous other occasions. Far from being an equal, Ireland had been conquered twice over and the policy of plantation pursued throughout the sixteenth century had clearly situated it as a colony. The Irish people were not entitled to the same rights and prerogatives because they were not English, despite their claims to the contrary.

From the late seventeenth century on, debates about Ireland's constitutional relation to England increasingly dominated both public discourse and Anglo-Irish self-representation. After the 1707 union of Scotland and England, these questions took on even more importance. Wounded pride at being excluded from the new "Britain," concern over the economic policies pursued by the British government, and resentment over English, rather than Anglo-Irish, appointments to key positions in the Irish government led to increasing agitation for parliamentary reform. Other issues of concern for "patriot" writers included the repeal of restrictive trade legislation, such as the Cattle and Woolen acts. These demands for free trade and legislative independence were circumscribed, though, by a continuing affiliation with Britain. As Jim Smyth remarks, "The closeness of settler identification with the 'mother country' is worth underlining, not least because in the headlong pursuit of the 'ideological origins' of protestant nationalism it is perhaps too easily lost sight of; more so because it set limits to the aspiration to legislative 'independence'—separatism was not envisaged—and helps to explain the seeming ambivalence of their constitutional posturing."[24] Seen from another perspective, the Anglo-Irish could not afford to break from England, for they depended on its cultural superiority, military might, and economic stimulus. The Protestant elite were unwilling to give up its identification with freeborn Englishmen, but opinions differed on whether to ground this assertion on parliamentary union or sovereignty.

The outpouring of literature on the subject in the eighteenth century by Jonathan Swift, George Berkeley, and other lesser-known "patriots" appealed to a unified "Irish" nation, an alliance of social, economic, and religious interests, to resist oppression by Britain and assert Ireland's rightful status with respect to, or within, the British Parliament. Swift's *Drapier's Letters* are perhaps the most well-known texts in this tradition, but Swift does not represent the majority voice in either tone or principles. Works by Samuel Madden, John Trenchard, and Berkeley suggest both the more dominant line of thought and the diversity of perspectives associated with constitutional nationalism.[25] Each of these writers appealed to a shared sense of community; and this language of an "inclusive" Irish identity, though perhaps not envisioned as extending to all members of the populace equally, was a significant touchstone for the development of Irish nationalism in the late eighteenth century. Perhaps even more importantly, the agitation for free trade and legislative independence produced victories in the later part of the eighteenth century. In 1779, rioting in Dublin helped Henry Grattan persuade the Irish Parliament to pass a short money bill and to vote for free trade with Britain. The ongoing war with the American colonies created a favorable climate for Irish demands, and the British government granted this concession. In 1782, Grattan followed with a

Declaration of legislative independence that led to the repeal of both Poynings' Law and the Declaratory Act subordinating the Irish Parliament to the British. The success of the Anglo-Irish in winning equality in trading rights and a greater measure of legislative autonomy from Britain fostered a stronger sense of Irish political identity.

And yet, the eighteenth century culminated in union with, rather than independence from, Great Britain. The Anglo-Irish failed to capitalize on the accomplishments of the 1780s for a variety of reasons, including the inability of their leaders to foster this nascent national identity. Initially, the American and French revolutions inspired movements dedicated to political independence. Many observers in Ireland and America drew parallels between the two. As Neil York remarks, "the American colonies served as a rallying cry among disgruntled Irishmen, inside Parliament and out."[26] Francis Dobbs attributed Grattan's success in securing the 1782 Declaration of Independence to the American political crisis, musing "it was on the plains of America that Ireland obtained her freedom."[27] While both Protestants and Catholics took up the ideals of republicanism, the latter stood to gain particularly from new configurations of political affiliation opened up by the French Revolution. As Kevin Whelan suggests, the rebellion of a predominantly Catholic population against a Catholic monarch indicated a willingness to break from the direction and influence of Rome. Irish Catholics could argue that their religious identification need not direct their political allegiances.[28]

Perhaps the most significant contribution of the American and French revolutions to Irish political identities was the formation of the United Irishmen in 1791. Initially grounded in commonwealth principles of limited monarchical rule, equal rights for all men, and religious toleration, the United Irish philosophy quickly mutated into radical republicanism. The militancy of the United Irishmen had predecessors in the agrarian conflicts of the 1760s. Price inflation and other disruptions in local grain and lease markets following the repeal of the Cattle Acts led to rural unrest and the formation of secret societies, which used violence and intimidation to prevent enclosure, protest taxes, and influence landlord-tenant relations. These secret societies, which included the Whiteboys, the Oakboys, and the Steelboys, represented regional responses to local grievances. Another wave of agrarian violence occurred in the 1770s, prompting the emergence of Protestant organizations such as the Peep o'Day Boys (later renamed the Orange Order). Ulster Catholics formed the Defenders in response and this movement spread across the country. The principles of Defenderism eventually included a broad range of emancipation measures, such as Catholic right to bear arms, thus integrating the traditional concerns of agrarian secret societies (taxes, rents, prices, and landlord-tenant relations) with revolutionary ideals.

Along with Defenderism, the Volunteer movement was an important precursor of radical republicanism. The Volunteers were established in Ulster in the late 1780s as an independent militia to supplement an Irish army depleted by the American war. Composed of respectable and middle-class members of Irish society, the organization primarily served purposes other than actual defense of the Irish nation. In R. F. Foster's words, "Volunteering was a great psychological affirmation: of citizenship, of 'patriotism', of exclusive identity."[29] Initially a government-supported Protestant militia with a loyalist bent, the Volunteers quickly became affiliated with political reform movements. In 1783, when leaders of the Volunteer movement met to draft a detailed plan for parliamentary reform, the issue of Catholic emancipation provoked a split within the organization. Fundamentally, the language and platform of the Volunteers assumed the continuance of Protestant political and social dominance. Theobald Wolfe Tone, James Napper Tandy, and Thomas Russell, who supported the full inclusion of Catholics into the Irish nation, founded the United Irishmen as an offshoot of the Volunteers. In his resolutions for the society, Tone declared that parliamentary reform would be neither "practicable, efficacious, or just, which does not include Irishmen of every religious persuasion." With this bold call for the equal treatment of "all sects and denominations of Irishmen" in political, legal, and social structures, Tone and the United Irishmen articulated the most inclusive sense of national identity up to that point.[30]

Among more conservative segments of the Protestant population, the Catholic emancipation movement produced widespread anxiety about the growing threat to Anglo-Irish structures of power. The association and collaboration of United Irish and Defender organizers was further cause for concern, and contributed to growing tensions between parliamentary and civil officials, and reform leaders. These fears were confirmed in 1793, with the passage of a Catholic Relief Act granting the right to vote to male property holders and repealing many of the remaining penal laws. The act was pushed through the Irish Parliament by British influence, leaving the Protestant community feeling betrayed and besieged. The British government's heavy-handed approach ultimately backfired, as David Dickson has noted, since the act depended on the willingness of Protestant gentry and corporations to grant life-leases to Catholic tenants, open guilds to Catholic members, and accept Catholics as jurors.[31] The Relief Act thus failed to bring real emancipation or to redistribute social and political power, and this led to further resentment and disillusionment among Catholics.

By 1795, the prevailing mood was that of dissatisfaction with the ruling parties and representatives of the British government, along with a dose of Protestant anxiety about the political future of the status quo. A cycle of skirmishes between Defenders, United Irishmen, Orangemen, among others, and military forces led to government repression, which in turn fostered increasing separatism and militancy within these organizations. Many of the measures taken by the government were drastic: taking oaths of allegiance to secret societies became a capital crime; radical leaders were harassed and their houses burnt; presses were destroyed and newspapers suppressed. In 1793 and 1794, numerous Defender and United Irish leaders were arrested and executed or exiled. Forced underground, the United Irishmen plotted a rebellion with French support. After fleeing the country, Tone returned to lead an invasion attempt at Bantry Bay in 1796. But stalled by bad weather, the rebels never touched ground. In 1797, the government declared martial law and began seizing guns from the Irish population. Attempts at insurrection in 1798 were weakened by this disarmament and by the arrest of Defender and United Irish leaders a month before the planned attacks. As a result, Marianne Elliott notes, "The rebellion was not a United Irish one as it would have been a year earlier, but a protective popular uprising which a spent United Irish leadership failed to harness."[32] Fighting occurred in four sections of the country, with the most significant conflict taking place in Wexford at Vinegar Hill. The revolt resulted in approximately thirty thousand deaths, along with the execution or transportation of hundreds of rebels and sympathizers.

The events of 1798 were cataclysmic for both the Irish and the British. In the realities of conflict, the radical alliance of diverse religious, social, and economic groups collapsed. Sectarian violence reemerged, especially in rural areas. For Catholics, the rebellion demonstrated "that when the link with Britain and the Crown was threatened, or the superior status of Protestants within Ireland was challenged, Catholics would be the losers."[33] For Protestants, 1798 fulfilled their ingrained stereotypes of a murderous Catholic population predisposed to mayhem and massacre.[34] For the British government, the rebellion demonstrated the need for drastic action to stabilize the political situation. Britain could not allow Ireland to become a back door for French invasion, nor did it wish to lose political and economic control over its restless neighbor. William Pitt, who had pressed for union since the 1780s, saw complete integration of Ireland within Great Britain as the logical solution. Under the directive of the

British government, the Irish lord lieutenant and his secretary bought the votes of Irish legislators to pass an Act of Union in 1800. As a result, the Irish Parliament was abolished, and Ireland was instead represented by one hundred members in the House of Commons, and thirty-two in the House of Lords. Ireland retained its legal system and judiciary, but legislative powers were transferred to Britain.[35]

Union with Britain offered the potential for profound changes in Anglo-Irish politics and political identity. As Kevin Whelan observes, union accomplished the goal of the United Irishmen to overthrow the existing power elite.[36] A new political affiliation was open to all members of Irish society and adopted by many, though the British persisted in regarding their compatriots as inferior in class and manners. But while union with Britain palliated the political crisis of the 1790s, in the long run it disregarded the fundamental problems troubling Ireland, such as Catholic emancipation, land ownership, and sectarian tensions.[37] At the turn of the century, Ireland struggled with famine, economic depression, and agrarian violence; throughout the first decades of the new era, these problems worsened, rather than improved.[38] Consequently, the constitutional conflicts of the eighteenth-century Anglo-Irish gave way to the nationalist movements of the nineteenth century.

Without doubt, our collection is founded on the scholarship which precedes it: the insightful analyses of ethnic and religious groupings among the inhabitants of early modern and eighteenth-century Ireland, of political arguments for Ireland's legislative independence, and of the ideological consequences of plantation experiments in Ireland for other British colonies. Yet, the wealth of scholarship on religion and politics in early modern and eighteenth-century Ireland can obscure the influences of other forces on Anglo-Irish identity. Two such areas explored in *Anglo-Irish Identities, 1571–1845* are economics and culture. Throughout this period, economic realities had a marked impact on the affiliation and self-identification of individuals, at once reinforcing and controverting religious or political influences. Policies pursued by the British government, such as plantation, prohibition of exports, management of currency and national finances, often served to polarize the Anglo-Irish community. Cultural considerations also played an important role in the alignment of individuals into social groups. The confrontation of Gaelic and English traditions was a particularly fertile ground for cultural ethnogenesis. The seventeenth century saw this conflict in oppositional terms and sought to displace native savagery with English civility. But as English literacy grew hand in hand with Anglo-Irish political dominance and stability, a nostalgic and romanticized view of Gaelic Ireland emerged. In the era of growing independence from England, the "English in Ireland" redefined themselves as culturally Irish.[39]

In *Anglo-Irish Identities, 1571–1845*, our contributors investigate how individuals experienced the ambiguities and conflicts of identity formation in a colonial society, how writers fought the economic and ideological superiority of the English, how the co-option of Gaelic history and culture was a political strategy for the Anglo-Irish, how literary texts contributed to the emergence of national consciousness, and so forth. In seeking to understand and trace the complex process of identity formation in early modern Ireland, the essays in this volume attest to its tenuous, dynamic, and necessarily incomplete nature. In examining a specific moment in the history of Anglo-Irish identity, one imposes limits on it. As Willy Maley has remarked, "even when this term does not imply a unitary Englishness and a monolithic Irishness, even when one speaks in terms of competing forms of Englishness in early modern Ireland, other identities, traditions, histories and ethnicities get left out of the grand oppositional narrative."[40] That which has been left out of our volume may later become central, and we hope that future studies will take up the task of elucidating the mutable discourse of Anglo-Irish identity.

Our collection begins with Susan B. Iwanisziw's essay on Hugh O'Neill and hostage diplomacy. Iwanisziw examines the historical experience of O'Neill as emblematic of both the key role that wards and hostages played in early modern politics and of the contested experience of identity in Ireland. She argues that his upbringing in a Protestant English household, combined with his continued affiliation with his noble Gaelic heritage, inculcated a sense of self that was both conflicted and protean. Iwanisziw discusses how O'Neill's wavering loyalties manifested themselves and suggests that the very instability of his own identity was one key to his failure to carry through his Gaelic-Catholic insurgency. She also explores the larger ideological role O'Neill has played in Irish identity over the past four hundred years. In particular, she describes his transformation into an icon of Irish nationalist ambition. Such portrayals, she argues, erase the aspects of O'Neill that embodied the complex divisions of identity in Ireland.

Margaret Mc Peake's "Strumpets, Wood Nimphs, and Contaminants: Representing Irish Women in New English Discourse, 1571–1601" takes as its point of departure not the identity of an individual, but rather the ways in which identity can be projected upon one group by another, an issue with particular force in a colonial situation. This is a topic to which several of the essays in this volume will turn. In this case, Mc Peake considers how the New English represented Gaelic women. She suggests that the depiction of native Irish women as sexually promiscuous, intellectually inferior, and emotionally inconstant laid the groundwork for even more serious charges of cannibalism, incest, and orgiastic behavior. By the latter part of the seventeenth century, however, Mc Peake shows that representational conventions shift to focus on their allure, and consequently their danger, to the New English colonists. In works such as Edmund Spenser's, women are imagined as a potential source of contagion that could overwhelm the English. Such images, Mc Peake contends, mirror the anxieties that the settlers in Ireland felt during the period.

Seeking to uncover the historical identity of Irish deist John Toland, Jeffrey R. Wigelsworth explores the complex ways in which Toland's sense of self was created and re-created throughout his life. Toland's identity, Wigelsworth argues, was a complex amalgam of his dissident religious convictions, flamboyant personality, political ambitions, and aspirations as a natural philosopher. These varied wellsprings of Toland's sense of self were variously combined and emphasized as the political and intellectual world changed during Toland's lifetime. By tracing the many groups to which Toland attached himself throughout his life and his varied identities, Wigelsworth provides a clearer sense of Toland's personal motivations and a reminder of the extreme complexities of identity in Britain and Ireland during the early eighteenth century.

In David Hill Radcliffe's examination of Irish and Scottish eclogues, we see the emergence of and conflict among national identities in England, Scotland, and Ireland. Taking the work of Edmund Spenser as his point of departure and moving through a wide range of lesser-known writers, Radcliffe observes the varied ways in which poets in the three kingdoms used the dialectical resources inherent in the eclogue both to attack traditional enemies and to imagine new political possibilities. As the eclogue evolved during the eighteenth century, new possibilities for political, social, and economic criticism emerged through the technique of localization. While these developments unfolded somewhat uniquely in England, Scotland, and Ireland, Radcliffe shows the poetic form was increasingly used to voice local dissent to the centralized English administration. He suggests that through this transformation into a genre dedicated to national character, local vernacular, and regionalism, the pastoral eclogue laid the groundwork for the romantic nationalism of the nineteenth century.

In his exploration of George Berkeley's understanding of himself in relation to the Irish, Scott C. Breuninger contends that Berkeley's thought gradually evolved as a result of both his changing personal situation and the shifting political, social, and economic climate in Ireland during the first several decades of the eighteenth century. Breuninger contextualizes this development as part of the larger conceptualization of "Irishness" during the time. He argues that while still a youth, Berkeley somewhat uncritically identified himself as "Irish" in contrast to the views of English thinkers. In his later years, however, Berkeley developed a more nuanced sense of self based on his continual engagement with both sectarian conflicts and economic disparities. Breuninger concludes that Berkeley eventually came to embrace a version of Irish patriotism founded upon his practical experiences of Irish poverty and political subordination.

In his essay on Jonathan Swift's reaction to the 1707 union of England and Scotland, Evan Davis examines the ways that the Act of Union figured into the development of Swift's individual and national Irish identity. In particular, Davis assesses how Swift's relationship with his Scottish friend John Arbuthnot evinced the personal, religious, and social tensions that stemmed from the political realignment of 1707. Davis argues that scholars have tended to overlook the importance of Scotland to Swift's analysis and critique of Anglo-Irish relations, in particular, the political and religious threats posed by the Union. By exploring some of Swift's lesser-known writings, such as the "Verses said to be written on the Union," Davis shows that Swift's concerns about the effect of the Union on the national character of England prefigured later critiques of English policy toward Ireland in his major works.

Virginia La Grand's study of the *Intelligencer* provides another perspective on how Swift sought to define his own identity in the context of a complex set of political, economic, and personal issues. La Grand focuses on Swift's self-articulation as a subject of the kingdom of Ireland and his representation of this political body as part of a composite monarchy owing allegiance to the English crown, but not subordinate to the English parliament. She suggests that this identity was undermined late in Swift's life by his disillusionment with English policy toward Ireland after the death of George I. Setting the *Intelligencer* into the larger context of Swift's political writings and contrasting his views in it with some of his earlier political essays, such as the *Drapier's Letters*, La Grand argues that Swift radically reversed himself to view Ireland as essentially a colonial outpost and to redefine himself as a member of an oppressed Irish people.

A parallel view of Swift is provided by Jill Marie Bradbury in her analysis of his economic writings on Ireland. Focusing on Swift's interpretation of the colonial domination and exploitation of Ireland by England, Bradbury shows how *Gulliver's Travels* represented a key turning point in his thought. While concerns with personal and political economy pervaded Swift's early works, these themes coalesce in *Gulliver's Travels* into a general attack on the colonial and commercial ambitions of the English. Bradbury suggests that *Gulliver's Travels* thus adumbrates Swift's later attacks on English mercantilist theories. At the same time, the narrative observes the complicity of the Irish in perpetuating their economic exploitation. The alienation and misanthropy so well known at the conclusion of *Gulliver's Travels* thus prefigures the disillusionment expressed in his later works on Irish problems.

In her study of Anglo-Irish identity in the latter half of the eighteenth century, Lesa Ní Mhunghaile examines a small group of Protestant antiquarians and historians. Her essay shows that even among this relatively small cohort, fractures existed that tended to run along sectarian lines. As the spectre of a Catholic rising faded in the aftermath of the Jacobite war, she argues, members of the Protestant Ascendancy felt their position secure and could validate their own legitimacy by identifying themselves with aspects the ancient Gaelic tradition of Ireland. This affiliation opened the possibility of a shared Protestant and Catholic sense of self. The moment was short-lived, however, as the political situation in Ireland became charged again in the 1780s and 1790s. Nonetheless, the work of this Anglo-Irish antiquarian society still had a tremendous impact on Irish literature and politics well into the nineteenth century.

Chris Nagle's analysis of critical responses to Sydney Owenson's *The Wild Irish Girl* teases apart the disparaging and laudatory responses to her work that have dominated since her own day. As a novel of many excesses, Nagle asserts, the book engendered immoderate criticism in response to this immoderation. Nagle argues that the inability of critics to completely distance themselves from indignation at Owenson's aesthetic derives from larger issues of gender, politics, and ideology. By appreciating Owenson's novel as a part of the literary tradition of sensibility, Nagle suggests that we can better understand and value Owenson's literary aims, techniques, and abilities.

Susan M. Kroeg's essay examines the use of marriage plots to represent and comment on the 1800 union of Ireland and England. Surveying recent scholarship on the topic, Kroeg suggests that the recurrence of incest motifs in Anglo-Irish novels demonstrates conflicted perspectives on the union. Owenson and Edgeworth were engaged in constructing their own "Irish" identity from opposite situations, but their concerns about the Act of Union converged. While Owenson feared unification would result in the destruction of local culture and traditions, Edgeworth doubted whether assimilation of the Gaelic Irish into a British identity could ever fully take place. Kroeg draws on Ellen Pollak's work to analyze how previously unremarked suggestions of incest in Owenson and Edgeworth's texts reveal the authors' misgivings about Ireland's integration into the United Kingdom.

David A. Valone concludes the volume with an examination of how British and Anglo-Irish political economists projected a contested identity upon Ireland during the era surrounding the Act of Union. His essay demonstrates how views of the Irish economy, especially those of T. Robert Malthus, have frequently been misconstrued in the literature about the Great Irish Famine. Valone argues that various ideologies of the Irish economy and of the economic prospects of the Irish peasantry existed during the early nineteenth century. Such alternative economic identities, however, were overshadowed by the dominant colonial discourse of famine that dates back to Edmund Spenser. When the blight struck in the 1840s, this ideology of famine played out in with catastrophic results.

Anglo-Irish Identities, 1571–1845 originated as a summer seminar sponsored by the National Endowment for the Humanities and run by Christopher Fox, Director of the Keough-Naughton Institute for Irish Studies at the University of Notre Dame. In compiling essays for this collection, we found ourselves ranging beyond the neat markers of centuries. Certainly, the events and concerns of the Tudor period in Ireland differed sharply from those of the seventeenth century, yet it is difficult to mark the beginning of one period and the end of another. The mid-sixteenth century saw a push to extend English control over Ireland, which was initially pursued equitably and peacefully through the practice of surrender and regrant. But widespread resistance to the spread of English influence among Irish lords led to a series of rebellions beginning in 1534 and culminating in the Flight of the Earls in 1607. Thus, between 1541 and 1607, many characteristic features of seventeenth and eighteenth-century public discourse on identity first emerged. Plantations and other developments of the seventeenth century are better understood in the context of the mid to late sixteenth century. Similarly, the period between the Act of Union and the Great Famine was an intermediary period, when old and new ideologies overlapped; when the course of events that would shape the nineteenth century had not yet become clear. It is for this reason that the final essays in our volume extend past the end of the eighteenth century, tracing the gradual yielding of one era into another.

NOTES

1. Such scholarship has made important contributions to the study of Irish identity despite its necessarily broader focus. See, in particular, Brendan Bradshaw and Peter Roberts, eds., *British Consciousness and Identity: The Making of Britain 1533–1707* (New York:

Cambridge University Press, 1998); Colin Kidd, *British Identities Before Nationalism: Ethnicities and Nationhood in the Atlantic World, 1600–1800* (New York: Cambridge University Press, 1999); and David Armitage, *The Ideological Origins of the British Empire* (New York: Cambridge University Press, 2000).

2. Political and ecumenical issues also receive excellent and insightful coverage in Tony Claydon and Ian McBride's collection *Protestantism and National Identity: Britain and Ireland c. 1650–1850* (New York: Cambridge University Press, 1998).

3. Two extensive and noteworthy studies are Toby Barnard, *Irish Protestant Ascents and Descents, 1641–1770* (Dublin: Four Courts Press, 2004) and Thomas Bartlett, *The Fall and Rise of the Irish Nation: The Catholic Question, 1690–1630* (Savage, Md: Barnes & Noble, 1992).

4. W. J. McCormack, *Ascendancy and Tradition in Anglo-Irish Literary History from 1789 to 1939* (Oxford: Clarendon Press, 1985), 88.

5. For a survey and discussion of this issue, see S. J. Connolly, *Religion, Law and Power, the Making of Protestant Ireland, 1660–1760* (Oxford: Clarendon Press, 1992), 103–5.

6. Ibid., 63.

7. Kidd, *British Identities*, 147.

8. However, Nicolas Canny suggests that this assimilation was primarily political, rather than cultural in nature, and greatly exaggerated by contemporaries: "by constantly seeking evidence of the alleged degeneracy of the Old English lords, the critics failed to recognize that the social trend which they were really witnessing was the fragmentation of Ireland into a sequence of political lordships." Lords of Anglo-Norman descent adopted the structures of Gaelic society as a means of maximizing their control over territories. "Early Modern Ireland, c. 1500–1700," in *The Oxford History of Ireland*, ed. R. F. Foster (New York: Oxford University Press, 2001), 90–91.

9. Henry VIII sought to quash the frequent rebellions of the Old English lords and Irish chieftains against the crown. In 1541, the Irish Parliament enacted legislation that transformed Ireland from a lordship to a kingdom ruled by the English monarch. The effect of such legislation was to bring all of Ireland under the authority of English law. Rights to land held under Irish law were thus invalidated, at least nominally. Through the policy of surrender and regrant, Irish lords were encouraged to swap their traditional titles and holding for English ones, which effectively brought them under the rule of the crown.

10. R. F. Foster, *Modern Ireland, 1600–1972* (New York: Penguin, 1988), 14.

11. Widespread crop failures and famine led to mass emigration from Scotland during 1695–98. Contemporary estimates ran as high as fifty thousand immigrants. See David Dickson, *New Foundations: Ireland 1660–1800*, 2nd ed. (Dublin: Irish Academic Press, 2000), 48.

12. Nicholas Canny, "Identity Formation in Ireland," in *Colonial Identity in the Atlantic World, 1600–1800,* ed. Nicholas Canny and Anthony Pagden (Princeton: Princeton University Press, 1987), 206.

13. Claydon and McBride, *Protestantism and National Identity,* 15. On the Catholic Church's internal split, see Foster, *Modern Ireland*, 47.

14. Canny, "Identity Formation," 180. This essay gives a detailed account of inquiries into the failure of the Irish plantations to produce the economic benefits touted by those who had promoted the settlements during the sixteenth century. Canny views these debates, which pitted Old and New English against each other in the form of reports to an investigative committee headed by Thomas Wentworth, Lord Deputy of Ireland, as integral to

the formation of Protestant self-image. The struggle of the New English against Wentworth, in particular, "set the final seal to the identity they had been fabricating over the past half century" as the exclusive defenders of the Irish commonwealth (197).

15. The Graces addressed Old English complaints about land tenure and holdings, reduced barriers to education, profession, and the holding of political offices, and generally promised an atmosphere of greater toleration. But Protestant reaction to the measures was vocal and strong, and the few token acts that were actually enacted did little to improve the situation of Catholics.

16. Foster, *Modern Ireland*, 85.

17. Kidd, *British Identities,* 154.

18. Connolly, *Religion, Law and Power*, 13, and Dickson, *New Foundations,* 4, 8.

19. The Catholic struggle continued on the popular level throughout the eighteenth century, as Éamonn Ó Ciardha has shown, though its leaders were never in a position to regain significant political power. See *Ireland and the Jacobite Cause, 1685–1766* (Dublin: Four Courts Press, 2002).

20. The Treaty of Limerick allowed Catholics who fought for James to leave Ireland for Europe, which resulted in the "Flight of the Wild Geese," or the emigration of thousands of Irish soldiers and gentry Catholics. Initially, the treatise also provided for legal toleration of Catholics. When confirmed by the Irish Parliament in 1697, many provisions were discarded or modified, ultimately producing little change in the situation of Catholics. Mike Cronin, *A History of Ireland* (New York: Palgrave, 2001), 78–79.

21. Kevin Whelan, *The Tree of Liberty* (South Bend: University of Notre Dame Press, 1996), 6.

22. Ibid., 38.

23. Neil Longley York, *Neither Kingdom Nor Colony: The Irish Quest for Constitutional Rights, 1698–1800* (Washington, D.C.: Catholic University Press, 1994), 18.

24. " 'No Remedy More Proper': Anglo-Irish Unionism before 1707," in Bradshaw and Roberts, *British Consciousness and Identity*, 308.

25. York, *Neither Kingdom Nor Colony*, 48–50.

26. Ibid., 106.

27. Francis Dobbs, *A History of Irish Affairs* (Dublin: M. Mills, 1782), 7–8.

28. Whelan, *Tree of Liberty*, 100.

29. Foster, *Modern Ireland*, 246.

30. Both excerpts from Tone quoted in Marianne Elliott, *Partners in Revolution: The United Irishmen and France* (New Haven: Yale University Press, 1982), 23.

31. Dickson, *New Foundations*, 198.

32. Elliott, *Partners in Revolution,* 166.

33. Cronin, *A History of Ireland*, 113–14. While the English government worked actively to pass the bill, it would be inaccurate to say that it forced union down the throats of the Irish populace. As recent writers have argued, the union could not have been passed without the presence of a large pro-union constituency in Ireland. See James Kelly, "The Act of Union: its origins and background," and Daniel Mansergh, "The Union and the Importance of Public Opinion," in *Acts of Union: The Causes, Contexts, and Consequences of the Act of Union*, ed. Kevin Whelan and Daire Keogh (Dublin: Four Courts Press, 2001).

34. James Kelly, "'We Were All to have been Massacred': Irish Protestants and the Experience of Rebellion," in *1798: A Bicentenary Perspective*, ed. Thomas Bartlett, David Dickson, Dáire Keough, and Kevin Whelan (Dublin: Four Courts Press, 2003), 313.

35. Cronin, *A History of Ireland*, 116.

36. Kevin Whelan, "The Other Within: Ireland, Britain and the Act of Union," in *Acts of Union,* ed. Whelan and Keogh, 19.

37. Cronin, *A History of Ireland*, 116–17

38. Whelan, "The Other Within," 21 and 31.

39. Connolly, *Religion, Law and Power*, 123–24.

40. "The British Problem in Three Tracts on Ireland by Spenser, Bacon, and Milton," in Bradshaw and Roberts, *British Consciousness and Identity*, 170.

Hugh O'Neill and National Identity in Early Modern Ireland

Susan B. Iwanisziw

THE RELIGIOUS, ETHNIC, AND CULTURAL ELEMENTS CHARACTERISTIC OF Irish nationalism, which emerged as a potent force in the early nineteenth century, had begun to crystallize as early as the revolt of 1641.[1] An English-language drama that analogizes that revolt—Henry Burkhead's *A Tragedy of Cola's Furie, or Lirenda's Miserie* (1646)—shows that the Catholic confederation of Gaels and the Old English owed much to the militancy of the Gaelic lord Hugh O'Neill (1550–1616), who led the resistance to New English encroachment in Ireland from 1592 to 1603.[2] This closet drama was printed without the publisher's imprimatur in Kilkenny and dedicated to Lord Herbert, who signed a controversial and short-lived treaty to accord Irish Catholics the freedom of worship in 1645. The play celebrates the confederation's gains in the initial stage of the revolt from 1641 to 1646, when Catholics united to protest the religious policies of the English parliament in Ireland. A New English governor of Lirenda (or Ireland) recalls Hugh O'Neill's furious valor during his victory over the English at the Blackwater in 1597, when "*Tyrona* ledd on by some vaine prophesie or other, did strive by dint of sword to assure himself the Northern Crowne."[3]

The "Northern Crowne" is a metonym for the legendary Gaelic overkingship of the O'Neills, a rank Hugh O'Neill acquired at the death of Turlough Luineach in 1595; however, for a mid-century audience or reader O'Neill would have symbolized Catholic Irish unity rather than purely Gaelic power. His 1607 assurance to Philip III of Spain that all Irish Catholics were of "one mind" and "very united" was a brave hope manifest in this confederation.[4] This joint revolt of 1641 led to intense negotiations during the course of hostilities for the reestablishment of Gaelic and Old English political authority in Ireland and for the enactment of statutory religious toleration. While shortly rendered moot by developments in England, these negotiations nevertheless laid the groundwork for an Irish nationalism under the banner of Catholicism.[5]

Hugh O'Neill proves an apt starting point to assess this precursive stage of Irish national identity, which could only come into being with some degree of unification among Ireland's diverse people. Until his rise to power, the disparate cultures of the Gaels, Anglo-Norman, New English, and Ulster Scots had never been unified by the religious, linguistic, political, or historical cohesiveness reflective of national identity.[6] But, possessed of a hybridized identity by virtue of his youth spent, in part, as a vulnerable member of the Catholic clan system of the Gaels and, in part, as a hostage-cum-ward within the Protestant community of the Pale, O'Neill entered into adulthood equipped to play a significant role in Irish politics. Doubtless, he had greater ambition for his own empowerment than he ever achieved, but he became the catalyst for the emergence of two of the core characteristics of Irish national identity: a cohesive version of Irish history, established around his own involvement in Irish affairs, and a common religion in Catholicism.

As D. George Boyce and Patrick J. Corish put it, a national identity is not necessarily about political independence but about a self-image accepted by members of a group who define their culture as the national one and their group as the legitimate inheritors of the homeland.[7] The English in Ireland and the Gaels had not, in O'Neill's lifetime, seen fit to unite under this rubric: most of the English, whether Catholic or Protestant, chose to cleave to an English identity.[8] In the creation of its own national identity, England foisted its language, its political system, and its religion on to the disparate cultures of Ireland. But the strategies of Anglicization and Protestant reformation were far from accomplished when O'Neill, already middle-aged, led a rebellion against Queen Elizabeth and took the first steps toward discarding an apparently cohesive colonial identity and orchestrating, however inadvertently, the genesis of Irish nationalism.

Between 1568, when he left the Pale to return to Ulster, and 1592, when he rebelled against English domination, O'Neill appeared to have fixed upon a colonial identity as an officer of the crown.[9] His subsequent repudiation of this identity illuminates Homi L. Bhabha's notion of colonial mimicry, which he argues arises as an ironic compromise in the "civilizing mission." O'Neill's maturation in New English households, his apparent adoption of English values, and his early acquiescence to Protestantism all predicted the success of crown strategy in shaping him into the ideal colonial subject—that is, "a reformed, recognizable 'Other,' *as a subject of a difference that is almost the same, but not quite*."[10] It was, however, the liminal space of the "not quite" that allowed O'Neill to break through his early conditioning and ally himself with the Gaels he had previously harried in the service of England. Although he stood a fair chance of diverting the course of English colonization and inaugurating, several hundred years before it materialized, an Irish national identity consonant with traditional Gaelic culture, O'Neill attempted, rather, to trade colonial masters in giving Ireland over to Spain.

A major contributor to the development of a national consciousness, or identity, in Ireland was Gaelic culture. The Gaels were divided by clan enmity, and, from the twelfth century onward, by a chief's collusion with or resistance to Norman invaders and their descendants. Nonetheless, the Gaels had long possessed a strong sense of cultural identity sustained by Brehon law and history relayed by clan poets, or bards, who created a sense of *natio*, or community, in their recitations of folklore and legends of tribal and dynastic origins. These origins were supposed to extend back to the arrival of the putative ancestor of the Gaels, Milesius of Spain. The twelfth century saw the rise of two Gaelic over-kingships based on descent from Milesius; in the north, the O'Neill clan claimed ancestry and rank from the younger son of Milesius.[11] The O'Neill (the tanist title for the elected chief) dominated Ulster, or the north and the eastern midlands, but decentralized government, the absence of a rule of primogeniture, and the militarism of the invaders all worked to undermine the cooperation necessary to drive out the Normans. After Ireland was annexed to England, it gained its own parliament in 1264, a legislative body from which Gaels were excluded until the time of Henry VIII, when the Gaelic lords who accepted the English policy of surrender and re-grant were raised to the rank of the peerage and accorded English titles to their traditional lands and seats in the Irish Parliament.[12]

The medieval period did not usher in the political or social unification of Gaelic and Old English factions despite a degree of racial and cultural intermixing, but Anglo-Norman power remained restricted to the Pale around Dublin and parts of the nearby counties of Meath, Kildare, and Louth.[13] Elsewhere, the Gaels pursued their traditional way of life. The O'Neills of Ulster, by and large, capitulated to English colonial authority, but they retained the legend of their origins, and the chief was still given the tanist title and, thereby, a position of great influence among the clans. Following the O'Neill rebellions of the sixteenth century, the terms of submission to the English monarch generally required the abolition of this title.

The vexing trajectories of Hugh O'Neill's personal history and his role in Irish history can be attributed to his hybrid identity, which developed from clan conflicts as well as his enforced English acculturation through hostage and wardship diplomacy in colonial Ireland. Hugh was born into a family riven by dynastic rivalry, and his father was murdered when he was about nine years old. At that point, Sir Henry Sidney, the Lord Deputy of Ireland, took Hugh in and he spent the rest of his childhood in the Pale. Sidney claimed that he "bred" O'Neill in his own house because he was poor and friendless, and certainly his intervention preserved the boy from the dynastic malice of his uncle, Shane O'Neill.[14] But taking the boy into wardship was as much a matter of policy as it was of compassion. Throughout early modern Europe, hostages were routinely given into the charge of the more powerful or victorious principal to cement an agreement or an alliance: sometimes principals, more usually the sons of principals, they served as pledges in a pan-European system of military honor.[15] As a queen's ward, O'Neill was situated with government interests in mind and educated in accordance with his rank. He converted to Protestantism and assimilated English culture in the household of Giles Hovenden, a New English settler.[16] Returning to Ulster in his adulthood, for many years O'Neill abetted the English policy of plantation and Gaelic "civilization": he was, to all appearances, a successfully acculturated colonial subject.

Hostage diplomacy and wardship were critical strategies in English-Irish relations, premised on anglicizing the Gaelic Irish through the joint policies of acculturation and reform. In his memoirs, Sidney notes that he took hostages whenever he subdued Gaelic rebels who gave their oath of future loyalty to the English monarch: most of these boys were transferred to English or Anglo-Norman households where they served as pages and servants.[17] O'Neill was a ward rather than a military hostage, but the two conditions were similar, differentiated mainly by the fact that a hostage's father (or official guardian) was still living.[18]

Through his sponsorship of Hugh, Sidney prevented Turlough Luineach from claiming the boy's rights to the baronage of Dungannon and the family land around the Blackwater.[19] Besides ensuring the boy's physical safety and securing a portion of his familial inheritance, Sidney's strategy served to intimidate O'Neill's kinfolk. Hugh was set up as a dynastic rival, endowed by the crown with an English education, significant properties, and a military subsidy, for the purpose of preventing the rise of a single, strong leader within the Shane and Turlough factions of the O'Neill clan.

Later in his life, O'Neill publicly objected to the queen's hostage and wardship policies in his "Articles intended to be stood upon" of 1599, in which he demanded the return of all Gaelic pledges. He reiterated his objection to the English "seduction" of Gaelic children in a letter to the Spanish Council of State in 1615. Nevertheless, he was similarly embroiled in strategies of child-exchange in order to cement alliances and dependencies.[20] This dislocation between public show and personal practice remained typical of his behavior, and it muddies the distinctions we would like to draw between his sincere values and canny strategizing.

Upon his return to Ulster in 1568, O'Neill quickly grabbed up lands to consolidate his authority as major landowner. As a former ward more or less keeping to the path set for him, he garnered more power and titles from the English: for his efforts in defending the Pale from Gaelic rebels, he was granted a lieutenancy in 1584. Appointed the Earl of Tyrone, he became a Peer of the Irish Parliament the following year. Evidently dissatisfied with his rewards, he fomented rebellion in 1592. Three years later, his clan elected him to the position of The O'Neill. With his English titles came military power, wealth, and an international stature, but with the Ulster title came control of the most vigorous Gaelic polity in Ireland.

After 1592, O'Neill began to figure prominently in official English records when he publicly spurned Protestantism, Queen Elizabeth, and her administrators in Ireland by joining forces with the Gaels in an attempt to cast off his English servitude, if not the appurtenances of his colonial identity. We know from Sir John Harrington's account of his visit to O'Neill's household in 1599 that his sons, unlike their Gaelic neighbors, wore "English clothes like a nobleman's sons, with velvet jerkins and gold lace," and both were learning English.[21] Despite his alliance with the Gaels, O'Neill maintained the sort of noble English household familiar to him since childhood. Surely, his repudiation of English authority arose when he realized that he would always remain a second-class subject—a colonial subject—in the queen's Ireland.

Despite his ancient kingship rights, perhaps it was unfeasible to promote an independent Ireland under his own rule; but O'Neill gambled for more than heavenly rewards when he colluded with Spain and the Vatican, and, around 1595, accepted their aid in a plot to overthrow the English colonial project and, by secret agreement, Queen Elizabeth herself. Assured of Spanish military assistance, O'Neill refused to be cowed by Elizabeth's anger, brazenly declaring that the rebels would "draw themselves to a more nearness of loyalty to her Highness" only if she authorized "free liberty of conscience" in Ireland and a royal pardon for himself, his family and the other rebellious Gaels.[22] In 1595, then, we find the first indication of his adherence to one of the principles for which he came to stand in Irish national discourse: the right to practice Catholicism. Despite an ensuing peace treaty, O'Neill reneged, and the Nine Years War continued. The pope issued a crusade indulgence and Spanish aid materialized in 1601, but these measures proved inadequate to defeat the English forces.

Persecuted by New English administrators after his submission to King James, O'Neill fled Ireland with Rory O'Donnell and their entourage in 1607. It seemed that O'Neill had failed both the Gaels and the Catholic Church in his stated aim of driving the English and their Protestant faith from Ireland. Stripped of his possessions and privileges, he died in Rome in 1616, a pensioner of Philip III. At this stage of his life, he was almost as helpless to control policy in Ireland as when he was a child taken into wardship. However, his failure in action does not imply a failure in influence.

Notwithstanding his military and diplomatic impotence in the courts of Europe, O'Neill remained a significant figure for generations of men and women concerned with Irish political empowerment because the conditions under which he had entered into history had been set to paper and disseminated at home and through the courts of Europe. After his exile, he appears in Irish writings as the figurehead for cultural unity and the Counter-Reformation in Ireland; moreover, writers representing English, Spanish and papal interests variously acknowledged and represented him in diplomatic papers. The conflux of correspondence, proclamations, history, and literature permitted the consolidation of manifold viewpoints, which proved far more potent in initiating the rise of a pan-Irish national consciousness than did Gaelic-language literature alone.[23]

Insofar as traditional Gaelic culture culled little respect from contemporary Europeans, while in exile O'Neill would have publicly conformed to continental habits of dress, language, and religious decorum. From the time of his childhood, social and political exigency had demanded this type of shape-shifting since many of his roles, like his avowed loyalties, were incompatible. For the purpose of securing allies or otherwise promoting his purposes, he had taken on, sometimes simultaneously, the mantles of an English aristocrat and military officer, a Gaelic prince, an oppressed recusant, a Gaelic rebel, a European warmonger, a diplomatic adviser to the Spanish court, and a Counter-Reformation insurgent on behalf of the Vatican. The ways in which he played these roles, along with the ways others represented him in his various guises, illuminate the enduring mutability of his personal identity. Although he has left behind no private meditations from which we might elicit his own sense of self or purpose, we can piece together from his official documents two of his paramount difficulties in dealing with his hybrid, or splintered, identity. If a national identity can be inferred from the shared mode of dress, language, religion, cultural history, and political system of a people, it is clear that O'Neill's primary difficulty was settling upon a consistent and appropriate cultural-national identity with which to deal with the multiple states to which he owed allegiance or sought to manipulate for his own advancement. The second was his difficulty in reconciling his status to his ambitions. Recent interpretations of the historical record suggest that his insurgency on behalf of the Catholic Church was a means rather than an end. If so, did he conceive of himself as a Gael seeking to re-empower Gaels in the European milieu, or as a European prince justified by birth, talent, and courage in exerting his own authority over the Irish people by whatever means came to hand?[24]

There are two major periods from which we can draw materials to evaluate O'Neill's ever-shifting identity and his contribution to the genesis of an Irish national consciousness. The first is the period (1592–1606) from the beginning of the Nine Years War to his submission under James I. At this point, he loosened his English moorings and sought cultural recognition among Gaels and Spaniards. Many of his own letters and proclamations during this time establish his wavering loyalties and changeable priorities. The second period spans the years of his exile from 1607 to 1616. Correspondence from this time reveals a consolidation of his objectives: one was the restoration of Catholicism to Ireland; the other was the protection of Gaels and, significantly, of other Irish Catholics from encroachments on their lands and freedom.

From O'Neill's own writing and English responses to his actions between 1592 and 1603, we can track his inability to steer a direct course to autonomy on his own behalf or for his Gaelic allies. In this period, the primary roles he took on were that of Gaelic lord fighting for the cultural freedom of his people in the exercise of religion and politics, and European warmonger inciting the Spaniards to invade Ireland and conquer England. English contempt for O'Neill's duplicity is understandable, for even as he treated with the English for pardons for himself and his fellow rebels in 1595, he kept up a secret correspondence with the Spanish king for soldiers, money, and arms "to restore the faith of the Church, and to secure Philip a kingdom."[25] Was this hedging of his bets made in the service of his own promotion, as the English supposed, or a genuine commitment to his countrymen? Whichever motivation was uppermost, he made a clever appeal for personal and Gaelic empowerment in his "Articles" of 1599. On the one hand, for the Gaels (cast as his confederates in furthering his authority in Ireland) he demanded the appointment of only high-ranking individuals as governors of Ireland; that other officials be "Irish men," or Gaels (possibly also the Old English); that all principal governments were to be controlled by "Irish" noblemen; and that half the soldiers and officers resident in Ireland should be "Irish men." He also demanded of Elizabeth that she allow Catholicism to be openly preached, that the pope govern the

Church of Ireland, and that England return all church lands seized during the Reformation to the Catholic Church.[26] Pertaining as much to his own ambitions as to the grievances of the Gaels, his demands to elevate them in the English administration and to restore their religious freedom suggest a significant threat to crown security. Moreover, rather than working for England's colonial expansion or fostering cooperation in Ireland, Gaels restored to their traditional faith and trained in colonial service would be well placed to assist in the Spanish colonial administration that O'Neill was urging upon Philip III.

As it turned out, the Spanish defeat at Kinsale in 1601 led to O'Neill humbling himself to King James in 1603 and renouncing Spanish and papal support, the traditions of his own clan, and the cultural independence of the Gaels. Suing "to be restored to his former dignity and living," he repudiated all dependency on foreign powers, vowed to "continue a loyal subject to the King's person, crown, and prerogative, and laws," and abandoned "the name and title of O'Neale." In addition, he promised to aid the English in advancing peaceful government by promoting the abolition of "barbarous customs contrary to the laws" and erecting for Gaelic people "civil habitations."[27] Within a span of eight years, he had multiplied the conditions for religious freedom in Ireland, yet elicited no improvement; stymied Gaelic territorial sovereignty by proposing to give Ireland to Spain; promoted the Gaelicization of the New English administration in Ireland, yet betrayed—in words if not (again) in deed—the Gaels and the culture he claimed to represent. Subsequently, he broke faith with James I and fled Ireland in 1607.

These broken covenants might well have tarnished his reputation and impeded an early genesis of national consciousness, but the illusion of his extraordinary contribution to the Irish cause was upheld after his flight through his own exilic correspondence, the writings of the Old English cleric Peter Lombard, and the poems and histories of Gaelic bards. In these texts, O'Neill takes on new mantles: a vengeful prince sullenly stirring up international warfare to bring about his glorious homecoming; a self-appointed military and spiritual adviser the Spanish king; the savior of the Gaelic people and other Irish, Scots, and English Catholics; an insurgent of the Counter-Reformation on behalf of the Vatican; and an impoverished Gaelic-Catholic nobleman yearning to go home and willing to do or say almost anything to achieve that end.

In his exilic correspondence compiled by Micheline Kerney Walsh, we can see how O'Neill ultimately traded his personal ambition for the security and spiritual freedom of the Gaels.[28] After he fled Ireland, neither Philip III of Spain nor the pope encouraged further action to promote war with England or the reestablishment of Catholicism in Ireland. O'Neill knew that he had only two options for escaping the tedium of exile: the route of submission to England, secret Catholicism, and English oversight among his own people in colonial Ulster; or a glorious restoration following a successful Spanish-papal intervention in Ireland. Hopes for the latter were quashed by Philip III's consistent refusal to meet with him or allow him freedom of movement. In the end, Philip tied him to Rome, far from any center of Gaelic resistance and, when James I offered reconciliation, dissuaded O'Neill from accepting. Nevertheless, O'Neill sent a barrage of letters and memoranda (many of them jointly with the Earl of Tyrconnell) encouraging Spanish intervention in Ireland and volunteering his military expertise. In these communications, O'Neill adopts a multitude of poses. At times, he appears a pitiful Gaelic exile; a grieving father; a dupe of the Spanish crown; a lord of ancient and proud lineage, related by blood to the Spaniards; an Irish historian; or the voice of retribution. His range of negotiation tactics goes from explanation to appeal, from threat to accusation.

Ever a warmonger, O'Neill advises Philip how best to conquer England, Ireland, and Scotland and simultaneously warns him of the dangers posed by an aggressive England. He raises the stakes by invoking a wrathful God ready to punish Philip for his neglect of Irish souls. Some letters contain accounts of Gaelic history to remind the king of the Milesian inheritance, the ancient brotherhood of Spain and Ireland, and the sacrifices the Gaels made for Catholicism; some document Gaelic disenchantment with Spanish promises and describe the oppressive conditions under English rule, which only Philip, in the service of God and the Church, can revoke. His requests for aid, when not aiming to shame Philip, accuse him, subtly, of perfidy. O'Neill claims that he and the rebellious lords had acted in the Nine Years War as subjects of the Spanish kings—"by order and persuasion" of Philip II and Philip III; and he reminds Philip III time and again that the lords might have come to honorable terms with the English crown had they not trusted to the Spanish monarch's promises. These letters clearly document O'Neill's increasing promotion of Catholicism and papal authority in Ireland, but whether from genuine commitment or sly policy is difficult to determine.

In his *De Hibernia Insula Commentarius* (p. 1632) Peter Lombard settles on O'Neill's guise as a Counter-Reformation hero. His history bears tribute to O'Neill's reputation, character, and aims, yet he observes, nonjudgmentally, the protean nature of the man: "if it were necessary for the matter in hand to appear serious or joyful, pleased or angry, he can most readily and in the most natural manner exhibit these emotions. Indeed, he quite captivates the feelings of men by the mobility of his looks and countenance, and wins the affections of his soldiers or strikes terror into them."[29] It is this ability to act any part with apparent sincerity that served O'Neill well in his multiple roles. Lombard clearly understands the nature of his hero's character and the influence of his childhood in shaping it: "In his early years he was instructed in his native land in those exercises and studies usual there for noblemen, and suitable to his years and opportunities and proper to one destined to his rank in life. When a little older, he came under English influence, under their tutelage was trained in their military art, and polite or courtly fashions, and made such strides towards distinction in both that he was made Baron of Dungannon."[30] Lombard believes O'Neill's bicultural education had groomed him perfectly for Irish military and diplomatic leadership in the service of the church: "he is most thoroughly versed in the politics and affairs not only of Ireland but also of England, in all matters relating to peace and war."[31] Lombard's partiality causes him to enhance O'Neill's Gaelic heroism and princely deportment, but also to ignore many of his weaknesses, duplicities, and reversals the better to construct the myth of his dedication to the Counter-Reformation. Biased by his vested interest in the restoration of Catholicism in Ireland, Lombard contributed substantially to the idealization of O'Neill's championship of the Catholic faith. Since the preservation of this faith was, indeed, the unifying concept in an embryonic nationalist consciousness by the time of the 1641 revolt, O'Neill was easily slotted into the role of Irish defender of the faith. Irish history from both Gaelic and Old English sources began to converge in this acknowledgment of his service to Catholicism.

Literary representations of O'Neill changed after the flight of the earls in 1607, as Marc Caball, Eleanor Hull, Aodh de Blácam, and Breandán Ó Buachalla have shown.[32] Before 1607, Gaelic poets, regardless of clan affiliation, had praised his devotion to the cause of the Gaels.[33] Afterward, they began to represent O'Neill as a prince tragically prevented from ushering in Irish independence and reestablishing Catholicism as the national religion. Marc Caball asserts that "early modern Irish nationalism" began to take root after the earls' exile, gaining momentum during the rebellion of 1641–49, and that this sense of national cohesiveness hinged on the coalescence of three concepts: "the indivisibility of Gaelic cultural integrity, territorial sovereignty, and the interlinking of Gaelic identity with profession of the Roman Catholic faith."[34] Before his flight, O'Neill's haphazard record with respect to Gaelic cultural autonomy and Irish territorial sovereignty would have made a rather unconvincing argument for any Irish national sensibility; after his exile, it was, so to speak, a different story. As did Lombard, the bardic poets were apt to gloss over the confusions, lapses, and betrayals of O'Neill's past and remake him as a consummate Gael.

Bardic chroniclers mythologized the exiled earls, their focus less on the restoration of Catholicism than an elegaic mourning for the dissolution of Gaelic autonomy and culture. These writers ensured that the reputations of O'Neill and the other rebels were magnified and celebrated. Tadhg Ó Cianáin, a poet attached to the Maguire clan, wrote a history in 1608 that renewed hope for European intervention when he describes the honorable welcome extended to the earls in Europe.[35] No bards attached to O'Neill's household have appeared as compelling witnesses to their lord's glorious exploits or abasements, but many poets, even those affiliated with viable clans, turned from compositions focused on their tribal affiliation to cast light on political, cultural, and religious changes throughout Ireland. Among such poets as Eoghan Rua MacA'Baird, Fearflatha O' Gnímh, and Andrew MacMarcus, Fearghal Og Mac-a-Ward composed several poems about Ireland's grief and the hope of O'Neill's return: "Fruits are coming, verdure's coming (with all shelter, with all growth), on a sweet voiced wind a-westward, to us over streaming tides."[36] And Eochy O'Hosey exhorted O'Neill to return before "Inisfail" perish, censuring all the great septs that, through disunion, brought about Ireland's ruin.[37] Caball views such personal and pan-Irish mourning as an important step in the development of Irish national consciousness.[38] Insofar as this mourning regularly invoked and glorified O'Neill's history, bardic poetry enhanced his reputation among the Gaels who remained in Ireland and, reciprocally, focused and tempered the exiled lord's public commitment to his people and their religion.

In the poems and histories of others, O'Neill's loyalty to Catholicism and Gaelic culture was pared of any ambiguity. After 1641, when English-language literature praising the Irish rebels became available, this corpus created the foundation of his reputation, especially after printing presses outside the Pale were licensed to operate. After 1643, Irish printers could finally publish books that challenged the dominant English discourse. One such work, Henry Burkhead's *A Tragedy of Cola's Furie*, purports to be a history of ancient, foreign conflicts. The plot analogizes the joint Gaelic/ Old English protest against the religious repressions perpetrated by Charles I, and the confederate characters are careful to insist upon their continuing loyalty to the English crown. The plot, focused on the initial stage of the rebellion from 1641 to 1646, favors their goals in its depiction of major battles against England's royal and parliamentary factions. In this play, his reputation already polished and refined by the literature and histories that sprang up to document his life, O'Neill appears as a symbol of just chastisement. Governor Berofus observes when he hears the news of an impending confederate attack, "now me thinks the terrour of this sudden hell-bred newes, strikes neere my heart, then all the legions of [Tyrone's] furious traine, could at that instant when Black-water-Fort, prov'd fatall to the most and best of ours."[39] O'Neill's nephew Owen Roe O'Neill, who goes by the name of Abner, is an incarnation of Hugh's best attributes. Burkhead's depiction of the O'Neills elides the Gaelic and Old English suspicions that imperiled Hugh's chances of success—and, which, indeed bedeviled Owen—in favor of a furious Catholic-Irish proto-nationalism: "our quarrell is religious, in maintenance whereof we are already sworne without equivocation."[40] Unfortunately, the playwright's hope for a Catholic Ireland was to be short-lived. Just three years after publication of the play, Oliver Cromwell arrived to chastise, in turn, the Gaelic and Old English rebels.

O'Neill's hybrid identity, derived from his Gaelic childhood and English wardship, permitted him the scope to assume diverse roles in pursuit of his own and his people's freedom from English oppression. But his loyalties were diffused by his early conditioning: his attachment to his Gaelic-Catholic heritage had been shattered during his early years, in part by the hostility of his kinfolk and in part by his English upbringing, which opened up vistas beyond traditional clan expectations. His championship of Gaelic culture and Catholicism came to him by default rather than principle, when his ambitions in the courts of England and Spain failed to materialize. He opted for the retrograde path—the Milesian inheritance and Spanish colonialism—because he never learned how to discipline the conflicting multicultural components of his ever-shifting identity into the agency and keenness of purpose required to forge an independent Irish nation. His return to his natal culture involved a weary, lifelong journey that never brought him home. Yet, however dismal his end, his struggles were not unavailing. His enduring legacy for the Catholic people of Ireland was the seeding of two core elements of Irish nationalism: the beginning of a cohesive mode of Irish history and Irish allegiance to Catholicism.

Notes

1. Liam Kennedy, *Colonialism, Religion and Nationalism in Ireland* (Belfast: Institute of Irish Studies, 1996), xiii.

2. Henry Burkhead, *A Tragedy of Cola's Furie, or Lirenda's Miserie* (Kilkenny: n.p., 1646). Short Title Catalog Part 2, Reel 174, No. 10.

3. Ibid, 4.

4. See his and Rory O'Donnell's 1607 letter to Philip III in Micheline Kerney Walsh, *"Destruction by Peace": Hugh O'Neill After Kinsale* (Ireland: R. & S. Printers, 1986), 192.

5. D. George Boyce, *Nationalism in Ireland*, 3rd edition (London: Routledge, 1995), 18.

6. Patrick J. Corish, "The Origins of Catholic Nationalism," in *A History of Irish Catholicism*, ed. Patrick J. Corish (Dublin: Gill & Son, 1968), 2.

7. Boyce, *Nationalism in Ireland,* 18; Corish, "Origins of Catholic Nationalism," 1–3.

8. Boyce, *Nationalism in Ireland*, 41–43.

9. Boyce notes that a colonial identity is felt by a group whose national identity originates in the mother country but whose cultural identity has been shaped by the colonial environment. Boyce, *Nationalism in Ireland,* 18–19.

10. Homi Bhabha, *The Location of Culture* (London: Routledge, 1994), 85–86.

11. Ibid, 26.

12. Hiram Morgan explains the English policy of "Surrender and Regrant" and the Gaelic system of tanistry in *Tyrone's Rebellion* (Bury St Edmunds: Boydell Press for the Royal Historical Society, 1993), 16–19.

13. Boyce, *Nationalism in Ireland*, 38, 41–42.

14. Morgan, *Tyrone's Rebellion*, 214.

15. The treatment of such hostages was codified throughout Europe. See Hugo Grotius, *The Law of War: A Documentary History*, ed. Leon Friedman (New York: Random House, 1972), 1:37, 93, 144–46.

16. It was once assumed that Sidney raised O'Neill in England, but Morgan's contention that he was actually the ward of Giles Hovenden is now generally accepted. While O'Neill was raised within the Dublin Pale, he spent time in England (in 1567–68, 1587, and 1590) at court and in the aristocratic households of Sidney and the Earl of Leicester, where he would have been instructed in courtly service. He became the first Irish lord widely endorsed as an accomplished Renaissance prince, although, as Morgan observes, he was not trained in chivalric warfare as befitted a European aristocrat. Morgan, *Tyrone's Rebellion*, 92–93, 97, 217–18.

17. Ciaran Brady, ed., *A Viceroy's Vindication? Sir Henry Sidney's Memoir of Service in Ireland, 1556–78* (Cork: Cork University Press, 2002), 88–89.

18. Evidence is scanty, but an entry in *The Sidney State Papers 1565–70*, ed. Tomás Ó Laidhin (Dublin: Dublin Stationery Office for the Irish Manuscripts Commission, 1962) strongly suggests that Irish boys were treated as both wards and hostages (132–33). While hostages were acquired ad hoc or by treaty in times of military conflict, conditions of wardship were determined in the early modern era by an official inquisition by the Court of Wards and Liveries.

19. Brady, A *Viceroy's Vindication?*, 54–55.

20. See Hugh O'Neill, "Articles intended to be stood upon by Tyrone" in Constantia Maxwell, ed., *Irish History from Contemporary Sources (1509–1610)* (London: Allen & Unwin, 1923) 183; Walsh, "*Destruction by Peace*," 348; *Calendar of State Papers for Ireland* (Nendeln, Liechtenstein: Kraus Reprint, 1974), 2:110; Morgan, *Tyrone's Rebellion*, 193, 205, 212. Moreover, O'Neill's objection to English policy had a personal edge: after his exile, Sir Tobias Caulfield took O'Neill's son Conn from his foster family and held him at Charlemont Fort; thereafter the boy was sent to Dublin, then to Eton College, and finally to the Tower of London. Walsh, "*Destruction by Peace,*" 137–38.

21. Sir John Harrington, *Report of a Journey into the north of Ireland* (1599), in Maxwell, *Irish History*, 338.

22. Hugh O'Neill, "Demands made by Tyrone" (1595), in Maxwell, *Irish History*, 182.

23. Benedict Anderson, *Imagined Communities: Reflections on the Origin and Spread of Nationalism* (London: Verso Editions, 1983), 17–41. Anderson notes that nationalism had to wait for widespread literacy and a commercial print culture that could create, for ordinary people, an imaginative identification with a national community to supplant the moribund hierarchical systems of the past.

24. Thomas J. Morrissey, *James Archer of Kilkenny: An Elizabethan Jesuit* (Dublin: Grenville Printing, 1979), 17.

25. Letter of Tyrone and Tyrconnell to Philip III (1959), in Maxwell, *Irish History*, 187.

26. O'Neill, "Articles intended to be stood upon by Tyrone," in Maxwell, ed., *Irish History,* 182–83.

27. *Calendar of State Papers for Ireland*, 1:13–14.

28. "O'Neil's Letters and Memorials," in Walsh, "*Destruction by Peace,*" 144–380.

29. Peter Lombard, *The Irish War of Defence, 1598–1600: Extracts from the* De Hibernia Insula Commentarius *of Peter Lombard,* ed. and trans. Matthew J. Byrne (Cork: Cork University Press, 1930) 27.

30. Ibid., 29.

31. Ibid., 27.

32. See Marc Caball, *Poets and Politics: Reaction and Continuity in Irish Poetry, 1558–1625* (Cork: Cork University Press, 1998); Eleanor Hull, *A Text Book of Irish Literature*, vol. 2, 1908 (New York: AMS Press, 1974); Aodh de Blácam, *Gaelic Literature Surveyed* (Dublin: Talbot Press, 1933); Breandán Ó Buachalla, "The Gaelic Response to Conquest," *New Perspectives on Ireland,* ed. Daltún Ó Ceallaigh (Dublin: Elo Press, 1998), 52–97.

33. Hull, *Text Book of Irish Literature*, 172–73.

34. Caball, *Poets and Politics*, 151.

35. Tadhg Ó Cianáin, "The Flight of the Earls" (1608), in Maxwell, *Irish History*, 205.

36. Blácam, *Gaelic Literature Surveyed*, 105, 139; Hull, *Text Book of Irish Literature*, 166.

37. Blácam, *Gaelic Literature Surveyed*, 143

38. Caball, *Poets and Politics*, 99–104.

39. Burkhead, *Tragedy of Cola's Furie*, 4.

40. Ibid, 19; Corish, "Origins of Catholic Nationalism," 17.

Strumpets, Wood Nimphs, and Contaminants: Representing Irish Women in New English Discourse, 1571–1601

Margaret Mc Peake

EDMUND CAMPION, WILLIAM STANYHURST, JOHN DERRICKE AND EDMUND Spenser all utilize representations of Irish women's bodies to rhetorically configure a relationship between the colony and that which lies outside of it, or the boundary between "civilization" and "barbarism." These manuscripts reveal how the dominant anxieties that faced New English commentators changed in the period 1571–1601, and how these changes are graphically represented through the figurations of women utilized in the texts. While earlier writers such as Campion and Stanyhurst represent Irish women as signifiers of sexual barbarism, toward the end of this period Irish women and their sexualities figure as a source of danger and contamination powerful enough to jeopardize the colony itself.

Edmund Campion's *History of Ireland*, composed in 1571,[1] represents an important contribution to the foundation of a New English history written in Ireland. In 1570, Campion went to Dublin to work with the Stanyhursts and the Lord Deputy, Sir Henry Sidney, on the establishment of a university. It was during this time that he undertook the writing of his *History of Ireland,* which was influential for both Raphael Holinshed and Richard Stanyhurst. Central to Campion's account is his interest in representing the Irish character, something which is also a mainstay of the classical and Anglo-Norman commentators who he references. In the context of this discussion, Campion is particularly focused on areas of transgression and taboo. To this end, he includes a rendering of Strabo's account of the Irish proclivity for public lasciviousness and incest. Campion's version illustrates how gendered terms are important to the characterization of excess, transgression, and taboo: "the Irish were great gluttons, eaters of man's flesh, and counted it honorable for parents deceased to be eaten up of their children, and that in open sight they meddled with their wives, mothers and daughters."[2] In addition to the charge of cannibalism in the above extract, the emphasis on sexual transgression, represented through public sex and incest "with wives, mothers and daughters," underscores the way in which a barbarous sexuality is imagined through the bodies of women as the signifiers of transgression. In other words, brothers, fathers, and husbands are not the named partners here, but rather their female counterparts.

The sexually transgressive continues as a theme in Campion's narrative in the way that sexual promiscuity is represented as a mainstay of Irish character. The figures of the "strumpet" and the "whore" become signifiers of Irish promiscuity in Campion's *History*:

> Strumpets are there too vile and abominable to write of, which not only without fear, but also without remorse, do advance themselves of numbering what noblemen have had liking to their bodies. He that can bring most of his name into the field, base or other, triumpheth exceedingly. For increase of which name, they allow themselves not only whores, but also choice and store of whores. One I hear named which hath (as he calleth them) more than twenty wives in ten places.[3]

Again, a primary sign of transgressive sexuality is found in the figure of a woman, in this case, the "strumpet" whose possession of an ungoverned sexuality places her almost beyond the realm of Campion's representation. This description of the strumpet is one which betrays a profound discomfiture with the prospect that Irish society is aligned around an axis in which possession of women's bodies could be beyond the governance of husbands, as defined and practiced in English society.[4]

In the above excerpt, both sexes are upbraided for either "numbering what noblemen have had liking to their bodies," in the case of Irish women, or "nam[ing] which hath (as he calleth them) more than twenty wives in ten places," in the case of Irish men. While the woman, characteristically, is the sex that falls under the weight of the derogatory term "strumpet" or "whore," the suggestion is that both Irish men and women are charged in equal measure with a lack of interest in sexual monogamy. By labeling women as "strumpets" when they boast of desiring noblemen, Campion's description may betray a criticism of interrelationship and intermarriage between Palesmen and Irish women, as a consequence of a relative lack of English women in the colony. This topic will continue as a theme for later commentators, such as John Derricke, and will become an obsession for Edmund Spenser. In addition, the description of Irish women's promiscuity may simply concern an anxiety about Irish fecundity. Whether or not they are producing "hybridized" children with the New English, Irish women, as a result of their sexual activity, are adding to the number of children who will be counted as those "beyond the Pale." This anxiety is also found in Campion's description of Irish men said to have a "choice and store of whores"—linked to their desire to produce as many children as possible: "He that can bring most of his name into the field, base or other, triumpheth exceedingly." This touches on a sore point for the New English at this time: relative numbers. In the 1560s and 1570s, inhabitants of colonial settlements in Ireland were outnumbered exponentially by the indigenous population.[5] This suggested increase in population, a virtual inevitability as a result of the behavior alleged by Campion, could do nothing but stoke paranoia about the danger of these reproducing Irish for the future of the English colony.

An overarching political correlative of Campion's representation of the Irish as promiscuous is the way in which the Irish are also perceived as faithless partners in their negotiations with English representatives of the crown. Sexual promiscuity is understood, in roughly analogous fashion, as political faithlessness. The Irish can not be trusted because they are prone to forget their promises to the English crown. As Shirley Adawy Peart asserts, "The theme of inconstancy appears in most of the writings on Ireland by English men. An inconstant woman is seen as a threat to male authority; Ireland, associated with inconstancy, posed a challenge to England."[6] A glaring example of Irish political inconstancy in the years immediately previous to Campion's composition could have been easily located in the actions of Shane O'Neill in popular imagination.[7] Ungoverned women in Irish society embody a version of the colonial allegory for Campion, referencing his concern about the ungovernability of the society for the English.

Richard Stanyhurst, influenced by the work Campion composed while his houseguest in Dublin, authored *Two Bokes on the Histories of Ireland.* Though not published in its own right until 1633, aspects of Stanyhurst's work were included in *Holinshed's Chronicles*, first published in 1577. Of the *Chronicles*, Stanyhurst compiled "The Description of Ireland" and the third book of the "History." In this way, Stanyhurst's *Two Bokes* were made widely influential in the late sixteenth century, and the representations of Irishness and Irish women they contained gained wide currency. Like Campion, with whom Stanyhurst lived in Dublin, he also characterizes Irish sexual practice in addition to marriage patterns:

> In olde tyme they much abused the honourable state of marriage, either in contractes vnlawfull, eetyng the degrees of prohibition, or in diuorcementes

> at pleasure, or in retaynyng concubines or harlots for wyues: yea euen at this day where the clergy is fainte, they can be content to marry for a yeare and a day of probation, and at the yeres ende, or any tyme after, to returne hir home with hir marriage goodes or as much in value, vpon light quarrels, if the gentlewomans friends be vunable to reuenge the iniury. In lyke maner may she forsake hir husband.[8]

Stanyhurst focuses on his perception of the irregularity and looseness of marriage bonds in Ireland, in relation to English practice. He narrates how "concubines or harlots" become wives, evidencing an anxiety about their lack of correlation between women's sexual experience and their marriageability. While uninterested in an accounting of sexual perversions such as incest and public sex which Campion enumerates, Stanyhurst similarly describes the potential for impermanent marriage contracts in Ireland. These differences in the definition of marriage as well as in the fitness of sexually experienced women to enter into the marriage contracts are at the center of Stanyhurt's account.

As Liam Miller and Eileen Power note, "The work of Stanyhurst and Campion is firmly interrelated. This may not, however, have been immediately obvious to contemporary readers of the *Chronicles*, as Campion's *Two Bokes of the Histories of Ireland* was not published until 1633, almost seventy-five years after it was written."[9] These narratives functioned as a means of informing the English about Irish geography, character, and history. Each was composed between 1565 and 1571, years which were full of uncertainty about the way forward for colonial administrations.[10] In this context, both writers pay attention to representations of women's sexualities, their alleged promiscuities and their profiles for marriage. Such representations, while more virulent in Campion than in Stanyhurst, are the foundation for the subsequent tradition of representing Anglo-Irish interrelations, as well as the anxieties of the New English in Ireland, via Irish women's bodies. Later narratives, more focused on explicitly political agendas in their representations, and more presently concerned with the relationship between New English and Irish populations, will take their discussions of Irish women's sexualities to another level—as dangerous mediums of contagion and death for the English colony.

John Derricke's account, *The Image of Ireland, With a Discouery of Woodkarne,* composed in 1578 and published in 1581, is one such narrative in which Irish women are identified as a danger to the colony. *The Image*, written in a verse-narrative form, is as explicitly didactic as Campion's and Stanyhurst's works, yet differs in its intended audience. Instead of writing a descriptive text about the Irish for an audience in England,

Derricke writes an extended warning for the New English in Ireland. Derricke, appointed in November of 1569 to a post in Drogheda to serve as a custom's collector on wine at ports, was probably in Ireland from 1569 to 1578. *The Image* was completed during "the year before the outbreak of the Desmond Rebellion and published [] in the wake of the massacre at Smerwick, in the midst of acute English anxiety about Spanish and French invasions."[11] Despite the violence immediately surrounding the work, Moroney observes the absence of any acknowledgment of this context by Derricke in the text of the *Image*:

> despite the three-year gap between the date of composition (1578) and the date of publication (1581), Derricke chose not to update his representation of the state of Ireland to include references to either the ongoing rebellion or the recent and abortive invasion attempt. Instead he gives his attention on Sir Henry Sidney's military triumph over rebellious Irish chieftains like Rory Og O'More, and his political victory over Turlough Luineach O'Neill, both of which predate the larger and more dangerous uprising.[12]

Such an acknowledgment is important in understanding the intent of the *Image* for Derricke, and is linked to how this work functions very differently than the texts which have been discussed so far. While accentuating the suppression of a rebellion, which is old news, Derricke advises the men of the soldiers of the Pale to whom the work is addressed about how to best preempt further attack—stay away from Irish women. He diverts attention away from present internal threats, and toward a battle won long ago, as a means of suppressing anxiety about a current state of uncertainty for the New English in Ireland. Simultaneously, Derricke utilizes representations of Irish women as a stand-in for the threat to the New English, thereby displacing the present threat of rebellion onto the sexualized figure of the Irish woman as temptress.

The vision of Irish women represented by Derricke differs greatly from that found in Campion or Stanyhurst in several important ways. Derricke is the first among these writers to both acknowledge the desirability of Irish women and explicitly link this to their danger for the colony. To this end, recognizing the beauty and allure of Irish women, whom he metaphorically refers to as "wood nimphs," is foremost in the piece. Imagining Irish women bathing, Derricke writes:

> Ah wouldn't revive a manne half dedde?
> to see those naked sprites?
> To see what games they can devise,
> and sundrie pastymes make:

Twould cause I doe assure you,
    a horse his alter brake.
To daunce attendance on these Dames,
    with recurrent service then:
To waight upon them in that case.

In addition to this attention to the pleasing nature of their bodies to the observer's eye, found in the narrative, Derricke's *Image* also includes a satirical celebration of Irish nimphs'/women's other positive dimensions. He moves from recognition of their physical attractiveness, to a lauding of their sexual proclivities:

O nimphes of lastying memorie,
    your vertuous actions rare:
With venus for integritie,
    I freely make compare.
With Venus for agilitie,
    (speake I of veniall sinne:)
In her celestiall paradice,
    ought you to enter in.
For you are they which store the ground
    with fruites of your encrease:
And make it daiely to abounde
    (meane I with rest and peace)?
With little nimphes and mountaine Gods
    transformed now and then:
From Bores to beares, and yet sometyme,
    resembling honest men,
Form whence there flowes as from a spring,
    an other generation.

Irish women's sexual proclivities lead to their fecundity—the real object of concern for Derricke in the passage. The concern about Irish women's fecundity is not just about the increase in population; instead, Derricke draws attention to the kind of population to which they give birth. The nimphs bring forth the next generation of "bores to beares," the fighters who are the enemies of Derricke's audience—the men of the Pale. Derricke's use of Classical allegory to praise Irish women underscores the movement in this work away from Campion and Stanyhurst's focus on Irish women's sexual barbarism, and toward a more humanized representation of Irish women as attractive. This is despite their role in creating another generation of potential warriors against whom Palesmen are opposed. As he goes on to say:

Who as thei growe in elder yeres
and springing rise in strength:
So doe their worke the Realmes anoye,
and hindreance at the length.
So doe thei worke the landes decaie,
procurying what thei canne:
The ruine and undoying quight,
of many an honest manne . . .
And since the pale is offed plag'de
with suche a hellishe sorte:
Let that suffice, and let us all,
be warn'de by true reporte.

There is no indication that the offspring of Irish "nimphs," whether hybridized or not, will be raised as members of the Colony—despite the possibility that they are fathered by Palesmen. Instead, the nimphs' offspring are represented, summarily, as being formed wholly by the values of their Irish mothers. Consequently, they will become the fighters who batter at the edges of the Pale which Derricke wishes to defend. Further, they produce "the landes decaie," hinting at a kind of contamination Spenser will take up as a major theme in *A View of the Present State of Ireland*.

It is at this point that the narrative turns clearly didactic in tone, and gives evidence for the intended audience that Derricke was trying to reach through *The Image*. Once the 'nimphs'/women have been identified as the sources of the danger who need to be guarded against, Derricke tells his audience about how to accomplish this:

So shalle we shonne the dangerous snares,
our secret foes have sette:
And overpasse the hunter coiles,
and foulers cratie neete.
So shall wee flie the traiterous grinnes,
that treasons might procure:
And in a towne of strong defense
our [] all assure
Wee knowe by good experience,
it is a dangerous thyng:
For one into his naked bedde;
A poysning Tode to bring
Or els a deadly crocadile,
when as he goesth to reste:
To lead with hym, and as his mate,
to place next to his breste.

English men of the Pale are entreated by Derricke to resist Irish women as they would poisonous creatures. The long rhetorical buildup in the work is to underscore this point—Irish women are the dangerous threat to the colony which must be resisted in order to ensure its future.

Once the key point of this section is articulated, Derricke develops a more directly admonishing tone toward his intended audience:

> Then since the harme is manifest,
> content with willyng minde:
> To ridde your handes from such a sorte
> for catte will after kinde.
> And be not witched evermore
> within their eternall sight:
> for why should men of th'English pale,
> in such a crewe delight
> Or eke repose such confidence,
> in that unhappie race:
> Such mioscheef lurketh oftentimes
> even in the smoothest face?

Derricke arrives in a rhetorical stance which bestializes Irish women by virtue of their potential for treasonous behavior enacted against the colony. Yet, Derricke's representation of Irish women both encompasses a recognition of their attractiveness and their danger—they are alluring, yet they also produce the next generation of fighters, and in the meantime, they are betraying female counterparts of those fighters who need to be resisted as poisonous and deadly beasts. Derricke's image of Irish women engages in the Irish nimphs' attraction as a means of trying to transform that source of attraction into repulsion for his audience. Such repulsion could persuade the New English men of Derricke's audience to forestall their attraction to Irish "nimphs" and instead install a preference for women of their own "kind" in its place.

Despite the fact that Derricke did not update the text of *The Image* to include details of current dangers for the English in Ireland, what is communicated through these images is a concern about the future of the colony mediated through representations of Irish women. The audience for the piece is being asked to respond to such concern by ceasing to consort with Irish women, and hence foreclosing on the possibility for betrayal. This suggests the text's underlying anxieties about creating firm boundaries between groups, but not about cultural/genetic contamination of the English colony, which is a later concern for Edmund Spenser. Instead, the focus here is pragmatically about the ability to survive betrayal and rebellion, rather than about withstanding the pollution of Irish blood and customs which travel through the bodies of Irish women, according to Spenser.

Edmund Spenser was an employee of the Elizabethan administration when he came to Ireland as Lord Lieutenant Grey de Wilton's private secretary, and someone who spent upward of twenty years of his life on the island. In *A View of the Present State of Ireland*, composed in 1596,[13] Spenser considers the problem of Ireland's incomplete conquest, and the best ways in which to complete it.[14] The role of language acquisition holds a chief place in the dialogue regarding the means by which the Anglo-Norman population has been "degraded" or made impure through association and breeding with the native Irish after their plantation in Ireland. Since the question of how this older conquest went wrong is central to his preoccupations, Spenser is much concerned with the ways in which such corruption by Gaelic identity can be withstood. It becomes necessary to posit an entrance point for this hybridization/degradation of the distinctions between conqueror and conquered, English and Irish—the binaries of division upon which the official colonial campaign insists. If the beginning of such corruption can be pinpointed, then the communication of other markers of Irishness can be contained and kept alien so that the Elizabethan conquest does not similarly fall victim to the conquerors becoming "more Irish than the Irish" themselves.

In the quest to understand how the Anglo-Normans of the older conquest became "impure" through their association with the "meere Irish" population, Irenius's character isolates the practices of fosterage and intermarriage as contaminating points of contact with the "outside" population. One can argue that the actual disruption, the colonizer's fear of assimilation, is beyond the limits of full representation. Instead of dealing with this threat fully, Spenser uses the body of the Irish woman as a metaphor for the fear of contamination.

According to Spenser's construction of the problem, language is the medium through which contamination travels. The vessel which mediates language is the body of a woman. Therefore, the anxieties latent in the project of conquest are externalized onto the contaminating body of the Irish woman:

> I suppose that the cheife cause of bringing in the *Irish* language, amongst them, was specially their fostering, and marrying with the *Irish*, the which are the two most dangerous infections, for first the Childe that suckethe the milke of the nurse must of necessitye learne his firste speache of her, the which being the first that is enured to his toungue is ever after moste pleasinge unto him In so much as thoughe he afterwardes be taughte *Englishe* yet the smacke of the first will allwayes abide with him and not

> onely of the speach, but allsoe of the manners and Condicions. For besides that, yong Children be like Apes, which will affect and imitate what they see done before them, especially by theire nurses whom they love so well, they moreover drawe into themselues, together with their sucke, even the nature and disposicion of their nurses: for the minde followeth much the temparature of the body: and also the words are the Image of the minde, So as they proceeding from the minde, the minde must be needes affected with the wordes So that the speache being *Irish*, the heart muste needes be *Irish*, for out of the abundance of the harte the tongue speaketh.[15]

A breakdown within the Manichean world of the colonial interchange is explained by Spenser through the further construction of a binary explanation. The body of the English colony is contaminated through contact with the influence of an Irish woman's body. In encapsulating "disfiguration"/ degeneration in this way, Spenser's representation of the Irish woman as source of contamination dematerializes her figuration. She comes to stand as an abstracted sign of the body, not as an anthropomorphized representation of woman. This is further connected to the project of colonialism, to dehumanize the outside/alien to the extent that it becomes possible to rationalize its containment and domination.

Spenser, therefore, characterizes the abstracted body of the Irish nurse as a source of contamination, a medium of impurity who transfers, in addition to her milk, a language and mind-set which are foreign. Interestingly, the milk itself is not understood to be the contaminating agent. Instead, the contamination of language and disposition occurs, not as a result of direct contact with the body, but as a by-product of the intimate relationship between child and nurse. As Julie Costello notes, "This concern that the child might pick up the language habits of its nurse reveals Spenser's deeper anxieties about children learning to love 'things Irish'—his fears that milk might be thicker than blood."[16] Consistent with his abstracted representation of the nurse's body, Spenser is not concerned with the physical contact of the nurse/child relationship, but instead, with the communication of "influence" in this context. The nurse's ability to mold, through a kind of osmosis, the character of the child, is the threatening aspect of the dynamic between nurse and child. This concern about the feared primacy of "nurture" over "nature" will also be found in Spenser's later focus on marriage as another means through which the culture of the English planters in Ireland can be penetrated by Irish culture. Spenser insists that the influence of the Anglo-Norman (Old English) population by the Irish population is a gendered process. According to Spenser, the Anglo-Normans were made "more Irish than the Irish themselves" through the penetrative influence of Irish culture mediated through the figure of a woman.

Such a response can be better understood if contextualized within the historical moment of the 1590s. As G. A. Hayes-McCoy argues, "The salient feature of the last decade of the century was the resistance shown by Gaelic Ireland to the completion of the Tudor conquest."[17] In this sense, *A View of the Present State of Ireland* is also the product of the increasingly pressurized colonial dynamic resulting from Elizabethan policies in Ireland. Spenser, by virtue of his position within the administration, is implicated in these policies. The difficulty encountered in regularizing a colonial presence, coupled with the disturbing example which the Anglo-Norman (Old-English) population offered for the new settlers, created the colonizers' sense of themselves as an embattled minority needing to defend their position within Irish society, and the borders of their identity, ever more closely. Within this environment, the image of the female Irish body becomes the focus of anxiety about the incomplete conquest. For Spenser, this focus is what needs to be engaged in order to solidify the boundary between Old English and Native Irish populations. If this metaphorical point of contact/contamination can be controlled, the larger project of finishing the conquest will also be within reach. In this sense, then, the battle against "infection" is a microcosm of the larger battle to control the island. What must be guarded against, specifically, is the communication of an infectious "Irishness" which has the potential to remake the colonizers in an Irish image, thereby neutralizing the goal of the Elizabethan colonial project. As Andrew Murphy comments: "What Irenius appears to be attempting in this passage is to venture *beyond* a theory of assimilation of the Old English to a suggestion that it is, in fact, possible—through something like an intersection of culture and nurturance—for the Old English in some literal way to have *become* Irish (as distinct from a process of assimilation, by which they would become *like* the Irish)."[18]

The contaminating force of the Irish woman's body is not limited to the transference of milk and influence associated with the wet nurse's liminal position between native and Old English populations. Spenser continues his focus on the Irish woman as the locus of infection through his explanation of the way that intermarriage functions to corrupt the English population:

> The next is the marrying with the *Irish*, which how dangerous a thing it is in all common-wealthes, appeareth to every simplest sense, and though some great ones have perhaps used such matches with their Vassals, and have of then neverthelesse raised worthy issue, as Telamon did with *Termessa*, *Alexander the Great* with *Roxane*, and *Julius Caesar* with *Cleopa-*

> *tra*, yet the example is so perillous, as it is not to be adventured: for in stead of those few good, I could count unto them infinite many evill. And indeed how can such matching succeede well, seeing that commonly the childe taketh most of his nature of the Mother, besides speach, manners, and inclynation, which are (for the most part) aggreable to the conditions of their mothers: for by them they are first framed and fashioned, so as what they receive once from them, they will hardly ever forgoe.[19]

Despite the few great examples of favorable progeny resulting from coupling between conqueror and vassal, by far the most evidence exists, according to Spenser, to insist on the policing of sexual alliances. He assumes that the type of marriage/sexual union to be guarded against occurs between an Irish woman and an Old English (Anglo-Norman) man. The reverse is never considered by Spenser in his reconstructed interaction with past marital and sexual alliances.[20] So, in Spenser's social history, the Irish woman is again situated as the contaminating medium of identity which must be resisted in order to prevent the Old English community's degradation. She has the power to shape the content of the child's mind, beginning with its speech and continuing with its "manners and inclination." Just as in Spenser's consideration of the wet nurse, "nurture" ultimately takes precedence over "nature"—the child's character is not inherited, but rather shaped through exposure to his/her mother. The dialogue briefly considers that laws have already been passed against such intermarriage, and yet "for what doe Statutes availe without penalties, or lawes without charge of execution?"[21] Such laws are ineffectual in that they are not enforced. In either the case of intermarriage or fosterage, it is the influence of an Irish woman which communicates "Irishness," according to Spenser, and therefore the degradation of the English population, as well as the negation of the Elizabethan colonial project. At a moment when the success of that project is in severe jeopardy, imagining the body of the Irish woman as a metaphorical source of contamination and defeat is a means by which Spenser manifests his anxiety associated with the colonial project.

A line of development can be drawn between the earlier narratives of Campion and Stanyhurst through to the later narratives of Derricke and Spenser. This developmental understanding of New English writing between 1571 and 1601 analyzes representations of Irish women's bodies and sexualities as a means of gauging how the writers under consideration characterize Irishness and its threat to the future of the colony. Campion and Stanyhurst represent Irish barbarity through sexual deviance, focusing on the figure of the "strumpet" or "whore" as most emblematic of that category. Derricke and Spenser locate danger to the colony in the bodies of Irish women who threaten the boundary of the Pale. For Derricke, this is a literal threat—through betrayal and rebellion. For Spenser, it is a threat which arrives through genetic/cultural contamination. The increasing pitch of the threat ascribed to Irish women in these work is directly related to the literal level of threat to the colony present on the ground at the moments in which the works are written. What starts out as a tactical representation of difference for Campion and Stanyhurst in writing colonial history ends up as a figuration of potential extinction for Spenser in a political missive. The constant in these works is how Irish women inevitably and variously signify incivility, rebellion, contamination or extinction and hence continually represent New English anxieties about their place in Ireland.

Notes

1. "Despite its unevenness and sketchiness, and even though it remained in manuscript until 1633, the History exerted considerable influence. Most immediately, Raphael Holinshed and Richard Stanyhurst borrowed extensively from it in compiling their contributions to the Irish volume of Holinshed's *Chronicles of England, Scotland and Ireland*. The History also circulated among several of the later writers, a fact suggested by their allusions to and borrowings from it. Spenser particularly seems indebted to it." James P. Myers, *Elizabethan Ireland: A Selection of Writings by Elizabethan Writers on Ireland* (Hamden: Archon Books, 1983), 22.

2. Myers, *Elizabethan Ireland,* 26.

3. Ibid., 30.

4. Although there was an articulation of different types of marriage, and wider possibility for divorce instigated by women under Brehon law, there is no evidence to suggest that marriage was not an expected and integral part of Irish cultural practice at this time.

5. "Irish towns could not be called large compared to their English counterparts—even Dublin had only the population of an English county town. For Ireland though, they were unusual concentrations of people. No proper or reliable figures exist or are ever likely to exist for the country's population at this time but a figure of 1 million has been estimated giving a density of 31.25 people per square mile compared to 156.25 today. Since there was little urban development in Gaelic areas, the contrast with the largely urbanised settler areas was strong." Anthony Sheehan, "Irish Towns in a Period of Change, 1558–1625," in *Natives and Newcomers: essays on the making of English colonial Society, 1534–1641*, ed. Ciaran Brady and Raymond Gillespie (Dublin: Irish Academic Press, 1986), 98.

6. Shirley Adawy Peart, *English Images of the Irish, 1570–1620* (Lewiston: Edwin Mellen Press, 2002), 75.

7. Steven Ellis notes the contradictory nature of O'Neill's efforts, directed both for and against crown interests: "In Ulster, Shane O'Neill consolidated his position on the pretext of doing service. He besieged and captured Lifford, ransomed O'Donnell who went to court to seek Elizabeth's support, and plundered Carlingford. But, then, to the government's satisfaction, he attacked the Scots and eventually in May 1565 decisively defeated them at Glenshesk in North Antrim: James and Sorley Boy MacDonald were captured and

two MacLeod chiefs." Steven Ellis, *Tudor Ireland: Crown, Community and the Conflict of Cultures 1470–1603* (London: Longman, 1985), 249.

8. This section is from the description, which Stanyhurst wrote, along with Book III of the History, 115.

9. Liam Miller and Eileen Power, "Introduction" in *Holinshed's Irish Chronicle* (Dublin: Dolemen Editions, 1979), xiv.

10. The political will of the crown administration, growing out of the uncertainty in this period, is characterized very differently by Ciaran Brady and Nicholas Canny: "This pervasive sense of failure posed a particularly acute problem when viewed in relation to the other discoveries noted above. Had these been aggressive, tough-minded individuals determined to initiate a new military conquest in the island, then their experience of confrontation, disappointment and defeat would have been readily enough accounted for. But they were not: they were instead conservative constitutionalists, seeking to revitalize a political culture that had once existed in most parts of the island by reform, persuasion and the minimum of coercion. This determined gradualism only made the universal hostility which they confronted, and their failure to overcome it, all the more difficult to explain." Ciaran Brady, *The Chief Governors: The Rise and fall of reform government in Tudor Ireland 1536–1588* (Cambridge: Cambridge University Press, 1994), xii.

On the other hand: "Thus, while recommending a middle course, Philip Sidney knew, as his father had done since the 1560s and as Spenser was to recommend in the 1590s, that the best course of action for the queen was 'by direct conquest to make the country hers, and so by one great heap of charges to purchase that which indeed afterwards would well countervail the principal.' " Nicholas Canny, *Making Ireland British, 1580–1650* (New York: Oxford University Press, 2001), 63.

11. Maryclaire Moroney, "Apocalypse, Ethnography, and Empire in John Derricke's *Image of Irelande* (1581) and Spenser's *View of the Present State of Ireland* (1596)," *English Literary Renaissance* 29, no. 3 (1999): 365.

12. Moroney, "Apocalypse, Ethnography, and Empire," 366.

13. It was not ultimately printed until 1633.

14. Nicholas Canny and Andrew Carpenter, eds., "The Early Planters: Spenser and his Contemporaries," *The Field Day Anthology of Irish Writing,* vol. 1 (Derry: Field Day Publications, 1991), 175.

15. Edmund Spenser, *A View of the Present State of Ireland* (Oxford: Clarendon, 1970), 47.

16. Julie Costello, "Maria Edgeworth and the Politics of Consumption: Eating, Breastfeeding, and the Irish Wet Nurse in *Ennui*" in *Inventing Maternity: Politics, Science, and Literature, 1650–1865,* ed. Susan C. Greenfield and Carol Barash (Lexington: University of Kentucky Press, 1999), 180.

17. G. A. Hayes-McCoy, "The completion of the Tudor conquest, and the advance of the counter-reformation, 1571–1603," in *A New History of Ireland,* vol. 3 ed. T. W. Moody (Oxford: Clarendon Press, 1976), 115.

18. Andrew Murphy, *But the Irish Sea Betwixt Us: Ireland, Colonialism, and Renaissance Literature* (Lexington: University of Kentucky Press, 1999), 73.

19. Spenser, *A View of the Present State of Ireland,* 48.

20. As is supported by various examples which Edmund Curtis gives elsewhere, the gender of those involved in Gaelic/Anglo-Norman intermarriage was not marked at the time. In other words, Anglo-Norman women intermarried with the Gaelic population, as well as their male counterparts. "The Gaelic and the Norman lords, indeed, in their use of

the Irish language, their patronage of Brehons and bards, their standing forces and love of local independence, were becoming almost indistinguishable, and the prohibition of intermarriage and fosterage went by the board. Ireland became a chequerboard for an aristocracy derived from both races, in many ways, acting together, though for long the 'Old English' boasted that they were the blood of the Conquest and thought themselves a superior race." *A History of Ireland* (London: Routledge, 1988), 136.

21. Spenser, *A View of the Present State of Ireland,* 48.

Fashioning Identity in Eighteenth-Century Politics: The Case of John Toland

Jeffrey R. Wigelsworth

SINCE HIS DEATH, THE IRISH-BORN DEIST JOHN TOLAND (1670–1722) HAS been viewed in widely divergent terms.[1] The diarist Thomas Hearne called him "a very ingenious man, but of most vile principles." Conversely, one eighteenth-century bookseller in London claimed Toland's reputation "hath received so great a Brightness from his own Pen, that it needs no auxiliary Light to increase its Lustre."[2] This same difference of opinion regarding Toland is found among historians. Some view him as a covert atheist and persistent liar, others as a political radical determined to topple existing institutions, while recently a more nuanced Toland is emerging, one who cannot be described with facile labels.[3] In order to begin to answer the question of who was John Toland it is necessary to refocus our attention away from modern perceptions of him and engage with his own efforts at identity creation. Thus, this chapter is concerned with the identity of an infamous individual rather than group or national identity that is the subject of other chapters within this book.

Current scholarship suggests that individual identity is formed through an internal process of self-fashioning and through membership in particular groups. Jan E. Stets and Peter J. Burke put it as follows: "the core of an identity is the catergorization of the self as an occupant of a role, and the incorporation, into the self, of the meanings and expectations associated with that role and its performance."[4] Steven Shapin has applied a similar notion of identity to early modern figures. He argues that "identity has to be continually made, and is continually revised and remade, throughout an individual career in contingent social and cultural settings."[5] We will see that Toland employed this strategy of identity fashioning through association (claimed and legitimate) with a variety of changing groups both inside and outside of England.

By using Toland as an example we are able to see how early modern thinkers wished to locate themselves in their society. In this chapter, I examine Toland's manuscripts and published works, in an attempt to answer the following two questions: (1) what identities did Toland want to construct through his attempts to insinuate himself into various groups after 1696 and the publication of his most famous book *Christianity not Mysterious*; and (2) what was his ultimate goal? That Toland changed his identity during his life is not surprising. Recently Amin Maalouf has argued that "Identity isn't given once and for all: it is built up and changes throughout a person's lifetime." What is more, a person's overall identity might be composed of various identities that are emphasized or downplayed depending on the situation in which a person is found. Consider Stuart Hall's assessment that identity is "increasingly fragmented and fractured; never singular but multiply constructed across different, often intersecting and antagonistic, discourses, practices and positions."[6]

Toland's earliest identity is matter of speculation. He was likely the bastard son of an Irish Catholic priest and raised in the north of Ireland where he became fluent in several Gaelic dialects. Around his sixteenth birthday Toland renounced the religion of his father. His first widely noticed identity was forged during his time at Oxford through the perception of others and Toland's own actions. Toland spent much of 1693 in Holland, ostensibly training as a Presbyterian minister at the University of Leiden. In reality, he had been imposing himself upon men with whom John Locke had associated during his self-imposed exile following the Exclusion Crisis. Later that year Toland returned to England.[7] Failing to secure employment in London, he traveled to Oxford in early 1694 with the intent of using his language skills to compose a dictionary, which used linguistic evidence, to demonstrate that Ireland had been an original colony of Gaul and therefore reveal Irish independence from England. Persistent accounts of Toland's irreligious actions, such as "burning a Common-Prayer-book," troubled Edmund Gibson, future bishop of London, who kept a close eye on him.[8] Gibson sent frequent reports to Arthur Charlett, Master of University College, Oxford, including biographical details. While studying in Scotland (1688–89), Toland had purportedly "got a rable together, and at the Head of them in the Market place burn't the Pope; upon wch occasion he made a formal Speech against the then Magistrates o' the Town for being Episcopal." Thus, Toland appeared anti-prelatic if not anti-priest and so distressed Gibson that he appointed several persons to collect information.[9] Toland took notice of these characterizations of him and responded in a letter to an anonymous recipient that "The irreligion laid to my charge, is as much owing to the malice of my enemies, as the reputation of my parts and learning to the goodness of my friends."[10] At this early stage of his life, Toland seems to be aware of the importance of association for his identity.

Toland's actions spoke louder than his words. From Oxford, Charlett wrote to Archbishop Tenison in October 1695 that Toland had become "so publick and notorious here, that the late Vice-Chancellor ordered him to depart this place, wch he accordingly promised to do, and did for some time, but afterwards in ye V-Cr's absence returned." Other witnesses described "upon Oath, of [his] Trampling on ye Common prayer book, talking against the Scriptures, . . . railing against Priests in general, with a Thousand other Extravagancys as hi[s] common Conversation." What was worse, Toland claimed friendships with "great men" and "pretended to great Intrigues and correspondencys. . . . ." This kind of "insolent carriage," which the work of Anne Goldgar has demonstrated, did indeed leave Toland "contemptible, both to ye Scholars and Townsmen." Others, including George Ashe, bishop of Derry and the nonjuring divine Henry Dodwell, also tracked the movements of a man who aroused much interest.[11]

Aside from being seen as a braggart, Toland became known around Oxford as a "man of fine parts, great learning and little religion," who was composing a book "to show, that there is no such thing as Mystery in our Religion."[12] Thus, even before he began a career as polemic author, Toland was infamous. With the release of *Christianity not Mysterious, or a Treatise Shewing That There is Nothing in the Gospel Contrary to Reason, Nor above it that no Christian Doctrine can be Properly Call'd A Mystery* (1696), Toland's perceived Oxford identity as a heretic was cemented throughout Britain and would taint others against him for the rest of his life. First appearing anonymously, Toland affixed his name on the title page of the second printing because he hoped to capitalize on the notoriety the book generated for its unknown author.

Toland's non-mysterious religion had its basis in a conception of God "who has enabled us to perceive Things, and form judgments of them, has also endu'd us with the power of suspending our judgment about whatever is uncertain." Whatever aspect of religion that cannot be known with certainty need not be known; it is unimportant. Toland asked, "to what end should God require us to believe what we cannot understand?" God does not conceal elements of Christianity required for its correct practice. That this is not widely known among Christians was the fault of ambitious and cunning priests who added mysteries to religion in order to vindicate and secure their privileged position as interpreters. What was more, priests opposed all honest inquiry into religion, branding all those who attempt to do so as atheists or heretics.[13] With his book, Toland believed he had done a great service to Christianity and would later view himself in the tradition of Martin Luther.

Toland returned to Ireland in early March 1697 eager to exploit his new fame. His aim, as we will examine momentarily, was to become secretary to John Methuen, the new lord chancellor. Toland chose a volatile time in which to insert himself into the midst of Anglo-Irish politics. In 1697, the Irish Parliament would ratify the Treaty of Limerick and cheaper woolen exports, which competed with those from England, were soon to cause political tensions as the English Parliament raised the specter of punitive duties.[14] William Molyneux, the philosopher and MP in the Irish Parliament, advised Locke that Toland was in Dublin but the reason was uncertain: "He is know[n] to be of no fortune" or employment.[15] Locke replied that care ought to be taken with Toland, whom he feared had an "exceeding great value of himself." Spending more time with Toland, Molyneux concurred: "He has raised against him the Clamours of all Partys; and this not so much by his Difference of Opinions, as by his Unreasonable Way of Discoursing, propagating, and Maintaining it." Toland's views were only part of the issue; more problematic was the choice of venue to pontificate his ideas. "Coffee-house and Publick Tables are not," Molyneux wrote, "proper Places for serious Discourse relating to the Most Important Truths." What was worse, a "Tincture of Vanity appear[ed] in [Toland's] Conversations, it disgusts many that otherwise have a due Value for his Parts and Learning." Despite Molyneux's request for Locke to help stop Toland's impudence, the aged philosopher replied that Toland would ignore "my friendly admonishments."[16] Locke then urged his compatriot to distance himself from Toland. Political practicalities may further account for Molyneux's reluctance to be associated with someone as controversial as Toland. When, in the course of the woolen dispute, the English Parliament ruled that its legislation took precedent over its Irish counterpart, Molyneux composed *The Case of Ireland's Being Bound by the Acts of Parliament in England Stated* (1698), which asserted Irish legislative independence.[17]

Authorities in Ireland were also keenly interested in Toland. Rumors concerning the contents of his book raised the suspicions of the Committee of Religion and an investigation soon followed. Toland recounted these events in a later publication referring to himself in the third person: "Mr. Toland was scarcely arriv'd in that Country, when he found himself warmly attack'd from the *Pulpit*. . . . ." He was surprised at this treatment because the Revolution of 1688 had supposedly guaranteed the freedom of religion which he advocated. What was more, Protestantism as envisioned by the original reformers demanded honest inquiry into religion. Toland submitted that he simply followed their example. This justification did not halt an inquest, which began on August 14, 1697. After deliberating for three weeks, the committee ruled "*That the Book entitul'd* Christianity not Mysterious, *containing Several Heretical Doctrines contrary to the Christian Religion and the establish'd Church of* Ireland, *be publickly burnt by the hands of the Common Hangman.*" Furthermore, it was ordered that Toland himself be taken into custody and prosecuted. Toland noted that he "took care to prevent" capture and fled to England.[18]

In the months following the combustible reception of his book in Ireland, Toland continued to defend its contents and presented himself as a modern-day reformer, a seventeenth-century Luther, the same identity he sought to fashion with *Christianity not Mysterious*.[19] When arguments based on religious freedom and toleration failed to win over his critics, Toland defended himself with appeals for an unrestrained press. It was, he contended, only through printing that knowledge increased. Specifically, Toland believed religious knowledge, the kind he hoped to disseminate in *Christianity not Mysterious*, only proliferated in a nation containing no restrictions on printing. He reminded readers that "The Reformation is wholly owing to the Press." Moreover, "This the brave *Luther* did singly and by himself in defiance of the whole Church, and this any Man now hath the same right to do: So that it's evident the Freedom or Restraint of the Press depends on this single Question, Whether we ought to be free, or Slaves in our Understandings?" As did Luther, so did Toland. By presenting himself as a member of this Protestant movement, Toland attempted to secure legitimacy for his works in that he would carry the identity of a Reformer, an example of Stret and Burke's notion of "the self as an occupant of a role."[20]

When the Lower House of Convocation tried and ultimately failed to censure *Christianity not Mysterious*, Toland explicitly defended his work for the last time in *Vindicius Liberius: or, M. Toland's Defence of himself, Against the late Lower House of Convocation* (1702).[21] Growing tired of repeated explanations and clarification of purpose, Toland stated that he believed "ample Satisfaction" had been given to all Christians who might have been offended at his honest, if ill-received, attempt to promote personal investigation into religion. This same work also serves as a point of divergence. It ended with a definition of correct government—"the Power of all Governors is originally conferr'd by the Society, and limited to their Safety, Wealth, and Glory"—and praise for the future ruling line of England, the House of Hanover, which promoted this form of government.[22]

Toland's purpose in returning to Ireland in 1697 was political. Not waiting to be offered a job from Methuen, Toland boasted of his expected position. William Simpson, a baron of the Exchequer, wrote to Toland alerting him that "Mr. Methuen as well as all your other Friends agree in censuring your Conduct Since you come to Dublin. They say you have acted a part very different from what was given you to be & that it was no way fit for a private man who tho no public employment, . . . to pretend to any at present, nor to own any hopes or Expectation of any. . . ." Toland's claim, Simpson scolded, drew "Censure upon" him but more importantly "There have been some Complaints made to Mr. Methuen of your dealing with several people. . . . ." An anonymous letter sent in June 1697 also warned Toland that his actions bore on both him and those with whom he wished to become associated. Methuen ultimately provided him nothing official. We may also note that when Molyneux required protection from an irritated English Parliament for his forceful assertion of Irish rights, it was Methuen who stemmed the tide of retributive desires from his fellow MPs.[23] It is likely that Methuen saw the inclusion of Toland into this circle as an unneeded distraction.

Failure in Ireland did not prevent Toland from pursuing his ultimate goal of crafting for himself the identity of political adviser. Fulfilling this desire through attempts at association with English and later German politicians characterize Toland's remaining years. All other identities created by him should be seen as subservient to this greater goal. The object of this strategy was firstly the English MP Robert Harley. During the election of 1698 Toland issued a pamphlet which urged voters to choose "fit and proper Representatives for the ensuing Parliament." This election came on the heels of the Treaty of Ryswick, which ended the Nine Years War (1689–97). Questions of war financing dominated sessions of Parliament and allowed those who supported William III's war effort to curry favor with the monarch: chiefly, Whigs of the so-called Junto. Opposed to the Junto Whigs, whom Toland presented as interested only in preserving their place and not the welfare of England, was a coalition of Old Whigs and Tories, led by Harley. Thus, Toland composed this present work to support Harley's cause by describing the rival Junto as unfit to govern.[24]

The following year (1699) Toland contributed to the standing army controversy with *The Militia Reform'd: or, an Easy Scheme of Furnishing England with a Constant Land-Force, capable of prevent or to subdue any Forein Power*. While the need for a standing army during the Nine Years War was obvious, the usefulness of maintaining it in the post-1697 era was uncertain. The Junto refused any reduction of the army as did William who believed it would encourage French aggression. Harley led the opposition once more, arguing that standing armies increased the power of the king at the expense of parliament; moreover, for an island nation, the Royal Navy and a militia of citizens was a sufficient safeguard.[25] Toland agreed with Harley and proposed a model for such a militia, based on a Roman example, which he outlined in ten propositions. This literary support for Harley's position earned Toland his covert patronage and furthered his attempts to become an adviser to the English government through Harley.[26]

In late March 1700, Toland again addressed the day's political climate with his edition of James Harrington's *The Oceana*. Harrington had come to prominence in 1656 with a depiction of the ideal commonwealth Oceana in the book of the same name. The intent of the work was to demonstrate that in a true republic military might also belonged to the members of that republic in the form of a militia. Toland dedicated his edition to "The Lord Mayor, Aldermen, Sherifs, and Common Council of London." The happiness of Londoners, Toland asserted, was a direct reflection of the goodness of the laws governing them and proof of the righteousness of London's government.[27] The key to all this was the propagation of liberty. Thus, any writer who promoted such a stance also must be good for the nation. Here Toland attempts to advance his own usefulness to the aldermen and mayor by inserting himself and his goals with theirs. As Shapin argues, identity in early modern Europe was created through political and cultural associations. Thus, Toland hoped to support his political adviser identity through perceived links with Harley and London's government.

At least one alderman was impressed with Toland's words. Sir Robert Clayton, former mayor of London, entered a motion in May 1700 to pay Toland for the kindness shown the "Mayor & Alderman in dedicating Harrington's Works to them." Another alderman retorted that similar motions in the past had come to nought because "the City was poor, and had no money for such uses." Furthermore, it was objected that why should Toland who "had printed a very bad book" be rewarded when other authors, who had written "a good sermon," received nothing. The sticking point seemed to be *Christianity not Mysterious*, which inhibited Toland's efforts at overt political reward. The alderman did, however, note that Clayton himself "had enough of his own, and he was willing to join in recommending Mr T case to Sir R. own generousity." Not surprisingly, "the Matter was dropped."[28] Toland would have to seek other avenues of advancement and other ways in which to secure his identity as political adviser.

In 1701, Toland published a book which would change the direction of his life and the focus of his political ambitions and his desired identity.[29] In *Anglia Libera: or the Limitation and Succession of the Crown of England*

Explain'd and Asserted, Toland articulated his support for the Act of Settlement (1701) and the House of Hanover as the heir to the English crown. He asserted that political theory supported the implication of the act, a fact confirmed by the action of English nobility in 1688–89. They were, Toland stated, "hearty Friends to the Liberty of the People, so zealous for preserving the *Protestant* Religion on both Home and Abroad. . . . ." Such behavior had been described a generation earlier by Harrington, who had, Toland reminded readers, outlined in *Oceana* how a force might be raised to defend the rights of citizens.[30] Toland concluded the book by urging goodwill toward the matriarch and her kin of the House of Hanover: it is "highly necessary that the Names of the Princess Sophia and her Issue be inserted in our public Prayers, with the rest of the Royal Family." By passing the governance of England to Protestants from Hanover, Toland suggested it would maintain the balance of power in Europe by curtailing France's and the pope's goal of Catholic dominance.[31] He left readers to consider that the Act of Succession did more than secure Protestantism in England, it secured the safety of all Europe. Toland's cause of identifying himself as Harley's spokesperson was giving way to his new hope of carving a niche as Hanoverian advocate, though his overall identity fashioning remained unchanged.

Based on the contents of *Anglia Libera* and at the urging of Harley, Toland traveled with the mission sent to Hanover in July 1701, to present the act to the electress Sophia.[32] Before arriving on the Continent, Toland's reputation preceded him. Sophia's privy counselor, the famed natural philosopher Gottfried Wilhelm Leibniz, received a warning from Baron Schütz that English bishops hated Toland as did many ministers of state. Furthermore, Schütz hope Leibniz would encourage Sophia to keep her distance from such a controversial figure.[33] The strongest rejoinder received prior to arriving in Hanover came from the third Earl of Shaftesbury who feared that Toland might display the same impolite behavior shown in Oxford. Shaftesbury was grandson to the famed first earl who had taken a lead role during the unsuccessful attempt to exclude James Duke of York from the throne. He frequently supported young men with promise and did so for Toland even though, according to Thomas Birch's later recollections, "he never had any great opinion of him. . . . ." It was through Shaftesbury that Toland had first met Harley.[34] The earl reminded Toland that "You are now in a great Scene of Affaires and Providence has assign'd you a great Part in them." Indeed, more than Toland's personal reputation lay in his actions.

> I hope you will remember that as you are the more rais'd, you are the more bound to preserve a Character such as becomes a Man who supports the

> Cause of Religion, Liberty and Vertue, and that it is not only your own and a few Friends' Reputation that is hazzarded but that your Native Country and the Lovers of it as well as all those of right Principles whome you represent to persons abroad, all these are engag'd with you and their Fame and Reputation in the Protestant World and amongst that Free People where you are known, does in a great manner depend on your Behaviour.[35]

Toland ignored Shaftesbury's advice and seemed to revert to his Oxford identity of braggart, but was actually taking the first steps toward cementing his identity as Hanoverian political champion in England. He included himself in all aspects of the mission using the opportunity to discuss philosophy and politics with the royal family. Such manners received notice back in England. Sophia herself related to the Duke of Newcastle that Toland had "made me a faithful representation" of the role Newcastle had played in securing the act.[36] This mention of Newcastle to Sophia was likely an attempt to gain the duke's favor as had been the dedication to him in *Anglia Libera*. Toland returned to England with great admiration for the Hanoverians and a new target for his political desires and new avenue for his desires.

In March 1702, two days after William III's death, Toland dispatched a letter to Shaftesbury requesting an introduction to Lord Halifax, a member of the former Junto. Despite siding against the Junto during the 1698 election and the debates over the standing army, Toland asked that Shaftesbury recommend him to Halifax and that Shaftesbury present the peer a copy of an unnamed book, perhaps *Anglia Libera* or *Vindicus Liberius*, which would have been politically fitting to his desires. Anticipating a prompt reply, Toland wrote that he would wait for Halifax outside of his lordship's home or at the Grecian Coffeehouse. The turbulent events of the day caused Shaftesbury to delay acting upon Toland's request. As he put it in a belated letter to Halifax: "I promised the person who sent this enclos'd to me, that I would present his Book to your Lordship and afterwards himself: but in this confusion of affaires I forgot both: so chose to send you this, as a less trouble to you than a visit on this account."[37] Once again Toland's attempts at advancement met with little success because Halifax seems never to have contacted Toland and there is no further letters from Toland on this matter.

After his attempts to secure a permanent position with the English government had failed and with the coronation of Queen Anne ushering in a new political and religious climate, Toland sailed to the Continent eventually turning up in Utrecht in mid-August of 1703. His allegations of association with important men followed him there. Toland's claimed alliance with Harley raised the suspicions of the latter's political rivals, the Duke of

Marlborough and Sidney Godolphin. Marlborough dispatched agents to Utrecht in order to mug Toland with the goal being to have him rethink his political company. Toland described the beating, to an unnamed correspondent, as occurring after a prolonged "Sickness, and passing over the brutal violence that was us'd against me in Such a Condition, either shows their gross partiality, or that I need not apprehend any Blemish to my Reputation from their Judgements." Despite the intention, Toland viewed his bruises as badges of honour and proof that his work was worrying those who would limit personal freedom. He assured his correspondent that "those Gentlemen's opinions of me, may ever prove my greatest uneasiness, being at present the least Thing in my Thoughts."[38] True to his words of defiance, Toland returned to England when a triumvirate, composed of Harley, Godolphin, and Marlborough ascended to the reigns of government. He arrived expecting a job, only to be dismayed when he found Harley employing Daniel Defoe's literary skills. Harley, who was then secretary of state, heard from an anonymous informant that "John Toland is in England and hard at work at his pen." William Nicolson, bishop of Carlisle, also learned of Toland's return during a conversation with Gibson. Afterwards Nicolson met with the archbishop of Canterbury who "assured [him] of Mr Toland's being out of Countenance at Hanover" due mainly to "his Knavery."[39] The news eased the three men's worries over Toland's potential political influence, albeit only temporarily.

Once more having failed to find English government employment, Toland turned his attention to the future rulers. During his visits to Hanover, Toland debated natural philosophy (science) with Sophia Charlottte, queen of Prussia (and daughter of the electress) and her counselor Leibniz. Toland's *Letters to Serena* (1704) was the result.[40] In composing this book for the queen, whose intellect received constant praise in his accounts of Hanover, Toland was attempting to establish a position next to persons of imminent political importance by presenting himself as an authority in the natural philosophy of the nation Sophia and her family would rule. Indeed, when the electress died in 1714, Toland lamented that she would never become queen of England and that his chance for a life of ease at court died with her.[41] *Letters to Serena* described his own unique description of matter and motion, which he tied to Isaac Newton's *Principia*. Just as priests obscured the intended clarity of Christianity, Toland believed philosophical authorities had done the same to the book of nature; and thereby prevented natural philosophers from acknowledging the notion of matter and motion he articulated.[42] Only in an atmosphere of intellectual freedom, as Toland described in his political works, can philosophers have a complete idea of matter. By linking his work to Newton, who was actively engaged in the priority dispute with Leibniz over the calculus, Toland may have been attempting to drive a wedge between Leibniz and the Hanoverian court in that Toland could be seen as a philosopher at home in English learned circles and not the divisive force Leibniz was certain to be.

His zeal to act as a kind of English spokesperson for the Hanoverians led Toland to publish a further account of the potential benefits of their rule in Britain. *An Account of the Courts of Prussia and Hanover* (1705) presented Toland's impressions of Hanoverian governance and described the laws through which a king ought to preside over the nation. Monarchs guide their subjects the same way that "God himself preserves the World by the Oppositions of Heat and Cold, of Gravity and Levity, of Hard and fluid Bodys, whence proceeds the admirable Harmony of all things." There was no "Prince at present in Europe, who has a nobler and greater Soul then Frederic the First." It was by the "King of Prussia's Genius" that the ideal kingdom existed in that nation; the same condition would too exist in England when the Hanoverians succeed to the crown. Key to the enviable management that this house brought to their subjects was "the intire Liberty of Conscience which all good Christians enjoy in this place, and throout all his Majesty's Territorys. . . ." There was, Toland asserted, no forced religious conformity in Prussia: people were permitted the use of their reason to find their own way to God and the religion which seemed best to them. He then went on at some length lauding the erudition of Sophia Charlotte. Her desire for learning influenced the choice of political advisors: "I need but name Monsieur Leibniz for an Example, who is here a Privy Counsellor and an Assistant in the Court of Chancery . . . " although, Toland conceded, "I cannot agree to his Metaphysical Notions. . . ."[43] This subtle challenge to the advice provided Sophia Charlotte by Leibniz is likely another attempt by Toland to obtain a court position for himself. Here identities of natural philosopher and political adviser unite in pursuit of a larger goal.

Not entirely certain of Hanoverian favors, Toland's desire to find government employment required that he consider alternatives and reshape his identity. This is evidenced by two notes he sent to Shaftesbury in late October 1705. Toland opened the first by referring to the letter Shaftesbury had sent prior to his trip with the Act of Settlement delegation. He assured the earl that "your Lordship's frank manner for chideing me for real or imaginary faults, has not diminisht, but rather increast that Confidence." Attempting to distance himself from his past Oxford identity as a boastful irritant, Toland alerted Shaftesbury to the fact that he was "not sauntering any longer in Coffeehouses, nor keeping so much tattling Company as I formerly us'd. . . . ." As he had done with past critics, he dismissed them with the claim that they did not know the real Toland. However, Shaftesbury too might not have been privy to the real Toland. In a letter sent to an unknown recipient on June 26, 1705, Toland expressed none of the reservations which he professed to Shaftesbury: "I am not asham'd to own, that I had not so much wisdom and discretion, as I had Sincerity and Zeal, in the management of my opinions."[44]

Conditions changed following the initial October letter. Toland now wrote with enthusiasm to Shaftesbury that "I am now in some manner altering my Circumstances: for what my Lord Somer's Ministry, wou'd not give me, and what I wou'd not ask my Lord Nottingham's Ministry, the present Ministry unsought has offer'd, and I am willing to accept." As to the exact nature of the appointment with Harley, Toland would not reveal in print. At the very least Toland hoped that this opportunity would allow him to "begin on clear ground" in the opinions of others.[45] Perhaps past perceived identities could be forgotten by Toland's contemporaries and he could begin fresh in their eyes. Acquaintances carried on further attempts on Toland's behalf to repair his damaged reputation. Elisha Smith wrote to Thomas Hearne, antiquarian, nonjuror, and at this time assistant keeper of the Bodleian, in early 1706 with just such a goal. After relating the many conversations he had with Toland, Smith advised Hearne that perhaps the public was too harsh in condemning Toland as a heretic. "I think myself oblig'd to vindicate him from ye mistaken prejudicies y[e] would has received concerning his Religion Since y[e] Publication of his first Book *Xtianity not Mysterious* he is very sensible of it & has confessed to me that those were only his Juvenile Thots at 25 & waits only for an opportunity to Convince Y[e] world how much they have mistaken him from that Book." Smith further assured Hearne that "I firmly believe him to be a man of Rel[igion]. & of y[e] Faith of Y[e] Church of Engl[and]." Hearne was unmoved and would later describe Toland as a "Sorry Wretch."[46] First impressions of Toland remained lasting impressions.

In early January 1707, the fourth Viscount of Netterville wrote Harley advising him that rumors of Toland's service to the minister was a frequent topic of discussion in political circles. Toland was seen as "Secretary Harley's champion." Later in the month, Harley admitted to Lord Raby, English ambassador in Berlin, that he had indeed covertly employed Toland on various occasions.[47] Toland had traveled to the Continent in early 1707 with the intent of meeting again with Sophia and her family. While abroad, he wrote to Harley expressing his disappointment at having not obtained a permanent position: "I think I may without fearing the least imputation of vanity, look on myself as much more deserving on many other accounts not fit to be named at present, and great deal more capable in all respects, than several in the long list of such as have been employed in that space of time." Apparently Toland felt somewhat uncomfortable asking "the best friend I have upon earth" for more money when Harley had already "supplied me now for two years out of your own pocket, in diet, clothes, lodging, and all other expenses." As to the reports of his actions during his trip, Toland assured Harley that "I am not going nor shall go either to Berlin or Hanover. . . . ."[48]

Not one to let a promise stand in the way of his political desires, Toland did not keep his word. After spending a few weeks in September at the court of John William, elector palatine of the Rhine, Toland requested a letter of recommendation to Sophia. William asked the electress "without any delay, to receive the said Toland into your mighty protection and powerful patronage." If she did this service, William predicted Sophia would not regret it.[49] Harley soon learned that Toland was indeed in Berlin and, what was worse, claimed to be acting on behalf of the English government. Erasmus Lewis, MP and under secretary of state, dispatched a brief account of Toland's latest actions in October 1707. An acquaintance had related to Lewis, who passed it along to Harley, that "Toland has come here from the Court at Dusseldorf, where the Elector made him considerable presents." Sophia herself was suspicious of Toland's unexpected arrival. The bishop of Spiga revealed to her at some length how he believed that Toland schemed the recommendation out of William. It seems Toland's claims of favor with politically great persons were as boastful as they had been thirteen years earlier in Oxford. This was not a surprising strategy. Shapin has demonstrated that socially lesser persons were untrustworthy; however, by linking (or in Toland's case asserting a link where none existed) with a person of higher social standing, men like Toland could potentially raise their status and legitimize their writings and identity.[50]

Leibniz too composed a description of Toland's arrival in Hanover and why the elector of Palatine might wish to support Toland, which he dispatched to Ambassador Raby at the end of December. He opined that the "Elector had an object of his own to serve, which was to . . . help to disabuse the English who have looked upon him as a persecutor of the Protestants." William belonged to the Catholic House of Palatinate-Neuburg and under his rule Calvinists were increasingly being exiled and barred from participating in government. By sponsoring Toland to the potential future ruler of England, Leibniz believed that the elector was attempting to appear friendly to all Protestants. In exchange, Toland had apparently composed a tract justifying Charles's actions with Protestants. This hypothesis was seconded from Berlin in a letter to Arthur Charlett, which lamented that "Mr. Toland I moan has lately been here coming from ye Palatine Court whose proceedings against ye Protestants we hear Mr. Toland has . . . defended & receiv'd great gifts for his pains."[51]

It was a mutually beneficially relationship of patron and penmanship. Toland's claim of identity as a Reformer, crafted in 1697, seems to have given way to that of a strategizing political author for the palatine elector. However, he miscalculated. The Hanoverian court "despis'd so mercinary a Pen yt cou'd write in favour of ye Elector Palatin's Persecuting ye Protestants, & put him off. . . . ." Toland's practice of supporting himself as a sort of quill-for-hire had cost him seriously in this case. He tried to balance one identity too many. This episode marked the end of his association, limited though it was, with the Hanoverians. Indeed, when George I succeeded to the English throne in 1714, he and his advisers explicitly prohibited Toland from attending court.[52]

Leibniz also reported that while at Hanover, Toland continually "insinuated to us here that since the change of Ministry in England he is in favour at Court, that he is employed by the Ministers."[53] Lord Raby wrote Leibniz in reply to this and related that Toland continued to claim "that he was employed by the English Ministry." Frustrated by this perpetual boasting, Raby advised Leibniz that he had initiated an end to it by dispatching a report to Harley. Erasmus Lewis passed the letter to Harley relating that Raby strongly urged him to "acquaint you with the great injustice done you by Mr. Toland." In reply to Raby's report, Harley disavowed any part in sending Toland to the Continent, rather he had initiated obstacles to stop Toland's travel.[54] Raby hoped this denial would finally halt Toland's vanity and self-promotion. Toland's unending statements about Harley's patronage and political favor raised the suspicions of other English politicians especially those who sparred with Harley for position. During August 1708, when Toland was in Holland, Marlborough and Godolphin kept close tabs on him because if he was indeed in Harley's service, it behooved them to keep abreast of their rival's overseas activities.[55] It seems that some took Toland's asserted political connections at face value.

With the election of 1710 returning a Tory majority, Harley's star was again on the rise. Toland seized the opportunity which events provided and wrote a letter of support to his former secret patron. From Leiden, he sent "Congratulations on Harley's happy return to the management of affairs and the disgrace of his enemies, confidently predicted and wished for by the writer."[56] After waiting a little less than a year with no improvement in his situation, Toland reminded Harley, now Earl of Oxford, of the service he might perform for the government. "It were strange if a person of my liberal education and experience in foreign Courts . . . should not be found useful in some things to so learned as well as so politic a Minister."[57]

By December 1711, Toland wrote with worry that Harley believed reports of his conduct. Toland feared he had been "abandoned as it were in my greatest need."[58] Toland wrote again on December 7 claiming that reports of his distaste for Harley's plans to end the War of the Spanish Succession (1702–13) through secret negotiations with France were indeed true and that his only friend in this matter was "the house of Hanover . . . and much less any peace that gives up Spain and the Indies to a Prince of the house of Bourbon, or to any French Prince whatsoever." He asked Harley to "consider whether it be advisable in any ministry to carry on a thing so perfectly disgusting to the next successor?" Among the potential members of the Grand Alliance who would be left to battle the French alone were troops led by Prince George of Hanover who feared a separate peace between England and France meant an end to the Hanover Succession and the proclamation of James III as King of England. To dissuade these feelings, Toland suggested that Harley "ought to dispatch me privately this minute to Hanover; where you'll find me as secret, as I hope to be successful . . . to clear up some things there. . . ."[59] Much to Toland's chagrin Harley ignored his volunteer role in international relations. Here we see identities in conflict: adviser to Harley versus adviser to Hanoverian monarchs, although the greater identity of political adviser remained intact.

Throughout 1712, Toland sent repeated requests to Harley for employment, asserting that Harley's reputation as a supporter of the Hanoverian succession was being eroded by enemies. Toland offered to secure Harley's character abroad for a salary of £200. The outcome was predictable: Harley ignored Toland. The year 1714 witnessed the start of the Hanoverian age in England and the end of whatever relationship still existed between Toland and Harley. In *The Grand Mystery Laid Open*, Toland repeated that a Protestant succession was secured through the efforts of the entire nation. Standing in the way was allowing one MP, who had "the purse and the prerogative at his disposal," to control the fate of the nation for the benefit of his party.[60] Toland not very subtly chastised Harley and his action ending the War of the Spanish Succession by making unfulfilled promises to Jacobite and overtures to the Pretender.

Harley also came under attack in *The Art of Restoring. Or, the Piety and Probity of General Monk In bringing about the Last Restoration* in which Toland contrasted the end of the Cromwellian commonwealth against the present political situation with Harley standing in for Monk. So corrupt had government become, claimed Toland, that only one's attitude toward the French identified him or her as a friend or enemy of England and the Hanoverian succession. He also claimed that the only support that Harley had for his platform was from papists and Jacobites. Against this impending Catholic usurping, he urged "every wise and generous *Briton*," to "lay aside their insignificant Piques, and all unite for the Preservation of their RELIGION and LIBERTY, which entirely depend (under God) upon maintaining the SUCCESSION, as is establishe'd by so many Laws in the serene *Electoral* House of HANOVER."[61] Toland, thus, abandoned Harley and his hope of establishing an identity as an English political adviser.

Now eager to secure his identity as Hanoverian advocate, Toland produced *The State Anatomy of Great Britain. Containing a particular account of its several interests and parties, their bent and genius* (1717), a description of the political landscape in England, which offered unsolicited advice to George I on which of the two parties were likely to support his reign. Remaining true to past description of Hanoverian monarchs as best embodying the characteristics of an ideal government, Toland believed that for George I "the Happiness, Ease, and Prosperity of his people, shall be the chief care of his life."[62] To fulfill this potential, George needed to choose advisers and ministers who shared this vision.

In explicit contrast to Tory High-Churchmen whom Toland argued brought divisions into the nation through their demands for religious exclusion and claims of Dissenter deviousness, he assured the new king that all variety of Dissenter were faithful to him. In spite of this fact, the Test Act (1673) still prohibited all but communicant Anglicans from any civil office. Toland urged George I to consider that the proliferation of the act "*is a Political Monopoly:* and they who wou'd confine all civil Employments to one sect, must be of opinion. . . ." Those who supported the act were also those who cried "Church in Danger" even though Dissenters were no religious threat, only a political one. Dissenters were Whigs and by preventing their holding of major positions, the Tories and High-Churchmen ensured these positions for themselves. Toland asked readers to consider that the real threat to England came from the very people who claimed to safeguard its religion. How could the monarch trust any who refused to swear allegiance to him while at the same time holding fast to their oaths given to the Stuarts who would certainly make England a Catholic state if given the chance. Toland's arguments attracted many readers, both supporters and critics; within a month of publication an eighth edition was ready for sale.[63]

Toland replied to critics of this book, who included Harley's onetime champion Defoe, with a second volume in April 1717. He repeated that the only purpose contained in the first volume was a demonstration of "from what fallacies and mistakes, from what wrong principles and pestilent projects, proceeded all the opposition to his Majesty and his illustrious family. . . ."[64] This desire is also seen in his unpublished scheme to regulate English newspapers. Though Toland had championed an unrestricted press in 1698, when it suited his purposes, defending George I—as the first Hanoverian king—became more important. It was, he suggested, time to "put the public Newspapers under some better regulation" regarding their attacks on the government and the king's person. As many papers seemed to conceive themselves having a "special privilege, to the damage of the King and Subject," Toland believed that guidelines must be established, not to end freedom of press but to halt seditious journalism. To this end, he proposed an act restricting periodical publishers to the use of stamped paper along with suitable penalties if unstamped paper was used. This would cease the "distracting plague of those Journals, which are the Scandal of this King George's reign, in which they all had their rise to disturb, and to the best of their powers, to destroy it."[65]

Toland and Edmund Gibson had a greater personal association than might be imagined. During June and July of 1694 they spent much time discussing natural history. It is well known that in 1695 Gibson issued a new edition of William Camden's *Britannia*, a sixteenth-century geographical and historical account of Britain. To accomplish this task, Gibson relied upon the talents of many scholars, including Toland who was to guide the section of the book concerning Ireland. Charlett remembered that Toland "courted" Gibson who "very little valued his Learning to which he so much pretended."[66] The two unlikely partners did not remain so for very long. Gibson was irritated with Toland's suggestion that they revise a manuscript catalog of English historians, which Gibson owned. The final break between the two occurred when Toland apparently uttered unfavorable comments regarding Camden which he unsuccessfully retracted. The loss to Gibson's endeavor was perhaps not a great one. When Toland initially arrived in Oxford he met and befriended Edward Lhwyd, antiquarian and Keeper of the Ashmolean. Lhwyd and Toland had many conversations about geology, but Lhwyd confessed to a friend that Toland was "not conversant in these studies, and endeavours to perswade us" as to his abilities.[67]

In his last years, Toland returned to studying the ancient history of Ireland, though he had never really abandoned it. Initial results of this research appeared in the second part of *Nazarenus* (1718) as "An Account of an Irish Manuscript of the Four Gospels." Toland's use of and fluency in Gaelic would have been viewed with suspicion in England because the language was seen as inherently Catholic and a barrier to bringing Protestantism to the nation.[68] Toland presented this "Summary of the ancient Irish Christianity" as a matter of fact either to be accept or rejected based on a reader's own reason. The first remarkable item of the original religion was the complete lack of ceremonies and the emphasis the Irish placed on reading "the *Scriptures* in the vulgar tongue." Moreover, the customary trappings of contemporary Christianity were absent: clergy wore no "gorgeous vestments." The "Church was esteem'd to be, not a political empire, or an organiz'd society with a proper subordination of officers and subjects; but the congregation of the faithful thro-out the world. . . ."[69] The implied conclusion was that ancient Gaelic religion was indeed the religion Toland advocated in his earliest writings; thus he appeared as a salvager of Irish religious antiquity.

The other result of his fascination with Irish history and archeology was *A Specimen of the Critical History of the Celtic Religion and Learning: Containing an Account of the Druids &c.*, dedicated to his friend and benefactor Lord Molesworth, which circulated in manuscript before being published in 1726 as part of a posthumous collection of Toland's writings.[70] His intent remained the description of ancient Celtic culture and religion "in a clearer light than anyone has hitherto done." Divided into three parts, each addressed to Molesworth, the book first considered Druid religion before moving to the archeological remains of Druid culture still present in Britain before concluding with an analysis of Druid mythology.[71] The work also contained the comparative dictionary, which Toland had initiated during his Oxford stay some twenty-five years earlier. Toland's letters reveal that he had been working on the Druid history project at least during 1718–19 and certainly before. He advised a correspondent that "I have been a great while upon a work so as all real lovers of learning will be glad to see . . . My subject is *the history of the Druids, as a critical account of the antient Celtic Religion & Literature*." Similarly, Toland revealed in another letter "my design to writing *the History of the Druids* . . . has been long in my thoughts." To this end, Toland said he had collected many relics and artifacts to supplement his written material.[72]

Toland's presentation of himself as an authority on ancient Gaelic peoples and traditions continued in a collaborative journey in erudition he took with Molesworth. During late 1720 and early 1721 they exchanged a copy of Martin Martin's *A Description of the Western Islands of Scotland* (revised edition 1716), in which each man wrote marginal comments and assessments of Martin's abilities as a scholar. We know which annotations they composed because Toland helpfully "thought fit to distinguish [Molesworth's] by L. M. and my own by J. T." This was an important venue for Toland, as Justin Champion argues, because exchanging books created a "theatre for the performance of intellectual charisma."[73] There is little doubt that Toland aimed to create within the margin notes a sense of superiority for his own impending history. He wrote in the preface "The Subject of this Book deserv'd a much better Pen." What is more, many of Toland's marginalia ask Molesworth to "See my History of Druids." However, if Champion is correct and Toland did intend to circulate the book among a wider audience than merely himself and Molesworth, then these comments take on greater importance. By drawing attention to his history as superseding Martin's, Toland is advertising himself and his credentials as an Irish linguist and antiquarian to all those who would see the book and would have their interests piqued to see his forthcoming history of the Druids. As Shapin has demonstrated, personal identity may also be made through the act of making one's private knowledge public.[74]

Toland and Molesworth joined in a more widely known effort in the name of Ireland in 1720. In the spring of that year, the English Parliament in Westminster passed the Declaratory Act, which asserted the legislative authority of George I and the British Parliament over the Irish Parliament in Dublin. At Molesworth's behest, Toland composed *Reasons most Humbly offered to the honourable House of Commons, why the bill Sent down to them from the most honourable House of Lords, entitul'd, An act for the better Securing the dependency of the Kingdom of Ireland upon the Crown of Great Britain, should Not pass into Law*, which urged a repudiation of the act in the name of Irish liberties.[75] English political desires and the identity accompanying them, which had ultimately come to nought, were abandoned in favor of Toland's becoming a champion of Ireland in the model of Molyneux whom he had alienated some twenty-five years previously. Interestingly, Molesworth as an English MP had also actively protected Molyneux in 1698 from parliamentary action and it was now he who encouraged Toland to publish this latest work in the name of Irish independence. It would seem that Toland was now, during his last years, in the position he coveted in 1697: squarely in the middle of Anglo-Irish politics.

Toland's final months and the course of the illness which claimed his life is traced through the last letters he exchanged with Molesworth who expressed growing concern as Toland deteriorated.[76] Though he was near death, Toland was still much absorbed with his history project: "I am far advanced in my history of the Druids, which will either be a thin folio or a thick quarto, with about 26 copper cuts." Toland then assured Molesworth that he would soon be able to "to puruse my Manuscript."[77] He died on March 22, 1722, with both his history unfinished and his identity still a matter of conjecture.

During his life Toland existed, and sought to exist, simultaneously as a member of several groups, which he emphasised or abandoned, as events and opportunity demanded in pursuit of his larger goal. After 1696, and the notoriety which befell him as the author of *Christianity not Mysterious*, he attempted to create the following identities: modern-day Reformer, political secretary and pamphleteer for the English MP Robert Harley, defender of the Hanoverian succession, natural philosopher, and, in his last years, Irish historian and advocate. These, however, ought to be seen for what they were: aspects of a single desired identity of political advisor. These efforts at self-fashioning crossed geopolitical boundaries, political affiliations, and confessional allegiances the acknowledgment of which results in a figure more complicated that past scholarship might indicate. At any one time Toland juggled more than one aspect to his desired identity, historians must attempt to do the same. In his epitaph Toland provided advice for historians: "If you would know more of him / Search his Writings."[78] Despite the intervening two and two-thirds centuries of research and interest in these writings, we are still searching for him.

NOTES

For their aid I gratefully acknowledge Justin Champion, Larry Stewart, and Alison Jeppesen. David A. Valone and an anonymous referee offered sage advice. Financial assistance came from the Social Sciences and Humanities Research Council of Canada, the Calgary Institute for the Humanities, and the Department of History, University of Saskatchewan. All quotations retain original spelling, italic words and underlining. In all dates the year is taken to begin on January 1, rather than March 25. Some of the material in this chapter is taken from my book *Deism in Enlightenment England: Theology, Politics, and Newtonian Public Science* forthcoming from Manchester University Press and is used here with permission.

1. The English language biographies are: Robert E. Sullivan, *John Toland and the Deist Controversy: A Study in Adaptations* (Cambridge: Harvard University Press, 1982); Stephen H. Daniel, *John Toland: His Methods, Manners, and Mind* (Montreal: McGill-Queen's University Press, 1984); Robert Rees Evans, *Pantheisticon: The Career of John Toland* (New York: Peter Lang, 1991); Justin Champion, *Republican Learning: John Toland and the Crisis of Christian Culture, 1696–1722* (Manchester: Manchester University Press, 2003).

2. Thomas Hearne, *The Remains of Thomas Hearne*, ed. John Buchanan-Brown (London: Centaur Press, 1966), 440 [November 23, 1734]; William Mears, *An Historical Account of the Life of Mr. John Toland* in *The Theological and Philological Works of the Late Mr. John Toland* (London, 1732), 2.

3. David Berman, "Disclaimers and Offence Mechanisms in Charles Blount and John Toland," in *Atheism from the Reformation to the Enlightenment*, ed. Michael Hunter and David Wootton (Oxford: Clarendon Press, 1992); Margaret C. Jacob, *The Radical Enlightenment: Pantheists, Freemasons and Republicans*, rev. 2nd ed. (Morristown, N.J.: Temple

Publishers, 2003); Justin Champion, "John Toland, the Druids, and the Politics of Celtic Scholarship," *Irish Historical Studies* 32 (2001): 321–42.

4. Jan E. Stets, and Peter J. Burke, "Identity Theory and Social Identity Theory," *Social Psychology Quarterly* 63 (2000): 224, 225.

5. Steven Shapin, *A Social History of Truth: Civility and Science in Seventeenth-Century England* (Chicago: University of Chicago Press, 1994), 127.

6. Amin Maalouf, *In the Name of Identity: Violence and the Need to Belong*, trans. Barbara Bray (New York: Penguin, 2000), 23; Stuart Hall, "Who Needs 'Identity'?" in *Identity: A Reader*, ed. Paul du Gay, Jessica Evans, and Peter Redman (London: Sage Publications, 2000), 17.

7. Philippus van Limborch to John Locke, July 24/August 3, 1699; Limborch to Locke, July 25/August 4, 1693; Benjamin Furly to Locke, August 9/19, 1693, in *The Correspondence of John Locke,* 8 vols., ed. E. S. De Beer (Oxford: Clarendon Press, 1967–89), 6:661; 4:704–5, 710–11.

8. Bodleian Library, Oxford, [Bod.] Ballard MS 5 f. 27.

9. Bod. Rawlinson MS D. 923 f. 314r. See also BOD Ballard MS 5 f. 47r.

10. John Toland to ?, n. d. in *A Collection of Several Pieces of Mr. John Toland,* 2 vols. (1729; facsimile reprint, New York: Garland Publishing, 1977), 2:302.

11. Dr. Charlett to Archbishop Tenison, October 25, 1695 in S. R. Maitland, "Toland," *Notes and Queries* 4 (1862): 7. Anne Goldgar, *Impolite Learning: Conduct and Community in the Republic of Letters, 1680–1750* (New Haven: Yale University Press, 1995), 158, 165, passim. For Ashe and Dodwell see Bod. MS Eng. Let. C 28 ff. 27r–v; Bod. MS Eng. Let. C 29 f. 23.

12. A_A_ to John Toland, May 4, 1694; For Mr. Toland, May 30, 1694 in *A Collection of Several Pieces*, 2:295, 312.

13. John Toland, *Christianity not Mysterious, or a Treatise Shewing That There is Nothing in the Gospel Contrary to Reason, Nor above it that no Christian Doctrine can be Properly Call'd A Mystery* (London, 1696), 20, 143, 145, 70–71, 168.

14. Patrick Kelly, "Recasting Tradition: William Molyneux and the Sources of *The Case of Ireland . . . Stated* (1698)," in *Political Thought in Seventeenth-Century Ireland: Kingdom or Colony*, ed. Jane H. Ohlmeyer (Cambridge: Cambridge University Press, 2000), 84–86.

15. William Molyneux to Locke, March 16, 1697; Molyneux to Locke, May 27, 1697; Molyneux to Locke, April 6, 1697, in *Correspondence of John Locke*, 6:40–41, 133, 83.

16. Locke to Molyneux, May 3, 1697; Locke to Molyneux, June 15, 1696, in *Correspondence of John Locke*, 6:105–6, 143, 144.

17. David Hayton, "Ideas of Union in Anglo-Irish Political Discourse, 1692–1720: Meaning and Use," in *Political Discourse in Seventeenth- and Eighteenth-Century Ireland*, ed. D. George Boyce et. al. (New York: Palgrave, 2001), 150; Kelly, "Recasting Tradition," 83.

18. John Toland, *An Apology for Mr. Toland, In a Letter from Himself to a Member of the House of Commons in Ireland; written the day before his Book was resolv'd to be burnt by the Committee of Religion* (London, 1697), 4, 11, 14, 22, 24–25, 51.

19. John Toland, *A Defence of Mr. Toland, In a Letter to Himself* (London, 1697), 1–2, 5, 13.

20. John Toland, *A Letter to a Member of Parliament, Shewing, that a Restraint on the Press Is Inconsistent with Protestant Religion, and dangerous to the Liberty of Nation* (London, 1698), 4, 11–12; Stets and Burke, "Identity Theory and Social Identity Theory," 224.

21. Bod. Ballard MS 6 ff. 51r–v; J. C. D. Clark, *English Society 1660–1832: Religion, Ideology and Politics During the Ancien Regime*, 2nd ed. (Cambridge: Cambridge University Press, 2000), 334.

22. John Toland, *Vindicius Liberius: or, M. Toland's Defence of himself, Against the late Lower House of Convocation* (London, 1702), 9, 26, 28, 29.

23. British Library [BL] Additional MS 4292 ff. 27r–v, 28r–v; J. G. Simms, "John Toland (1670–1722), a Donegal Heretic," *Irish Historical Studies* 16 (1968/69): 309; Daniel, *John Toland*, 151; Kelly, "Recasting Tradition," 103–4.

24. John Toland, *The Danger of Mercenary Parliaments* (London, 1698), 1. Tim Harris, *Politics under the Later Stuarts: Party Conflict in a Divided Society 1600–1715* (London: Longman, 1993), 64–65; Mark Kishlansky, *A Monarchy Transformed: Britain 1603–1714* (London: Allen Lane The Penguin Press, 1996), 303; J. H. Plumb, *The Growth of Political Stability in England 1675–1725* (London: Macmillan, 1967), 133; Champion, *Republican Learning*, 55–65.

25. Plumb, *Growth of Political Stability*, 121, 134; Lois G. Schwoerer, "The Role of King William III of England in the Standing Army Controversy 1697–1699," *Journal of British Studies* 5 (1966): 75–78; J. A. Downie, *Robert Harley and the Press: Propaganda and Public Opinion in the Age of Swift and Defoe* (Cambridge: Cambridge University Press, 1979), 30–31.

26. Toland, *The Militia Reform'd*, 17–84; Evans, *Pantheisticon*, 47.

27. J. G. A. Pocock, *Politics, Language and Time: Essays on Political Thought and History* (New York: Atheneum, 1971), 113–14, Paul Kleber Monod, *The Power of Kings: Monarchy and Religion in Europe, 1589–1715* (New Haven: Yale University Press, 1999), 197. John Toland, ed., *The Oceana and Other Works of James Harrington Esq*, 3rd ed. (London, 1747), i.

28. Bod. Ballard MS 4 f. 54.

29. The *Post Boy,* June 19, 1701; The *Post Man,* June 19–21, 1701.

30. John Toland, *Anglia Libera: or the Limitation and Succession of the Crown of England Explain'd and Asserted* (London, 1701), 1, 2, 6, 56, 59.

31. Toland, *Anglia Libera*, 106, 141, 144.

32. Sullivan, *John Toland and the Deist Controversy*, 16; Daniel, *John Toland*, 9.

33. E. J. Aiton, *Leibniz: A Biography* (Bristol: Adam Hilger, 1985), 260.

34. Birch's recollections are in BL Add. MS 4254 f. 188r; Lawrence E. Klein, *Shaftesbury and the Culture of Politeness: Moral Discourse and Cultural Politics in Early Eighteenth-Century England* (Cambridge: Cambridge University Press, 1994), 14; Champion, *Republican Learning*, 32–33; Sullivan, *John Toland and the Deist Controversy*, 12.

35. Public Records Office, London, [PRO] 30/24/21, f. 23.

36. Sophia, Electress of Hanover, to the Duke of Newcastle, October 10, 1701, in *Report on the Manuscripts of his Grace The Duke of Portland, K. G., Preserved at Welbeck Abbey*, 8 vols. (London: Ben Johnson & Co., 1907), 2:180.

37. BL Add. MS 7121 ff. 61, 59; Harris, *Politics Under the Later Stuarts*, 151; Kishlansky, *Monarchy Transformed*, 306–7.

38. BL Add. MS 4465 f. 3r. Edmund Ludlow, "A Voyce from the Watch Tower, Part Five: 1660–1662," in *Camden Fourth Series,* vol. 21, ed. A. B. Worden (London: The Royal Historical Society, 1978), 45. On Harley and Marlborough see Brian W. Hill, *Robert Harley: Speaker, Secretary of State and Premier Minister* (New Haven: Yale University Press, 1988), 92–95. Toland's beating is also mentioned in a letter from Dr. William Stratford to Edward Harley, the 2nd Earl of Oxford, July 14, 1726. Stratford recalled that in 1703

Toland was "cudgelled most severely by some of Marlborough's ruffians." *Manuscripts of his Grace The Duke of Portland*, 7:441.

39. Evans, *Pantheisticon*, 99. On Harley and Defoe see Hill, *Robert Harley*, 86–87, 89; Downie, *Robert Harley and the Press*, passim; Anon. to Robert Harley, July 5, 1704 in *Manuscripts of his Grace The Duke of Portland*, 4:98. Clyve Jones and Geoffrey Holmes, eds., *The London Diaries of William Nicolson Bishop of Carlisle 1702–1718* (Oxford: The Clarendon Press, 1985), 215 [October 26, 1704].

40. Simms, "John Toland (1670–1722)," *Irish Historical Studies* 16 (1968/69): 315. See the letters Leibniz and Toland sent to Sophia Charlotte in *Die Philosophischen Schriften von Gottfried Wilhelm Leibniz,* vol. 6, ed. C. J. Berhardt (Hildesheim: Georg Olms Verlag, 1961), 508–21. John Toland, *Letters to Serena* (1704; facsimile reprint. Stuttgart-Bad-Cannastatt: Fredrich Formmann Verlag, 1964), preface; Michel Fichant, "Leibniz et Toland: philosophie pour Princesses?," *Revue de Synthèse* 116 (1995): 421–39; BL Add. MS 4465 ff. 44, 45; Champion, *Republican Learning,* 52–55, 169.

41. John Toland, *An Account of the Courts of Prussia and Hanover* (London, 1705), 32; Toland, *Collection of Several Pieces*, 2:431–32.

42. Toland, *Letters to Serena*, 171. See also Jeffrey R. Wigelsworth "Lockean Essences, Political Posturing, and John Toland's Reading of Newton's *Principia*," *Canadian Journal of History* 38 (2003): 521–35.

43. Toland, *An Account of the Courts of Prussia and Hanover*, 1, 10, 18, 55.

44. PRO 30/24/20 f. 105. Toland to Mr. ***, June 26, 1705 in *A Collection of Several Pieces*, 2:338.

45. PRO 30/24/21 f. 237. See also Angus McInnes, *Robert Harley, Puritan Politician* (London: Victor Gollancz, 1970), 83n; Hill, *Robert Harley*, 98.

46. Bod. Rawlinson MS C. 146 f. 47; Rawlinson MS D. 401 f. 30.

47. John Netterville to Robert Harley, January 14, 1707, Harley to Lord Raby, 1707 in *Manuscripts of his Grace The Duke of Portland*, 8:279; 4:289–90; Evans, *Pantheisticon*, 123; Daniel, *John Toland*, 142.

48. Toland to Harley, May 16, 1707, in *Manuscripts of his Grace The Duke of Portland*, 4:408, 409, 410.

49. BL Add. MS 4295 f. 15.

50. Erasmus Lewis to Secretary Harley, October 11, 1707 in *Manuscripts of his Grace The Duke of Portland*, 4:456; Agostino, bishop of Spiga, to electress Sophia, October 22, 1707, in *State Papers and Correspondence Illustrative of the Social and Political State of Europe from the Revolution to the Accession of the House of Hanover*, ed. John M. Kemble (London: John W. Parker and Son, 1857), 459, 60. Shapin, *A Social History of Truth*, 355–407.

51. Bod. Ballard MS 27 ff. 37v–38r.

52. Ibid., 27 f. 41v.

53. Leibniz to Lord Raby, December 29, 1707, in *State Papers and Correspondence*, 462–63.

54. Erasmus Lewis to Harley, May 29, 1708, in *Manuscripts of his Grace The Duke of Portland*, 4:491; Lord Raby to Leibniz, January 17, 1708, in *State Papers and Correspondence*, 464–65.

55. Marlborough to Godolphin, August 2/13, 1708; Godolphin to Marlborough, August 8, 1708; Godolphin to Marlborough, November 30, 1708; Marlborough to Godolphin, December 9/20, 1708, in *The Marlborough-Godolphin Correspondence*, 3 vols., ed. Henry L. Snyder (Oxford: Clarendon Press, 1975), 3:1059, 1066, 1165, 1171.

56. Kishlansky, *Monarchy Transformed*, 332; Toland to Harley, August 22, 1710, in *Manuscripts of his Grace The Duke of Portland*, 4:572.

57. Toland to the Earl of Oxford, June 6, 1711, in *Manuscripts of his Grace The Duke of Portland*, 5:4.

58. Toland to the Earl of Oxford, December 3, 1711, in *Manuscripts of his Grace The Duke of Portland*, 5:120.

59. Toland to the Earl of Oxford, December 7, 1711, in *Manuscripts of his Grace The Duke of Portland*, 5:126, 127; Kishlansky, *Monarchy Transformed*, 334.

60. Toland to the Earl of Oxford, c. 1712 in *Manuscripts of his Grace The Duke of Portland*, 5:258–60; John Toland, *The Grand Mystery Laid Open: Namely, by Dividing of the Protestants to Weaken the Hanover Succession, and by Defeating the Succession to Extirpate the Protestant Religion* (London, 1714), 3–4, 12–14, 15.

61. John Toland, *The Art of Restoring. Or, the Piety and Probity of General Monk In bringing about the Last Restoration* (London, 1714), viii, 2, 41, 38.

62. John Toland, *The State Anatomy of Great Britain. Containing a particular account of its several interests and parties, their bent and genius*, 4th ed. (London, 1717), 4.

63. Toland, *The State Anatomy of Great Britain*, 32–33, 81; The *Postman,* February 23–26, 1717.

64. John Toland, *The Second Part of the State Anatomy, &c* (London, 1717), 7, 8; Daniel Defoe, *An Argument Proving that the Design of Employing and Enobling Foreigners, is a Treasonable Conspiracy . . . With an Appendix; Wherein an insolent Pamphlet, Entitled, The Anatomy of Great Britain in Anatomiz'd* (London, 1717), 50; Maximillian E. Novak, *Daniel Defoe Master of Fictions: His Life and Ideas* (Oxford: Clarendon Press, 2001), 204.

65. BL Add. MS 4295 ff. 49r, 50r–v.

66. Stan A. E. Mendyk, *"Speculum Britanniae": Religional Study, Antiquarianism, and Science in Britain to 1700* (Toronto: University of Toronto Press, 1989), 213, 323n. 34; Charlett to Archbishop Tenison, October 25, 1695 in Maitland, "Toland," 7.

67. Bod. Ballard MS 5 ff. 50, 58. Edward Lhwyd to Dr. Lister, March 13, 1693/94, in *Life and Letters of Edward Lhwyd*, 232–33; Alan Harrison, "John Toland's Celtic Background," in *John Toland's Christianity Not Mysterious: Text, Associated Works and Critical Essays*, ed. Philip McGuinness, Alan Harrison, and Richard Kearney (Dublin: The Lilliput Press, 1997), 247. The dispute centered on "A Letter from Sir Robert Redding, late S. R. S. concerning Pearl-Fishing in the North Ireland, communicated by Dr. Lister, R. S. S.," *Philosophical Transactions* 198 (March 1693): 663–64.

68. Champion, "Toland, the Druids, and the Politics of Celtic Scholarship." John Toland, *Nazarenus, or, Jewish, Gentile, and Mahometan Christianity*, ed. Justin Champion (1718; Oxford: The Voltaire Foundation, 1999), 194. T. C. Barnard, "Protestants and the Irish Language, c. 1675–1725," *Journal of Ecclesiastical History* 44 (1993): 243–72; Karl S. Bottigheimer, "The Failure of the Reformation in Ireland: *Un Question Bien Posée*," *Journal of Ecclesiastical History* 36 (1985): 196–207.

69. Toland, *Nazarenus*, 199, 207–8, 211, 215, 217, 219.

70. John Toland, *A Specimen of the Critical History of the Celtic Religion and Learning: Containing an Account of the Druids &c.*, in *A Collection of Several Pieces*, 1:1–183. The manuscript title page and outline of contents is found in BL Add. MS 4295 f. 61r.

71. For a discussion of the contents see Champion, "Toland, the Druids, and the Politics of Celtic Scholarship," 331–32.

72. BL Add. MS 4465 ff. 13, 16. See also BL Add. MS 4465 f. 19 and Add. MS 4295 f. 27r.

73. Bod. Gough Scotland 185: Martin Martin, *A Description of the Western Islands of Scotland* (London, 1716), preface. This is an exact copy of the original housed in the British Library (C.45.C.1). Justin Champion, "Enlightened Erudition and the Politics of Reading in John Toland's Circle," *The Historical Journal* 49 (2006): 111–41. The quoted phrase is found in an earlier version of Champion's article.

74. Champion, "Enlightened Erudition;" Shapin, *A Social History of Truth*, 126.

75. Isolde Victory, "The Making of the Declaratory Act of 1720," in *Parliament, Politics and People: Essays in Eighteenth-Century Irish History*, ed. Gerard O'Brien (Dublin: Irish Academic Press, 1989), 9, 26.

76. *A Collection of Several Pieces*, 2:484–90; BL Add. MS 4465 ff. 27r–29v, 37r.

77. BL Add. MS 4465 f. 36r.

78. BL Add. MS 4295 f. 76.

Sawney and Dermot: Locality and National Identity in Irish and Scottish Eclogues

David Hill Radcliffe

Eighteenth-century British poets pursued competing national identities in a series of eclogues that thoroughly recast pastoral uses of dialogue, description, topics, and metaphor. The Anglo-Irish and Scottish eclogues display little consensus about what it meant to be Irish or Scottish, or, for that matter, about the nature of pastoral. From the contentious variety of these poems emerged key components of literary nationalism: particularity in descriptions of customs, language, and places, the elevation of vernacular poetry to literary status, and the reconceptualization of "simplicity" as cultural holism as opposed to bumpkin ignorance. Scottish and Anglo-Irish pastorals stood in an asymmetrical relationship: while North Britons could draw upon vernacular traditions in Scots poetry, the Anglo-Irish had only their English tradition to draw upon—at least until Scots pastoral began making inroads in Ireland. That late development was hardly unprecedented, for verses, ideas, and even poets had always circulated among the nations. Like Britain, the complex and mutable eighteenth-century eclogue was ever a work in progress.

Edmund Spenser supplied the prototype. In the *Shepheardes Calender,* the "new poete" gave form and substance to a distinctly national and Protestant literature by recasting classical, Continental, and English sources in an English idiom. In the *Faerie Queene*, pastoral romance allegorizes political differences as fairy fictions in which the noble and repulsive aspects of colonial adventure engage in fearsome combat. *Colin Clouts Come Home Againe* renders the concept of "home" thoroughly problematic: is home Ireland, or England, or some imaginary place? Eighteenth-century eclogues were likewise concerned with the appropriation of tradition, conflicts between realism and idealism, and the uncertainty of local attachments. Scottish and Anglo-Irish pastoralists crafted complex identities from local, national, and cosmopolitan traditions, invented pastoral fictions to praise or damn political regimes, and used pastoral juxtapositions of art and nature to underscore contrasts between imperial civilization and native custom. Scottish pastoralists might embrace the vernacular idiom as a way of differentiating themselves from the English, while Anglo-Irish pastoralists might embrace English traditions to differentiate themselves from the vernacular idiom. Or not: Scottish and Irish pastoral poets might identify themselves as British citizens, or reject national and imperial ties by identifying themselves as humanists, Jacobites, or cosmopolites. The divided loyalties apparent in Spenser's verse are not far to seek in eighteenth-century Scottish and Irish eclogues.

While Spenser had introduced dialect pastoral in the *Shepheardes Calender*, locality became an issue in English pastoral verse only after Ambrose Philips and other English Whigs began using descriptive specificity to differentiate "British" pastoral from classical and French models.[1] The author of *The Guardian* No. 30 (April 15, 1713) argued that "There are some things of an established nature in Pastoral, which is essential to it, such as a Country Scene, Innocence, Simplicity. Others there are of a changeable kind, such as Habits, Customs, and the like. The difference in Climate is also to be considered, for what is proper in *Arcadia*, or even in *Italy*, might be very absurd in a colder Country."[2] Descriptive specificity usually involved a low stylistic register. In "A Pastoral Poem on the Union [of the English and Scottish Parliaments]," published in *The Observator*, Roger opines that "A Country Fellow ought to tell a Country Story like himself" (March 12, 1707). The poem describes an expansive allegorical prospect extending from "Northern Orcades to Southern Wight" before diving into low particularity when "Albia" ridicules the "High-Church Cormorants and Burrards" who "squirt on honest People as they fly."[3] The Proem to John Gay's *Shepherd's Week* (1714) mocks Philips's call for local specificity: "Thou wilt not find my Shepherdesses idly piping on oaten Reeds, but milking the Kine, tying up the Sheaves, or if the Hogs are astray driving them to their Styes. My Shepherd gathereth none other Nosegays but what are the growth of our own Fields."[4] Yet Gay's own burlesque pastorals set new standards for graphic, racy particularity.

In Ireland and Scotland too, local places and customs were being introduced into pastoral eclogues. *A Pastoral in imitation of the First Eclogue of Virgil: inscrib'd to the Provost, Fellows, and Scholars, of Trinity College, Dublin; by Murroghoh O Connor* (1719) takes up the emigration issue. Virgil's Tityrus and Meliboeus become Murroghoh and Owen, Milesian gentlemen dispossessed by their landlords, the trustees of Trinity College.

Murroghoh, the putative author of the poem, has been reinstated, while Owen is left to utter Meliboeus's complaint, rendered into the local idiom:

> My old Acquaintance, and my dearest Friend,
> My Murroghoh! what Joys on you attend!
> Ten thousand Blessings seem at once to shine
> Upon your Farm and House of Ballyline.
> Since you're restor'd to Native Land and Ease,
> The World's your own, and use it as you please:
> Now tell the Glories of your noble Name,
> How Prince O'Connor from Hispania came. . . .[5]

Murroghoh's patronage relationship represents things as they ought to be but Owen's situation—he considers emigrating to France "with Satchel cram'd with Books, | With empty Pockets, and with hungry Looks"—represents things as they are.[6] Owen underscores his painful separation with an artful hemistich:

> Adieu my dear Abode –
> I shall no more with Brogue Boan Scribiogh climb
> Steep Mulloghbert, enthron'd on Top sublime,
> Head of my Clan. . . .[7]

Yet with all its Irish particularity, Murroghoh's address to the scholars of Trinity ultimately requires a rhetoric of Virgilian humanism to establish common ground with the college fellows.

Cosmopolitan humanism also figures in two Irish Protestant burlesques influenced by John Gay. The characters and manners in James Ward's mock-heroic *The Smock-Race, at Finglas* (1716) are not merely marked as Irish, but as urban or rural, genteel or rustic, protestant or Catholic: "Poor Paddy swears his whole Week's Gains away, / While my young Squires blaspheme, and nothing pay."[8] Nicolas Brown's *The North-Country Wedding* (1722) is an early example of what would become something of a set-piece in Anglo-Irish writing. The poem gently mocks the elevated pride of the decayed Old Irish like the knight Mc Farrel: "Proud of his Birth, in Majesty he stalks, / Snuffs, and looks big, and glories in his Name, / His Name being all which he is Heir to now."[9] Like Gay's burlesque, these poems by Trinity-educated clergymen rejoice in the happy coincidence of classical and contemporary characters; they have Irish subjects but do not, like Murroghoh's, use the cosmopolitan tradition to bridge national differences because the burlesque locates the simple characters and artful narrators on different planes.

The case is somewhat different in Swift's "A Pastoral Dialogue" (1733). Congleton senses ridicule of Ambrose Philips and the Moderns: "There is no question of his [Swift's] attitude toward a modern, anglicized pastoral; in it he presents contemporary rustics of the coarsest kind to show the absurdity of the rationalistic doctrine."[10] As with Gay, so with Swift: "When you with Oonah stood behind a ditch, / I peep'd, and saw you kiss the dirty bitch." But while low, Swift's dialogue is not burlesque since it makes no allusions to Philips or other pastoralists. Swift's particularity works differently, as when Dermot is discovered weeding the "Court of Gosford Knight." Gosford is not in Ireland but in East Lothian, a fact that lends sly point to Dermot's selectivity: "No more that Bry'r thy tender Leg shall rake: / (I spare the Thistle for Sir Arthur's sake)."[11] Resentful at laboring for a foreign master, he leaves the "foreign" weed standing alone in prickly arrogance. The point at issue is not a literary quarrel with Philips but a political quarrel with Scotland to which Swift alludes by being particular about his weeds. Swift's rhetorical strategy differs from those of Murroghoh, Brown, and Ward: ignoring classical pastoral, he explores common ground between the Anglo-Irish and native Irish by coding his sentiments in their idiom.

The status of Britain was also a subject of contention in Scottish pastorals. Allan Ramsay, the reviver of Scots verse, began a series of eclogues on British subjects with *Richey and Sandy, A Pastoral on the Death of Mr. Joseph Addison*.[12] The speakers are Alexander Pope and Richard Steele, fantastically metamorphosed into Scottish shepherds speaking a patois of Scots and English. The odd confluence of high and humble emblematizes a union not to be confused with uniformity. The following year Joseph Mitchell published *The Doleful Swains*.[13] In this piece, Willie, Davie, and Mungo complain of the loss of a girl, a lamb, and a bag of gold, having been betrayed, respectively, by a false friend, a murderous dog, and a scheming Laird. The singing contest, in Scots, is adjudicated by one Bellair. Mitchell published his poem in London with a translation on facing pages. But Bellair's polished English, common to both versions, indicates which is the superior partner in the Union (Mitchell would later cast his lot with Robert Walpole). In 1721, Ramsay published *Robert, Richy and Sandy. A Pastoral on the Death of Matthew Prior* in London.[14] Once again Ramsay challenges his readers with unity-amid-incongruity: the Dublin-born, ultra-Whig Steele is made to praise Prior's skills in negotiating the much-despised Treaty of Utrecht. Ramsay, unlike Mitchell, was politically ambidextrous; as did Swift, he cultivated personal and literary ties with England while asserting local independence.[15]

In 1720, Ramsay had published at Edinburgh *Patie and Roger*, an eclogue presenting a low and national subject without burlesque: "Her Coats were kiltit, and did sweetly shaw / Her straight bare Legs, which whiter were than Snaw."[16] This became the germ of *The Gentle Shepherd* (1725), in which the eponymous Patie discovers his genteel origins and as the poet's Jacobite friends might express it, "comes into his own again." Ramsay's pastoral romance about reclaiming a legacy became a landmark poem in Scottish literature. Like Spenser, Ramsay was Janus-faced, looking backward to high-antique tradition and ahead to demotic realism. In Scotland, Spenser's diction had the advantage of resembling the language spoken in the streets. Where else but Edinburgh could the local vernacular pass for a classical tongue? Ramsay opined that "The Scoticisms which perhaps may offend some over-nice ear, give new life and grace to the poetry, and become their places as well as the Doric dialect of Theocritus."[17] He himself was the first of a long series of Scottish poets of humble origins to write literary poetry in Scots—real-life "gentle shepherds." While proletarian pastoral was mostly a late-century phenomenon, Ramsay found early emulators in a shadowy coterie of Edinburgh tradesmen (Alexander Pennecuik, Alexander Maben, Thomas Blair). He pointed the way to recasting the formerly courtly tradition of Scots poetry as a new kind of national literature, at once old and new, provincial and classical, popular and polite.

If these early-century eclogues illustrate how quickly local particularity was taken up in eighteenth-century pastoral, they also show that there was no correspondence between the use of this mode and any particular national or political ideology. Pastoral poetry was literally and figuratively all over the map.

There was no Irish equivalent to Allan Ramsay, and dialect pastoral (as opposed to song) is consequently scarce. This is perhaps surprising since the Irish brogue was a frequent subject of mirth on stage and in novels and periodicals.[18] Possibly the Anglo-Irish were disinclined to burlesque the Irish-inflected English for which they were themselves ridiculed. Certainly the linguistic situation was different: Ramsay and his contemporaries wrote in Scots, English, or both depending on whether they were thinking of themselves as Scots, Britons, or both. By contrast, Gaelic was unintelligible to all but a few of the Anglo-Irish and there was no court tradition to lend literary authority to Irish-inflected English. While working-class literacy in lowland Scotland was high, such was not the case in Ireland, making reciprocity between social ranks divided by ethnic and religious differences all the more difficult. With little native tradition of its own, eighteenth-century Anglo-Irish poetry had to become "British" before it could become Irish.

This process is exemplified in the careers of two Anglo-Irish pastoralists, John Cunningham (1729–73) and Thomas Stratford (1735–95fl.). Cunningham, the son of a Dublin wine-cooper, came from the same social class as Ramsay and had the same kind of limited education. His father was reportedly of Scottish origins; Joseph Ritson, who knew him, reports that Cunningham's parents were Catholics.[19] After some juvenile verses gained him access to the Dublin theater, the poet pursued a career as an actor in Edinburgh and the north of England before retiring impoverished to Newcastle. In the 1760s, Cunningham became the best-known pastoral writer in Britain, developing an extremely popular lyric mode of pastoral out of William Shenstone's "Pastoral Ballad." In contrast to the poems we have been considering, Cunningham's pastorals reject geographical particularity, adopting a restricted range of diction and imagery at once simple and artificial, familiar and fantastic. Like the anapestic quatrains in which they are written, the ballad mode was insistently repetitious, returning readers again and again to the jessamine bowers of an idealized yet recognizably British version of Arcadia. Cunningham deliberately excludes public matters from his verse, as he explains in his most famous lyric, first published March 12, 1763, in the *St. James's Chronicle*:

I said,—on the banks of the stream,
I've pip'd for the shepherds too long!
Oh grant me, ye Muses, a theme,
Where glory may brighten my song!

But Pan bade me stick to my strain,
Nor lessons too lofty rehearse;
Ambition befits not a swain,
And Phillis loves pastoral verse.[20]

Rather than national politics, Cunningham and his many imitators typically concerned themselves with the competing claims of wealth and taste, men and women, city and country. Few if any readers would have recognized Cunningham's verses as Irish. It is the absence of nationality that marks them for what they are: Anglo-Irish in their deracination and perhaps even Irish-Catholic in a response to emigration that treats "home" as a tenuous floating-island of the imagination. Cunningham's ballad style proved eminently exportable; it was particularly popular among provincial and semiliterate poets. The setting for pastoral ballads was simply "the plain," an undifferentiated space open to all comers.

The Rev. Thomas Stratford, the son of a Westmeath farmer, was educated at Trinity College; he translated three books of *Paradise Lost* into

Greek and may have been the Philisides who in 1758 rendered *The Shepheardes Calender* into blank verse, the measure employed in four remarkable pastorals first published in the *Dublin Mercury*.[21] These "Pastoral Essays" were begun during the Seven Years' War, which like Marlborough's wars seems to have triggered a turn to Spenser, Shakespeare, and Milton as prototypes for a distinctly "British" poetic. Frightened at the approach of a witch, Hobbinol recounts to Colinet how he had fled to a neighboring abbey where he was accosted by howling, strange lights, and "a tall ghost in majesty of woe" (July 4, 1769). In the concluding pastoral the ghost relates his history: once an English minstrel, he has been condemned to walk by night since the Norman conquest of Ireland. While living, he had refused to offer songs of praise to Ireland's venal tyrants and sought refuge in England under the Percys; he now awaits a time when Ireland's "mitred sires" will "Reanimate these ruins into form, / Like man in perfect renovation rouz'd" (April 5, 1770).

The meaning of this allegory is obscure, not least because of the Minstrel's tortured Miltonic syntax. But it points to Stratford's own search for patronage in the Irish church, as do the patriotic dedications: the second pastoral is dedicated to William Pitt, and the third to George Townshend, who had fought with Wolfe in Canada and was then Lord-Lieutenant of Ireland. The fourth is dedicated to "To their Graces the Duke and Duchess of Northumberland"; Hugh Percy had been Lord-Lieutenant of Ireland from 1763 to 1766. To the colonial government, Stratford proposes a Miltonic literary program to render Irish poetry properly "British" in opposition to France and Catholicism:

> Yet Merit pleads
> This bold emprize to spurn the Gothic yoke
> Of Rhyme, rude demon; which, when papal night
> Eclips'd the sun-bright radiance of the soul,
> Ruthless untun'd each weeping Muse's lyre,
> And sunk ev'n godlike Britons into slaves. . . .
> (April 5, 1770)

The dramatic situation in these gothic pastorals turns on an opposition between past and present, the ghost signifying the incomplete work of conquest. Though twice republished, Stratford's pastorals fell on deaf ears: the Percys patronized an English medievalist, Thomas Percy, who in 1782 became bishop of Dromore.

For these two Irish poets "British" pastoral had very different implications: for Cunningham abandonment of any pretense of national specificity, and for Stratford a very specific understanding of how places, persons, and nations are caught up in political history. But neither poet was prepared to identify themselves with Ireland as Ramsay had with Scotland.

The British empire was understood by many advocates to be an empire of commerce that would erode concepts of national identity and promote cross-border exchanges. In poetry, commerce was linked to georgic concepts of progress and refinement and opposed to pastoral concepts of atavism and simplicity. But by mid-century, distinctions between georgic and pastoral were eroding as writers thought through the implications of commercial empire. Spenser had set the precedent for mingling these genres; Pope refined Spenser's georgic "calendar" by condensing twelve months into four seasons, while Philips rendered his pastorals georgic by extending Spenser's descriptive particularity. This was taken to new extremes by mid-century pastoralists like Stratford, who could speak of Irish mountains that "silver'd o'er / With sidelong-streaming glories of the moon, / Swell into boundless prospect, as they sweep / In bold magnificence along the shore" (July 4, 1769). The pastoral ballad, while an oppositional genre to georgic, took refinement as one of its principal themes. Nor was georgic immune from mixture with pastoral; Cunningham's lyricism was likely an influence on Goldsmith's *Deserted Village* (1770): "How often have I paused on every charm, / The shelter'd cot, the cultivated farm, / The never failing brook, the busy mill, / The decent church that topt the neighbouring hill."[22] Goldsmith's poem resembles pastoral not only by omitting any account of labor, but in the generality of its description: it is notoriously hard to say whether Auburn is an English or an Irish village.

The conflation of pastoral and georgic is most obvious in a busy series of burlesque eclogues concerned with the division of labor and resulting differentiation of manners. This series, which began in London, includes "Warbletta: a Suburban Eclogue" (1733) about a ballad singer, "The Billingsgate Contest. A Piscatory London Eclogue" (1734) about fishwives, "A Covent-Garden Eclogue" (1735) about streetwalkers, "A Stage Eclogue" (1736) about players, and "A Wapping Eclogue" (1739) about sailors.[23] As the titles indicate, these burlesque poems are not only profession-specific, but place-specific. By mid-century, the locales in this series were extending beyond London. In "The Chairmen" (1760), "A. E." (Andrew Erskine) invokes a northern genus loci: "In Lothian's fields, whose ev'ry plain / Luxuriant smiles o'erspread with golden grain, / Built by the ancient Picts, Edina stands. . . ." Macewen and Macgregor, who earn their living hoisting the gentry up and down Castle Hill, are nonplussed by an outbreak of fair weather: "Behold yon beau array'd in chearful green, / Lo on his stockings not a speck is seen; / Where now he walks, I've view'd the filth so thick, / That there almost his spindle shanks would stick."[24] For pastoral simplicity, the poem substitutes the interconnected complexity of an economy situated a very particular place and time. In 1771, the *Dublin Mercury* published an anonymous times-of-day sequence that is similarly local and particular. In "Morning, or the Discovery," Lactea and Black Moll cross swords over the worthless boot-boy, Scobby; in "Evening, or the Politicians," Muzzle the tinker and Patch the cobbler repair to the alehouse for a political singing contest. In "Midnight, or the Wake"—the compulsory pastoral elegy—mourners lament the passing of Pitcherina, who in accordance with Irish tradition appears "stretch'd on houshold door."[25] Readers enjoyed seeing the verities of Theocritus tricked out in modern garb, but also the local manners distinguishing the Edinburgh and Dublin poems from their London equivalents.

If these town eclogues oppose provincial to metropolitan manners in a fairly simpleminded way, the subtleties of diction, tone, and character in Robert Fergusson's dialect poems elevate the town eclogue to high art. In "Mutual Complaint of Plainstanes and Causey, in their Mother-tongue" and "A Drink Eclogue" (1773), the prosopopeia presses georgic materialism to its limit. When Plainstanes (the sidewalk) complains of having to bear the weight of highland chairmen with their burdens, Causey (the roadway) will have none of it:

> Your libel I'll impugn verbatim,
> And hae a magnum damnum datum;
> For tho' frae Arthur's-seat I sprang,
> And am in constitution strang,
> Wad it no fret the hardest stane
> Beneath the Luckenbooths to grane?[26]

The conflation of Latin and Scots underscores the mixed genealogy of Scots pastoral, which threw high and low together like the promiscuous throng walking the streets of Edinburgh. Commercial crossing plays out differently in "A Drink Eclogue," where the traditional contest between goatherds and shepherds is reworked as a singing competition between Whiskey and Brandy. Nationality enters when Brandy (in broad Scots) begins to assume foreign airs and is debunked by the judge: "Will you your breeding threep, ye moungrel loun! / Frae hame-bred liquor dy'd to colour brown?"[27] "A Drink Eclogue" underscores both the reciprocity of provincial and international economies and the "taste" required to differentiate locality-specific products. But it does not claim the superiority of local whiskey to imported brandy: Fergusson, like Edinburgh, is too cosmopolitan for that.

Fergusson regarded national bigotry as a product of London manufacture. In "To Dr. Samuel Johnson: Food for a new Edition of his Dictionary," he yokes the Tory lexicographer responsible for the offensive definition of "oats" with Charles Churchill, the Whig who had "depicted pauperated swains, / With thraldom and bleak want reducted sore."[28] Londoners were notoriously reluctant to enter into reciprocal exchange with their northern neighbors. In Churchill's abusive *A Prophecy of Famine. A Scots Pastoral* (1763), pastoral burlesque was used to attack all things Scottish:

> SAWNEY as long without remorse could bawl
> HOME'S madrigals, and ditties from FINGAL.
> Oft at his strains, all natural tho' rude,
> The Highland Lass forgot her want of food,
> And, whilst she scratch'd her lover into rest,
> Sunk pleas'd, tho' hungry, on her SAWNEY'S breast.[29]

Through twenty-eight quarto pages—in length as in subject the poem is georgic—Churchill's satire makes abundant use of pastoral particularity. In *The Drivers* (1770), an anonymous contribution to the town eclogue series, an English carrier reports on his commercial travels in North Britain: "The most accursed spot in all Creation, / They're nasty too beyond imagination."[30] It was against this backdrop of English xenophobia that Robert Fergusson revived Scots dialect pastoral, which had lain fallow since Ramsay's time.

Not that Scottish pastoralists were above xenophobia themselves. Among Fergusson's imitators was "Aquilo," who in 1776 published an eclogue on the American rebellion. A "weird-wife" having prophesied conflict between Britain and her "bairns," the shepherds declare their intention "To make Britannia mistress o' her ain,": "Hegh! Dany, man, an' are we a' gaen' aff / To beat the wild Americans to caff?"[31] Ten years later this poem was refashioned in the *Berwick Museum* as "A Pastoral suited to the Times." Here, a group of shepherds opposed to lowering trade barriers band together to beat back the *Irish* threat. It required no great insight to prophesy war in 1776, but one is impressed with the weird-wife's capacity to successfully call the rebellion of 1798 in 1785:

> She goodlied out, that in the lift she saw,
> Irlan' wrestling 'gainst Britannia;
> Lords against Commons, Commons against king,
> English and Irish, down by turns each fling.
> She said, she saw the Magna Charta flame,
> Wi' ither sights, that makes me quake to name![32]

If it makes sense for shepherds to rail against the free flow of commerce (a georgic topic) one cannot but be impressed with the dexterity with which the border poet exemplifies the porosity of boundaries by "lifting" his poem from a metropolitan magazine. The redactor has changed none of the vernacular, which was as native to Berwick as to Edinburgh.

The prominence of the georgic topic of commerce in eighteenth-century eclogues is seen in occupation- and location-specific treatments of labor, in discussions of cosmopolitanism, national prejudice, and economic policy, in the very "exchange" of themes and formal qualities between the two genres. It would be a mistake to regard the authors of these piebald pastorals as indifferent to genre; on the contrary, pastoral and georgic are mixed precisely because their particular resources and associations were so useful for writing about the effects of commerce on nationality. The real inconsistency lies in the writers' attitudes toward commerce, which vary without much respect to national origins.

Yet emigration, a kind of commerce in human persons, is consistently rejected in pastoral poetry. Virgil's eclogue recounting Meliboeus's loss of his Sabine farm became the prototype for long series of emigration pastorals, among them Murroghoh O Connor's. Emigration is the theme of Goldsmith's *Deserted Village*, which, though a formal georgic, is conventionally pastoral in its hostility toward commerce and in particular toward emigration. Thomas Coombe published *Edwin: or the Emigrant. An Eclogue* (1775) as a sequel in which Goldsmith's villagers are murdered by savages in the Ohio Valley.[33] Coombe's life underscores the connection between the theme of exile and the circulation of poets: after being arrested in 1776 by the Philadelphia authorities on account of his Tory politics, this American poet became personal secretary to the lord lieutenant of Ireland and held a rectory in County Tyrone. Forced emigration was a frequent topic in Jacobite poetry, including W. Nisbet's "The Exile" (1780), a pastoral elegy modeled on Goldsmith. A Virginia planter lamenting his son's forced conscription into the Continental Army recalls his own youthful experience of rebellion and its unhappy consequences: "Erst had he shone among those hapless few / Of Scotia's sons to Stewart's cause how true!"[34] These Tory "eclogues" by Goldsmith, Coombe, and Nisbet register the effects of sending the Stuarts into exile: a leaden age of disruptive commerce, political oppression, and banishment to foreign climes.

Among the better-known emigration eclogues were those by George Gregory, Chatterton's first biographer. The son of a Wexford clergyman, Gregory was educated in Scotland and preached in the north of England before making his career in London as a lecturer at St. Giles Cripplegate and the London Foundling Hospital. The speakers in his "American Eclogues" (1783–84)—in effect sequels to Chatterton's "African Eclogues" —are African warriors enslaved on American plantations: "Lift high the scourge, my soul the rack disdains; / I pant for freedom and my native plains!"[35] While it would be a stretch to represent these characters as types of the oppressed Irish, the humanitarian views expressed by this Irish expatriate were likely shaped by experiences closer to home. Gregory's appeal to social justice and natural right is echoed in the dialect pastorals of John Learmont (1791), a gardener working in or near Edinburgh. "The First of Spring" responds to the threat of war with France, Britain's traditional enemy, by declaring himself a pacifist: "How stupit is't, whan men for sordit gain, / Mak empires mourn their usefu bairnies slain?"[36] One might contrast the implicit subterfuge of Swift's Dermot with the explicit class-resentment of this real-life gardener, related in "New Year's Day, an Eclogue":

> The grit-man's gate obsequious rowes the hinge
> For lordly guests — while servants to them beenge,
> An' stow the board wi' mair than it dowe had,
> While countless teinds gang supperless to bed. . . .[37]

Learmont makes his appeal to the Rights of Man in subliterary Scots without the least suggestion of national pride. In this context, Scots dialect pastoral acquires a striking new meaning: rather than locality or simplicity it signifies class, and that with a rural cosmopolitan's awareness of rebellious events unfolding in France.

Late-century eclogues introduce a new kind of pastoral dualism, reconceptualizing the pastoral opposition between nature and art as a juxtaposition between "things as they are" to things as they ought to be in an egalitarian social system. The Irish schoolmaster Samuel Thomson recasts the traditional contrast between the learned poet and the simple speaker when he addresses his *Poems on Different Subjects, partly in the Scottish Dialect* (1793) to the "unletter'd swains, / My gay coevals, on our northern plains."[38] The famous opening of Spenser's *Shepheardes Calender*—"A Shepeheards boye (no better do him call)"—is construed literally:

> To you, ye Rustics of the present Age,
> In life's low vale, I dedicate my page;
> Sworn foe to Pride, and every selfish aim,
> A shepherd lad—he seeks no better name:
> With hat in hand presents his rural lays,
> And begs your patronage and honest praise.[39]

Thomson was the rare Irish pastoralist who (sometimes) writes in dialect, though as a Presbyterian he was the exception proving the rule. While Thomson's demotic verse is a far cry from what Cunningham and Goldsmith were writing a generation earlier, he was, like them, a man without a country. Or, as an Ulster Scot, he might be considered as a man of two countries (Thomson's ties to Scotland were strong and he traveled to Scotland to meet his idol, Robert Burns). Or he may have considered himself a citizen of a nation yet unborn, for Thomson was a United Irishman attempting to join Presbyterians and Catholics under the banner of the Rights of Man.[40] Identifying himself with Colin Clout on the one hand and the Irish peasantry on the other, Thomson idealistically tries to close the gaps arising from class divisions and multinational identities.

While Thomson's poetry lacks political grit, revolutionary attitudes are very apparent in the *Hibernian Eclogues* (also 1791) by Thomas Atkinson, an English-born United Irishman. "Connor, or the Peasant's Complaint" is an emigration eclogue blasting the landholding class in echoes of Goldsmith's *Deserted Village*; "Phelim and Doran, or the Panegyrist" imitates Virgil's Pollio eclogue, imagining a king who will restore peace and abolish the established church in Ireland; the prophecy improbably unites a Jacobitical rhetoric of sacral kingship with a Jacobinical project of world revolution. In the third eclogue, Patrick replies to Dermot's account of his starving family with a proposal to fly to "Where men disdain to bear oppressive laws, / Where Gallic lillies blush in freedom's cause."[41] The fourth, modeled on Pope's "Autumn," is a lover's complaint possibly intended as political allegory. Hugh Mulligan is equally emphatic in *Poems chiefly on Slavery and Oppression* (1788). Like Atkinson, Mulligan adopts Pope's times-of-day motif, but he sets each eclogue in a different locale: America, Africa, Asia, and Europe. Britain has exported oppression all around the globe, but in Ireland its legacy has been to export the populace as well, a point made by a speaker returning from fighting Britain's wars to find himself a stranger in his own land: "From camps return'd, no former friends I found, / For Desolation silent stalk'd around; / Thro' distant climes my sad companions roam / In search of freedom, lost, alas! at home."[42] There is nothing formally innovative about Mulligan's topographic pastorals; the novelty lies in the implicit identification of the condition of Ireland with the condition of the world.

Scottish and Irish eclogues of the 1790s are typical of a broader trend in which regional, national, and transnational identities strengthened as poets questioned the authority of imperial government. The most important and widely disseminated pastorals of the era were Robert Southey's "Botany Bay Eclogues" (1794) which describe the corrosive effects of empire on provincial people who suddenly find themselves transported to the farthest reaches of the globe. Across the Atlantic, the fashion for ethnographic-humanitarian protest eclogues was mocked by the *Port Folio* in an 1801 article on "Esthonian Poetry," one of its frequent attacks on the president of the United States. Jefferson's Anglophobic taste for Ossian is ridiculed in a "Song of a Female Orphan": "The sparrow-hawk has five, beside herself: the duck always goes in pairs. I am quite alone; I have no father, no mother. To whom shall I lament my woes? To whom shall I unbosom my distress? Behind whom shall I run, when people scold me?"[43] Simplicity can be deceptive: in these lines a Philadelphia journalist attacks a Virginia planter for harboring French sympathies in a parody of a forged translation of ancient Scottish poetry that ridicules the simplicity of American emulators of England's Lake Poets—all presented as the sentiments of those who "inhabit the upper regions of the Gulph of Finland." A nation of emigrants, the United States was both removed from and thoroughly entangled with the matter of Britain as treated in pastoral verse.

"Esthonian Poetry" exposes a limitation of humanitarian pastoral: where the issue is the rights of man, ethnographic particularity tends to be superfluous. This is not the case with what might be called "bardic pastoral," the other major late-century development. Rather than appealing to universal rights, bardic pastoral appeals for authority to national customs and traditions for which ethnographic context is essential. Already, eighteenth-century eclogues had assembled key components of nationalist poetics: landscape descriptions, peculiarities of language, manners, belief and superstition, and the reconstitution of "simplicity" as sincerity or suffering innocence. To render pastoral nationality into pastoral nationalism, bardic pastoral had only to replace allusions to Theocritus and Virgil with allusions to writers in a national tradition, to identify pastoral speakers with the collective voice of the nation, and to revalue rustic superstition as inspired vision.

The key figure for bardic pastoral was James Macpherson, who responded to the dismantling of the Jacobite clans by publishing *Fragments of Ancient Poetry collected in the Highlands of Scotland* (1760). The *Fragments* recast material from Gaelic ballads as short monologues or dialogues that are, in effect, prose eclogues. Macpherson brilliantly extended the pastoral "pathetic fallacy" into an elaborate set of interlocking images in which landscape, atmospheric effects, memories, songs, and supernatural events interact with uncanny reciprocity. The resulting uniformity of tone and emotion enabled readers to imagine "simplicity" not as ignorance or naiveté but as an informing holism that stamped a national character on societies regulated by traditions of extemporaneous song. As in Cunningham's pastoral ballads, there is a narrow range of diction and theme, hypnotic rhythm, and a lack of georgic specificity.[44] But the crucial matter was the appropriation of tradition as such, which Macpherson accomplished by offering his imitations and adaptations as "translations." The significance of this was immediately grasped in Ireland and England and the resulting controversies over historical authority aroused nationalistic passions in all three nations.[45]

Another significant figure in bardic pastoral was Robert Burns, who like Macpherson cast aside the trappings of the classical eclogue while recasting demotic poetry as high literature. Burns also had a precedent in Allan Ramsay's one excursion into bardic poetry, "The Vision," a Jacobite effusion concealed as an ancient Scots translation from a Latin original.[46] Unlike Ramsay and Macpherson, however, Burns claimed bardic status in his own right based on his relationship to vernacular tradition. In "The Vision," the muse Coila descends, wearing a mantle representing (in the manner of Ossian) the lights and shades, mountains and rivers of Scotland:

> All hail! my own inspired Bard!
> In me thy native Muse regard!
> Nor longer mourn thy fate is hard,
> Thus poorly low!
> I come to give thee such reward,
> As we bestow.[47]

Like an Old Testament prophet, Burns is summoned from obscurity to speak truth to kings. Fergusson had celebrated the lives of simple people in "The Farmer's Ingle"; but "The Cotter's Saturday Night" refashions this source into a heroic ode where humble characters, or (properly speaking) their manners and beliefs figure as full-fledged agents in politics and history. Burns did not compose pastoral eclogues, but read in the light of "The Vision" and "The Cotter," his entire corpus of songs, lyrics, and dialogues came to be regarded as pastoral; indeed his authority was such that the whole national tradition might be construed as informed by a pastoral genius. For example, Hector MacNeill's *The Pastoral, or Lyric Muse of Scotland* derives the genealogy of all Scottish poetry from an original shepherd modeled on Burns in a passage imitating "The Vision."[48]

Bardic pastoralists in Ireland operated under comparative disadvantages. Unsettled constitutional questions made it difficult for poets to appropriate the past while speaking for the nation as a whole. Nor did Anglo-Irish "bards" have a centuries-old nationalist tradition to work with. Thomas Stratford attempted to carve out a literary identity for Ireland by inventing a British tradition from elements of Spenser, Shakespeare, and Milton. Spenser was the obvious candidate for foundational status in a specifically Anglo-Irish tradition. But Denham, Congreve, Swift, Parnell, and Concanon had shown little interest in Spenser, whose poems had never been published in Dublin. The first Anglo-Irish poets to claim Spenser's legacy were mid-century romantics, among them Stratford and Philip Doyne, whose *Triumph of Parnassus* (1763) derives the genealogy of English poetry from Gaelic as well as British origins. Imparting national trappings to an imperial state, Doyne imagines Spenser celebrating the birth of an heir to the House of Hanover:

> First, from Armulla's dale the shepherd came,
> Who after Chaucer sung his mystic lay;
> (Ierne's boast, and Colin clout his name)
> He kept his flocks along the Mulla's shore,
> Under the foot of Mole. . . .[49]

John Ball later wrote "To the River Slaney" (1771), a fine pastoral elegy for Doyne that strives, like Ossian and Burns to read a national literary tradition into and out of the Irish landscape:

> I mark old Toscar's gleaming Cloud,
> A beck'ning Form is on the Ray:
> I hear a calling Voice aloud—
> And shall I raise great Spenser's Lay?
> And gives he me his Pipe to play?
> And does he join his Pen to mine?—
> Ah! where will thee thy Love betray?
> It was not Colin, 'twas thy Doyne![50]

The passage appropriates the conclusion of "The Bard," substituting a specifically Irish tradition for the Spenser-Shakespeare-Milton triad in Gray's original. If Anglo-Irish Spenserianism failed it was not for want of trying. But the literary community was too small, it had no strong poet, and it lacked the connection to vernacular poetry that sustained Scottish nationalism.

The failure of bardic pastoral in Ireland is vividly illustrated in the career of Thomas Dermody (1775–1802), briefly lifted to international status by patrons believing they had discovered untutored national genius. Over the course of a short and unhappy life, Dermody published a substantial number of odes and epistles, sonnets, satires, and descriptive flights of fancy. In place of "standart Habbie," he composed in variations of the

Spenserian stanza; instead of vernacular superstitions, he appropriated fairy folkways from Spenser, Shakespeare, and Milton. In accordance with his patrons' wishes, he presented himself to the world as a new Colin Clout: "The strain, a shepherd-boy hath sung erewhile, / All by the side of some romantic hill, / (His flock at feed,) perchance, may gain a smile."[51] But rather than drink from the high fount of ancient poetry, the wayward youth preferred imbibing at Dublin taverns and coffeehouses, living and dying a sad travesty of Burns. Like Dermody himself, Irish Spenserian poetry left little of note behind. Its pastoral bards would not or could not align themselves with the populace in a way permitting them to speak for the nation. Ireland acquired a more authentic voice in the character of Thaddy in Maria Edgeworth's *Castle Rackrent* (1800), where the dialectical ambiguities of eighteenth-century eclogue are given full play in a work that has little to do with the visionary holism of bardic poetry.[52]

With the turn of the nineteenth century, the formal eclogue slipped into precipitous decline, abandoned even by the Scottish and Irish autodidacts who were among its last practitioners. Pastoral may have fallen victim to its own success: by the end of the eighteenth century it was practiced in modes so diverse, and in generic combinations so diffuse, that the eclogue, like the georgic, ceased to be a distinct form. But the legacy of British pastoral flourished in a general modal shift toward green landscapes of the imagination, a limited range of topics (romantic poets, like Sicilian shepherds, avoided didactic subjects), simplified diction and syntax, characters in humble life, and the contemplative attitude associated with pastoral leisure. The topics developed in pastoral were divided and multiplied in other genres: landscape verse, metrical romance, lyric songs, regional novels. If the rhetorical display and complex irony typical of pastoral eclogue came to seem "artificial" to nineteenth-century readers, its concerns with simplicity, tradition, and locality were matters of all-consuming interest. Through eighteenth-century pastorals, simplicity came to be identified with national character, tradition with vernacular customs, and landscape with political geography. The success of Irish and Scottish literary nationalism in the romantic era owed more than a little to the forgotten eclogues of the eighteenth century.

NOTES

1. James Edmund Congleton, *Theories of Pastoral Poetry in England 1684–1798* (Gainesville: University of Florida Press, 1952), 75–76.

2. *The Guardian*, ed. John Calhoun Stephens (Lexington: University Press of Kentucky, 1982), 129.

3. "A Pastoral Poem on the Union," *The Observator*, March 12, 1707.

4. John Gay, *The Shepherd's Week. In Six Pastorals* (London, 1714), sig. A4r.

5. Murroghoh O Connor, *A Pastoral in Imitation of the First Eclogue of Virgil: Inscrib'd to the Provost, Fellows, and Scholars, of Trinity College, Dublin* (1719); reprint, *Miscellaneous Poems . . . published by Mr. Concanen* (Dublin, 1724), 308–9.

6. Ibid., 316.

7. Ibid., 317.

8. James Ward, *The Smock–Race, at Finglas: With Some Other Poems and Translations* (1716); reprint, *Miscellaneous Poems* (see n. 5), 323.

9. Nicholas Brown, *The North-Country-Wedding, and the Fire, Two Poems in Blank Verse* (Dublin, 1722), 4.

10. Congleton, *Theories of Pastoral Poetry*, 84.

11. Jonathan Swift, *Miscellanies. The Third Volume* (1733); reprint, *Poems*, ed. Harold Williams (Oxford: Clarendon Press, 1966), 3:882, 81.

12. Allan Ramsay, *Richy and Sandy, a Pastoral on the Death of Mr. Joseph Addison* (Edinburgh, 1719).

13. Joseph Mitchell, *The Doleful Swains: A Pastoral Poem. Written Originally in the Scotch Dialect, with an English Version* (London, 1720).

14. Allan Ramsay, *Robert, Richy, and Sandy. A Pastoral on the Death of Matthew Prior, Esq; Dedicated to the Right Honourable Person Design'd by the Old Shepherd* (1721), reprint, *Poems*, ed. Burns Martin and John W. Oliver, 5 vols. (1951–61).

15. On Ramsay's "English" crossings, see Carol McGuirk, "Augustan Influences on Allan Ramsay," *Studies in Scottish Literature* 16 (1981): 98.

16. Allan Ramsay, *Patie and Roger: A Pastoral Inscribed to Josiah Burchet Esq. Secretary of the Admiralty* (Edinburgh, 1720), 9.

17. Allan Ramsay, *Poems by Allan Ramsay* (1721); reprint, *Poems* (see n. 14), xix.

18. Andrew Carpenter, *Verse in English from Eighteenth-Century Ireland* (Cork: Cork University Press, 1998), 10–11.

19. Joseph Ritson, *The Letters of Joseph Ritson Edited Chiefly from Originals in the Possession of His Nephew* (London, 1833), 1:iv.

20. John Cunningham, "Corydon: A Pastoral. To the Memory of William Shenstone, Esq.," *St. James's Chronicle or British Evening Post*, March 12, 1763.

21. Thomas Stratford, "Four Pastoral Essays," *Dublin Mercury*, March, 18, 1769, July 4, 1769, March 29, 1770, April 5, 1770.

22. Oliver Goldsmith, *The Deserted Village, a Poem* (London, 1770), 1.

23. "A Covent-Garden Eclogue," *Universal Spectator and Weekly Journal*, April 26, 1735; "A Wapping Eclogue," *Universal Spectator and Weekly Journal*, November 10, 1739; "Lunny, Lightwit, and Common Sense. A Stage Eclogue, in Imitation of Virgil's 3d Pastoral," *The Prompter*, February 13, 1736; "The Billingsgate Contest. A Piscatory London Eclogue," *Universal Spectator and Weekly Journal*, May 25, 1734; "Warbletta: A Suburban Eclogue," *The Grub-Street Journal*, July 19, 1733.

24. Andrew Erskine, "The Chairmen: A Town-Eclogue," in *A Collection of Original Poems. By the Rev. Mr. Blacklock, and Other Scotch Gentlemen* (Edinburgh, 1760), 180, 82.

25. J. N., "Evening; or, the Politicians: An Eclogue," *Dublin Mercury*, October 8, 1771; J. N., "Midnight; or, the Wake. An Eclogue," *Dublin Mercury*, August 22, 1771; J. N., "Morning; or the Discovery. An Eclogue," *Dublin Mercury*, August 15, 1771; J. N., "Night, or the Charm: An Eclogue," *Dublin Mercury*, September 7, 1771.

26. Robert Fergusson, "Mutual Complaint of Plainstanes and Causey, in Their Mother-Tongue," *Weekly Magazine or Edinburgh Amusement*, March 4, 1773, 306.

27. Robert Fergusson, "A Drink Eclogue," *Weekly Magazine or Edinburgh Amusement,* November 11, 1773, 210.

28. Robert Fergusson, "To Dr. Samuel Johnson: Food for a New Edition of His Dictionary," *Weekly Magazine or Edinburgh Amusement*, October 21, 1773, 114.

29. Charles Churchill, *The Prophecy of Famine. A Scots Pastoral* (London, 1763), 14.

30. *The Drivers: A Dialogue* (Cambridge, 1770), 8. A London newspaper recalled the Bute era in connection in objecting to the dissolution of the Irish parliament; an Irishman observes, "'Tis plain, that YOU SCOTCH have turn'd most out of place, / If WE turn the rest out, by similar grace, / Pray what's to become of JOHN BULL?" "Pat's Query on the Union," *The Morning Herald*, February 2, 1799.

31. Aquilo, "A Pastoral, Suited to the Times. In the Caledonian Dialect, with a Glossary," *Weekly Magazine or Edinburgh Amusement*, January 25, 1776, 145.

32. "A Pastoral Suited to the Times," *Berwick Museum* 1 (1785): 262.

33. Thomas Coombe, *Edwin: Or the Emigrant. An Eclogue. To Which Are Added Three Other Poetical Sketches* (Philadelphia, 1775).

34. W Nisbet, "The Exile," in *Poems; Chiefly Composed from Recent Events* (Edinburgh, 1780), 95.

35. George Gregory, "American Eclogues. Eclogue I. Morning; or the Complaint," *Gentleman's Magazine* 53 (1783): 1043, George Gregory, "American Eclogues. Eclogue Ii. Evening; or the Fugitive," *Gentleman's Magazine* 54 (1784).

36. John Learmont, *Poems Pastoral, Satirical, Tragic, and Comic* (Edinburgh, 1791), 121.

37. Ibid., 195.

38. Samuel Thomson, *Poems, on Different Subjects, Partly in the Scottish Dialect* (Belfast, 1793), sig. A3v.

39. Ibid., sig. A3r.

40. Tim Burke, " 'yet Tho' I'm Irish All without, I'm Every Item Scotch within': Poetry and Self-Fashioning in 1790s Ulster," *John Clare Society Journal* 22 (2003): 37.

41. Thomas Atkinson, *Hibernian Eclogues. To Which Are Added, Miscellaneous Poems* (Dublin, 1791), 3, 9, 15. Atkinson's fate is obscure; he published a poem ridiculing Edmund Burke's defense of chivalry (for which he was warmly lauded in the *Dublin Evening Post*, May 19, 1791) but was not heard from again.

42. Hugh Mulligan, *Poems Chiefly on Slavery and Oppression, with Notes and Illustrations* (London, 1788), 18.

43. "Esthonian Poetry," *The Port Folio* 1 (1801): 16.

44. See David Hill Radcliffe, "Ancient Poetry and British Pastoral," in *From Gaelic to Romantic: Ossianic Translations*, ed. Fiona J. Stafford and Howard Gaskill (Amsterdam: Rodopi, 1998).

45. On this controversy viewed from the Irish perspective see Clare O'Halloran, *Golden Ages and Barbarous Nations: Antiquarian Debate and Cultural Politics in Ireland, c. 1750–1800* (Cork, Ireland: Cork University Press in association with Field Day, 2004), 99–113. For the Scottish perspective see Kristmannsson Gauti, *Literary Diplomacy*, (New York: Peter Lang, 2005), 1:97–108.

46. Allan Ramsay, *The Ever Green, Being a Collection of Scots Poems* (Edinburgh, 1724), 1:211–30.

47. Robert Burns, *Poems Chiefly in the Scottish Dialect* (Kilmarnock, 1786), 92.

48. Hector MacNeill, *The Pastoral, or Lyric Muse of Scotland; in Three Cantos* (Edinburgh, 1808).

49. Philip Doyne, *The Triumph of Parnassus, a Poem. On the Birth of His Royal Highness the Prince of Wales* (Dublin, 1763), 6.

50. John Ball, Odes, Elegies, Ballads, Pictures, Inscriptions, Sonnets (Dublin, 1775), 55.

51. Thomas Dermody, *Poems: Consisting of Essays, Lyric, Elegiac, &C.* (Dublin, 1792), sig. B2r. See James Grant Raymond, The *Life of Thomas Dermody: Interspersed with Pieces of Original Poetry, Many Exhibiting Unexampled Prematurity of Genuine Poetical Talent; And Containing a Series of Correspondence with Several Eminent Characters*, 2 vols. (London, 1806).

52. Except insofar as it engages an antiquarian tradition common to Irish poetry and fiction. See Katie Trumpener, *Bardic Nationalism: The Romantic Novel and the British Empire* (Princeton: Princeton University Press, 1997), 60–61.

Berkeley and Ireland: Who are the "We" in "We Irish think otherwise"?

Scott C. Breuninger

DESPITE BEING ACKNOWLEDGED AS ONE OF THE GREATEST IRISH THINKERS, until recently George Berkeley has been relatively neglected in the land of his birth. Although steps have been taken to rectify this omission—such as deciding to name the library at Trinity College after Berkeley and issuing a special stamp bearing his likeness in honor of his bicentenary in 1985—a marked hesitancy to associate "the good Bishop" with Ireland remains. Studies of Irish history often tend to downplay his Hibernian connections, only mentioning in passing that he was the author of "some Irish tracts."[1] At best, these studies mine his influential economic treatise, *The Querist*, for contemporary commentary while making little effort to place this work within the context of his larger projects. At worst, he is not mentioned at all. In philosophy, Berkeley's Irish connections receive similarly scant attention. Traditional histories of philosophy cast him as the "middle British empiricist," forming the central link in a philosophical chain running from Locke to Hume.[2] By focusing almost exclusively on Berkeley's identity as a "British empiricist," philosophers have done a great disservice to a man whose work was embedded within Irish matters.

Writing as a student at Trinity in 1707, Berkeley rejected the contemporary theories of Locke and Newton with the claim that "we Irish men can conceive no such lines."[3] It was this brazen refutation of the dominant English philosophy that earned Berkeley praise from William Butler Yeats as a "fierce young man" whose intellectual struggles (along with Swift) concerned "all those who feel a responsibility for the thought of modern Ireland."[4] Yet, as a Protestant Anglo-Irish figure, the question of "which" Ireland he chose to identify with remains open. This problem is exacerbated by the fact that over the course of his career, Berkeley eventually became one of the leading figures of the Irish Church, fixated upon the social and economic welfare of the nation. This essay will trace the development of Berkeley's engagement with Irish matters, paying particular attention to his changing attitudes toward the sectarian and class differences that plagued Irish society. His proscriptions for the economic well-being of his native land illustrate Berkeley's espousal of a vision of Irish "patriotism" grounded in practical recognition of the challenges facing Ireland as a whole. While this mature position contained elements of religious prejudice, these were tempered by a greater concern for creating a self-sufficient state able to weather the storms of social upheaval.

Part of the problem of identifying the Irish aspects of Berkeley's work stems from the contentious nature of notions of Irish identity during the early eighteenth century. As a leading member of the Church of Ireland, Berkeley's legacy has been linked to debates concerning the Protestant Ascendancy and its role in Irish history. While this is an important consideration, it is also crucial to explore the ways in which Berkeley himself understood his place within Irish culture. Berkeley was born in Thomastown and spent most of his life in Ireland, including his education at Trinity and his later ecclesiastical post at Cloyne. Given this close personal connection with Ireland, it is essential to see how he defined himself and his project—in other words, to explain to whom he was referring when he wrote "we Irish think otherwise" and what this came to mean to him over the course of his career.

During the early years of the eighteenth century, a great deal of inconsistency and confusion surrounded Irish Protestants' use of the term "Irish." David Hayton has called attention to the fact that between the 1690s and the 1720s, political and economic issues drove an important shift in the terms used by Anglo-Irish Protestants to identify themselves, as they moved away from regarding themselves as the "English Interest in Ireland" and toward the gradual adoption of the mantle of the "Irish interest."[5] During this transitional period, thinkers such as Archbishop William King and Jonathan Swift displayed a bifurcated vision of "Irishness": a type of dual identity dependent upon specific contexts. King, for instance, alternatively referred to Protestants as "the people of Ireland" and to Catholics as "the Irish."[6] Likewise, although Swift addressed the fourth of his *Drapier's Letters* to "the whole people of Ireland," he later referred to the Catholics as "the Irish" and to Protestants as "the true English people of Ireland."[7]

This habit of thinking about nationality in two keys should be remembered when considering Berkeley's sense of identity, as his choice of words may have been—like King's and Swift's—partially dependent upon the context of his statements. At the same time, we must recognize shifts in Berkeley's own attitudes toward Ireland, since over the course of his life Berkeley moved from being a student at Trinity to an influential bishop in Cloyne, and his experiences over this period altered his understanding of Irish identity.

With these considerations in mind, this essay will begin by briefly discussing some of the problems facing the articulation of "Irishness" during the first half of the eighteenth century. Notions of Irish identity during this time were particularly raucous and this will help contextualize Berkeley's sense of self-definition with regard to Ireland. During the course of his career, Berkeley's written references to Ireland display a distinct shift, moving from a close connection with all of Ireland to one much more located within the Protestant Irish community. While part of this transition may be explained through reference to his increasingly high profile within the Church of Ireland, this movement reflects a general change in his attitude toward social policy: a move away from abstract theorizing to more concrete and practical plans for the amelioration of the ills that he saw besetting Ireland. While it is difficult to generalize from Berkeley's experiences to the situation facing other Protestant Irish during this time, this explication of a specific case may help provide a richer context for further thought on this issue.

Contemporary discussions concerning Irish identity during the early eighteenth century often run aground upon questions of terminology and inclusion. An important point of contention in this controversy over the "Irishness" of various figures centers on the definition of the "Anglo-Irish" interest in Ireland during the early eighteenth century. For many modern writers, the taint of "English" or "Protestant" affinities often is enough to exclude historical figures from representing the "true" nature of Ireland.[8] As a result, historians of eighteenth-century Ireland are confronted with the problem of determining the "Irish" credentials of their subjects, in light of present-day concerns.

A key factor in this debate stems from the fact that the governing class of Ireland during this time was the "Anglo-Irish." While this terminology appears to suggest a purely ethnic category, its use typically has been expanded to include a religious dimension, stressing the Protestantism in general and Anglicanism in particular of its subjects.[9] However, this tactic poses the problem of eliding the socioeconomic disparities within the Irish Protestant community, placing the Protestant landed elite on a par with their poorer brethren. While religious preference certainly played an important role in determining one's self-identity at this time, historical inquiries that downplay the economic gap within this community threaten to overemphasize religious bonds. One technique to avoid this pitfall involves the use of the term the "Anglo-Irish ascendancy," thereby defining this group "along social and political, rather than ethnic, lines."[10] By highlighting the socioeconomic position of this group, "ascendancy culture" is located within the country houses and estates of the wealthy, begging the question of whether an ethnic or religious component need be included at all. Nonetheless, the more common "Protestant Ascendancy" has flourished despite being a term that only came into use during the 1780s.[11]

Historians have raised a number of questions concerning how the concept of the "Protestant Ascendancy" was constructed, primarily focusing upon the methodological slippage attendant to the anachronistic application of this term to early eighteenth-century individuals. Taking aim at the work of Roy Foster and James Kelly, W. J. McCormack forcefully argues that the notion of an "ascendancy culture" has too often been used unreflectively and without concern for the context within which this idea developed.[12] McCormack stresses that the phrase "Protestant Ascendancy" was first publicly used by Sir Boyle Roche in the Irish House of Commons in February 1782 and notes that its modern use to describe the early eighteenth-century elite raises problems concerning the continuity and persistence of this group throughout the century. McCormack contends that the ideological concept of the "Protestant ascendancy" should be dated to 1792, within an "urban and mercantile, even commercial" context.[13] Thus, he argues that advocates of earlier figures such as Swift "as a spokesman for the protestant ascendancy have now even fewer legs to stand on."[14]

In response to McCormack's attack, Kelly strongly defended both the origins of the ideological concept of a "Protestant ascendancy" amid the paper war of 1786–88 and the belief that this term may be usefully applied to earlier periods of Irish history. Drawing upon the work of Jacqueline Hill, Kelly argues that this notion was articulated as "part of the wider response of Irish Protestants to the challenge posed to their traditional dominance by the repeal of the Penal Laws and other demands for change."[15] Although determining when this ideological construction entered into popular use is an important issue, for the purposes of considering the context within which Berkeley lived, Kelly's second point is more pertinent. Acknowledging that the term "Protestant ascendancy" was a late development, Kelly is careful to point out the wide variety of contemporary labels that were used to describe this group. For instance, immediately following the Revolution of 1688/89, Anglicans residing in Ireland were typically referred to as the "representatives of England in Ireland," later being seen as "the Protestant and English interest of Ireland."[16] Kelly argues that while these settlers were dependent upon the English crown for their protection, the evolution of the relationship between Ireland and England eventually "drove a wedge between them and, as a result they were inclined increasingly . . . to describe themselves simply as the 'Protestant interest.'"[17] Kelly notes that during the reigns of Queen Anne and Kings George I and II, this formulation was commonly used to indicate the dominant Anglican elite. In the end, he concludes that the idea of the "Protestant ascendancy" should be seen as "part of the ongoing evolution of conservative Protestant thinking in the late-eighteenth century."[18]

Against this interpretation, Joep Theodoor Leerssen places Irish Protestant thought within an international context, specifically a notion of "patriotism" premised upon civic virtue, the pursuit of the common good, and active citizenship.[19] As explained by Leerssen, the idea of Irish "patriotism" provides a useful tool for discussing Berkeley's Irish identity. Noting that the ideological connotations of the term "Anglo-Irish" have too often resulted in a "binary polarity" between "pro-English/anti-native Irish 'Ascendancy' interests" and an "anti-English/pro-Irish 'National' interests," Leerssen contends that this division fails to account for the diversity of attitudes held by pro-Irish individuals of English descent.[20] By locating the idea of Irish "patriotism" within the broader context of European thought, Leerssen attempts to prove that this concept was a precursor of moderate liberalism, not extreme nationalism.[21] While this idea typically drew upon traditions of individual liberty and the common good, among Anglo-Irish patriots the historical record circumscribed this affinity. Unable to cite Irish examples of these beliefs, many Anglo-Irish writers were forced to appeal to the English historical tradition, including the Magna Carta and the Glorious Revolution, to support their constitutional claims. Not only did this strategy allow them to highlight their own Englishness against the backdrop of the native Irish majority, but it also provided a storehouse of traditional English liberties to which they could claim inheritance.[22] The main problem with this tactic centered on the fact that these individuals also needed to account for Irish constitutional thought, much of which had been repudiated by the events of 1688/89.[23] By seeking to explain the position of these patriots straddling English and Irish thought, Leerssen contends that Irish patriot discourse was "by necessity remarkably a-historicist," on the grounds that it could not draw upon pre-1688 Irish thought without evoking fears of Catholic resurgency.[24]

Leerssen observes that early eighteenth-century notions of patriotism were often premised upon a sense of "disinterested service to one's country."[25] Although we shall see that Berkeley's references to the plight of the native Irish often were tarnished by prejudice, they were still premised upon the desire to help improve the overall health and security of the island: a task that he saw as cutting across class and sectarian differences. This goal was evident in many of Berkeley's works, as he presented a moderate vision of patriotism grounded in practical concerns for improvement and the public good. For instance, in the dedication to his *New Theory of Vision*, he contended that a "true patriot" has "the interest of the publick at heart, and omits no means of informing himself what may be prejudicial or advantageous to his country, in order to prevent the one and promote the other."[26] Likewise, in his *Maxims Concerning Patriotism*, Berkeley gave further voice to this idea, defining a patriot as "one who heartily wisheth the public prosperity, and doth not only wish, but also study and endeavour to promote it."[27] In each of these cases, chosen from both his early and later writings, it is possible to see that his hopes for the general welfare of Ireland provided the underpinning of his engagement with Irish matters. In this respect, Leerssen's notion of Irish patriotism seems to aptly describe some of Berkeley's attitude toward his homeland, as evidenced by his interest in the practical improvement of Ireland, at least in comparison to Britain.

Although Berkeley often repeated his love of Ireland, over the course of his lifetime there was a shift in his use of the term "Irish" and his sense of personal affinity with this identification. While a young student, Berkeley unreflectively identified himself as "Irish," particularly in contrast to the tenets of English philosophy, but also in the sense that he wrote with great passion of his "Irishness."[28] Although relatively few in number, these early references to Ireland did not indicate an appreciation for the sectarian differences within the nation, rather they generally assumed that the island formed a cohesive whole distinct from Britain. As the Bishop of Cloyne, Berkeley displayed a more nuanced use of the term—continuing to embrace "Irishness" against the economic powers of Britain, but further distinguishing between the "inhabitants of Ireland" and the "native Irish" on both economic and religious grounds. In the end, Berkeley sought to improve the situation of all Irish people, but in the process his self-identification shifted along with his evolving understanding of contemporary political realities. As a result, the "Irish" he spoke of as a youth condensed, becoming the "Irish" led by the Church of Ireland and who feared the influence of Britain over Ireland. These impressions hold true in examining Berkeley's Irish education, during which time he composed his philosophical system.

In his brief survey of Irish philosophy of this time, David Berman identifies two main strands of thought, both of which took Locke as their point of departure and sought to combine theology with philosophy in a distinctively "Irish" manner.[29] The first of these positions was associated with liberal Enlightenment values such as toleration, rationalism, and critiques of religious dogma in favor of natural religion. This group of "left-wing Lockeans" not only included such political luminaries as William Molyneux and Robert Molesworth, but also philosophical and religious figures like Thomas Emlyn, Francis Hutcheson, and Robert Clayton.[30] In their own ways, each of these thinkers used Lockean principles to defend individual liberty and valorize the rational pursuit of knowledge; however, the most influential representative of this tradition was John Toland. Hailed as the "father of Irish philosophy," albeit a "hated father," Toland's *Christianity not Mysterious* (1696) sparked a heated Irish reaction that melded philosophy and theology.[31] In response to the so-called Deist debate, the second stream of Irish thought coalesced, which Berman associates with more "conservative" or "traditional" "Counter-Enlightenment" values of extreme empiricism, fideism, and intolerance. According to Berman, writers and theologians such as William King, Peter Browne, and Edward Synge appropriated a "right-wing" version of Lockeanism to defend religion against the assaults of Toland and his followers.[32]

Within this framework, Berman is careful to note that Berkeley was an exception since he did not fit neatly into either of these categories. For instance, while his thought contained "important rationalistic and empiricistic elements," he simultaneously rejected fideism and had little patience for religious toleration.[33] Berman claims that he is best understood as "mediating between the left-wing Lockeanism of Toland and Emlyn and the right-wing Lockeanism of Browne, King, and Synge."[34] Thus, it was through this *via media* that Berkeley drew from both camps to produce his distinctive contributions to philosophy and theology. Both groups of thinkers identified by Berman provide an essential context for explaining Berkeley's early writings. As a student and fellow at Trinity, Berkeley was both aware of and personally knew many of the key figures associated with these strands of thought—traditions that were distinctively "Irish" in their orientation. While constructing his main philosophical texts, the issues and concerns at play in these debates concerning the role of reason in religion, the limits of human knowledge and perception, and the use of language all informed his understanding of the relationship between philosophy and religion.

Through his espousal of an idealism (or immaterialism) grounded in Irish debates and concerns, Berkeley challenged English thinkers with a model of understanding dramatically at odds with the dominant empiricism. As a result, Harry Bracken has claimed that Berkeley is best understood as an "Irish Cartesian," whose work was more inspired by continental thought, applied to the Irish context, than that of England.[35] In this respect, Berkeley's early forays into philosophy indicate that he understood his intellectual heritage as stemming from an Irish confluence of ideas: while a student, "we Irish" implied a philosophical identity founded in opposition to English thinkers, not in agreement with them. Still, after 1713, when Berkeley left Ireland, he was no longer a student and thus those modern studies of his work that ignore his post-1713 writings fail to capture the more socially engaged Berkeley known to his contemporaries.

If we turn to Berkeley's personal writings concerning his native island, we can see that his correspondence shows that he thought of himself as an "Irishman" whose interests were opposed to those of England. Until 1713 Berkeley had never left Ireland and his letters reflect his great devotion to the island and its people. Even after he began his period of extensive continental travel, his letters continued to compare Ireland favorably to the areas he was exploring—betraying a wistful nostalgia for the land he had left and to which he would eventually return.

The most telling of these letters evoke an awareness of contemporary Anglo-Irish disputes and a clear siding with the "Irish interest." In a 1711 letter to his lifelong correspondent Lord Percival, Berkeley wrote to thank him for his efforts "in behalf of our country" against a "bill for the further impost on Irish yarn."[36] At this point the British Parliament was proposing to increase the duty on Irish-spun wool, following a 1710 law that had prohibited the import of hops from any country other than England.[37] Two years later, after his arrival in London, Berkeley's letters continued to display an interest in the economic plight of Ireland. Again writing to Percival, he expressed fear that the French would implement a plan to import sixty thousand head of cattle, mostly from Ireland. Although it is doubtful that the British government would have allowed such a scheme, Berkeley was concerned that this operation would not only allow the French to "rival us in our beef trade" but also feared that such wholesale exports would have the even more dangerous effect of lessening the Irish stock.[38]

Berkeley's early correspondence also contains elements that suggest a more personal appreciation for Ireland, one that failed to mention the sectarian divisions within it. Shortly after his arrival in London, Berkeley wrote a letter to Percival filled with longing for his native land. Not only did he miss the fellowship of his friends, but he also wrote more pragmatically of his desire for "fair weather, which we have had as little of here as ever I knew in the worst season in Ireland." Taken as a whole, his experience in England made him feel "more in love with my own country than I was before."[39] For his part, Percival took care to point out that although England may seem to be "a more kindly soil" for Berkeley's work than the country of his birth, "we on this side will insist on it that the plant is our own . . . that you are of Irish growth."[40] At least in his personal life, the young Berkeley believed himself to be "Irish" in both philosophical and personal senses.

After leaving Dublin in 1713, Berkeley's attitudes toward Ireland and his use of the term Irish slowly began to change, as he came to recognize the importance of the religious differences within the land. By the 1730s, when he was appointed bishop of Cloyne, Berkeley had spent considerable time in London and had embarked on his ambitious missionary venture to Rhode Island that ultimately fell through due to funding problems.[41] The mature Berkeley who took office in Cloyne still cared deeply for Ireland, but this interest was now tinged with a more practical outlook shaped by his experiences on both sides of the Atlantic. Berkeley's later references to the Irish people displayed his fears of the social ills he saw besetting Ireland in general and his pastoral charges in particular. In this context, as a highly placed member of the Church of Ireland with many social responsibilities, Berkeley was forced to confront the differences between the Protestant and Catholic Irish interests, as well as those between different economic groups. He still showed concern for the "inhabitants of Ireland," but this was balanced by economic proposals specifically aimed at the "native Irish."

With a few exceptions, studies of early eighteenth-century Irish economics have often overlooked the important theoretical advances generated in response to the problems besetting the nation.[42] The overwhelming impression of Ireland's economy during this time, as relayed by contemporary observers, was of a "poor and backward" nation.[43] While some historians have argued that the Irish economy was not in as dire a state as conveyed by writers of the time, it was still a far cry from the level of prosperity enjoyed by her neighbors. For many Irish writers, this economic problem was symptomatic of a deeper political one: namely, the influence and power exerted by Britain over the island. Pressure on Irish trade from the Westminster Parliament had slowly increased, since the 1663 prohibition of live cattle exports, to include more strict enforcement of the Navigation Laws and the 1699 Woolen Act.[44] When coupled with the prohibitive duties on the import of Irish goods to England, these measures were believed to strike at the heart of Irish trade.

As James Kelly has noted, while the first two decades of the eighteenth century were generally good, by the end of the 1710s the collapse of prices and a series of poor harvests "exposed the weaknesses of the Irish economy and plunged the nation into crisis."[45] Irish frustration with Britain's unsympathetic attitude was further acerbated during the early 1720s, with the eruption of the Bank Controversy (1720–21) and Wood's halfpence affair (1723–25).[46] In 1720 a proposal was advanced to establish a National

Bank in Ireland modeled on the Bank of England that would, so argued its supporters, essentially be a private corporate bank whose main customer was to be the Irish government.[47] The problem with this plan, from the perspective of Irish "patriots," was the fear that the British would manipulate it to perpetuate the poor state of the Irish economy, as they had with earlier trade restrictions.[48] This persistent distrust of British motives also colored the debate over the introduction of Wood's halfpence, sparking a flurry of tracts against the establishment of this coin.[49]

The Irish writers who confronted the challenge of placing their nation on the track for growth during the 1720s and 1730s shared a number of concerns about this issue. The individuals who composed the "Irish School" shared an abiding concern for improving the economic condition of their state. Many of them were members of the Dublin Society, an improving organization founded in 1731 by Thomas Prior and Samuel Madden for the express purpose of encouraging Irish economic development.[50] Likewise, most of these figures had attended Trinity College together and were devout Anglicans. Although the foci of their investigations differed, they shared a common method of eschewing grand theories in favor of solving immediate, practical problems.

One prominent factor undermining the Irish economy, according to members of the Irish School, lay in the great sums of money "that our Gentlemen abroad draw yearly out of the Kingdom."[51] In addition to recognizing the dangers posed by the lack of currency, thinkers such as Prior also took aim at the prevalence of luxury spending among the Irish gentry. Here, the brunt of their scorn was reserved for the absentees, whose "extravagance," "vanity," and "luxury" contributed to the "impoverishment and ruin of their native country."[52] In a similar manner, Arthur Dobbs railed against the overwhelming consumption of luxury by the wealthy and its more widespread influence upon Irish society. According to Dobbs, it was essential that Ireland "retrench" against luxury spending, "before idleness and debauchery prevail too far among the middle and lower ranks of men" since these people "readily follow the examples of those of higher station."[53] This fear of the creeping desire for luxuries was also exhibited by the anonymous author of 1730 tract, *The Present State of Ireland Consider'd*. The author of this piece not only pointed out that the absentees "annually draw immense sums out of the Kingdom, none of which ever returns," but also highlighted the fact that they were the primary cause of "large importations of consumable commodities, the true fuel of luxury."[54] Going one step further, this tract argued against the "pleasure which attends luxury, the Bane of every State," since it promotes "luxury in your inferiors, by their following" the examples of the gentry.[55]

Berkeley's collection of essays, *The Querist*, reflected many of these concerns. Published over the course of three years (1735–37), this text is an important work in the history of Irish economics and is guided by his proscriptions for the revitalization of Ireland, helping to illuminate the mature Berkeley's understanding of Irish matters. Generally speaking, his queries addressed two social groups: the "inhabitants of Ireland" and the "native" or "common" Irish. He used the first of these terms primarily to designate everyone on the island, Protestant and Catholic, while the latter solely signified the Irish Catholics. If we look more closely at the contexts within which he raised these issues, it is possible to gain a fuller sense of his mature attitudes toward notions of "Irishness" and "patriotism," as well as his own place therein.

In *The Querist*, Berkeley's sporadic references to the "inhabitants of Ireland" or to "our people" occur at points where he contrasted the economic interests of Ireland (as a whole) with those of Britain. He took issue with the Irish strategy of raising large numbers of sheep, suggesting that too much dependence upon the wool trade could be dangerous to "Ireland" and to "the Irish."[56] He further claimed that the whole nation should work together (vis-à-vis Britain), asking "whether anything can be more ridiculous than for the north of Ireland to be jealous of a linen manufacturer in the South?" (Qu. 95). Likewise, Berkeley sought to encourage domestic consumption, by both Protestants and Catholics, in order to raise the living standards of everyone (Qu. 127). In this sense, he considered himself "Irish" when the interests of his native land were placed into juxtaposition with those of Britain. This is the Berkeley cited by those who have enshrined him in the pantheon of early Irish economic protectionists and it would thus seem as though Berkeley harbored an inclusive attitude toward "Irishness"; at least when faced with economic issues close to the hearts of Irish Protestants.

Although the meaning of Berkeley's message was somewhat obscured by the rhetorical style of his queries, his goal of ameliorating the problems facing the Irish economy, as a whole, was clear. In this respect, Berkeley may be seen as an "Irish economic nationalist" who sought to improve the Irish economy against that of Britain. Echoing sentiments common to the Irish School, Berkeley's analysis focused upon unemployment, fiscal policy related to the balance of trade, and the advisability of monetary institutions, such as a national bank, for Ireland. Surveying the general economic condition of Ireland, Berkeley expressed dismay for the fact that the bulk of the Irish (Catholic) population remained mired in poverty, despite being blessed with abundant natural resources. He wondered "whether we are not in fact the only people who may be said to starve in the midst of plenty?"[57] In a similar vein, he asked "whether it be not a new spectacle under the sun, to behold, in such a climate and such a soil, and under such a gentle government, so many roads untrodden, fields untilled, houses desolate, and hands unemployed."[58] Berkeley's response to this situation focused upon two main segments of the Irish population. First, he lamented the poor living conditions of the bulk of the Irish Catholics, but also suggested that their plight was partially of their own making due to their moral (and presumably religious) failings. At the same time, Berkeley took aim at the luxurious lifestyles of the Anglo-Irish gentry (at home and abroad) for placing their own personal interests above those of the nation and for failing to recognize their moral duty to assist others within Ireland, showing the concern for the "common good" associated with Leerssen's notion of "patriotism."

In *The Querist*, Berkeley articulated a two-pronged plan for improving the economic health of the nation and the well-being of its inhabitants. Expanding upon the arguments of his 1721 *Essay toward Preventing the Ruin of Great Britain*, Berkeley's strategy centered on a carefully nuanced interpretation of the dangers and benefits luxury could hold for a developing economy.[59] In making this argument, Berkeley displayed a newfound appreciation for the benefits of "low-level" luxury on a strictly economic level. Suggesting that the Irish needed to cultivate a "taste for prosperity" among the laboring classes, Berkeley displayed a willingness to adopt tactics absent from his earlier forays into economic writing. Still, while this limited embrace of "reasonable fashions" indicated that Berkeley was able to recognize the importance of "appetites" as a spur to industry, he was careful to note that the stimulation of demand should only be targeted at the lower classes. Thus, Berkeley's encouragement of new wants was tempered by his moral disdain for luxury, particularly the spending patterns of the Irish gentry and their taste for foreign goods. In the end, he sought to counterbalance the creation of new wants among the lower classes by reigning in the luxurious expenditures of the gentry. By encouraging the consumption of domestic goods, Berkeley hoped to make it possible for the Irish to "live cleanly and comfortably, till the land, and reap the fruits of it," even "if there was a brass wall a thousand cubits high round this kingdom" (Qu. 134).

Underlying Berkeley's plans was a sophisticated understanding of the needs of a developing economy. Contending that the health of the economy was dependent upon the employment of its people, Berkeley asked "whether there ever was, is, or will be, an industrious nation poor, or an idle rich?" (Qu. 1). Rejecting the common assumption that gold and silver were the yardsticks of a state's economic well-being, Berkeley stressed the idea that "human labour" is "the true source of wealth" (Qu. 42). By redefining a nation's prosperity in terms of the activities of its citizens and not in terms of specie, Berkeley shifted his analysis away from traditional concerns for the "balance of trade" and made it possible to look within Ireland for the solutions of its problems. The presence, or absence, of metallic specie was no longer the primary determinant of a state's economic power, but rather the industriousness of its inhabitants. By thus refocusing attention upon the domestic conditions within Ireland, particularly the work habits of the labor force, Berkeley made it possible to identify the specific problems facing his homeland and suggest targeted solutions for them.

From this vantage point, Berkeley trained his eye upon the chronic unemployment of Ireland and identified what has since been termed the "perverse supply curve of labor."[60] Accepting a long-standing commonplace, Berkeley recognized that once the workforce achieved a minimum standard of living, it was difficult to induce individuals to increase their labor. While he certainly acknowledged that involuntary unemployment was a serious problem, the prevalence of voluntary unemployment troubled him, which he explained by singling out the faults of the native (Catholic) Irish. Addressing this problem, Berkeley asked "whether the bulk of our Irish natives are not kept from thriving, by that cynical content in dirt and beggary which they possess to a degree beyond any other people in Christendom?"[61] Berkeley saw this endemic lack of industry among Irish laborers as part of a vicious circle, by which the poor lacked incentives to improve their standard of living, thus encouraging idleness and resulting in economic stagnation. He suggested that "nastiness and beggary . . . extinguish all . . . ambition, making men listless, hopeless, and slothful" (Qu. 61). Faced with this state of affairs, Berkeley sought to introduce psychological spurs to the industry he believed so essential for the development of the Irish economy.

Berkeley contended that the easiest and most effective way to encourage industry was to stimulate demand for a higher standard of living. Keying in on the low expectations of the bulk of the Irish population, he suggested that introducing the desire for new commodities would provide the motivation needed to eliminate idleness. Berkeley asked "whether the creating of wants be not the likeliest way to produce industry in a people? And whether if our peasants were accustomed to eat beef and wear shoes they would not be more industrious?" (Qu. 20). While the introduction of beef and shoes may not seem to be "luxurious" by today's standards, the fact that they represented a move from mere subsistence is indicative of Berkeley's belief that moderation was the key to a stable economy.

Berkeley expressed this notion of moderation by suggesting that "comfort" was the watchword by which commercial society should be governed. Asking "whether comfortable living doth not produce wants, and wants industry, and industry wealth?" Berkeley highlighted the cumulative effects that minute improvements in the standard of living could produce (Qu. 107). Through the process of stimulating and expanding the wants of the population, Berkeley hoped to break through the cycle of poverty and idleness that had become entrenched throughout the Irish countryside. It is worth noting that Berkeley's focus on the standard of living may have drawn upon the "Discourse of Trade" literature that had flourished during the late seventeenth and early eighteenth centuries.[62] Berkeley, like thinkers such as Nicholas Barbon and Dudley North, believed that once the poor were driven to acquire "incentive" goods, they would be self-motivated toward industry and thus eschew the idleness previously common throughout the nation, in effect using an economic carrot to lure them from their "innate" disposition toward sloth.[63] Berkeley articulated the end-result of this shift in values by asking, "suppose the bulk of our inhabitants had shoes to their feet, clothes to their backs, and beef in their bellies, might not such a state be eligible for the public, even though the squires were condemned to drink ale and cider?" (Qu. 112).

This last query suggests the second aspect of Berkeley's plan: a concerted effort to stamp out the luxury of the Protestant gentry classes. Berkeley, along with most of his fellow Irish economists, castigated the "Irish squires" who preferred costly French wines as symptomatic of a more general economic problem facing Ireland. While Berkeley's earlier writings on luxury had a strong moral component, *The Querist* grounded his position in considerations of the effects of foreign luxury goods upon the well-being of the nation as a whole. Asking "how far the vanity of our ladies in dressing, and of our gentlemen in drinking, contributes to the general misery of the people?" Berkeley identified the two foreign imports that he believed to be most widespread and detrimental to Ireland (Qu. 102). Berkeley contended that consumption of both French fashionable lace and claret illustrated the widespread "vanity" of the Irish, rather than any true necessity, and posed a grave danger to the state. Berkeley argued that the Irish gentry failed to recognize that Ireland's economy was substantially different than those of its trading partners. Thus, when the upper classes began "imitating those neighbours in our fashions, to whom we bear no likeness in our circumstances," Berkeley asked "whether we are not undone by fashions made for other people? And whether it be not madness in a poor nation to imitate a rich one?" (Qu. 17 and 140).

At the heart of Berkeley's critique of foreign luxuries was an appreciation for the national interest, rather than sectarian or class ones, thus indicating his greater allegiance to Ireland as a whole, rather than "Protestant Ireland" in particular. By spending their fortunes on foreign delicacies, the Irish gentry were ignoring the needs of their countrymen and thus undermining efforts for national improvement. It is important to note that Berkeley's argument against foreign trade was not premised upon mercantilist concerns for the flow of money, but rather upon the needs of the domestic population. Taking aim at the habits of the gentry, Berkeley asked "whether the vanity and luxury of a few ought to stand in competition with the interest of a nation?" (Qu. 167). Rejecting this proposition, he asserted that "national wants ought . . . to be the rule of trade . . . and the most pressing wants of the majority ought . . . to be the first considered."[64] In a vivid image encapsulating this idea, Berkeley questioned "whether she would not be a very vile matron, and justly thought either mad or foolish, that should give away the necessaries of life from her naked and famished children, in exchange for pearls to stick in her hair, and sweetmeats to please her own palate?" (Qu. 117). Berkeley believed that by sending essential Irish goods abroad to pay for imported luxuries, the Irish gentry were irresponsibly squandering the opportunity to improve the wealth of the nation and dooming the bulk of the population to poverty.

Berkeley proposed a number of measures that could potentially alleviate this situation. First and foremost were plans for encouraging the demand for domestic manufactures, which he believed would spur production and industry throughout the nation. Berkeley contended that while "fashion" created "appetites," it was possible for "the legislature to interpose in the making of fashions; and not leave an affair of so great influence to the management of women and fops, tailors, and vintners" (Qu. 13). Placing great stock in a dynamic vision of national growth, Berkeley suggested that once the process of national rejuvenation began, it would quickly pick up momentum and "become more and more considerable" (Qu. 591). Thus, he claimed that even the smallest first steps of the Irish government could eventually have important ramifications for the national economy.

For Berkeley, a key tactic was the creation of a moderate "general good taste" that placed value on domestically produced commodities (Qu. 15). He repeatedly compared Irish goods with foreign ones, pointing out that the quality of the former often surpassed that of the latter. By substituting Irish goods, such as tiles and plaster, for foreign ones, such as Norwegian fir, Berkeley believed domestic production would increase and unemployment be ameliorated. This, in turn, would spur industry and encourage the widespread consumption of Irish goods. Furthermore, Berkeley hoped that Ireland would develop new areas of manufacturing, which could provide an important addition to the nation's wealth. Thus, Berkeley argued that rather than "fold our hands, and repine that we are not allowed the woollen [trade]," the Irish should seek to "strike out and exert [themselves] in permitted branches of trade" (Qu. 73). By seeking to expand the sphere of Irish manufactures, Berkeley hoped to stimulate demand among the poor, which would spur them to the industry needed to acquire these goods. As a result, rates of employment, production, and standard of living in Ireland would all rise.

Although Berkeley's plans generally favored using positive incentives to encourage industry—stimulating demand through new "fashions" and "tastes" and highlighting the value of Irish goods—he was keenly aware of the powerful role that the state could play in this process. If the carrot did not entice the Irish poor to industry, Berkeley was willing to use the stick. After asking "whether the public hath not a right to employ those who cannot or who will not find employment for themselves," Berkeley suggested that "temporary servitude" might be the "best cure of idleness and beggary" (Qu. 382 and 383). More chillingly, he wondered if "all sturdy beggars should not be seized and made slaves to the public for a certain term of years?" (Qu. 384). Less dramatically, Berkeley also suggested that the state could take more prosaic actions aimed at reigning in excessive spending. Recalling some of the plans advanced in his 1721 *Essay*, he noted that "nations as wise and opulent as ours . . . have made sumptuary laws," and asked "what hinders us from doing the same?"[65] In this manner, by encouraging the consumption of Irish manufactures and seeking to limit that of foreign goods, Berkeley hoped to lay the foundation for a strong economy in Ireland.

Nonetheless, while Berkeley may have thought of Ireland as a whole when confronted with England, he also distinguished between the Irish Protestants and the "native" or "common" Irish Catholics when faced with situations within Ireland. Seeking to improve the lot of these "poor illiterate natives," Berkeley raised a number of suggestions aimed at alleviating their more pressing burdens. In addition to his economic arguments, he also advanced a moral argument targeted at "our old native Irish," since he believed them to be "the most indolent and supine people in Christendom" (Qu. 357). Berkeley identified two possible sources of this lack of industry, first asking "whether our natural Irish are not partly Spaniards and partly Tartars; and whether they do not bear signatures of their descent from both these nations?"[66] This question led Berkeley to the second possible source of the "native's" "sloth," namely their Catholicism.

Taking aim at the religion of the "native Irish," Berkeley believed that the state should implement plans so "that our Irish natives should be converted, and the whole nation united in the same religion, the same allegiance, and the same interest" (Qu. 289). From this point, we can see a division in Berkeley's thought, as he disengaged the "interests" of the Catholic Irish from their Protestant countrymen, privileging the latter group. At the core of this scheme was the use of the Irish language by Protestant missionaries, to make it easier to "convert the natives" (Qu. 261). Berkeley believed that not only adults, but the children of the natives should be targeted, asking "whether a sum which would go but a little way toward erecting hospitals for maintaining and educating the children of the native Irish might not go far in binding them out apprentices to Protestant masters?" (Qu. 259). Despite having a personal reputation for great generosity in Cloyne, among both Protestants and Catholics, Berkeley's sectarian (and racial) opinions emerged to differentiate between varying degrees of "Irishness," with religion being the final determining criteria. While he ultimately hoped for improvements in the general welfare of all inhabitants of Ireland, he did not view them as all existing on the same plane. As he came to view the economic plight of Ireland in increasingly stark terms, Berkeley sought to encourage different strategies of improvement toward particular groups (especially the "native Irish" and absentee gentry). Still, a key component of Berkeley's writings during this time stressed the need for the improvement of his homeland as a whole, a goal in line with Leerssen's idea of Irish "patriotism."

With regard to Ireland, it appears clear that there was a shift in Berkeley's use of the term "Irish" and his sense of personal affinity toward this identification, over the course of his lifetime. While a young student, Berkeley unreflectively identified himself as "Irish," particularly in contrast to the tenets of English philosophy, but also in the sense that he wrote with great passion of his Irishness. As the Bishop of Cloyne, Berkeley displayed a more nuanced use of the term—continuing to embrace "Irishness" against the economic powers of England, but further distinguishing between the "inhabitants of Ireland" and the "native Irish." This movement reflects a larger transition in Berkeley's thought: away from abstract theorizing and toward more concrete, practical engagement with the social problems facing Ireland during this time. In the end, Berkeley sought to improve the situation of all Irish people, but in the process his self-identification shifted along with his evolving understanding of contemporary political realities. As a result, the "Irish" he spoke of as a youth became, in his maturity, the "Irish" led by the Church of Ireland and those who feared the influence of England over Ireland.

Berkeley hoped to both raise the standard of living at the bottom of Irish society and lower it among the gentry, resulting in a more moderate society with a much more equitable distribution of wealth. He imagined "a society or nation of human creatures, clad in woollen cloths and stuffs, eating good bread, beef and mutton, poultry and fish, in great plenty, drinking ale, mead, and cider, inhabiting decent houses built of brick and marble, taking their pleasure in fair parks and gardens, depending on no foreign imports either for food or raiment," and then asked his reader "whether Ireland be not as well qualified for such a state as any nation under the sun?" (Qu. 123 and 124). The answer, according to Berkeley, was a resounding "yes" and marked the goal of his hopes for the Irish economy and people.

NOTES

1. For instance, see R. F. Foster, *Modern Ireland, 1600–1972* (London: Penguin, 1988), 170. For a critique of this view, see Richard Kearney, "George Berkeley: We Irish think otherwise," in *Postnationalist Ireland: Politics, Culture, Philosophy* (London: Routledge, 1997), 145–56.

2. For a critique of this tradition of interpretation, see David Fate Norton, "The Myth of 'British Empiricism,' " *History of European Ideas* 1 (1981): 331–44.

3. George Berkeley, entries 392–94 and 398, *Philosophical Commentaries* (1706–9), in George Berkeley, *The Works of George Berkeley, Bishop of Cloyne*, 9 vols., edited by A. A. Luce and T. E. Jessop (Edinburgh: Thomas Nelson, 1948–57), 1:47. Hereafter I shall be citing from this edition of Berkeley's *Works* in my notes.

4. W. B. Yeats, "Introduction" to J. M. Hone and H. M. Rossi's *Bishop Berkeley* (London: Faber & Faber, 1931), reprinted in W. B. Yeats, *Essays and Introductions* (London: Macmillian, 1969), 396–97.

5. David Hayton, "Anglo-Irish Attitudes: Changing Perceptions of National Identity Among the Protestant Ascendancy in Ireland, ca. 1690–1750," *Studies in Eighteenth Century Culture* 17 (1987): 147.

6. King to Southwell, March 13, 1708, and King to St. George Ashe, April 20, 1708, quoted in S. J. Connolly, "Swift and Protestant Ireland: Images and Reality," in *Locating Swift: Essays from Dublin on the 250th Anniversary of the Death of Jonathan Swift, 1667–1745*, edited by Aileen Douglas, Patrick Kelly, and Ian Campbell Ross (Dublin: Four Courts Press, 1998), 41.

7. Cited by Hayton, "Anglo-Irish Attitudes," 149. For more information concerning Swift's attitude toward the relations between Ireland and England, especially the influence of Molyneux's *Case* upon his *Story of the Injured Lady*, see Joseph McMinn, "A Weary Patriot: Swift and the Formation of an Anglo-Irish Identity," *Eighteenth Century Ireland* 2 (1987): 103–13.

8. For the relevance of this problem for the study of Berkeley, see Kearney, *Postnationalist Ireland*, 145–56.

9. Beckett argues that the "Anglo-Irish [were] the Protestant community that dominated Ireland in the eighteenth century and those who inherited and maintained its tradition in the changed and changing circumstances of a later age." More recently, D. George Boyce has

suggested that the Anglo-Irish were defined by place and faith: "one had not only to be born in Ireland, but also to be born an Anglican." Terence De Vere White also uses the term "Anglo-Irish," but uses it in both an economic and religious context. J. C. Beckett, *The Anglo-Irish Tradition* (London: Faber, 1976), 11. D. George Boyce, *Nationalism in Ireland* (London: Croom Helm, 1982), 106. Terence De Vere White, *The Anglo-Irish* (London: Victor Gollancz, 1972).

10. A. P. W. Malcomson, *John Foster: The Politics of the Anglo-Irish Ascendancy* (Oxford: Oxford University Press, 1978), xvii–xix.

11. S. J. Connolly, *Religion, Law, and Power: The Making of Protestant Ireland, 1660–1760* (Oxford: Oxford University Press, 1992), 104.

12. W. J. McCormack, "Eighteenth-Century Ascendancy: Yeats and the Historians," *Eighteenth Century Ireland* 4 (1989): 160–61.

13. Ibid., 162.

14. Ibid., 164.

15. James Kelly, "Eighteenth-Century Ascendancy: A Commentary," *Eighteenth Century Ireland* 5 (1990): 173–74. Also, see Jacqueline Hill, "The meaning and significance of 'Protestant ascendancy,' 1787–1840," in Lord Blake, *Ireland after the Union* (Oxford: Oxford University Press, 1989).

16. Kelly, "Eighteenth-Century Ascendancy," 174–75.

17. Kelly notes that the formulation "Protestant interest" did not include Presbyterians. Also, he highlights the fact that the "use of the comparatively neutral word 'interest' masked the determination of Irish Protestants to maintain and, where possible, to strengthen their economic, social and political dominance in Ireland." Ibid., 175–76.

18. Ibid., 179.

19. Joep Theodoor Leerssen, "Anglo-Irish Patriotism and its European Context: Notes towards a Reassessment," *Eighteenth-Century Ireland* 3 (1988): 7–24. This idea is more fully explained in Leerssen's *Mere Irish and Fíor-Ghael: Studies in the Idea of Irish Nationality, its Development and Literary Expression prior to the Nineteenth Century* (Notre Dame: University of Notre Dame Press, 1986).

20. Leerssen, "Anglo-Irish Patriotism," 8.

21. Leerssen associates the concept of "patriotism" with "middle-class, enlightened, complacent in its economic security, joining the notion of individual liberty with that of social consensus and government accountability, aiming to ensure stability and to prevent or alleviate disaffection by reconciling the interests of the state and of the body of its citizens." Ibid., 15.

22. Ibid., 21.

23. See S. J. Connolly, "The Glorious Revolution in Irish Protestant political thinking," in S. J. Connolly, ed., *Political Ideas in Eighteenth-Century Ireland* (Dublin: Four Courts Press, 2000); Robert Eccleshall, "Anglican Political Thought in the Century after the Revolution of 1688," in D. George Boyce, Robert Eccleshall, and Vincent Geoghegan, eds., *Political Thought in Ireland since the Seventeenth Century* (London: Routledge, 1993); and J. I. McGuire, "The Church of Ireland and the 'Glorious Revolution' of 1688," in Art Cosgrove and Donal McCartney, eds., *Studies in Irish History, Presented to R. Dudley Edwards* (Dublin: University College, 1979).

24. Leerssen, "Anglo-Irish Patriotism," 22.

25. Ibid., 10.

26. George Berkeley, *An Essay towards a New Theory of Vision* (1709), in *Works*, 1:162.

27. George Berkeley, *Maxims Concerning Patriotism* (1750), in *Works*, 6:254.

28. George Berkeley, *Philosophical Commentaries*, entries 392–94, in *Works*, 1:47.

29. See David Berman, "Enlightenment and Counter-Enlightenment in Irish Philosophy," and "The Culmination and Causation of Irish Philosophy," *Archiv für Geschichte der Philosophie* 64 (1982): 148–65 and 257–79 [respectively]; and "The Irish Counter-Enlightenment," in Richard Kearney, ed., *The Irish Mind: Exploring Intellectual Traditions* (Dublin: Wolfhound Press, 1984). Also, see Thomas Duddy, *A History of Irish Thought* (London: Routledge, 2002), 124–43 and Terry Eagleton, *Crazy John and the Bishop, and other Essays on Irish Culture* (Notre Dame: University of Notre Dame Press, 1998), 17 ff.

30. Although his *Case of Ireland Stated* (1698) may have forged his reputation in Ireland, Molyneux's contributions to theories of perception were also very important, best summarized by the thought problem named for him. In philosophical terms, Ernst Cassirer has suggested that "*The New Theory of Vision*, which forms the prelude to Berkeley's philosophy, and contains all his ideas implicitly, is nothing but an attempt at a complete systematic development and elucidation of Molyneux's problem." Ernst Cassirer, *Philosophy of the Enlightenment* (Princeton: Princeton University Press, 1950), 109. For a reading of Molyneux's *Case of Ireland* informed by considerations of "Irish" identity, see Thomas McLoughlin, *Contesting Ireland: Irish Voices against England in the Eighteenth Century* (Dublin: Four Courts Press, 1999), 41–64.

31. David Berman, "The Irish Freethinker," in *John Toland's Christianity not Mysterious: Text, Associated Works, and Critical Essays*, edited by Philip McGuinness, Alan Harrison, and Richard Kearny (Dublin: Lilliput Press, 1997), 224.

32. Berkeley's relations with these figures, many of whom were his direct superiors while at Trinity, were contentious at best, with disputes ranging from the philosophical (the meaning of the term "infinity") to the more personal (the "irregularities" associated with Berkeley's ordination that led King to order him to be prosecuted in his court). See David Berman, *George Berkeley: Idealism and the Man* (Oxford: Clarendon Press, 1994), 17–18. Also, see Jackson Hershbell, "Berkeley and the Problem of Evil," *Journal of the History of Ideas* 31 (1970): 543.

33. Berman, "Enlightenment and Counter-Enlightenment," 150.

34. Ibid., 163. Also, see Berman, "Culmination and Causation," 257.

35. Harry Bracken, "George Berkeley: The Irish Cartesian," in Kearney, *The Irish Mind*, 107.

36. Berkeley to Percival, June 3, 1711, in *Works*, 8:47.

37. Connolly, *Religion, Law, and Power*, 107.

38. Berkeley to Percival, April 16, 1713 and May 7, 1713, in *Works*, 8:65–66. On English policy toward Irish cattle, see Connolly, *Religion, Law, and Power*, 52.

39. Berkeley to Percival, August 7, 1713, in *Works*, 8:70.

40. Percival to Berkeley, May 14, 1713, in B. Rand, *Berkeley and Percival* (Cambridge: Cambridge University Press, 1914), 117.

41. For information on this trip, see Edwin Gaustad, *George Berkeley in America* (New Haven: Yale University Press, 1979).

42. Notable exceptions are the works of Patrick Kelly and George C. Caffentzis. See Patrick Kelly, "Ireland and the Critique of Mercantilism in Berkeley's *Querist*," in *George Berkeley: Essays and Replies,* ed. David Berman (Dublin, Irish Academic Press, 1985), and George C. Caffentzis, *Exciting the Industry of Mankind: George Berkeley's Philosophy of Money* (Boston: Kluwer Academic Publishers, 2000).

43. Foster, *Modern Ireland*, 197.

44. The Woolen Act prevented the "exportation from Ireland of all goods made or mixed with wool except to England." Note that the action against the export of woolens to England was not so much desired by the English government, as Bristol merchants and various interests in the woolen interest in southwest England had been pressing for this action since 1695. L. M. Cullen, *An Economic History of Ireland since 1660* (London: B. T. Batsford, 1972), 34 ff.

45. James Kelly, "Jonathan Swift and the Irish Economy in the 1720s," *Eighteenth Century Ireland* 6 (1991): 8–9.

46. The roots of the former existed as early as 1719, when the merchant bank of La Touche and Kane began operations and soon offered banker's notes for its customers. See L. M. Cullen, "Landlords, Bankers, and Merchants: The Early Irish Banking World, 1700–1820," in A. E. Murphy, ed., *Economists and the Irish Economy from the Eighteenth Century to the Present Day* (Dublin: Irish Academic Press, 1984), 26–30. Also, see C. George Caffentzis, "Why Did Berkeley's Bank Fail? Money and Libertinism in Eighteenth-Century Ireland," *Eighteenth Century Ireland* 12 (1997): 100–115.

47. Joseph Johnson, *Bishop Berkeley's "Querist" in Historical Perspective* (Dundalk: Dundalgan Press, 1970), 45 ff. Caffentzis, "Berkeley's Bank," 102–5.

48. One of the leaders of the opposition to the bank, Hercules Rowley, suggested that "if the intended Bank prove advantageous to us by increasing our trade and encouraging our manufactures—and should in the least interfere with or hinder the trade of England, then we may expect they will procure a Repeal of Charter, and so cramp our trade and discourage our manufactures as to render them impracticable. If it happens to impoverish us, and drain our little substance into Great Britain, then indeed we may be sure of a continuation." Hercules Rowley, *An Answer to a Book entitled "Reasons offered for erecting a bank in Ireland*" (Dublin, 1721), 5. Cited in Johnston, *Berkeley's Querist*, 47, and Caffentzis, "Berkeley's Bank," 103.

49. David Dickson, *New Foundations: Ireland 1660–1800* (Dublin: Irish Academic Press, 2000), 72. Also see Caffentzis, *Exciting the Industry of Mankind*, 66 ff and Kelly, "Critique of Mercantilism," 107.

50. It should be noted that Berkeley had known both Prior and Madden since their time at Trinity where they were close friends. A. A. Luce, *Life of Berkeley: Bishop of Cloyne* (New York: Thomas Nelson and Sons, 1949), 30–33. Also, see Salim Rashid, "The Irish School of Economic Development: 1720–1750," *Manchester School of Economic and Social Studies* 56 (1988): 345–69; James Livesey, "The Dublin Society in Eighteenth-Century Irish Political Thought," *The Historical Journal* 47 (2004): 615–40; and K. Theodore Hoppen, *The Common Scientist in the Seventeenth Century: A Study of the Dublin Philosophical Society, 1683 – 1708* (Charlottesville: University of Virginia Press, 1970).

51. Thomas Prior, *A List of the Absentees of Ireland, and the Yearly Value of their Estates and Incomes Spent Abroad. With Observations on the Present State and Condition of that Kingdom* (Dublin: R. Gunne, 1729), preface. Note Prior's use of the term "abroad" to indicate landowners residing in England.

52. Ibid., 26, 27, 31.

53. Arthur Dobbs, *An Essay on the Trade and Improvement of Ireland* (Dublin: J. Smith, 1729), 52.

54. Anon., *The Present State of Ireland Consider'd* (London, 1730), 19, 21.

55. Ibid., 22.

56. Berkeley, Queries 88, 89, and 490 of *The Querist*, in *Works*, 6:112 and 145. Subsequent quotations from this work are cited parenthetically in the text (Qu.).

57. Berkeley, Query 446. This sentiment is echoed in Berkeley's *Word to the Wise* (1749), in *Works*, 6:235–36.

58. Berkeley, Query 418, *Querist*, in *Works*, 6:139. Also, note query 138, "Whether there be any other nation possessed of so much good land, and so many able hands to work it, which yet is beholden for bread to foreign countries;" and query 143, "Whether a foreigner could imagine that one half of the people were starving, in a country which sent out such plenty of provisions?"

59. For a brief analysis of this piece, see Patrick Kelly, "'Industry and Virtue versus Luxury and Corruption': Berkeley, Walpole, and the South Sea Bubble Crisis," *Eighteenth Century Ireland* 7 (1992): 57–74.

60. Hutchison, "Berkeley's *Querist*," 56–57. Also, see Douglas Vickers, *Studies in the Theory of Money, 1690–1776* (London: Peter Owen, 1960), 148.

61. Berkeley, Query 19. Compare this with his later contention that "our poor Irish are wedded to dirt upon principle." Berkeley, *Word to the Wise*, in *Works*, 6:242.

62. For instance, Dudley North argued that "the main spur to trade or rather to industry and ingenuity is the exorbitant appetites of men which they will take pains to gratify, and so be disposed to work, when nothing else will incline them to it; for did men content themselves with bare necessities, we should have a poor world." Dudley North, *Discourses on Trade* (London, 1691), 27. For an overview of this literature, see Andrea Finkelstein, *Harmony and the Balance: An Intellectual History of Seventeenth-Century English Economic Thought* (Ann Arbor: University of Michigan Press, 2000).

63. For instance, Barbon argued that fashion "is the great Promoter of Trade, because it occasions the Expence of Cloaths before the Old ones are worn out: It is the Spirit and Life of *Trade*; It makes a Circulation, and gives a Value by Turns, to all sorts of Commodities; it keeps the great Body of *Trade* in Motion." Still, it should be noted that while Berkeley may have been willing to accept this aspect of Barbon's argument, he objected to the valorization of luxury that formed the core of his analysis. See Nicholas Barbon, *A Discourse of Trade* (London: Tho. Milbourn, 1690), 34.

64. "Whether national wants ought not to be the rule of trade? And whether the most pressing wants of the majority ought not to be first considered?" Berkeley, Query 168, *Querist*, in *Works*, 6:119.

65. Berkeley, Query 103. Also, see Berkeley, *Essay toward Preventing the Ruin of Great Britain* (1721), in *Works*, 6:76.

66. Berkeley, Query 512. Note that this concern about the racial heritage of the "native Irish" was repeated in Berkeley's earlier religious text, *The Alciphron* and later appeared in his *Word to the Wise*. See Berkeley, *The Alciphron* (1732), in *Works*, 3:262, and *A Word to the Wise*, in *Works*, 6:236.

The Injured Lady, the Deluded Man, and the Infamous Creature: Swift and the 1707 Act of Union

Evan R. Davis

JONATHAN SWIFT'S *STORY OF THE INJURED LADY*, AN ALLEGORY OF IRELAND, Scotland, and England on the eve of Anglo-Scottish Union, has been read almost exclusively as the first of Swift's Irish tracts, a foreshadowing of his emergence two decades later as the Drapier Dean. Carole Fabricant argues that the tract "suggests the extent to which Ireland's oppression at the hands of England was a deeply rooted and abiding preoccupation of Swift's throughout his lifetime," Claude Rawson calls it "Swift's first essay on Irish affairs," and Rick Canning, in the most trenchant recent account of *The Injured Lady*, labels it Swift's "earliest treatment of Irish grievances."[1] To be sure, the tract does function this way, denouncing a history of English colonial rule in Ireland and targeting the abuses of absentee landlords, the Woolen Act of 1699, unwarranted treatment by the lord lieutenant, and "an hundred other Hardships."[2] But there is a procrustean quality to this narrative about Swift's emergence as an Anglo-Irish writer, for while it accommodates Swift's critique of English oppression, it has precluded a full consideration of his relationship to Scotland by bracketing the 1707 Act of Union as a mere "occasion" for the text.[3] The full title of the tract—*The Story of the Injured Lady. Being a true Picture of Scotch Perfidy, Irish Poverty, and English Partiality*—suggests that in 1707 Swift was thinking not in binaries but in triplets, and that Scotland figured centrally in his analysis of Anglo-Irish relations. In terms of the allegory, the Lady (Ireland) is injured not only by her oppressive Lover (England), but also by "the infamous Creature" (Scotland), who has duped her lover into a promise of marriage. Besides downplaying the role of Scotland, critics committed to a narrative of Swift as an Irish patriot have tended to set aside his other work on Anglo-Scottish Union, his "Verses said to be Written on Union," in which Swift awkwardly negotiates between English and Anglo-Irish identity. Both the avoidance of Scotland in *The Injured Lady* and the neglect of "Verses on Union" spring from the mistaken assumption that Scotland, while a marginal interest for Swift, did not fundamentally affect his understanding and presentation of his own national identity. To understand the emergence of Swift's Anglo-Irish identity, we need to understand his long-standing objections to Scotland and the Scots.

Those objections have been brought to light by Christopher Fox, whose essay "Swift's Scotophobia" describes the origins and repercussions of Swift's enduring antipathy toward the Scots. In 1695, Swift took his first parish in the prebend of Kilroot, on Ireland's northeastern coast; not only were Anglicans in the minority there, but because it was a year of famine in Scotland, Swift witnessed wave after wave of Scottish Presbyterians emigrating from southwestern Scotland. As Fox argues, "Swift's lifelong dispute with the Scots was first and foremost a *political* one, and a high stakes game at that."[4] Concerned that Ulster Scots would attempt to abolish episcopacy in Ireland as it had been abolished in Scotland, Swift expressed his anxieties in a range of texts, from his satiric characterization of Jack in *A Tale of a Tub* to his vituperative marginalia about Scots in his copies of Whig histories of England to his late *Memoirs of Captain Creichten*, a pro-Episcopalian retelling of the anti-Presbyterian battles in Scotland. Fox raises the question of "whether we can properly understand Swift's views of Ireland, or of England, without taking Scotland into account."[5] I will argue that we cannot, for Swift's own Anglo-Irish identity, just beginning to be articulated in *The Injured Lady*, is constructed only with Scotland as a critical third term.

As the subtitle of Linda Colley's book *Britons: Forging the Nation 1707–1837* suggests, the 1707 Act of Union provided the legal foundation for a conception of Britishness that would develop over the next century. But while Swift's writings of 1707 bear out the importance of union, they also, by displaying its effects on Ireland, prompt us to recognize that, as Jim Smyth has argued, "the superimposition (or forging) of a British identity was a project (or process) flawed at its inception."[6] Writing in the wake of J. G. A. Pocock's seminal 1975 essay, "British History: A Plea for a New Subject," historians including Smyth have increasingly argued that Britishness cannot be adequately understood as a function of England's occasional interaction with its "Celtic fringe" but rather should be viewed within the interrelations of England, Ireland, and Scotland. Though New British History has been much more transformative in historical than literary circles, its emphasis on the ways in which the three kingdoms "interacted so as to modify the conditions of one another's existence"—can illuminate the anxieties about national identity manifested in Swift's 1707 works.[7]

Swift's animosity toward Scotland did not, of course, preclude his close friendship with individual Scots, most notably John Arbuthnot, whose own response to Union sets Swift's in relief. Like Swift, Arbuthnot responded to the turmoil in Scotland and Ireland that accompanied the Ascension of William and Mary by moving to England, where he subsequently advanced in powerful English circles, being named to the Royal Society in 1704 and appointed Physician Extraordinary to the Queen in 1705. While Swift was in Dublin writing his bitter denunciation of Union, Arbuthnot was heartily embracing it from London and celebrating a vision of pastoral England as an antidote to Scotland's economic woes. In Arbuthnot's *Sermon Preached to the People at the Mercat Cross of Edinburgh, on the Subject of Union*, issues of trade and sovereignty are draped in the vestments of a sermon; in Swift's *Injured Lady*, religious concerns emerge within an allegory of a soured romance. Yet despite their contrary purposes and methods, the incipient union forces both writers to foreground their own national identities.

Of the two Anglican writers, it might be expected that the religious consequences of Union would echo more lastingly with Arbuthnot. As part of the ecclesiastical settlement of 1689–90, prelacy in Scotland had been abolished and the Presbyterian Church restored. As one contemporary Scottish Episcopalian described the events of 1690, "The Church of Scotland is at this time under the Claw of an inraged Lion; Episcopacy abolish'd, and its Revenues alienated; the Clergy routed, some by a form of Sentence, and others by violence and popular Fury; their Persons and Families abused, their Houses ransak'd, their Gowns torn to pieces, with many other Injuries and Indignities done them."[8] By late summer and early fall of 1690, all Scottish ministers were required to swear allegiance to the Presbyterian Kirk; among those who refused to conform and subsequently lost his living was John Arbuthnot's father, the Reverend Alexander Arbuthnot. Of his three sons, two later supported the Jacobites; the third, John, left Scotland for London.

Yet despite being titled a sermon, Arbuthnot's contribution to the debate avoids almost entirely the effects of union on the established church of Scotland. Indeed, Arbuthnot's is not an authentic sermon at all, nor was it preached in Edinburgh, though it was first published there in 1706. Given the actions of some Edinburgh mobs, even if Arbuthnot had been in Scotland, preaching a pro-union sermon would scarcely have been prudent.[9] Sermons opposing union, however, were ubiquitous, and Arbuthnot's nominal appeal to scripture may have caught the attention of readers who had been inundated by the ecclesiastic debate. But from the outset, he makes clear his intent to frame the issue as an economic one. "I have chosen," he writes in his opening paragraph, "an Apocryphal text [from the book of Ecclesiasticus], because my subject is not sacred, but secular."[10] Arbuthnot selects a text that can be easily assimilated into an economic discourse—"Better is he that laboureth, and aboundeth in all things, than he that boasteth himself, and wanteth bread"—and proceeds to advocate union on the basis of economic, not ecclesiastical, grounds (397).[11] Despite its abundant natural resources, Arbuthnot argues, Scotland is scarred by poverty, famine, and political mismanagement; an incorporated union—the only mechanism that will open trade and enable Scotland to prosper—has been hampered by unwarranted worries about increased emigration to London, by groundless fears about taxes, and, most of all, by a misplaced national pride. While praising Queen Anne as coming from "the ancient line of our own Monarchs" and claiming that "None can have a greater value for the noble achievements and honour of our ancestors than I have," he resists the tendency to let pride in a Scottish past slide into a misguided boastfulness about present Scottish independence and sovereignty, which he describes as "precarious, imaginary, and fantastical" (403). Only at the conclusion of the pamphlet, in the weakest part of his text, does Arbuthnot grudgingly address himself to Presbyterians worried about the loss of power in a British Parliament: "To such as are afraid of the Church and religion, I shall only say, that the religion of the Church of England is imposed upon no man within the dominions of England. As for the squeamishness of sitting in Parliament with prelates, and the fear of being disarmed of all other weapons, but what are allowed by the Gospel; these are such unchristian dissuasives from an union, that to mention them only is to refute them" (407). Though some Scottish Episcopalians opposed union, Arbuthnot was one of many who hoped that despite the treaty's explicit recognition of the Scottish Kirk, Episcopalians would nonetheless receive increased tolerance from a united parliament.[12] As well, his advocacy may have been a response to the desires, if not the demands, of his current employer, Queen Anne, who in her coronation speech had publicly declared her intention to pursue union.

Arbuthnot's *Sermon Preached at the Mercat Cross* minimizes the divisive ecclesiastical dilemmas posed by the Act of Union, but its sermon form is central to its rhetorical effect. By addressing his audience as a preacher speaking to his congregation, Arbuthnot is able to manipulate the distance between himself and his Scottish readers. From the sermon's opening address— "Dearly Beloved Countrymen and Fellow Citizens"—

Arbuthnot identifies himself as a Scot speaking to Scots, an effect compounded by the frequent use of the pronouns *we* and *our* to refer to Scots and *they* and *their* to refer to English. But at the same time, in the role of a preacher, he can also berate the Scots in the second person, criticizing his readers' "matchless ignorance and stupidity" and admonishing them that "You are used only as tools and machines" (402, 406). These changing pronouns, as we will see, superficially resemble the changing pronouns in Swift's writing, where, uneasy about aligning himself too closely with either side of the Anglo-Irish split, Swift at times seems uncertain about just which community he is imagining with his *we*.[13] But for Arbuthnot, the modulating pronouns do not reflect an uncertainty about his own national identity; his *we* is consistently Scottish, while his *you* indicates not a new identity but rather a new perspective, that of a writer who combines the sympathy of a native Scot with the ostensibly disinterested judgments of an outsider.[14]

It is as an outsider that Arbuthnot is able to critique what one historian has described as "the false consciousness of an impoverished backwater promoted by her vested interests, nobles and clerics whose pathetic ambition was to continue 'to insult over slaves and beggars.' "[15] To do so, he dissevers political and economic independence from Scottish identity, thus undermining the argument of anti-Union Scots such as Lord Belhaven who argued that the loss of the former would entail the loss of the latter.[16] Arbuthnot does not deny that union will alter the sovereignty of both Scotland and England: "I would ask any reasonable man, do we lose our sovereignty in any other sense than England does? Is there not a new title, new seal, new arms, and the same changes for them as for us? for I take an incorporating union to be, as if two pieces of metal were melted down into one mass; neither can be said to retain its former form or substance, as it did before the mixture" (402).[17] Yet even as its sovereignty is altered, Scottish identity remains distinct: "The country, the people, are not annihilated; nor does an union cause all the worthy deeds, that have been done at any time by the Scottish nation, to be forgotten" (403). But such an assertion of national identity depends on an embrace of the national past that for Swift will prove untenable.

It serves Arbuthnot's purposes to vary his address to Scottish readers, sometimes stressing his common national identity, sometimes confronting them from the distance of the second person, all the while maintaining a third-person distance from the England he praises and inhabits. But because of his complicated relationship with both England and Ireland, Swift rarely enjoyed the stability that pervades Arbuthnot's work, whether he was trying to present himself as an Englishman or, later in his life, as the defender of Irish liberty. This volatility accounts for much of the dynamic quality of Swift's Irish tracts, a fact that becomes clear when we read his satire not simply as "an attack upon discernable, historically authentic particulars . . . plainly existent in the world of reality," but rather as "a rhetorical means to the production of difference in the face of a potentially compromising similarity."[18] Swift's works on the Act of Union evince not only an attack on the malfeasance of England and Scotland but also an attempt to distinguish himself from facets of both England and Scotland that have become dangerously familiar to him. Complicating matters further, the attraction and repulsion, sympathy and attack in these works operate within a triangle of England, Ireland, and Scotland. As the relationships between and among the kingdoms shifted in the first decade of the eighteenth century, so too did Swift's perception of his own national identity. Even while attempting to distance himself from England and Scotland, he reveals his affinity with both. It is the moments when he most insistently attacks Scotland that he most sympathizes with England, and when he most directly attacks England that he identifies with Scotland.

This tendency of Scotland to unsettle Swift's relationship to both England and Ireland is evident in his "Verses said to be written on Union," written in 1707 but unpublished in his lifetime. In it, Swift characterizes Anglo-Scottish Union as beset by unstable doubleness, culminating in an extended metaphor of an ill-fated twin-hulled vessel that subverts the smooth-sailing ship of state. Because it is not particularly well known, I include the full poem here:

> The Queen has lately lost a Part
> Of her entirely-*English* Heart,
> For want of which by way of Botch,
> She piec'd it up again with *Scotch*.
> Blessed Revolution, which creates
> Divided Hearts, united States.
> See how the double Nation lies;
> Like a rich Coat with Skirts of Frieze:
> As if a Man in making Posies
> Should bundle Thistles up with Roses.
> Whoever yet a Union saw
> Of Kingdoms, without Faith or Law.
> Henceforward let no Statesman dare
> A kingdom to a Ship compare;
> Lest he should call our Commonweal
> A Vessel with a double Keel:
> Which just like ours, new rigg'd and man'd,

And got about a League from Land,
By Change of Wind to Leeward Side,
The Pilot knew not how to guide.
So tossing Faction will o'erwhelm
Our crazy double-bottom'd Realm.[19]

In the year before the poem was written, Daniel Defoe had praised the Act of Union in terms of the wholeness it would bring to the island: "The Island will be One, the Government One, the Treasure One, the Military Power One; their general Commerce undivided and In Common."[20] Swift, by contrast, condemns union precisely for its unstable and ill-formed doubleness. The "clumsy patch" of Union both exposes the crown's loss of the episcopacy in Scotland and also ironizes Anne's claim in her coronation speech that her heart was "entirely English."[21] Insofar as the binary images refer to Scotland and England, they establish the speaker as an Englishman critical of union, one who wants his nation to be single rather than double. Ireland, it would seem, has been excluded from the poem altogether by the metaphors, which can accommodate two, but not three, kingdoms. Taken together, the speaker's identification with England and the poem's exclusion of Ireland leads Irvin Ehrenpreis to argue that the poem "represent[s] not an Irish but an English protest against the event" and to judge Swift in particularly harsh psychological terms: "A pathetic side to the poem," he claims, "is the author's identification of himself with 'our commonweal' of England. Just as victims of long persecution tend to adopt the standards of their persecutors, so Swift, whose failure to win the posts he desired was partly due to his Irish birth and education, clung to the picture of himself as entirely English."[22]

But the question of the speaker's national identification is more complex than Ehrenpreis allows. Whatever the speaker's position vis-à-vis the new union, it is deferred for over half the poem: no pronoun at all appears in the first fourteen lines. Only in line fifteen— "Lest he should call our commonweal"—does it become clear that the speaker is part of the now-doubled nation, an Englishman lamenting union with Scotland. But no sooner has that identity been established than Swift destabilizes it in the possessive pronoun "ours" of the line "which just like ours, new rigg'd and man'd."[23] Without explanation, the referent of *ours* has shifted, the speaker now claiming an affinity with "Ireland and the new order which followed the victory of William III."[24] The Kingdom of Great Britain, that is, resembles the precarious position of Anglo-Ireland. In the terms of the metaphor, the double-keeled vessel of Anglo-Scottish Union resembles a specific Anglo-Irish vessel, one designed in Dublin by Sir William Petty.

Well-known as Cromwell's chief demographer, Petty had experimented with twin-hulled vessels from the 1660s through the 1680s, their successes being overshadowed by their well-publicized failures. In 1665, he raced his sixty-foot *Experiment* against three comparably weighted ships from Dublin to Holyhead. As the Royal Society reported, "Sir William's men, for want of dexterity to shift their sails, stopped twice in the wind, and ran back near a quarter of a mile, in one of which errors, one of her rudders was broken, she also grated twice on the shoal ground, and by reason of the sudden flaws of wind, the sheet of the mainsail did sometimes break loose; and the men wore yet confounded (in this new way) in the names of the ropes."[25] When Swift was seventeen, Petty suffered a final setback with the sinking of *St. Michael the Archangel*, a failure that put an end to catamaran design in England for two centuries. It was not only the novelty of the design that must have caught Swift's eye, but the language associated with it as well. Petty described his vessel as a "fantastical double-bottomed machine," an apt description for Swift of the Anglo-Scottish Union that he saw similarly destined to flounder. When the poem shifts, therefore, from "our commonweal" to "just like ours," the speaker's imagined community is shifting as well. In the final couplet, Swift attempts a further shift back to an English, now British, speaker, as he predicts the outcome of union in "our crazy double-bottom'd Realm." Within this poem, Swift's problem is not, as Ehrenpreis would have it, that Swift excludes Ireland and speaks in the assumed voice of the "entirely-English," but rather that he cannot speak with a single voice that is either consistently English *or* Anglo-Irish. The Act of Union, in other words, prompts Swift first to avoid any claim of national allegiance at all and then to veer back and forth in uncertain waters.[26]

Written shortly before "Verses on Union," after the Act of Union had been passed but before it had been implemented, *The Injured Lady* likewise underscores the way that Swift's sense of national identity is transformed by Anglo-Scottish Union. The tract is a mock epistle from a Lady (Ireland), seeking advice from a Gentleman about her mistreatment at the hands of her Lover (England), and also about her quarrels with her Rival (Scotland), who has tricked the Lover into a promise of marriage. Both Scotland and the Scottish Kirk figure prominently, yet both tend to be overlooked or downplayed by literary critics. Rick Canning, for instance, frames the allegory as a triangle of the Lady Ireland and two men, her inconstant Lover, England, and her loyal Friend, who he reads as a stand-in for the Ascendancy. "The question," Canning writes, "is therefore not 'Should any man guide the frail damsel Ireland [but rather] *Which* man should guide her?' "[27] This Lady/Lover/Gentleman triangle (rather than the

Lady/Lover/Rival triangle) reflects Canning's reading of the political situation that Swift faced: "The Ascendancy faced two major challenges to its control of Irish affairs. The first challenge was English power . . . The second challenge came from the other direction, from Ireland's Catholic majority."[28] But for Swift, there was clearly a third challenge: the Scottish Presbyterians who emigrated in large numbers toward the end of the seventeenth century and whose domination of the Ulster province worried Swift even more than the Catholic majority.[29] If, to an Anglican in Ireland, the Catholics were "a Lion . . . bound fast with three or four chains, his Teeth drawn out, and his Claws pared to the Quick," the Scots were "an angry Cat in full Liberty at his Throat."[30] Swift always supported the Penal Laws, but he was equally insistent on the Test Act, which he viewed as a bulwark against Scottish Presbyterians.

> They bring with them from *Scotland*, a most formidable Notion of our Church, which they look upon, at least, as three Degrees worse than Popery; and it is natural it should be so, since they come over full fraught with that Spirit which taught them to abolish Episcopacy at home. . . . I do not see how it can be otherwise, considering their Industry and our Supineness, but that they may, in a very few Years, grow to a Majority in the House of Commons, and consequently make themselves the National Religion, and have a fair Pretense to demand the Revenues of the Church for their Teachers.[31]

Swift's fear that episcopacy could be challenged in Ireland as it had been in Scotland was complicated by his recognition that the continued survival of the Church of Ireland depended upon English troops being stationed there. The Irish Parliament could not risk the aggressive actions of its Scottish counterpart, whose passage of the 1703 Act of Security threatened the Hanoverian succession that had already been approved in Westminster.[32] As well, Swift was clearly frustrated that England had united with Scotland rather than with Ireland. It is one of the underappreciated twists of Swift's life that the writer who would later style himself the defender of Irish liberty was, like most of his Ascendancy peers, in 1703 an advocate for the union of England and Ireland. But the Irish parliament's petition for union had been summarily rebuffed by England, making the 1707 Anglo-Scottish Union all the more exasperating.[33]

Read in binary terms of England and Ireland, *The Injured Lady* appears to be essentially an anti-English tract. But alongside his extensive criticism of England, Swift levels equally specific charges against Scotland: Scotland has threatened to withdraw from the Hanoverian succession; the Scots are responsible for both the Great Fire and the beheading of Charles I ("for which I think, and so doth all the Country, that she ought to be answerable"); despite the Act of Union, Scots remain loyal to the exiled Pretender; finally, and most significantly for Swift, the Scots, committed to the Solemn League and Covenant, seek to bar Episcopacy not only from Scotland but from England and Ireland as well. Echoing the question in "Verses on Union," "Whoever yet a Union saw / Of Kingdoms, without Faith or Law?" the Lady observes, "She [Scotland] is of a different Religion, being a Presbyterian of the most rank and virulent Kind, and consequently having an inveterate Hatred to the Church; yet, I am sure, I have always been told, that in Marriage there ought to be an Union of Minds as well as of Persons" (4). If Swift had seen the Act of Union as a mere occasion to attack English actions in Ireland, he presumably could have devised an allegory that did not entail such attention to Scotland. Yet notwithstanding the tract's sustained attack on England – characterized as an inconstant, unreasonable, and deceitful lover—it is the rival, Scotland, who is described in the most detail: "she is tall and lean, and very ill-shaped; she hath bad Features, and a worse complexion; she hath a stinking Breath, and twenty ill Smells about her besides, which are yet more insufferable by her natural Sluttishness; for she is always very lousy, and never without the itch" (3).

The triangulated allegory reflects Swift's understanding of the political dynamics of Union, but it also creates a potential problem for the Scotophobic Swift; namely that readers will compare the grievances of the two women. English restrictions on trade, after all, had damaged the Scottish economy as well as the Irish one, and the economic condition of Scotland was worse than in Ireland during the 1690s.[34] It is this possibility that Swift attempts to finesse by underscoring the differences between the injured Lady and her infamous Rival. After he establishes the basic elements of the allegory in the first two paragraphs, but before he enumerates grievances against England, Swift pauses to differentiate between the two women: "Before I enter into the Particulars of this Gentleman's hard Usage of me," the Lady writes, "I will give a very just and impartial Character of my Rival and myself" (3). The comparison, not surprisingly, is hardly "just and impartial." The rival is unpardonably corrupt, both by birth and by experience. She is ugly, smelly, sluttish, and lice-ridden; "As to her other Qualities, she hath no Reputation either for Virtue, Honesty, Truth, or Manners; and it is no Wonder, considering what her Education hath been. Scolding and Cursing are her common Conversation. To sum up all; she is poor and beggarly, and gets a sorry Maintenance by pilfering whereever she comes" (3–4). The Lady then gives her "own Character . . . with Modesty and Truth": "I was reckoned to be as handsome as any in our Neighbourhood, until I became pale and thin with Grief and ill Usage. I am still fair enough, and have, I think, no very ill Feature about me. They that see me now will hardly allow me ever to have had any great Share of Beauty; for besides being so much altered, I go always mobbed and in an Undress, as well out of Neglect, as indeed for want of Cloaths to appear in" (4). The differences seem sharp: natural deformity worsened by vicious education on the one hand, natural beauty tainted by mistreatment on the other. But beneath those differences, even prompting their articulation, are noticeable similarities. Whereas the Rival "hath bad Features," the Lady lacks "any great Share of Beauty"; whereas the rival has a "sorry Maintenance," the Lady "go[es] always mobbed and in an Undress"; whereas the Rival feels "inveterate hatred to the church," the Lady feels "invincible hatred to that Lady" (3–4). This is not to say that Swift equated Ireland and Scotland, but that when contemplating the effects of English policy in the two kingdoms, he recognized enough similarity that he felt obliged to disown it.

Indeed, Swift's Scotophobia leads him not only to distance himself from Scotland but also to commiserate with England, in a gesture that would be inexplicable in a straightforwardly anti-English tract. The threat that Scotland poses to England is established at the outset of the letter, where the Lady observes that her Lover's house is separated from her Rival's only by "an old broken wall" (3). In terms reminiscent of "Verses on Union," the Lady sympathizes with the Lover, whom she imagines as a fool deluded by a knave: "in the Midst of this my Situation, I cannot but have some Pity for this deluded Man, to cast himself away on an infamous Creature, who, whatever she pretendeth, I can prove, would at this very Minute rather be a Whore to a certain Great Man, that shall be nameless, if she might have her Will" (8). Swift's argument is somewhat misleading here—the English ministry pursued union to preempt precisely the Jacobite threat that the passage invokes—but it reflects the effect of Scotland on his expressed attitude toward England.

Characteristic of Swift's analysis of Irish problems, the Lady reveals herself to have been too passive in her response to the Lover. She admits that "being young and foolish, [she] too readily admitted" his advances and that she remained loyal long after she should have resisted him. The Lady's weakness, however, seems to be compensated for by the firm logic of her Friend, who in *The Answer* proposes that she make four clear resolutions, signifying four proposals for Ireland: to insist upon an independent parliament with a single king (thus pursuing Molyneux's claim that Ireland was not a colony but a separate kingdom with the same king and anticipating Swift's own later objections to the term "dependent kingdom"); to resist trade restrictions of the Woolen Act; to force Irish office-holders to live in Ireland; and to deny the English Parliament's assertion of legislative authority in Ireland. In part because these are all proposals that Swift will advocate and refine throughout his career, Canning reads the Friend as an allegorical representation of "a manly resolute Ascendancy," presented as the plausible alternative to English power. "The lady's weakness calls for some form of male authority," he writes, "and since English authority is selfish and cruel, the Ascendancy's alternative authority appears benign, natural, and paternal."[35] Canning recognizes that the proposals rest on a "fantasy of independence": the Ascendancy's continued rule depended on the enforcement of English troops. But he does not hesitate to attribute those proposals unproblematically to Swift. Indeed, for Canning, the importance of the gendered allegory is that it enables Swift to "naturaliz[e] the Ascendancy's power while simultaneously validating its sense of oppression."[36] Swift intends, in other words, that the complaints about England in the Lady's letter be taken seriously, but also that the Ascendancy should appear to be the natural guide of Ireland as it addresses those complaints.

Even if we accept the association between the Friend and the Anglo-Irish ruling elite—the only figure in the allegory not explicitly identified—it is still important to notice how thoroughly the Rival Scotland undercuts the efficacy of the Friend's resolve. In the first half of his curiously divided letter, the Friend dwells overwhelmingly on the Lady's ill-advised relations with her Rival, asserting that it is those relations that have doomed her future with the man: "your invincible Hatred to that Lady," he writes, "hath carried your Resentments so high, as to be the cause of your Ruin." Poorly advised by "the pernicious counsels of some about you," the Lady has developed an "Aversion" toward her Rival, who she ought to have been imitating. The Lady's "unpardonable Weakness," therefore, consists in not recognizing that her actions are triangulated and that she needs to consider three variables, not two. "You know very well," he tells her, "that she began to apprehend he had Designs of using her as he had done you; and common Prudence might have directed you rather to have entered into some Measures with her for joining against him, until he might at least be brought to some reasonable Terms" (10). Having scolded the Lady for her missing the opportunities that her Rival presented and telling her disingenuously that "it is too late to reproach you with any former Oversights, which cannot now be rectified," the Friend turns in the second half of *The Answer* to the proposals outlined above, concluding with an enigmatic, perhaps threatening promise: "If the Gentleman refuses these just and reasonable Offers, pray let me know it, and perhaps I may think of something else that will be more effectual" (12). The apparent straightforwardness of the proposals, however, is compromised in several ways. Rhetorically, *The Answer* is overshadowed by the Lady's own telling of her story, by far the more vibrant and memorable of the two parts, so that the four proposals seem anticlimactic and less fully formed than the Lady's description of herself, her Rival, and her Lover.[37] Moreover, the Friend is counting on "just and reasonable offers," but the Lady has already raised the possibility that the Lover is bewitched and beyond reason: "I think, and so doth all the Country too, that the Man is possessed; at least none of us are able to imagine what he can possibly see in her, unless she hath bewitched him, or given him some Powder" (8). The Friend's appeal to reason, therefore, ignores a crucial point that the Lady has made: that the Rival, possessing a power akin to "That Spirit which taught [Scottish Presbyterians] to abolish Episcopacy at home," has so bewitched the Man that he will be unresponsive to reason. The proposals, then, are likely to falter when they encounter the reality of an England embroiled in both Irish and Scottish affairs.

Anachronistically, we might read the Friend's answer as an allegorical response to Swift scholarship that has assumed that Swift's national identity can be understood with reference to England and Ireland alone. As the Lady has missed opportunities by failing to see that her actions are intertwined with the relationship between her Lover and her Rival, so too Swift scholars have not fully appreciated the ways that Scotland conditions Swift's understanding of Anglo-Irish relations. In *Britons*, Linda Colley explicitly excludes Ireland from her analysis of the "forging" of a British identity in the eighteenth century: "The invention of Britishness," she writes, "was so closely bound up with Protestantism, with war with France and with the acquisition of empire, that Ireland was never able or willing to play a satisfactory part in it."[38] Her emphasis on a unifying Protestantism can account for pro-Unionists like Arbuthnot who grounded their arguments in trade rather than in the charged arena of religious controversy, but it makes little sense of Swift, for whom the religious divide signaled an irremediable split in the ostensible oneness of union. As the reconvening of the Scottish Parliament in 1999 and recent historiography bear out, the doubleness that Swift perceived would continue to haunt the forging of national identities in the emergent Britain.

Notes

I am grateful to the Huntington Library for a summer fellowship that supported the research for this essay, and to Julie Dugger and Jill Bradbury for reading early drafts.

1. Carole Fabricant, *Swift's Landscape* (Baltimore: Johns Hopkins University Press, 1982), 109; Claude Rawson, "The Injured Lady and the Drapier: A Reading of Swift's Irish Tracts," *Prose Studies* 3 (1980): 15; Rick G. Canning, "'Ignorant, Illiterate Creatures': Gender and Colonial Justification in Swift's *Injured Lady* and *The Answer to the Injured Lady*," *ELH* 64, no. 1 (1997): 77. See too Irvin Ehrenpreis, *Swift: The Man, His Works, and the Age*, vol. 2 (Cambridge: Harvard University Press, 1967), 170; Oliver Watkins Ferguson, *Jonathan Swift and Ireland* (Urbana: University of Illinois Press, 1962), 32; Joseph McMinn, ed., *Swift's Irish Pamphlets* (New York: Barnes and Noble Books, 1991), 22.

2. Jonathan Swift, *The Prose Works of Jonathan Swift*, ed. Herbert Davis, vol. 9 (Oxford: Shakespeare Head Press, 1948), 6. Subsequent quotations from this work are cited parenthetically in the text.

3. Carole Fabricant writes, "The specific occasion, the Union of England and Scotland, provides the work with its central theme and metaphor, but at various points becomes eclipsed by the more vivid accounts of the severe injuries sustained by the Lady at the hands of her oppressive lover over the years." "Swift the Irishman," in *The Cambridge Companion to Jonathan Swift*, ed. Christopher Fox (Cambridge: Cambridge University Press, 2003), 53–54. Without denying the force of Swift's critique of England, I will suggest that the aggressive portrayal of the rival, Scotland, is more central and more sustained than Fabricant's description implies.

4. Christopher Fox, "Swift's Scotophobia," *Bullan: An Irish Studies Journal* 6, no. 2 (2002): 45.

5. Ibid., 57.

6. Jim Smyth argues that Colley's account "underestimates the extent to which Anglo-Scottish relations were unresolved by the union." *The Making of the United Kingdom, 1660–1800* (London: Longman, 2001), 102.

7. Pocock, "Limits and Divisions of British History: In Search of an Unknown Subject," *American History Review* 87 (1982): 317. As Pocock notes, the use of the term "British" to encompass Ireland in the eighteenth century is problematic. Nonetheless, Pocock's alternative label—the "Atlantic Archipelago"—has found few followers, and the phrase "New British History" has become widely, though not universally, accepted.

8. John Sage, Thomas Morer, and Alexander Monro, *An Account of the Present Persecution of the Church in Scotland, in Several Letters* (London, 1690), preface. Referring to the treatment of Episcopalians by the rabblers, Swift transforms the tearing of clergy's gowns into Jack's tearing of his coat in *A Tale of a Tub*. See Fox, "Swift's Scotophobia," 47.

9. See Lester M. Beattie, *John Arbuthnot: Mathematician and Satirist* (Cambridge: Harvard University Press, 1935), 318.

10. John Arbuthnot, *The Life and Works of John Arbuthnot*, ed. George A. Aitken (New York, 1892), 396. Subsequent quotations from this work are cited parenthetically in the text.

11. Arbuthnot treats more famous texts in a similar fashion: "If, after all, you should want money to pay your taxes, I can propose no better expedient than that of the Gospel, 'Launch out into the Deep, and let down your Nets'; and you may fetch your tribute-money out of your fishes; for after an union, you will have stock to employ your people to catch them, and vent for them when they are catched" (400–401).

12. John Robertson, "An Elusive Sovereignty: The Course of the Union Debate in Scotland, 1698–1707," in *A Union for Empire*, ed. John Robertson (Cambridge: Cambridge University Press, 1995), 222. Robertson notes, for instance, that both Cromarty and Seton

were "Episcopalians of an erastian cast, and if they were careful not to be too explicit in 1706, the suggestion that a united parliament might use its sovereignty at least to enlarge the toleration enjoyed by Episcopalians was not far from the surface" (222). For an opposing reading of Episcopalian sentiment, see Murray G. Pittock, *Inventing and Resisting Britain: Cultural Identities in Britain and Ireland, 1685–1789* (New York: St. Martin's Press, 1997), 44.

13. Looking specifically at the fourth *Drapier's Letter*, Carole Fabricant describes the effect of Swift's slipping pronouns, which create "texts whose speakers at times embrace the collective category of 'us' (even on occasion expanding it to include Africans, American Indians, and others), while in other instances strenuously attempting to wrest a more limited 'us,' defined by its 'purer' English roots, from the undifferentiated 'us' of the 'native Irish.' " Carole Fabricant, "Speaking for the Irish Nation: The Drapier, the Bishop, and the Problems of Colonial Representation," *ELH* 66, no. 2 (1999): 343.

14. The most strategic manipulator of national identity in the union debate was Daniel Defoe. While still in London, Defoe had written two pamphlets favoring union, but he soon discovered how differently they had been received in Edinburgh: "I calculated those Essays principally for the *English* part, where I always expected the difficulty would lye . . . But I confess my self surpriz'd, when coming to Edinburgh, on some private Affairs of my own, I found my two Essays Re-printed here, and forwardly handed about as Argument against that very Subject they were written to Promote." Daniel Defoe, *An Essay at Removing National Prejudice against a Union with England. Part III* (1706). George Justice describes the challenge that Defoe, like Swift and Arbuthnot, faced in creating a coherent point of view in the midst of shifting national identity: "In his arguments, Defoe had to choose between a 'British' point of view and a self-consciously English point of view that would correspond with his known identity. . . . Either Defoe would become omniscient or he would participate in a dialectic between sincere, yet interested, parties. As it happened, Defoe waffled between a constructed 'British' point of view and the 'English' point of view that Scots forced upon him." George Justice, "The Production of Literature in Eighteenth-Century Britain" (Ph.D. dissertation, University of Pennsylvania, 1994).

15. Colin Kidd, *Subverting Scotland's Past: Scottish Whig Historians and the Creation of an Anglo-British Identity, 1689–1830* (Cambridge: Cambridge University Press, 1993), 38.

16. On the eve of union, Lord Belhaven addressed the Scottish parliament: "But above all, My Lord, I think I see our Ancient Mother Caledonia, like Caesar sitting in the midst of our Senate, Rufully looking round about Her, Covering Her self with Her Royal Garment, attending the Fatal Blow, and breathing out Her last." John Hamilton Belhaven, *Lord Beilhaven's Speech in Parliament, the Second Day of November 1706. On the Subject-Matter of an Union Betwixt the Two Kingdoms of Scotland and England* (Edinburgh, 1706), 6. It was this sort of vision that Arbuthnot's *Sermon* attempts to repudiate: "But as for our independency, so much boasted of, though it be most certainly true in itself, and undeniable in law, as well as justifiable from history, yet, at present it is in effect precarious, imaginary, and fantastical; and is no more than the privilege to be governed by a ministry under foreign influence. . . . Now in lieu of this titular sovereignty and imaginary independency, you acquire by a union true and solid power and dominion" (403).

17. Arbuthnot admits that this mixture of metals will not miraculously equalize Scotland and England: "whatever metal exceeded before the mixture, the same will exceed in the mass" (403). Yet even while acknowledging that Scots will be outnumbered twelve to one in the new British parliament, Arbuthnot avoids mentioning what he surely knew: that

while Union provided Scotland with sixteen peers and forty-five M.P.s, those representatives would remain largely in the pocket of the ministry. See D. Hayton and D. Szechni, "John Bull's Other Kingdoms: The English Government of Scotland and Ireland," in *Britain in the First Age of Party, 1680–1750: Essays Presented to Geoffrey Holmes*, ed. Clyve Jones (London: The Hambledon Press, 1987), 241–42.

18. Edward E. Rosenheim, *Swift and the Satirist's Art* (Chicago: University of Chicago Press, 1963), 25; Frederick Bogel, *The Difference Satire Makes: Rhetoric and Reading from Jonson to Byron* (Ithaca: Cornell University Press, 2001), 42.

19. Jonathan Swift, *Poems of Jonathan Swift*, ed. Harold Williams, vol. 1 (Oxford: Clarendon Press, 1938), 96.

20. Daniel Defoe, *An Essay at Removing National Prejudices against a Union with Scotland, Part II* (London, 1706), 9. Despite his claim of unity, Defoe was well aware that the new nation would not be unified to the extent that James I and VI had desired a century before. James had pressed for not only union of crowns and economies, but also of courts, religion, and education. See Mark Goldie, "Divergence and Union: Scotland and England 1660–1707," in *The British Problem, c. 1534–1707*, ed. Brenden Bradshaw and John Morrill (New York: St. Martin's, 1996), 221.

21. "Botch, n. —2. *fig.* a. A clumsy patch; a meaningless or unsuitable word added for the sake of rime or metre." *Oxford English Dictionary Online*, http://www.oed.com/ (accessed August 28, 2006).

22. Irvin Ehrenpreis, *Swift: The Man, His Works, and the Age,* vol 1 (Cambridge: Harvard University Press, 1962), 175.

23. Swift's shifting use of the pronoun "our" was brought to my attention by Richard Nash.

24. Harold Williams, ed. *Poems of Jonathan Swift* (Oxford: Clarendon Press, 1938), 1:96n.

25. Quoted in Ernle Dusgate Selby Bradford, *Three Centuries of Sailing* (London: Country Life, 1964), 30.

26. The metaphoric resonances of the poem continue to echo for Swift. In the following year, he returned to the image of the posies ("As if a Man in making Posies / Should bundle Thistles up with Roses"). But rather than being a simile of Anglo-Scottish union, they become an image of religious divisions within Ireland. In his *Letter Concerning the Sacramental Test Act*, it is the dissenters, particularly those from Scotland, who become the thistles: "If the Dissenters will be satisfied with such a *Toleration* by Law as hath been granted them in *England*, I believe the Majority of both Houses will fall readily in with it; farther it will be hard to perswade this House of Commons, and, perhaps, much harder the next. For, to say the Truth, we make a mighty Difference here between suffering Thistles to grow among us, and wearing them for Posies. We are fully convinced in our Consciences, that *We* shall always tolerate them, but not quite so fully that *They* will always tolerate us, when it comes to their Turn; and *We* are the Majority, and *We* are in Possession." McMinn, ed., *Swift's Irish Pamphlets*, 44.

27. Canning, "Ignorant, Illiterate Creatures," 81.

28. Ibid., 83.

29. David Dickson describes the "huge Scottish immigration of the 1690s" that bolstered the power of the General Synod of Ulster. He argues that "[i]n the next generation, the fall-off in immigration and the eruption of a series of doctrinal disputes was to make Presbyterianism far less menacing to the Anglican elite." David Dickson, *New Foundations: Ireland 1660–1800* (Dublin: Irish Academic Press, 2000), 61. As Fox points out,

however, Swift remained Scotophobic even after many Ulster Scots had emigrated to North America. Fox, "Swift's Scotophobia," 53.

30. Swift, *Prose Works,* vol. 2, 122.

31. Ibid., 116–17.

32. Ultimately the Act of Security led England toward Union by forcing the issue of succession. Allan Macinnes, "Union Failed, Union Accomplished: The Irish Union of 1703 and the Scottish Union of 1707," in *Acts of Union: The Causes, Contexts and Consequences of the Act of Union*, ed. Daire Keogh and Kevin Whelan (Dublin: Four Courts Press, 2001), 80–81; Jim Smyth, " 'No Remedy More Proper': Anglo-Irish Unionism," in *British Consciousness and Identity: The Making of Britain, 1533–1707,* edited by Brendon Bradshaw and Peter Roberts (Cambridge: Cambridge University Press, 1998), 306–7.

33. Smyth, " 'No Remedy,' " 302.

34. Hayton and Szechni, "John Bull's Other Kingdoms," 247.

35. Canning, "Ignorant, Illiterate Creatures," 81.

36. Ibid., 78. For an alternative reading of Swift as representative of his class and hostile toward Ireland, see Patrick Reilly, "The Displaced Person: Swift and Ireland," *Swift Studies* 8 (1993): 68–82.

37. Perhaps implying this unequal effect, in his edition of selected Irish tracts, Joseph McMinn prints *The Injured Lady* but excludes *The Answer*.

38. Linda Colley, *Britons: Forging the Nation 1707–1837* (New Haven: Yale University Press, 1992), 5, 8.

Notes from A Native Son: Swift's *Intelligencer*

Virginia La Grand

JONATHAN SWIFT'S FAMILY TRADITION AND CULTURAL IDENTITY WERE anchored in a political theory that he was forced to modify late in life. For most of his life Swift insisted that Ireland was a kingdom owing allegiance to the English, part of a composite monarchy, but not part of the Kingdom of England. He scorned the kind of colonial engagement he saw England and other European nations undertake in America and elsewhere.[1] Eventually and reluctantly, Swift came to feel that for the English government, Ireland was virtually one of its modern colonies rather than a sister kingdom or even a colony of the ancient kind planted by Greece and Rome. Swift never stopped referring to Ireland as "this Kingdom," but began writing about it as if it were on its own—just like "any" Country.[2] His collaboration with his Irish friend Thomas Sheridan in the *Intelligencer* marks the change in his political situation as he identifies himself with Ireland and attempts to build an Irish community of political responsibility focused in upper-class Ireland.

In its opening issues, Swift's Dublin weekly attempted to use satire as a way to unify the governing class. As Swift explains in his review of *The Beggar's Opera,* humor is "the best Ingredient towards that kind of Satyr, which is most useful, and gives the least Offence; which instead of lashing, Laughs Men out of their Follies, and Vices."[3] During the journal's publication, however, the overtly political anticolonial perspective that Swift shared with Sheridan became the dominant theme. The *Intelligencer* bears witness both to Swift's attempt to shape Ireland's governing class and to his identification with Ireland.

The *Intelligencer* began weekly publication on May 11, 1728. Its last issue appeared about December 20 in that year.[4] The journal is clearly designed to be one of the several periodicals oriented toward contemporary issues popular in England in the late 1600s and early 1700s. These publications were both commercial ventures and successful attempts to reshape London political discourse, as Brian Cowan argues: "the public sphere envisioned by the Spectatorial periodical essay was a carefully policed forum for urbane but not *risqué* conversation, for moral reflection rather than obsession with the news of the day or the latest fashions, and for temperate agreement on affairs of state rather than heated political debate."[5] Both English models and Swift's Irish version were political organs. Swift knew this well, having written a few essays for the *Tatler* in 1710, having watched the beginning of the *Spectator,* and having used the form in 1710 and 1711 for forty-five issues as the chief writer for the *Examiner.*[6] Cowan describes this "Spectatorial strategy" as its refusal to engage in overtly partisan politics, but points out that it led to "a political 'culture of critique' in eighteenth-century Britain."[7] This is precisely the effect Swift was hoping to create in the Dublin of his day.

Swift may have wanted to institute a Dublin *Spectator*, but he was not supported by the literary culture needed to carry on such a project. Nor did he intend the *Intelligencer* to be a major commitment of his time and effort. Years later, he told Pope that he had always hoped to hand it over to a younger editor.[8] While Swift began the paper, he left it to Sheridan's solo management for half of its publication period. Swift and Sheridan had originally planned to write alternate issues and managed to do so for the first seven issues. Of the journal's nineteen issues, Swift wrote nine, Sheridan wrote nine, and one was copied from a London paper. Even in the first issues authored by Swift, though, Sheridan wrote the introductions to some essays. After the first series of ten issues, Sheridan took almost complete control of the *Intelligencer*.

The permutations of Swift's tactics are difficult to trace in the *Intelligencer* until one notes that his contributions to the journal do not appear in chronological order. Specifically, the essay published as *Intelligencer* no. 15 interrupts the sequence. While the early *Intelligencer* essays show his original intention by addressing his readers as people interested in Ireland's cultural life, the later essays turn to more political and economic topics. Nevertheless, Swift's nine *Intelligencer* essays demonstrate a coherent political perspective.[9] Throughout, Swift focuses his attention on Ireland and its institutions. His personal identification with Ireland as the land of his birth and his residence becomes more clear and explicit in his final *Intelligencer* essay even as it focuses on the dismal state of the Irish economy. Swift's increasing concern with political and economic issues was prompted by contemporary events. The *Intelligencer*'s publication run coincided with a time of increasing economic distress. The crops of 1726 and 1727 had failed, people were starving, and there was a wave of emigration to America—particularly Protestants from the north of Ireland.[10] Swift would be moved by this famine to write his famous "Modest Proposal" in 1729. He also broke his habitual silence on Ireland in his correspondence with his English friend Pope:

> As to this country, there have been three terrible years' dearth of corn, and every place strewed with beggars; but dearths are common in better climates, and our evils here lie much deeper. Imagine a nation the two thirds of whose revenues are spent out of it and who are not permitted to trade with the other third. . . . what I have said requires forgiveness, but I had a mind for once to let you know the state of our affairs, and my reason for being more moved than becomes a clergyman, and a piece of a philosopher. (August 11, 1729)[11]

At this same time England was transitioning between the governments of George I and George II. Swift had hoped that a new government would mean a new attitude to Ireland, but in 1727 the newly crowned George II decided to retain Walpole as prime minister. This decision meant that Irish political and religious offices would continue to be part of Walpole's patronage system. *The Intelligencer* grows out of Swift's anger at this type of English domination of Irish political, religious, and economic institutions, as well as ignorance of the state of affairs resulting from this subjection. His anonymous pamphlet "A Short View of the State of Ireland," originally published on March 19, 1728, was reprinted as no. 15 of the periodical. In it Swift attacks the English perception that Ireland was prosperous and under-taxed, despite the country's obvious distress.[12] The *Intelligencer* perspective shapes his Irish writing even after the journal ceased publication. His pamphlet *A Modest Proposal,* for example, published in October 1729, picks up references to cannibalism from Sheridan's essay in the *Intelligencer* no. 6 and plays with the mercantilist economic theory that Swift uses in *Intelligencer* no. 15.

The formula of the periodical—its echo of Addison and Steele's *Tatler* and *Spectator*—puts Dublin into the same league as London. In the *Intelligencer* essays, Swift and Sheridan write satirically and critically about Dublin life, Irish politics, Irish politicians, and the Irish countryside. Swift's opening essay presents Dublin as a center of civil discourse by evoking the places in which such discourse goes on: the playhouse, churches, balls, assemblies, coffeehouses, meetings for quadrille, courts of justice, and the college.[13] He establishes a sophisticated upper-class persona in his inaugural essay. "Mr Intelligencer" will gather "Weekly Information of all *Important Events* and *Singularities,* which this famous *Metropolis* can furnish" so that "we hope to gather Materials enough to Inform, or Divert, or Correct or Vex the Town."[14] The tone of the opening is clearly an imitation of Mr Spectator who offered "to enliven Morality with Wit, and to temper Wit with Morality."[15] In keeping with Swift's appeal to Dublin society, most of the *Intelligencer* essays in the first series take up topics related to Irish high society—rural hospitality among the upper classes (no. 2), fashionable women's gambling (no. 4), the way to advance in the church (no. 7), political name calling (no. 8), and the education of the nobility (no. 9). These issues suggest that Dublin is a lively city with a thriving theater, coffeehouses, storytelling friends, and well-known street characters. The essays also depict a countryside where gentlemen can travel and can expect hospitality. Swift treats upper-class Ireland as a nation with a political identity, values, and culture. These essays are by and for Dubliners, and in them the voice of satire is the voice of love.

Swift's earlier pamphlets on Ireland take a harsher stance. In the *Drapier's Letters* (1724–25), he directed sarcasm, irony, and rage to the relationship between Ireland and England. These texts convey the impression that Ireland's most important attribute is its connection with England. Although the *Intelligencer* clearly indicates the current dismal state of the Irish economy through a description of roads thronged with people on the move to towns or to the American colonies, this situation is remarkable because it is a crisis. The country towns may be littered with ruins from Cromwell's invasion, but there *are* towns and ruins. In *Intelligencer* no. 6 Sheridan demonstrates this perspective on Ireland when he compares these ruins to the ruins Athenians left unrepaired after the Macedonian invasion.[16] The classical allusion has the effect of making Ireland and England the modern representatives of age-old conflicts, with Ireland as Athens, the invaded cultural center.

If the *Intelligencer* illuminates Swift's changing political identification, a topic that continues to exercise scholars, why has it been so little studied? The journal's publication history gives a simple explanation for its obscurity in the Swift canon: its pedigree was not clear. James Woolley's 1992 annotated edition is the first complete edition since 1729. Woolley traces the reasons why "scholars have been confused about what the *Intelligencer* was, when it was, and by whom it was written."[17] It was published by the Dublin printer, Sarah Harding—the widow of the printer who had been jailed for printing the *Drapier's Letters.* Woolley describes the paper as shabby, but he judges that it is "within the normal range of contemporary Dublin ephemeral printing."[18] There was no collected volume published in Dublin, but the paper was read in Dublin, and readers sent issues to friends in England and America. [19]

From London's point of view, the *Intelligencer* was Swift's work. Many of the undated individual issues were picked up and reprinted in London weeklies with hints that linked all of them to Swift.[20] A London volume of the collected papers—attributed to the author of *The Tale of A Tub*—was published in 1729 after the paper itself had ceased publication. That volume was reprinted in 1730, and soon afterward Swift tried to make sure that his essays were distinguished from Sheridan's, as Pope was preparing a joint volume of his and Swift's work.[21] The tradition of seeing the paper only as a place to find essays by Swift continued, with editors putting the essays into the context they saw as relevant. In the 1898–1907 edition of Swift's *Prose Works*, W. E. H. Lecky included Swift's *Intelligencer* essays in volume nine along with Swift's contributions to the *Tatler, Examiner*, and *Spectator*.[22] In 1964, Herbert Davis included them in the volume *Irish Tracts 1728–1733*.[23]

The publication of Swift's *Intelligencer* essays as individual items has determined why and how they are read, and only the review of *The Beggar's Opera* (no. 3) arouses much interest. Since the announced purpose of the *Intelligencer* was to be an entertaining cosmopolitan Dublin journal, it is not surprising that the individual essays Swift contributed to it pale in emotional force when compared to his other work of this period: the *Drapier's Letters* (1724–25), *Gulliver's Travels* (October 1726), and *A Modest Proposal* (1729).[24] Perhaps it should not surprise us that rage is easier to pick up across the centuries than the mixture of anger, humor, and irony that fills the pages of the *Intelligencer*.

Modern readers see the paper from London's point of view, but Swift did not write for London. Indeed, his starting a Dublin paper might have seemed like an alienation of affection to his London friends. We find that his comments to Pope about the *Intelligencer* downplay or disparage the paper. Swift complained to Pope that "only the Verses and of those not the four last slovenly lines" of Number 10 are his,[25] and he told Pope that Sheridan had used the "View of Ireland" as issue 15 "merely for laziness not to disappoint the town."[26]

Even Swift's collaborator, Sheridan, must have wondered how strongly Swift was committed to the paper. Although Swift wrote the first issue and last issue, he did not let the project keep him in Dublin. He spent the period from June 1728 through February 1729 visiting his friends the Achesons at Market Hill, leaving Sheridan to piece together the weekly issues. When Sheridan wrote him in July asking about contributions to the paper, Swift replied: "as to what you call my exercises [the *Intelligencer*], I have long quitted it; it gave me too much constraint, and the world does not deserve it. We may keep it cold till the middle of winter" (August 2, 1728).[27]

Swift's reply to Sheridan, seems not to have meant that he had completely lost interest—just that he did not want to take responsibility for the paper's management.[28] He was seemingly unaware that the paper had ceased publication in December 1728 when he sent the publisher a contribution in February 1729. Woolley notes that "Mrs Harding published Swift's poem separately in late January or early February 1728/29, mentioning in her colophon that at her shop 'Gentlemen may be furnished with the *Intelligencer*, from No 1 to No 19.' "[29]

Woolley argues that rather than wishing to end the paper, "Swift and Sheridan apparently changed their minds and planned a third series of the *Intelligencer.*"[30] A freestanding satire on one of Swift and Sheridan's clergy antagonists, Dean Smedley, appeared in May 1729 and invited contributions to "an *Irish* Dunciad" at the "Intelligencer."[31] Swift seems to have had topics in mind for more issues than were actually published.[32] The undated "Hints of Intelligencer Papers" taken from Swift's notebooks show that he planned to write about the education of ladies, "Beau's dresses," "Clergy preaching, bad Engl——&c," "improvements, penal clause, as to time &c for improvement & preservation of trees & their kinds—abuse Squires on this head."[33]

Not only the focus, but the persona Swift develops for the *Intelligencer* is different from that of the *Drapier's Letters*, his most famous earlier Irish pamphlets. Swift's general method for writing pamphlets, however, did not change. Swift's tactic, according to his biographer Irwin Ehrenpreis, was to "disguise himself as a superior member of the class he addressed."[34] The *Drapier* pamphlets, for example, were addressed to what Ehrenpreis calls "a sub-literary audience."[35] The speaker reduces "History, law and morality . . . to their humblest terms," while "emotions stream from every phrase."[36] Swift used this voice to brush aside rules of social politeness: "He has the confidence to name and characterize any person who belongs to his argument," from "the loathsome Mr Wood" to "the name of the King, which he treats with ostensibly respectful epithets only to undercut them by the boldness of the reference."[37] Summing up his analysis, Ehrenpreis says "Nothing in the Drapier's logic is so effective as his disorderly tone and lurid illustration."[38]

In contrast to his voice as the Drapier, Swift uses three different voices in his *Intelligencer* contributions—two of them constructed for the journal and one incorporated by the use of his "Short View" pamphlet. None of these voices in the *Intelligencer* has the Drapier's attractive exuberance. Mr Intelligencer is sarcastic and clever. He writes to the Dubliners who frequent coffee shops, a sophisticated upper-class audience of theatergoing, clergy-related English Irishmen and women.[39]

The second persona Swift constructed for the *Intelligencer* appears in no. 19—the final issue. Here Swift writes as an Irish landowner concerned by the shortage of cash and by the emigration to America. In this essay the speaker refers to the Drapier as one who raised the question of why Ireland has no mint.[40] The speaker, however, does not claim to be the Drapier, nor to be close to the merchant. His friends are close to the government. He reports a conversation with "A Person of Distinction" who "discoursed with the Lord Lieutenant, before his last Return to England."[41]

Swift's persona in *Intelligencer* no. 15—the reprinted pamphlet—is neither the urbane Mr Intelligencer, nor the disheartened landlord, but he is most certainly not the disorganized and enthusiastic seller of cloth. Instead he is logical and angry. An educated man who defines himself as Irish by birth and residence, he is aware of the laws of economics and knows that Ireland's prosperity or lack of prosperity is determined by the laws of economics common to all countries. He is at the end of his patience with the political obscurantism of those who will not name England as the source of Irish troubles. He brusquely lists the fourteen causes of national prosperity and baldly proves that none of them describe Ireland. He has no interest in games such as the Drapier's ironic pretense that the English King cared for Ireland's good. After one sarcastic paragraph he confesses that his "heart is too heavy to continue this Irony longer."[42]

In beginning the *Intelligencer*, Swift was trying a different approach to reforming the Irish governing class than he had in his *Drapier's Letters.* His theme in many of the early *Intelligencer* essays is the use of humor in political writing, and he practices what he describes. Beginning with the review of his friend John Gay's play, *The Beggar's Opera,* in *Intelligencer* no. 3, Swift argues that humor exerts a positive moral force in society. The whole community ought to see *The Beggar's Opera* because Gay has "placed vices of all Kinds in the strongest and most odious Light; and thereby done eminent Service, both to *Religion* and *Morality.*"[43] Its humor can unite all levels of society and all sorts of people. Humor in *The Beggar's Opera* explains the play's "prodigious success both here and in England."[44]

Swift himself had been criticized for having an unsuitable sense of humor ever since his authorship of the 1704 satire, *The Tale of the Tub,* had become known. In his two-part essay on discretion (*Intelligencer* no. 5) and clerical advancement (*Intelligencer* no. 7), he turns the tables on his critics by defining discretion as the vice of selfishness rather than as a virtue. Discretion has nothing to do with "*Genius, Learning, strong Comprehension, quickness of Conception, Magnanimity, Generosity, Sagacity*, or any other superior Gift of Human minds."[45] Discretion, however, does pay off in church politics. Ironically, then, Swift sketches the contrasting careers of *Corusodes*, the discreet clergyman who rises high although he "never understood a Jest, or had the least Conception of Wit"[46] and the indiscrete *Eugenio* who dies in an obscure parish because "he had written Verses, and particularly some wherein he glanced at a certain Reverend Doctor, famous for Dullness."[47]

Swift turns from talking about jests to employing them in his verse essays "Mad Mullinex and Timothy" (*Intelligencer* no. 8) and "Tim and the Fables" (*Intelligencer* no. 10). In these verses, Swift imagines a dialogue between the well-known Dublin street character "Mad Mullinex" and a politician, "Timothy." The street character cannot understand "Timothy's" worry over Jacobites: "Why ever in these raging Fits / Daming to Hell the Jacobits?"[48] Even a madman knows that there are no Jacobite threats, implies Swift. The danger to Irish unity comes not from imagined Jacobite rebels but from real politicians who perpetuate outdated party quarrels and who take personal offense at political fables.[49] Woolley's introduction to the essay traces the character "Timothy"—the Jacobite-hunter—to the Whig Irish privy councillor Richard Tighe whose political witch hunting had injured both Swift and Sheridan.[50] In the *Intelligencer* verse essays, Swift argues that Tim's accusations of Jacobitism merely obscure true political debate.

All of these essays imply a varied and cosmopolitan Dublin society. By creating the *Intelligencer,* Swift implicitly replaces London as the single focus of his print world. He attempts to establish an Irish space for discussion—a Dublin journal as the vehicle for political satire and social commentary, and an Irish group of readers in Dublin. Swift's attempt to establish a Dublin upper-class journal grows out of the radical change in his perception of the Irish situation with respect to England. He had grown up as a member of the English community in Dublin whose members saw themselves as participants in a civilizing mission, whose job it was to govern Ireland as part of a composite monarchy under the English King. Swift's early writing reveals his self-confident understanding of how barbarian lands become civilized[51] and his self-assessment as a member of the governing class of this composite kingdom. His first years as the dean of Saint Patrick's Cathedral brought him to feel that the Irish themselves were creating their own ruin. But later he came to feel that Ireland was more like a possession than a sister kingdom,[52] and that Ireland was not seen as a constituent of a composite monarchy by its English neighbor. His writing in the late 1720s shows his reaction to this realization. His references to England become enraged, and so do his references to the American colonies. Swift's personal motivation for his 1727/28 pamphlet "A

Short View" becomes clear when one reads it as the public presentation of material Swift had developed a year earlier (April 28, 1726) in a letter to Walpole about the Irish situation.[53]

In Swift's 1726 visit to London, his penultimate, he had attempted to convince Sir Robert Walpole, King George I's prime minister, to change the way England was treating Ireland. At this time, despite his antagonism to the Whig government of Walpole, Swift still formally assumed that he and Walpole shared a political theory which made them colleagues in their concern for both English and Irish well being. Swift managed to get a meeting with Walpole, but Sir Robert did not listen to him.[54] Back in Dublin, Swift wrote a long letter summarizing the perspective he had tried to give Walpole. He sent it to Lord Peterborough, the friend who had arranged Swift's interview with Walpole, for Peterborough to give to Walpole. Swift presents himself as an impartial informant: "my principal design was to set him right, not only for the service of *Ireland*, but likewise of *England*, and of his own administration."[55] The letter enumerates many causes of Ireland's woes—all of them having to do with English policy. Swift counts off systemic injustices of this policy: the restrictions on Irish trade, the appointment of Englishmen to Irish church, university, and government positions, the huge proportion of Irish wealth leaving Ireland for England, and the English refusal to give government employment to the children of Englishmen who had been appointed to government or church office in Ireland—the same list he would recite in his *Short View*. When summing up the causes of Irish poverty, Swift reports having said to Walpole, "I think it manifest, that whatever circumstances can possible contribute to make a country poor and despicable, are all united with respect to Ireland."[56] In his Irish pamphlet he put it this way: "our misfortune is not altogether owing to our own Fault, but to a million of Discouragements."[57]

Swift's letter to Walpole tries to appeal to shared norms of ethical behavior. He asks for justice for people like himself—the Englishmen born in Ireland. Swift states two grounds for his complaint. One ground is "the notions I had of liberty, a possession always understood by the British nation to be the inheritance of a human creature."[58] But his primary ground for appeal is England's violation of the universal norms of imperial action: "they [English born in Ireland] ought to be on as good a foot as any subjects of Britain, according to the practice of all other nations, and particularly of the Greeks and Romans."[59]

When Swift appealed to Walpole's knowledge of classical colonial practices, he was appealing to these practices as a shared conceptual framework, not as a description of Ireland's situation. In Swift's view, Ireland was not England's colony, but a kingdom that had submitted to the English king Henry II and more recently, to the English monarch under Henry VIII in 1541. There was a well-developed body of thought about England's relationship to both Scotland and Ireland in terms of composite monarchy. This perspective had been developed in Ireland in 1643[60] and 1660 and reworked in 1698.[61] The composite monarchy position which saw Ireland's loyalty due the English crown but not to the English parliament was argued during Swift's lifetime by William Molyneux—like Swift, an Englishman born in Ireland.[62] Molyneux argued that the relationship was one of "a dual monarchy, under which Ireland owed allegiance to the King of England but only in his inextricably linked capacity as King of Ireland."[63] He wrote to make a "defence of the legislative independence of the Irish parliament."[64] This pamphlet was well-known in England and aroused strong opposition there during Swift's lifetime. In 1698—when Swift was living with Sir William Temple—Molyneux's pamphlet was "severely censured by the English House of Commons."[65] Over the years it was frequently reprinted. Its assertions were formally denied by the "Declaratory Act of 1720 which expressly defined Ireland as a 'dependent' kingdom."[66]

The complementary model of Ireland as a semi-independent colony under the authority of the English parliament was also well developed in Swift's day, as David Armitage shows in his study, *The Ideological Origins of the British Empire.* Armitage points out that for more than a century, Roman colonial practice had been an explicit model for the relationship between the English crown and the other nations of the British Isles, Wales, Scotland, and Ireland: "The Anglo-Scottish debate of the 1540s introduced the concept of an empire of Great Britain into British political thought, and associated it for the first time with the Roman conception of a colony."[67] Armitage quotes the advice of Sir Thomas Smith, Regius Professor of Civil Law at Cambridge who became clerk of the privy council in March 1547. Smith advised setting up colonies in Ireland to bring it closer to England "to augment our tongue, our laws, and our religion in that Isle, which three be the true bands of the commonwealth whereby the Romans conquered and kept long time a great part of the world."[68] Armitage traces this discussion through Elizabethan and Jacobean times through the discussion in the Commonwealth over what kind of empire Britain could become. Specifically Armitage explains how Harrington's long treatise *Oceana* took up classical models of empire: "To 'take the course of Rome' would ensure the maintenance of liberty and the achievement of *grandezza*."[69]

Of these two models, Swift affirmed that of the composite kingdom, rather than that of the Roman colony. What he called "modern way of planting colonies" however, is still another kind of relationship. It earns his contempt, but it was the model the English were adopting for America and for Ireland. Swift's engagement in this argument is clearly evident in his *Drapier's Letter* "To the whole People of Ireland" where the Drapier indignantly rejects the claim "that Ireland is a "depending Kingdom."[70] Swift has the Drapier point out that when the English Parliament assumed the power to bind Irish law, "they were at first, openly opposed (as far as Truth, Reason, and Justice are capable of opposing) by the famous Mr Molineaux, an English Gentleman born here."[71]

Swift's political theory gave clergymen the role of conscience in the monarchy. When he traveled to England to petition Queen Anne for Church of Ireland parity with the Church of England in respect to church taxes, he felt that he was serving the Irish church.[72] When he lived in England he wrote as an Englishman, not as an immigrant or a foreigner. He stepped right into the center of political debate about England's European wars. His essays in the *Examiner* explain the system of limited monarch and established church that "we" have.[73]

Swift's 1726 failure with Walpole marked a defining moment in the collapse of his political worldview. Without moving physically outside the land of his birth, he suffered the shock of culture change as the relationship between Ireland and England worked itself out. The definition of culture provided by the anthropologist Mary Douglas helps conceptualize the change that Swift experienced. In her 1992 collection of essays *Risk and Blame,* Douglas defines a culture as a "system of persons holding one another mutually accountable."[74] When Swift attempted to talk to Walpole in 1726, Swift could at least for the sake of argument assume that he and Walpole belonged to the same culture.

Swift believed in a political and ecclesiastical hierarchy, and assigned blame to those who deviated from the hierarchy. In his first Irish pamphlets, Swift blamed the Irish Parliament, the ladies, the shopkeepers, the clergy, and the country landlords—as well as the appointed governors for unthinking destruction of the Irish. Gradually, however, Swift began to identify the colonizing power, England, as deviating from patterns of good government by setting up the conditions for the failure of the Irish economy. In his essay *Intelligencer* no. 19, Swift's landlord persona speaks of the "Hatred and Contempt born us by our Neighbors and Brethren, without the least ground of Provocation, who rejoice at our Sufferings although sometimes to their own Disadvantage." Swift came to see Ireland as a modern colony of England, and he came to see himself—someone born and raised in Ireland—as having the duty to speak out as a native son. In his post-*Intelligencer* pamphlets Swift addressed himself to Irish landlords rather than to the English.

Swift's appeal to a minimal standard of justice demanded a classical model of a colony, but facts on the ground outran the theory. Modern European colonization was redefining the idea of a colony. Swift's political writing resists both the modern kind of colony and the redefinition of Ireland's kingdom status. After his failure to influence Walpole Swift keeps on using the term "kingdom," but he can no longer pretend that Ireland is a kingdom under the care of the English King. Ireland's view of itself as a kingdom is belied by its de facto status. How can it be a kingdom if it is an "exception to all other states or monarchies that were ever known in the world"?[75] Again Swift mocks Irish pretensions to this term in *Intelligencer* no. 19, saying "Ireland is the first imperial Kingdom since Nimrod, which ever wanted Power to coin their own Money."

Thomas Sheridan, Swift's collaborator in the *Intelligencer*, was a well-known Dublin schoolmaster, and he had detailed knowledge of Roman colonization patterns as well as knowledge of the history of the English in Ireland.[76] Sheridan was twenty years younger than Swift, and the dean was Sheridan's patron as well as his friend.[77] Like Swift, Sheridan was a clergyman in the established church. Like Swift, he was a graduate of Trinity College, Dublin. But unlike Swift, his family had roots in the Irish countryside. Sheridan was one of Swift's guides to Gaelic Ireland when they traveled together on several occasions. Sheridan lent Swift his country home for the spring and summer of 1725. Furthermore, he claims to have introduced Swift to some of the local Gaelic-speaking farm workers when Swift stayed with him. Ehrenpreis quotes verse by Sheridan in which he says of Swift:

> So far forgetting his old station,
> He seems to like their conversation.
> Conforming to the tatter'd rabble
> He learns their Irish tongue to gabble.[78]

Thomas Sheridan, the Gaelic-speaking schoolmaster, could not have shared Swift's English perspective on colonization. From his point of view, colonialism wore an oppressive face whether it was Roman, Spanish, or English. Sheridan was very much the junior partner in the *Intelligencer*, but his insistently polemic approach to the journal eventually dominated Swift's attempt at setting up a circle of education through humor. Sheridan's editing forced Swift's work into an overtly political frame.

In the short life of the *Intelligencer* we can see a kind of tug-of-war between Swift and Sheridan. They are united in their view of Ireland's situation, and they are united in their desire to awaken a sense of political responsibility in the Irish governing classes. Where they differ is in strategy. Swift is trying to develop a sense of Irish identity in a cosmopolitan Irish upper class. Sheridan wants to focus on direct confrontation with England. Swift creates Mr Intelligencer as the journal's voice. Sheridan insistently exposes his collaborator as the Drapier. His introduction to Swift's reprinted pamphlet (*Intelligencer* no. 15) brings up Swift's work as the author of the *Drapier's Letters,* an identification Swift never makes. Sheridan spends another issue (no. 18) linking the *Drapier's Letters* to the Elizabethan attempt to dominate Ireland by diluting the coinage, and trying to raise support for a public celebration of the Drapier's birthday in Dublin.

Looking at Swift's essay published as *Intelligencer* no. 19 and at the pamphlets he wrote after the journal folded, it seems that Swift tacitly adopted Sheridan's Gaelic perspective on the colonial relationship between Ireland and England. He was pushed into the stance of lashing the Irish upper class rather than educating them by laughter. Woolley asserts, "of Sheridan's original compositions, none demonstrates more clearly than the *Intelligencer* the range of social and political concerns he shared with Swift."[79] Nevertheless, Sheridan's individual perspective shows up in his contributions that describe the Irish countryside and Irish history. Sheridan's *Intelligencer* essays reveal his identification with Gaelic Ireland over against the colonizing English. In *Intelligencer* no. 6, Sheridan shows both his concern for the Irish people and his perspective as a colonial subject in his striking descriptions of the Irish countryside: "We see in the several Towns a very few Houses scattered among the Ruins of thousands which he [Cromwell] laid level with their streets. Great Numbers of Castles! The Country Seats of Gentlemen then in Being, still standing in ruins, habitations for Bats, Daws, and Owls."[80] More vivid still is the description of the people he met on the road: "Six tattered Families flitting to be shipped off to the West-Indies. A colony of a hundred and fifty Beggars, all repairing to people our Metropolis. . . . Travellers enough, but seven in ten wanting Shirts and Cravats; nine in ten going barefoot, and, carrying their Brogues and Stockens in their Hands."[81] Sheridan's essay explicitly blames "*that Usurper Cromwell*" for the ruin of Irish churches, but his more generalized accusation against the English colonial enterprise reveals itself in the fable he writes for this essay.[82] In the fable, a "Colony of large Dogs" manages to displace the native dogs and set them quarreling over scraps and offal while the colonizing dogs live "in Peace and Luxury."[83] The terms of this fable would imply that the English—even a friend like Swift—were colonizing dogs.

Sheridan's Gaelic perspective resonates in the distinctions he makes between Celts and English in the history of England and in the history of

Ireland. In *Intelligencer* no. 6 he describes Ireland by alluding to the pre-battle speech of the Briton going into battle against the Romans "*Et ubi Solitudinem faciunt, id imperium vocant*" [when they make a wilderness they call it sovereignty].[84] In a much later *Intelligencer* issue (no. 18), Sheridan quotes the Elizabethan report about what happened in the late 1500s when the English fought rebellion in Ireland by devaluing Irish money. The Irish were driven to eating grass and to cannibalism: "All the publick Roads were strowed with Dead *Carcases* of miserable Wretches, whose Mouths were Green (as the Author expresses it) with their last meal of Grass. . . . and at the same time, a discovery being made of Twelve Women, who made a practice of stealing Children, to Eat them, they were all burned."[85] The Elizabethan action had been taken to put down an Irish rebellion, but Sheridan asserts that the rebels themselves— "the *Giraldies*, the *Tools*, the *Cavanaghs*, and the *Byrns* who were the Ring-leaders, were all of English Extraction."[86]

Swift's identification with England changed over the years, but this change was a redefinition of conceptual categories rather than the substitution of a fixed Irish identity for a fixed English identity. Most critical discussion about Swift's identity tries to determine whether Swift really identified himself with the whole Irish nation when he wrote his political pamphlets, or whether he spoke only for the Anglo-Irish segment of the Irish population. This topic is old, but it still generates interest, as we can see by two essays in the 2002 collection, *Representations of Swift* edited by Brian A. Connery.[87] Robert Mahoney summarizes the history of the issue and argues for an approach that can "incorporate ambivalence . . . to effect a compromise between the nationalist interpretive camp and that disposed to emphasize his hypocrisy."[88] Although it is hard to disprove "ambivalence," my analysis argues that Swift *changed* his position because he realized that the very terms of the argument had changed during his lifetime. The modern system of colonization under which he lived was radically different from the theoretical system of a composite monarchy that he had affirmed as a young man, and it was even different from the ancient system of colonization practiced by Greece and Rome.

In arguing for conceptual change in Swift's perception and self-understanding, I follow the lead of both Carole Fabricant and Irvin Ehrenpreis in looking at the words Swift used.[89] These scholars track the complexities of Swift's identification with the "whole Irish people" as a mental and emotional struggle for Swift in redefining the terms available to him. Swift's varying personal pronouns make it look as though sometimes he identifies himself with the Irish, but at other times with the English, as Fabricant demonstrates.[90] Fabricant shows that Swift's identity problem is not an individual issue, but is common to his social group. Bishop Berkeley demonstrates the same problem of identity in his *Word to the Wise: or an Exhortation to the Roman Catholic Clergy of Ireland.*[91]

Going beyond pronoun switches into the definition of concepts, Ehrenpreis argues that Swift redefines the word "people" in his fourth and fifth Drapier's letters so that it refers to all the productive elements of Irish society irrespective of their religion or national origin: "The word 'people' may have at least two senses. One is the 'true English' minority to which Swift belonged. . . . The other is the nobility, farmers, artisans, and so forth who lived in the kingdom and contributed to its prosperity."[92] Fabricant and Ehrenpreis argue that Swift's writing shows his shifting sense of himself, but Swift's uncertainties were not simply questions of personal allegiance within a stable political system. The political forms represented by the term "colony," "kingdom," and "country" were also changing at the time.

Swift and his contemporaries were familiar with discussions of definitions such as Locke's 1693 demonstration in his *Essay on Human Understanding* that no individual can define abstract nouns, so when we see Swift defining terms like "kingdom" or refusing labels such as "depending kingdom" we can assume that he knew how thin the ice was beneath his feet. Writers such as Swift and Berkeley were aware that the language was changing to reflect the new political realities, and they did their best to fight the changes. Swift's sense of his own identity may have changed in response to his situation, but the very categories of analysis, or at least the English words for these categories—terms like "kingdom," "colony," and "empire"—were being redefined by governments and events.

Swift's analysis of the Irish situation and his publication of the *Intelligencer* seem to coincide with Benedict Anderson's analysis of Spanish colonialism in his book *Imagined Communities*. Anderson points out that in the American colonies of European kingdoms administrative segregation created groups of disenfranchised colonial elites in political administration, armed forces, and church who "were to be economically subjected and exploited, but . . . were also essential to the stability of the empire."[93] These Spanish and English colonies in America were the modern kind of colony that Sheridan and Swift deplored.

In Ireland the same colonial mechanisms that motivated the Spanish in Latin America made the Anglo-Irish spend their time and money currying favor with the English power structure in London. By starting an Irish journal, the *Intelligencer*, Swift was taking the colonial next step toward making Ireland an independent nation—the development of a creole culture. Swift's Dublin paper demonstrates his growing awareness that both the two-kingdom and the colonial outpost frameworks on which he had built his life were obsolete. There might once have been a relationship between the English and Ireland that permitted Ireland to be a self-respecting part of a composite monarchy, but not in the current English colonization of Ireland. The fact that Irish Protestants—albeit the Ulster Presbyterians Swift disliked—were lining up for ship passage to America meant that, like it or not, Swift's homeland was part of this modern English colonial system.

If, as I argue, the *Intelligencer* marks a conceptual change and a political change in Swift's world, we should be able to see evidence of such a tectonic shift. I believe that two groups of texts do indeed show changes in Swift's perspective. The first group consists of the published and unpublished pamphlets from 1729. The second group consists of letters and pamphlets from 1733. Swift published the pamphlet for which he is most famous—"A Modest Proposal" in October 1729, but this savage indictment of Irish landlords was not his only pamphlet from that year. Swift wrote several more pamphlets after the *Intelligencer* ceased publication. At least three of them used the objective, educated, discouraged persona of his "Short View" (*Intelligencer* no. 15). The speaker has the same first-person despair as the speaker who said "my heart is too heavy to continue this Irony longer."[94] Swift wrote and left unpublished several weary and despairing pamphlets at this time: "Letter to the Archbishop of Dublin concerning the Weavers," two called "Answer to Several Letters from Unknown Hands," and the "Maxims Controlled in Ireland." It was Swift's cousin, Deane Swift, who published them in the 1760s.[95] In these works we can see more evidence that Swift had adopted the anticolonial perspective of his collaborator Sheridan. Swift seems to have abandoned his attempt to use laughter to unify the Irish governing class.

Swift's "A Modest Proposal" brought to life a new persona—the mercantile projector, full of calculations and profitable plans but blind to elementary human decency. This cheerful cannibal, whose blood-chilling computations of how many meals a family might make out of a year-old child, is replaced near the end of the essay by the same angry voice that appears in Swift's "A Short View" and his unpublished pamphlets:

> Therefore, let no Man talk to me of other Expedients: Of taxing our Absentees at five Shillings a Pound: Of using neither Cloaths, nor Household Furniture; except what is of our own Growth and Manufacture: Of utterly rejecting the Materials and Instruments that promote foreign Luxury: Of curing the Expensiveness of Pride, Vanity, Idleness, and Gaming in our Women: Of learning to love our Country; wherein we differ even from LAPLANDERS and the Inhabitants of TOPINAMBOO.[96]

Further evidence for Swift's changed perspective comes from a letter he wrote in 1732 to an Irish Catholic exile who had served the Pretender. Just as Swift was turning a genteel satirical eye on Dublin's upper class in the *Intelligencer*, Pope was publishing his *Dunciad* and Gay *The Beggar's Opera.* Swift wrote in response to the complaints against Gay's mockery of English politics. Swift presented Pope, Gay—and himself—as defenders of public morality: "You see Pope, Gay, and I, use all our Endeavours to make folks Merry and wise, and profess to have no Enemies, except Knaves and Fools."[97]

In this same letter, Swift analyzes the effects of the English occupation of Ireland:

> I cannot but highly esteem those Gentlemen of Ireland, who, with all the Disadvantages of being Exiles and Strangers, have been able to distinguish themselves by their Valour and Conduct in so many Parts of Europe. I think above all other Nations, which ought to make the English ashamed of the Reproaches they cast on the Ignorance, the Dulness and the Want of Courage in the Irish Natives, those Defects, wherever they happen, arising only from the Poverty and Slavery they suffer from their inhuman neighbours.

Swift's distancing himself from "the English" here is clear. Even more striking is his praise of the Irish.[98] We see the same matter-of-fact analysis in a published minor pamphlet Swift wrote in the 1730s. The pamphlet—addressed to the citizens of Dublin—points out that the two political parties in Dublin are not the Whig and Tory or any of the other dichotomies the reader might have expected, but "These English who happen to be born in this Kingdom" and "The Gentlemen sent from the other Side to Possess most of the chief Employments here."[99]

Swift has long been presented as a person made bitter by disappointed ambition, and only reluctantly an Irishman. Many of his own comments to his English friends encourage such a view. Less melancholy than this picture of Swift the exile is the postcolonial Swift. Swift's turn from allegiance to England to his identification as one born and raised in Ireland, his ability to collaborate with Sheridan, and his attempt to create a responsible governing class of English in Ireland place him at the head of the long and notable tradition of Anglo-Irish writers and their claim to being truly Irish.

Notes

1. Swift has Gulliver scornfully describe a 'modern colony' at the end of *Gulliver's Travels* (New York: Dover, 1996), 224. In the 1720 pamphlet *A Proposal for the Universal Use of Irish Manufacture* Swift complains that some previous government ministers "were apt, from their *high* Elevation, to look *down* upon this Kingdom, as if it had been one of their *Colonies* of *Out-casts* in *America.*" Joseph McMinn, ed., *Swift's Irish Pamphlets* (Gerrards Cross: Colin Smythe, 1991), 54.

2. Jonathan Swift and Thomas Sheridan, *The Intelligencer*, ed. James Woolley (Oxford: Clarendon Press, 1992), no. 15, 175. Hereafter quotations from the *Intelligencer* will be cited by issue number and page in the Woolley edition.

3. *Intelligencer* no. 3, 62.

4. Woolley's 1992 annotated edition of the *Intelligencer* provides modern readers the needed bibliographic support for reading the paper. Besides annotating the textual allusions to contemporary Dublin life, Woolley lists the author of each essay, investigates the evidence for each issue's date of publication, and argues that the nineteen numbered issues form two series. The first series—numbers one through ten—appeared between May 11 and mid-July 1728. The second series appeared between October 8 and December 10, 1728 (32–33).

5. Brian Cowan, "Mr Spectator and the Coffeehouse Public Sphere," *Eighteenth-Century Studies* 37 (2004): 351.

6. During Swift's 1710 trip to London on business of the Irish Church, he contributed to Steele's *Tatler.* Describing his essays to his close friend Esther Waters (Stella), he writes "Tell me how my shower is liked in Ireland: I never knew any thing pass better here. . . . Have you heard of the verses about the *Rod of Sid Hamet*? Say nothing of them for your life. Hardly any body suspects me for them, only they think no-body but Prior or I could write them." *The Journal to Stella, I*, ed. Harold Williams (Oxford: Clarendon Press, 1948), 65. Swift's enjoyment of the enterprise and its clandestine character was such that he did not acknowledge authorship even to Stella until the very end of his *Examiner* editorship (208).

7. Ibid., 360.

8. In a letter to Pope dated June 12, 1732, Swift writes, "Two or three of us had a fancy three years ago to write a Weekly paper and call it an Intelligencer. But it continued not long, for the whole Volume (it was re-printed in London and I find you have seen it) was the work of only two, myself and Dr. Sheridan. If we could have got some ingenious young man to have been the manager, who should have published all that might be sent to him, it might have continued longer, for there were hints enough, but the Printer here could not afford such a young man one farthing for his troubles, the Sale being so small, and the price one half-penny, and so it dropt." Alexander Pope, *Correspondence of Alexander Pope*, ed. George Sherburn (Oxford: Clarendon Press), 3:292.

9. The essays Swift wrote specifically for the paper were published as no. 1, 3, 5, 7, 8, 9, 10, and 19.

10. Woolley, "Introductory Note to *Intelligencer* 19," 204.

11. Letter dated August 11, 1729. F. Elrington Ball, ed., *The Correspondence of Jonathan Swift, D.D.* (London: G. Bell, 1913), 4:89.

12. Woolley quotes a pamphlet written by Archbishop King in 1721: "Tis a General opinion in Great Britain, and passes Current without contradiction; that Ireland is in a flourishing condition; that Whilst England has been oppressed and Deeply sunk in Debt by Excessive Taxes, Ireland has been at Ease." "Appendix A: Archbishop King on the Taxation

of Ireland," 227. Swift's 1728 "Short View" may have been a response to a March 1728 tract, *Seasonable Remarks,* and its exaggeration of Ireland's wealth. Swift's pamphlet began an exchange, which was "in the background by the time Sheridan reprinted the pamphlet as Intelligencer 15," Wooley, "Introductory Note to *Intelligencer* 15," 171, 170.

13. *Intelligencer* no. 1, 48.

14. Ibid.

15. Joseph Addison and Richard Steele, *The Spectator I*, ed. Donald F. Bond (Oxford: Clarendon Press, 1965), no. 10, Monday, March 12, 1711.

16. *Intelligencer* no. 6, 87.

17. Wolley, "General Introduction," 6.

18. Ibid., 36.

19. Ibid., "Áppendix D: Commentary in *Mist's* and *Fog's*," 236.

20. Woolley says, "Through London newspaper reprints the *Intelligencer* reached a far larger audience than through either the original Harding pamphlets or the Bowyer-David reprints of 1729 and 1730. The most important of the reprinting newspapers was *Mist's Weekly Journal*, an anti-ministerial paper with Jacobite leanings and an estimated circulation of 8,000–10,000. . . . *Fog's Weekly Journal* . . . appeared in September 1728 to replace *Mist's* after the government forced its cessation. . . . *Mist*'s and *Fog's* usually prefaced the reprinted *Intelligencers* with a hint at Swift's authorship (even though most of the reprinted papers were Sheridan's)." Ibid.

21. Swift lists his contributions in a letter to Pope on June 12, 1732. This is Swift's copy of the letter noted above in footnote 11. Jonathan Swift, *The Correspondence of Jonathan Swift,* ed. Harold Williams, 4:29–32.

22. Jonathan Swift, *Prose Works 9, Contributions to "The Tatler," The Examiner," The Spectator," and "The Intelligencer,"* ed. Temple Scott (London: George Bell, 1902).

23. Jonathan Swift, *Irish Tracts*, ed. Herbert Davis (Oxford: Blackwell, 1964).

24. The first five *Drapier's Letters* were written in 1724 and 1725 and published as a collected edition in 1725 according to Irvin Ehrenpreis, *Swift, The Man, his Works, and the Age* (Cambridge: Harvard University Press, 1983), 3:317. They aroused public opinion in Ireland against a proposed copper coin to be issued by William Wood, an English entrepreneur (ibid.,187). Their success made Swift a national hero. *A Modest Proposal* was published in October 1729. All of these pamphlets were printed in Ireland. *Gulliver's Travels* was published in London in 1726 according to Christopher Fox, ed., *Cambridge Companion to Jonathan Swift* (Cambridge: Cambridge University Press, 2003), xi.

25. *Correspondence,* ed. Williams, 4:30. This is part of Swift's attempt to disentangle his work on the *Intelligencer* from that of Sheridan, mentioned above in note 8.

26. Ibid.

27. *Correspondence,* ed. Ball, 4:41.

28. Swift's essay published as *Intelligencer 19*, was the paper's final issue. In this essay, Swift writes in the persona of "A. North," a landlord and Member of Parliament who complains about the lack of small coins and about the emigration to America from Ulster. Woolley suggests that the persona is modeled on Sir Arthur Acheson, with whom Swift had been staying for seven months, "Introductory Note to *Intelligencer* 19," 206.

29. Wolley, "General Introduction," 31.

30. Ibid.

31. Woolley publishes this satire as "*Intelligencer* 20," even though it went "entirely forgotten by the first generation of Swift's editors . . . [and] was first admitted to Swift's canon in 1779, in John Nichols's *Supplement* to Swift's *Works*." "Introductory Note to *Intelligencer* 20," 217.

32. His letter to Pope, quoted above in fn. 11 mentions that "there were hints enough" for a longer run of the journal.

33. Jonathan Swift, *Irish Tracts,* ed. Herbert Davis, 306.

34. Ehrenpreis, *Swift*, 3:207.

35. Ibid.

36. Ibid., 210.

37. Ibid.

38. Ibid., 211.

39. "In Lucass's by chance there lay the Fables writ by Mr Gay" (*Intelligencer* no. 10. 132). The final four lines which Sheridan added to the verse essay and Swift called 'slovenly' (see fn. 21 above) break out of this sophisticated voice into scatological invective.

40. *Intelligencer* no. 19, 209.

41. Ibid.

42. *Intelligencer* no. 15, 179.

43. *Intelligencer* no. 3, 63.

44. Ibid., 61.

45. *Intelligencer* no. 5, 79.

46. *Intelligencer* no.7, 95.

47. Ibid., 97.

48. *Intelligencer* no. 8, 104.

49. "The Tories! You are their Delight. / And should you act a diff'rent Part / Be grave and wise, 'twou'd break their Heart" (*Intelligencer* no. 8, 106). When Tim reads a copy of Gay's *Fables*, he takes the satire as a personal attack, but responds as though it is a party conflict: "*These Scriblers grow so bold of late/ Against us Ministers of State / Such Jacobites as he deserve,— / Dammee, I say, they ought to starve*" (*Intelligencer* no. 10, 133).

50. Wooley, "Introductory Note to *The Intelligencer* 8," 101–2.

51. The notes Swift made on English history show how he justified the Norman domination of Ireland. He tells how Henry II had taken up the challenge of civilizing Ireland from its "continual state of war" in Jonathan Swift, "Abstract and Fragment of History of England," *Miscellaneous and Autobiographical Pieces Fragments and Marginalia,* ed. Herbert Davis (Oxford: Blackwell, 1962). The Irish had submitted themselves to Henry's rule. Swift comments: "And indeed there is hardly any country, how renowned soever in ancient or modern story, which may not be traced from the like original. Neither can a nation come out from this state of confusion, until it is either reduced under one head at home, or by force or conquest becomes subject to a foreign administration" (5:76).

52. Swift's recognition of this change does not imply that the change started in his lifetime. Karl Bottigheimer points out that one explanation for the eclipse of the Anglo-Irish in Elizabethan times, is "the impact upon the English statesmen of Spanish New World colonial rule both in theory and in practice," in "Kingdom and Colony: Ireland in the Westward Enterprise, 1536–1660." *The Westward Enterprise,* ed. K. R. Andrews, N. P. Canny, and P. E. H. Hair (Detroit: Wayne State University Press, 1979), 51.

53. *Correspondence,* ed. Williams, 3:131–33.

54. Williams says, "Many rumours spread abroad of Swift's purpose in desiring to see Walpole—that he sought preferment for himself by conciliating the Prime Minister, that he was offered an English benefice at a price." (*Correspondence,* ed. Williams, 3:132 n 1).

55. *Correspondence,* ed. Williams, 3:132.

56. Ibid.

57. *Intelligencer* no. 15, 177.

58. *Correspondence*, ed. Williams, 3:132.

59. Ibid.

60. This perspective antedated 1643, as Nicholas Canny argues describing the Elizabethan period (quoted in Bottimger, "Kingdom and Colony," 50).

61. Patrick Kelly demonstrates this link in his study "Recasting a tradition: William Molyneux and the sources of *the Case of Ireland . . . Stated* (1869)," *Political Thought in Seventeenth-Century Ireland* (Cambridge: Cambridge University Press, 2000), 83–106.

62. Published in 1698, the essay was reprinted nine times to 1782, and Patrick Kelly calls it "the most significant Irish political pamphlet of the seventeenth and eighteenth centuries," 83.

63. Ibid., 90, 84.

64. Ibid., 84.

65. Ibid., 83 n.3.

66. Joseph McMinn, in Jonathan Swift, *Swift's Irish Pamphlets*, ed. Joseph McMinn, 79 n5.

67. David Armitage, *The Ideological Origins of the British Empire* (Cambridge: Cambridge University Press, 2000), 45.

68. Quoted in Armitage, *Ideological Origins,* 49.

69. Ibid., 157.

70. Swift "To the Whole People of Ireland." *Swift's Irish Pamphlets*, ed. Joseph McMinn, 79.

71. Ibid., 80.

72. Ehrenpreis summarizes Swift's political ideals at the time of his writing the *Examiner*: "he believes the national constitution is twofold, comprising the Established church as well as the machinery of state," Irvin Ehrenpris, *Acts of Implication* (Berkeley: University of California Press, 1980), 51.

73. Jonathan Swift, *The Examiner. Prose Works, 9*, ed. Temple Scott (London: George Bell, 1902), 9:92.

74. Mary Douglas, *Risk and Blame: Essays in Cultural Theory* (London: Routledge, 1992), 32.

75. Swift. "Short View." *Swift's Irish Pamphlets*, ed. Joseph McMinn (Gerrards Cross: Colin Smythe, 1991), 110.

76. Woolley's introduction to the annotated *Intelligencer* devotes fifteen pages to Sheridan, describing him as a "classicist, schoolmaster, translator, priest, poet, essayist, and wit," 6. Wooley also point out that Sheridan was a very successful schoolmaster as measured by the number of his students at Trinity College Dublin, 9.

77. Ehrenpreis summarizes the relationship as one of patronage: "He [Swift] admired Sheridan's skill as a teacher, respected his honesty, and felt protective in response to his poor health and fecklessness. He was godfather to Sheridan's third and favorite son; he was a debtor to Sheridan's vivacity, wit, and readiness to join Swift in the pursuit of trifles." *Swift,* 3:360.

78. Ibid., 367.

79. Woolley, "General Introduction," 24.

80. *Intelligencer* no. 6, 88.

81. Ibid., 89.

82. Sheridan's attribution is deliberately vague: "a *Fable* which I Read in a *Monkish Author.* He quotes for it one of the *Greek Mythologists*" (no. 6, 87). Woolley cannot find this in Aesop and suggests that it is one of Sheridan's personae. Woolley "Notes to *Intelligencer*

6," 91.

83. *The Intelligencer* no. 6, 87.

84. Woolley points out that Sheridan modifies material from Tacitus's *Agricola XXX*. Sheridan substitutes *solitudinem* for Tacitus's *pacem* (91). Woolley fails to point out that this particular comment on Roman imperialism is a pre-battle speech made by the Celtic leader fighting against the Romans. In context, the allusion looks like Sheridan's Celtic identification of the imperial Rome with imperial England.

85. *Intelligencer* no. 18, 198.

86. Ibid.

87. Brian Connery, *Representations of Swift*, ed. Brian Connery (Newark: University of Delaware Press, 2002).

88. Robert Mahoney, "Swift, Postcolonialism and Irish Studies: the Valence of Ambivalence," *Representations of Swift,* ed. Brian Connery (Newark: University of Delaware Press, 2002), 228.

89. Carole Fabricant, "Speaking for the Irish Nation" in Connery, 236–68.

90. Fabricant notes that in the *Drapier's Letters*—specifically *Drapier Four* in which the speaker complains that the English in Ireland are being conflated with the Savage Irish whom "our Ancestors conquered several Hundred Years ago"—Swift's speakers "at times embrace the collective category of 'us'—even on occasion expanding it to include African, American Indians, and other 'savages'—while in other instances strenuously affirming a more limited 'us,' defined by its 'purer' English roots," 242. Fabricant also points out the complexity of Swift's revelation of these ancestral roots. They go back to the Britons in Caesar's time who "painted their Bodies, or Cloathed themselves with the Skins of Beasts," 242.

91. Ibid.

92. Ehrenpreis, *Acts* 79/80.

93. Benedict Anderson, *Imagined Communities* (London: Verso, (1981) 1991), 58.

94. This phrase occurs in both *Intelligencer* no. 15 and in "A Short View," published in McMinn *Swift's Irish Pamphlets*, 111.

95. Joseph McMinn, appendix to Jonathan Swift, *Swift's Irish Pamphlets*, 183. McMinn says of the letter to the Archbishop, "An exasperated plea by Swift to the Archbishop to use his influence to promote economic and agricultural reforms." Of the first "Answer," McMinn says, "A weary review of the reasons for rising Protestant emigration from Ireland to the new colonies in America. Addressed to reformers like himself, Swift questions the very point of such appeals," 183.

96. Swift, "A Modest Proposal," *Swift's Irish Pamphlets*, ed. Joseph McMinn, 149.

97. *Correspondence,* ed. Williams, 4:50.

98. Ehrenpreis notes a similar attitude when he points out that in his 1735 edition of the Fifth Drapier letter Swift changes the term "rabble" (those eager to destroy images of William Wood) to "my faithful Friends the Common People" *Acts of Implication,* 82.

99. Swift, "Advice to the Free-Men of the City of *Dublin* in the Choice of a Member to Represent them in Parliament," *Irish Tracts 1728–1733*, ed. Herbert Davis (Oxford: Blackwell, 1979), 80.

Domestic, Political, and Moral Economies in Swift's Irish Writings

Jill Marie Bradbury

STUDIES OF THE ANGLO-IRISH IDENTITY OF JONATHAN SWIFT (1667–1745) have revealed a number of personas: "a coloniser, a colonist, an Enlightenment patriot, and an Englishman who became 'more Anglo-Irish than the Anglo-Irish themselves.' "[1] Swift's "ambivalences," to reference Robert Mahoney, are indicative of a specific moment in the development of British imperialism and Irish nationalism.[2] While his works invoked a broad social and political alliance among the "whole people of Ireland," such Patriot rhetoric belies the complexity of Swift's relationship to the Anglo-Irish and Gaelic communities. In what follows, I suggest that Swift's conflicted sense of identity marked his political economy, as well as his politics. Swift's writings on economic topics contributed to an emerging sense of Irish nationalism by articulating a communal response to the commercial, agricultural, and financial restrictions imposed by England. At the same time, the moralistic bent of these works suggests his frustration with the inability of the Irish to recognize and act in their own national self-interest. As a look at his financial records reveals, Swift personally struggled with and overcame the same factors he saw as obstacles to Ireland's ability to prosper in the face of English colonial domination. His eventual despair of persuading even the Anglo-Irish (let alone the natives) to see the political folly of their individual and collective actions is presaged in Gulliver's transformation into a misanthropic recluse. The alienated and embittered Gulliver is a figure for Swift's later disillusionment with the Irish populace; a "dis-identification" most acerbically detailed in *A Letter . . . Concerning the Weavers*.

A concern with economy, both domestic and political, pervaded Swift's life in many forms. Beginning in 1699, he kept detailed records of his household expenses for each year of his adult life. The extant volumes, though not complete, give an intimate view of his early domestic arrangements. Of particular interest in light of his published writings are the large purchases of English clothes he habitually made before returning to Ireland. Paul and Dorothy Thompson, modern editors of the account books, note, "It was Swift's custom, when leaving London for Ireland, to buy an unusual amount of clothing, which he may have felt was of superior quality to any he could get in Dublin."[3] Expenditures in 1704, 1709, and 1712 show a predilection for English goods at odds with Swift's published commitment to "buying Irish." The questions these purchases raise are not easily answered, though, for only a few volumes of the account books survive, nor do the entries for clothing expenditures in Ireland record whether they were for English or Irish goods. But the suggestion that Swift valued fine English products in his earlier years is supported by contemporary biographer W. H. Dilworth's remark that the young Swift was wont to save money only "to squander it away as soon as he reached London, upon a fine waistcoat, or some additional gaiety to his dress."[4] It is not surprising, then, that consumption of English goods became a prominent theme of his later writings on Irish economic issues.

By the time he became dean of St. Patrick's in Dublin, however, Swift had developed a strict method of personal economy which transformed frugality into charity. Both the account books and observations by his contemporaries attest to frequent and generous support for indigent members of his parishes. Careful economy allowed him to manage well on the meager funds he collected through church appointments. Notations of gifts such as "poor womn 2 s 8d 1/2" proliferate throughout the accounts.[5] In a letter to Alexander Pope, Swift claimed that he donated one-third of his annual income to charity, an estimate borne out by later editors of his accounts. His beneficence was also well known to his friends and acquaintances. Biographer John Hawkesworth described Swift's habit of making small loans out of his personal funds to deserving shopkeepers and tradesmen, his patronage of poor street peddlers, and regulation of beggars within the environs of St. Patrick's. Yet this generosity was always tempered by encouragement of proper work ethics. In Hawkesworth's words, "He was indeed diligent to relieve the poor, and at the same time to encourage industry, even in the lowest station."[6] Swift's zeal to encourage prudent personal economy was such that he fired his own servants if their expenditures exceeded the generous wages he paid them. For those who lived sparingly enough to accumulate a year's salary, he paid them interest on their savings.[7] Such liberality was funded through Swift's own parsimony.[8] After his death, Swift's entire estate went to charity as well, to establish a hospital for the mentally ill. Through careful financial management, he was able to live comfortably and better the lives of those in his community. This personal success in managing domestic economy was fundamental to Swift's public discussion of Ireland's political economy, as it fueled his conviction that the Irish people could overcome the political, legal, and economic disadvantages to material prosperity that they faced only through careful and disciplined habits of living.

After his appointment as dean of St. Patrick's, Swift took up public discussion of Ireland's political and economic affairs. The ten-year period of his engagement with these issues saw the publication of a remarkable series of works, such as *The Drapier's Letters*, *Gulliver's Travels*, *Maxims Controlled in Ireland*, and *A Modest Proposal*. His earliest works approach the problems of Ireland's political and economic situation obliquely. In *The Story of an Injured Lady* (1707), Swift discusses England's political subjection of Ireland allegorically. Ireland is the "Injured Lady," and England, the "inconstant Gentleman" who seduces and then discards her. Describing the abuses she has suffered, the Injured Lady complains that Ireland must export its products in their raw state and is unable to reap the economic benefits of manufacturing finished goods. This criticism of protectionist legislation passed by England, such as the 1699 Woolen Act, was a commonplace charge and Swift's objections lack both specific context and an underlying theory. Indeed, economic concerns are only of tangential interest in *The Story of an Injured Lady*, the bulk of which targets the political ramifications of Scotland and England's union in 1707.

The first tract focused solely on economic themes, *A Proposal for the Universal Use of Irish Manufactures*, was published in 1720. This pamphlet demonstrates Swift's increasing grasp of Ireland's complex situation and introduced several key elements of his economic views, such as the emphasis on "buying Irish" and the need to export goods rather than specie. The first two precepts were commonplaces in mercantilist writings of the seventeenth century and his commentary reveals a superficial understanding of economic theory at the time. While Swift attacked Irish landlords for pursuing markets (such as wool) that had been restricted by English laws, he did not recommend other industries the Irish might develop to boost their revenue from exports. Furthermore, in discussing the Irish trade with France, he admonished that it relied on the export of currency, rather than commodities. This concern with the seepage of specie from Ireland recurs at the end of the pamphlet, with the ironic remark that the problems with Ireland's money supply were worsened by export of specie and melting down of silver plate. But as Charles Davenant and others had come to realize by this time, the loss of specie from a kingdom was not in itself a cause for concern unless there was no corresponding influx of imports or profits from exports. English contemporaries, such as Sir Dudley North and Henry Martyn, were already moving beyond economic protectionism to acknowledge the dynamic nature of trade and its growth potential. Either Swift was unaware of works by Josiah Child, Nicholas Barbon, Davenant, and other exponents of "mercantilist liberalism," or he had not yet considered how these ideas would apply to Ireland.[9]

One noteworthy aspect of Swift's analysis of commerce in the *Proposal* is the attention he paid to the political aspects of economic behavior. With tongue in cheek, he writes, "It is wonderful to observe the Biases among our People in favour of *Things*, *Persons*, and *Wares* of all Kinds that come from England."[10] Not being immune from it himself, Swift understood both the cachet of English superiority and its role in the continued dominance of Ireland. The challenge was to convince his readers, the "Persons of Quality" who influenced public tastes, that their own self-interest lay in resisting colonial co-option through sumptuary discipline. Swift's appreciation of how sociopolitical power could be gained by molding and manipulating economic behavior is second only to Berkeley's later analysis in *The Querist*. But overall, Swift's early economic writings demonstrate only a limited understanding of the complex factors that hindered Ireland's agricultural and commercial development and tend, instead, to recycle stock complaints and remedies. While aspects of his views are present in the early works, it was through writing *Gulliver's Travels* and *The Drapier's Letters* that Swift came to a nuanced understanding of the *system* of exploitation under which Ireland labored.[11]

Gulliver's Travels and *The Drapier's Letters* touch on many of the issues raised in the Irish pamphlets. Domestic economy and consumption, foreign trade, money and finance, and territorial conquest all figure in Gulliver's many journeys. The novel delivers a scathing critique of England's maritime imperialism and a more general satire on the all-too-human lusts for money and material advancement. In several parts, it is also concerned with the serious problems contemporary Ireland faced. These issues are addressed more directly in *The Drapier's Letters*, which attacks the constitutional basis of England's legislative control of Ireland. Here, Swift tackles the complex concept of monetary value, bringing abstract issues of finance to a concrete level in his efforts to persuade the Irish and Anglo-Irish community to reject Wood's coinage, and renews his argument for domestic economy on the individual level as a strategy for regenerating domestic economy on the national level.[12] Both *Gulliver's Travels* and *The Drapier's Letters* follow the early tracts in articulating what we might call a moral economy. In the section on the Houyhnhnms, Swift described an idealized socio-economy that is agrarian, austere, and self-sufficient. While critics have argued that the Houyhnhnms are as much a satiric target as the other cultures Gulliver visits, their society is founded on the kind of virtuous and self-interested domestic economy that Swift both practiced and preached. Similarly, *The Drapier's Letters* reiterates his call for personal sacrifice and frugality in the name of political and national unity. Of the two texts, however, *Gulliver's Travels* ultimately reveals more about future developments in his economic thinking, for Gulliver's expulsion from the utopian world of the Houyhnhnms foreshadows Swift's eventual despair of and retreat from Irish affairs.

Among other things, *Gulliver's Travels* satirizes the massive apparatus of English mercantile colonialism. From the opening pages, Swift represents Gulliver's journeys as partaking in the English trading empire. Framed as a mock travel narrative, the text emphasizes the integral connections between exploration and commerce. As did the sixteenth-century merchant adventurers of the East India, Royal African, and South Sea companies, Gulliver undertakes his travels into new lands in search of discoveries, knowledge, and profits. Each of his voyages is motivated by desire for material gain, as well as curiosity and thirst for adventure. The biographical information at the beginning of his narrative emphasizes the importance of monetary considerations. During his apprenticeship to a surgeon, Gulliver studies navigation and subjects "useful to those who intend to travel, as I always believed it would be some time or other my Fortune to do."[13] Swift emphasizes the double meaning of the word "fortune" a few lines later, when Gulliver remarks that he eventually became a ship's surgeon on merchant vessels sailing in the East and West Indies to make "some additions to my Fortune" (40). Indeed, Gulliver is able to increase his financial position only through foreign trade, for though he tries several times to establish practices on land (i.e., in the domestic economy), business simply does not go well. Thus it is that he accepts the "advantageous offer" to serve on the trading ship bound for the South Seas that leaves him shipwrecked in Lilliput. At the start of part 2, Gulliver offers the explanation that, "having been condemned by Nature and Fortune to an active and restless life," he undertook a new voyage (91). For this voyage, he invests his stock, "Part in Money and Part in Goods, in Hopes to improve my Fortunes" (89). The third and fourth voyages bring a greater share of responsibility (and thus profit) in the trading enterprise. Part 3 sees Gulliver sharing in the command of a ship and taking charge of entrêpot trading. In part 4, he becomes captain of a vessel sailing to the South Seas to trade. Clearly, his lot in life is inextricable from his prospects in colonial enterprise.

Financially, Gulliver benefits from all but the last of his journeys. Upon leaving Lilliput, he takes sixteen cattle and sheep for improvement of the English breeds, and fifty pouches of tiny gold coins. Having first made "a considerable profit" exhibiting the cattle, Gulliver then sells them for six hundred pounds. Through "the Fineness of the Fleeces," the sheep will benefit both Gulliver and the woolen industry, the linchpin of the English economy (89). Curiosities and gifts of gold are also turned to advantage when he returns home from Brobdingnag and Luggnagg. At the end of part 4, however, Gulliver repudiates the monetary benefits of his journeys. Holding himself to the standards of Houyhnhnms, he asserts that he writes "for the noblest End, to inform and instruct Mankind" and "without any View towards Profit or Praise" (263). In this transformation, we see Swift's desire for the moral economy of the Houyhnhnms and yet, through the satiric framework of the narrative, his acknowledgment of its practical impossibility.

Swift uses Gulliver's transactions in foreign lands to critique not only the mercantile enterprise, but English and, more generally, European colonialism as well. Gulliver's sojourns often begin with stereotypical musings about the "savages" he expects to meet, but each travel reverses his views. Upon arrival in Houyhnhnmland, for example, he declares his intentions to submit himself to the first native he meets and to "purchase" his life with fetishes, the "Bracelets, Glass Rings, and other Toys, which sailors usually provide themselves with in those Voyages" (207). But when Gulliver does encounter the natives of the various lands he finds himself in, he acts in a manner contrary to that of the colonial aggressor. In Lilliput, he is tempted to exert his superior force but refrains, not simply from fear of their arrows, but also from "the Promise of Honour I made them." Having been fed and watered by their collective efforts, Gulliver considers himself "bound by the Laws of Hospitality" (44). Similarly, he refuses to act as colonial aggressor toward Belfuscu, declaring before the Lilliputian council that he "would never be an instrument of bringing a free and brave People into Slavery" (67).

His situation is inverted in Brobdingnag, where he finds himself an enslaved animal. In a typical Swiftian reversal, Gulliver becomes the kind of curiosity that he would bring home from his own travels. After being overworked to the point of near death by the farmer who finds him, Gulliver is purchased by the queen of Brobdingnag. Thereafter, he lives in a cage and often reflects on his disenfranchised status. Comparing himself to a tame Canary Bird, he remarks, "I was the Favourite of a great King and Queen, and the Delight of the whole Court, but it was on such a Foot as ill became the Dignity of human Kind" (138). The comparison is apt, for canaries are native to the Canary Islands, then a French colony. Gulliver's affinity with creatures from colonial lands is further emphasized by his traumatic abduction by a monkey, which treats him as its own offspring (123). While Carole Fabricant likens Gulliver's objectification in these scenes to the experience of the Irish, Swift's use of animals from foreign colonies to parallel his condition in Brobdingnag indicts European imperialism in general.[14] Gulliver's experience as an oddity allows him to see through the eyes of the Other, and his conversation with the king of Brobdingnag further develops this reversal of savage and European identities. Seen from the perspective of Brobdingnag's king, Gulliver's ilk are "the most pernicious Race of little odious Vermin that Nature ever suffered to crawl upon the Surface of the Earth" (130).

In Gulliver's residence with the Houyhnhnms, this transposition of human and animal, master and servant, civilized and savage takes new forms. From his initial identification of the Hooyhnhnms as animals, to his shocked recognition of the Yahoos as human beings, Gulliver's experience implodes his understanding of self and other. The resulting reification of the virtues and rationality of the Houyhnhnms persists even after he returns to England: he turns away in horror from his own reflection and is pleased to be told he walks and speaks like a horse. Far from promoting English and European civilization as superior to the other cultures he encounters, Gulliver's journeys end in his suggestion that Europe needs to be civilized by the Houyhnhnms (264). This reversal opens up textual space for the unsparing mockery of imperialist expansion that immediately follows. Swift singles out England for particular scorn, in Gulliver's remark that these "Scruples with relation to the distributive justice of Princes" who conquer other lands of course do not apply to the "*British* nation," whose monarchs are "an Example to the whole World for their Wisdom, Care, and Justice in planting Colonies" (265).

Throughout *Gulliver's Travels*, then, Swift develops a multifaceted critique of colonialism. The semantic play on Fortune as both fate and financial status in the opening pages can be read as a satire of manifest destiny, an expose of the profit motive that lay behind it. The respect Gulliver shows for the cultures and institutions that he encounters provides a moral counterweight to the exploitative behavior of European colonizers. These general themes take a specific Irish context in the *Drapier's Letters*. In this series of seven pamphlets on the Wood's halfpence patent, Swift refined his argument against the constitutionality of England's political, legislative, and economic dominance over Ireland. As Carole Fabricant notes, each letter addresses a different audience and Swift adapts his rhetoric to suit each.[15] While the third letter makes the most detailed and legalistic case for Ireland's equality with England, he takes pains in the first and fourth letters to make his reasoning intelligible for all ranks of Irish society. In doing so, as many scholars have noted, the *Drapier's Letters* contribute to the founding of Irish nationalism by appealing to a broad social and political alliance. But this shared identity is economic, as well. The Irish are united in the material consequences that will follow if Wood's halfpence were to become accepted currency. Swift's dramatization of Gresham's law (bad money drives out good) frequently emphasizes that Wood's coinage will impact all Irish citizens equally. Indeed, the Drapier confesses that "I have been sometimes tempted to wish that this Project of *Wood* might succeed; because I reflected with some Pleasure what a *Jolly Crew* it would bring over among us of *Lords* and *Squires* and *Pensioners* of *Both Sexes*, and Officers *Civil* and *Military*; where we should live together as merry and sociable as Beggars."[16] Swift calls on the higher classes of Irish society to recognize their shared interest with the lower classes in this matter; to put aside the divisions of rank and join with the "whole people of Ireland" in boycotting the base copper farthings. In this appeal to a unity of economic interest, Swift transcends his own identification with the Anglo-Irish elite and sets the stage for late eighteenth and early nineteenth-century nationalism.

In comparison with his earlier writings, Swift's integration of diverse issues into a single passage is one of the more striking aspects of these pamphlets. The first letter connects Ireland's inability to mint its own coin with the lack of political representation in England, and this to the problem of absentee landlords *(DL*, 5). Swift's urgent calls for national unity are based on the interrelated economic effects of Wood's halfpence. Once Ireland has been ruined by Wood's coinage, "*Gentlemen of Estates* will all turn off their *Tenants* for want of Payment . . . then they will turn their own *Farmers*, *as too many of them do already*, run all the *Sheep* where they can, keeping only such *Cattle* as are necessary" (*DL*, 7). The litany of consequences makes multiple points about contemporary economic problems, including the shift in land use from tillage to pasture, the racking of customary rents, the loss of profits from estates to consumer imports, and the general disintegration of traditional structures of economic interdependency. Rather than examining several topics sequentially, but discretely, the *Drapier's Letters* discusses multiple ideas relationally. The structural logic of the letters indicates a shift to a more systematic and integrated perspective than is seen in Swift's earlier writings. By depicting Wood's coinage as having causal reverberations throughout an entire socio-economy, he was able to make an even more effective argument for Irish unity against English oppression.

While the *Drapier's Letters* showcases Swift's greater understanding of Irish political economy, *Gulliver's Travels* contains a more general survey and critique of diverse kinds of political economy. Throughout the narrative, Swift indicates his preference for a pre-industrial, agrarian, and self-sufficient system. In the manner of sixteenth- and seventeenth-century travel narratives, Gulliver's accounts of the countries he visits detail their cultures, manners, morals, and public institutions. Description of the kinds of domestic and political economy practiced is central to this commentary. Among other topics, Gulliver surveys the lands, agricultural practices, domestic and vocational education of children, institutions of public charity, systems of taxation, and laws governing commerce. Throughout, he makes positive and negative comparisons to England and Europe that function as a vehicle for Swift's political satire. As with the descriptions of other British and European social institutions, Swift uses initially Gulliver's chauvinistic perspective to satirize Enlightenment pride in the superiority of the modern.

Allan Bloom has argued that the four books of *Gulliver's Travels* divide into ancient and modern models, with Swift expressing a strong preference for classical politics and philosophy (241). This general pattern holds as well in the various archetypes of political economy depicted. Thus, Lilliput and Laputa/Balnibarbi represent the flaws of English financial and mercantile policies. Gulliver views the laws and government institutions of Lilliput with respect, but describes them as degenerated from the original model by "the gradual Increase of Party and Faction" (73). For both the monarch and his ministers, public finance has become an instrument to manipulate to achieve personal motives, rather than for the good of the country as a whole. By linking the expense of maintaining Gulliver, who the Lilliputian king wishes to use to conquer Belfuscu, to public finance, Swift criticizes the Williamite innovation of funding wars through loans from the Bank of England.[17] Similarly, he uses Gulliver's description of Laputa to attack England's economic dominance over Ireland.[18] Laputa's king is uninterested in learning about the countries Gulliver has visited, being preoccupied with more abstruse matters of philosophy and mathematics (160). The king's indifference to good stewardship is manifest in the physical environment of the capital and its rural provinces. Though the land seems fertile, Gulliver remarks, "I never knew a Soil so unhappily cultivated, Houses so ill contrived and so ruinous, or a People whose Countenances and Habit expressed so much Misery and Want" (167).

In relating the kinds of social, political, and economic institutions he encountered during his travels, Gulliver has more appreciation for Brobdingnag. Through its monarch's naïve perspective on modern innovations of statecraft, Swift mocks English/European systems of government, institutions, and achievements. Public finance is shown to be a paradoxical concept when, despite Gulliver's explanation, the king "was still at a Loss how a Kingdom could run out of its Estate like a private Person." Similarly, Swift critiques European foreign policy through the king's query as to why countries become involved in affairs outside their borders, "unless upon the Score of Trade or Treaty, or to defend the Coasts with [their] Fleet" (131). In comparison to the other books, Gulliver does not describe Brobdingnag's economy or agriculture in much detail. He recounts that they value agriculture, husbandry, and manufacturing above all other pursuits and forms of knowledge, but he focuses more on the system of education than on the political economy of the country. As Brobdingnag seems to represent the most realistic, or perhaps, the most attainable ideal in the *Travels*, it seems odd that Swift would not take this opportunity to describe its political economy. The elision might be attributed to the negative focus of Swift's satire in general or to the limitations of his economic philosophy. Swift's Irish tracts as a whole are similar to his other works in presenting an unattainable ideal, rather than a pragmatic alternative to the systems he castigates.

It is in Gulliver's final voyage that Swift describes an idyllic socioeconomy. In narrating his life among the Houyhnhnms, Gulliver emphasizes the primitive aspects of their agriculture and industry. Uncultivated grains and grass grow in fields naturally demarcated by rows of trees, building materials are organic and unfinished, and rudimentary tools are shaped from flint. After some time, he adapts to this nonindustrial, noncommercial, and capital-free economy by manufacturing clothes from skins, shoes from wood, and bedding from hemp and feathers. Of his life among the Houyhnhnms, Gulliver remarks, "I had settled my little Oeconomy to my own Heart's Content" (249). His is a simple life taken up by the manufacture of goods to satisfy his basic needs, a prelapsarian diet of honey, milk, and bread, and freedom from the vices and passions of mankind (250). Through conversations with his "Master," Gulliver learns to see England and Europe as inferior to Houyhnhnm society, which is governed by friendship, benevolence, and a natural economy. The Houyhnhnms espouse the communitarian principle that "all Animals had a Title to their Share in the Productions of the Earth," though the relative enslavement of the Yahoos and the rigid vocational hierarchy among the Houyhnhnms themselves indicate that this is not an egalitarian society (229). Luxury commodities are unknown, as is also money, except in the negative analogy of the Yahoos' fascination with shiny, multicolored stones found in the fields (236).

In Gulliver's depiction of the Houyhnhnms, Louis Landa finds a rejection of contemporary commercial ideologies: "The economy of Houyhnhnmland is in effect a localized, idealized agrarian provincialism, far from the cosmopolitan ideal pervasive in the mercantile vision of an entire world providentially designed in a vast economic nexus and organized to bring the world into a state of universal amity."[19] The Houyhnhnms represent reason, moderation, and an abstemious lifestyle, all things Swift advocated as paths to solving Ireland's problems. Unlike the other societies, the Houyhnhnms are governed by a moral, rather than a political economy. Gulliver's narratives about Lilliput, Brobdingnag, and Laputa/Lagoda dwell on the topic of regnal "oeconomy," while his depiction of the Houyhnhnms emphasizes personal virtue and self-regulation. What Gulliver admires there is a political economy in which politics play no part. It is, rather, a moral economy arranged and managed according to the highest standards of rational behavior. And it was these standards to which Swift held the Irish in order to improve their material and political situation. While I agree with Landa that "the Houyhnhnms are norms to be taken seriously," I would add that the tenability of their system is undermined by Gulliver's eventual expulsion from it.[20]

In writing *Gulliver's Travels*, then, Swift considered an array of ways in which political, social, and economic institutions were intertwined. He indicated his preference for older models of husbandry, agriculture, industry, and trade, while at the same time casting doubt on the possibility of keeping any such complex arrangement free from the corrupting influence of human passions. *Gulliver's Travels* crystallized his perspective on the politics and economics of Irish-English relations, and this viewpoint marks his remaining treatises. In the tracts published after 1725, Swift stressed a new element in his discussion of Irish economic affairs. He had come to realize that the analytic generality assumed in conventional economic discourse served political purposes in England's rise to dominance as a world power. While authors emphasized the particularity and precedence of English economic interests when discussing commercial policy, their suggestions were justified as reflecting principles common to all nations. Swift's post–*Gulliver's Travels* writings disputed the concept of an abstract commercial polity by considering trade and national policy in terms of Ireland's situation as an English colony.[21] These works were, in Salim Rashid's words, "the inspiration" for an Irish school of economic development which sought appropriate solutions to the peculiar problems of their country.[22]

Swift did not reject outright the principles articulated by English writers. He accepted the mercantilist stress on self-sufficiency in domestic consumption, the condemnation of importing goods, the importance of exporting finished, rather than raw goods, and the benefits of keeping wealth in the kingdom. But he argued that Ireland's colonial status refuted other central "maxims" of seventeenth and early eighteenth-century thought, such as the belief in international trade as the key to national prosperity, the truism that people are the "riches of a nation," and the monetary and financial theories developed by English writers. In *A Short View of the State of Ireland* (1728) and *Maxims Controlled in Ireland* (1724), Swift argues that Ireland's constitutional subordination to England invalidated the supposedly general principles of economic growth. In refuting the mercantilist stress on international trade, Swift notes that a country subjected to the Navigation Acts was "denied the Liberty of exporting their native Commodities and Manufactures, wherever they please."[23] Ireland's political situation also thwarts the general rule that "the first Cause of a Kingdom's thriving is the Fruitfulness of the Soil, to produce the Necessaries and Conveniences of Life; not only sufficient for the Inhabitants, but for Exportation into other Countries," as well as the second principle of economic growth, "the Industry of the People, in working up all their native Commodities, to the last Degree of Manufacture."[24] While Ireland was well-endowed with natural resources that would yield products for manufacture and export, British laws discouraged the development of such industries. As a consequence, its commercial potential went to waste and its people without work.

In contrast to the mercantilist stress on increased trade, Swift advocated full employment and a strong agricultural sector as solutions to Ireland's economic distress. Yet Ireland was unable to employ its large population for lack of encouragement to manufacturing, and agriculture. Seeking opportunities for work, the Irish people emigrated to the outer colonies of the British empire. The Irish experience thus confuted another "undisputed Maxim in government, that the people are the riches of the nation."[25] Other hindrances imposed on the Irish economy by its political subordination to England included control over shipping, ports, and coinage. Ireland's inability to produce its own coin contributed to a chronic shortage of small change, which hampered market transactions.[26] Both the Irish economy and the coinage situation were worsened by the transfer of public funds, manufacturing profits, and rents to England via absentee landlords. As Swift concludes, "I would be glad to know by what secret Method, it is, that we grow a rich and flourishing People, without Liberty, Trade, Manufactures, Inhabitants, Money, or the Privilege of Coining, without Industry, Labour, or Improvements of Lands."[27]

Though Swift's writings after *Gulliver's Travels* emphasized the inapplicability of English ideas about national prosperity to Ireland, he continued to view the Irish as complicit in their economic woes. As Oliver Ferguson remarks, "Swift was realist enough to see that since no major change in England's Irish policy was possible, especially so long as it was directed by Walpole, the Irish should do what they could to help themselves."[28] Throughout his pamphlets, Swift targeted greed, vanity, indolence, and dishonesty as a chief source of Ireland's woes. He encouraged Irish farmers to follow sound agricultural practices and landlords to promote food production over cattle grazing and exhorted manufacturers to produce quality wares and merchants to engage in honest business practices. Moral economy was as important to Swift as it was to the Houyhnhnms. Swift also badgered the Irish to improve their situation by exercising control over their habits of consumption. Self-sufficiency was a recurrent and insistent theme in his later discussions of economic issues. In private correspondence, sermons, and published works, he urged the clergy, nobility, and gentry to set an example for the lower classes by wearing only Irish manufactures. At a time when English writers were beginning to concentrate on the mechanisms of commerce, Swift continued to focus on the actions of individuals as a means of achieving collective interests.

Swift's critique of English theories of commerce reaches its most impassioned peak in *A Modest Proposal* and the posthumously published *An Answer to the Craftsman* (1758). Stylistically similar to *A Modest Proposal*, *An Answer to the Craftsman* offers an ironic literalization of William Petty's proposal to depopulate Ireland for England's benefit. The projector-persona recommends converting all Irish land to cattle grazing, retaining only enough people necessary to manage the industry. The remainder of Ireland's population would be exported to serve as soldiers in foreign wars. Agricultural goods would be exported in their raw state to England alone, while only fully manufactured English goods would be imported. Only leather strips stamped in England would be allowed to circulate as money, while all taxes and rents would be sent to England. "That which maketh me more zealously bent upon this Scheme," the projector explains with typical Swiftian irony, "is my Desire of living in Amity with our neighbouring Brethren; for we have already tried all other Means."[29]

Earlier works such as *A Short View* and *Maxims* argue that conventional economic wisdom failed to address the Irish situation. *An Answer to the Craftsman* takes this argument to its logical extreme to show how policies guided by English theories would destroy Ireland's economy. Similarly, Swift's advocacy of commercial self-sufficiency as a means to rescue Ireland from its deeply entrenched economic woes reaches its zenith (or perhaps nadir) in *A Modest Proposal*. "Viewed from one angle, his plan was not altogether new," Ferguson comments; "it was but the logical extension of a plea Swift had made unceasingly to the Irish since 1720: domestic consumption of domestic production."[30] The despair and frustration vented in these tracts arose from Swift's success in being a rational and self-interested individual, when others could not or would not conform to such an ideal.

Gulliver's Travels played a central role in both Swift's commentary on Irish economic affairs and his ambivalent affiliation with Irish economic identity. Written during the period of his most intense involvement with Irish monetary, commercial, and agrarian difficulties, the text evinces a new level of sophistication in the critique of English mercantile colonialism. At the same time, *Gulliver's Travels* adumbrates Swift's eventual disillusionment with his public role as M. B. Drapier. At the end of his travels, Gulliver must live in England and write for the instruction of the degenerate Yahoos. As both Carole Fabricant and Patrick Reilly observe, Gulliver's final, reluctant recognition of kinship with both Yahoos and Houyhnhnms parallels Swift's own uneasy identification with the Anglo-Irish and native Irish communities.[31] Swift, like Gulliver, must live in exile, surrounded by people he viewed as degenerate and savage, and write for their edification. In the *Answer to a Letter From Unknown Hands*, Swift compared the intellect of the Gaelic Irish to that of animals. The native Irish are an "uncultivated people" living in an "idle, savage, beastly, thievish manner of life."[32] Reversing the *Drapier's Letters*, the final Irish tract turns this association of the Gaelic with savagery onto the nation as a whole. This rhetorical move suggests Swift's bitter frustration at failing to convince the Irish to adopt the models of moral, domestic and political economy presented in his Irish writings. In *A Letter . . . Concerning the Weavers,* he describes Ireland and the entire Irish population as a species apart from all others:

> I cannot reflect on the singular condition of this Country, different from all others upon the face of the Earth . . . without often examining, as I pass the streets whether those animals which come in my way with two legs and human faces, clad and erect, be of the same species with what I have seen very like them in England, as to the outward Shape, but differing in their notions, natures, and intellectuals more than any two kinds of Brutes in a forest.[33]

In this passage, the public-spirited Drapier has vanished, replaced by the misanthropic and alienated Gulliver.

NOTES

1. Eileen Douglas et. al., "Introduction" in *Locating Swift: Essays from Dublin on the 250th Anniversary of the Death of Jonathan Swift* (New York: Four Courts Press, 1984), 17–18

2. Robert Mahoney, "Swift, Postcolonialism, and Irish Studies: The Valence of Ambivalence," in *Representations of Swift*, ed. Brian Connery (Newark: University of Delaware Press, 2002), 230–31.

3. Paul and Dorothy Thompson, *The Account Books of Jonathan Swift* (Newark: University of Delaware Press, 1984), lxxix.

4. W. H. Dilworth, *The Life of Dr. Jonathan Swift* (London, 1758). Rpt. in *Three Biographical Pamphlets, 1745–1758* (New York: Garland Publishers, 1975), 15.

5. Thompson, *Account Books*, 13.

6. John Hawkesworth, *An Account of the Life of the Revd. Jonathan Swift* (London, 1755). Rpt. in *Three Biographical Pamphlets,* 35.

7. Hawkesworth, *Life of the Revd. Jonathan Swift*, 34.

8. "Swift turned all the evil of excessive frugality upon himself. It induced him to walk when he had been used to ride, and he would then say he had earned a shilling or eighteenpence which he had a right to do as he pleased with, and which he constantly applied to his usual charities, which by this expedient he could continue and yet expend less upon the whole than before" (Hawkesworth, *Life of the Revd. Jonathan Swift,* 36).

9. Patrick Kelly notes that the sale catalog for Swift's books contains titles by writers such as Child and Davenant, but suggests Swift did not engage with new theories of commerce discussed by English or Irish writers. Kelly asserts that despite the range of Swift's personal library, "there is little indication he was familiar with the more sophisticated Irish writings of the later 1720s and 1730s, such as those of Prior, Bindon, and Dobbs" ("Swift on Money and Economics," 141). A detailed discussion of "mercantilist liberalism" can be found in Terence Hutchison, *Before Adam Smith: The Emergence of Political Economy 1662–1776* (Cambridge: Basil Blackwell, 1988, rpt. 1991), 86ff.

10. Jonathan Swift, *Swift's Irish Pamphlets*, ed. Joseph McMinn (New York: Barnes and Noble Books, 1991), 53.

11. Swift's early economic writings also lack the coherence of an underlying model. In *A Proposal for the Universal Use of Irish Manufactures*, for example, commentary on the use of Irish goods is linked sequentially, but not logically, to arguments about the near-sightedness of Irish shopkeepers, the general exploitation of Ireland by England, the racking of the Irish peasantry by landlords, and recent proposals for a national Irish bank. Unlike Swift's later pamphlets, these discrete sections are not brought together into a methodical discussion of Ireland's economic problems. In some respects, the lack of an underlying model can be attributed to the state of economic thought in general. While economic historians frequently laud seventeenth and early eighteenth-century writers for developing a rudimentary model of an interrelated and self-adjusting economic system, much work during this period treated issues such as money, employment, prices, interest rates, trade levels, exchange rates, and so forth as independent variables. It is primarily from the 1750s on that we begin to see an interest in the general system of commerce, in works such as Cantillon's *Essay on the Nature of Commerce in General.*

12. The financial and monetary dimensions of Swift's appeal to an Irish national community are explored by Sean Moore in " 'Our Irish Copper-Farthen Dean': Swift's Drapier's Letters, the 'Forging' of a Modernist Anglo-Irish Literature, and the Atlantic World of Paper Credit," *Atlantic Studies* 2, no. 1 (2005): 65–92.

13. Jonathan Swift, *Gulliver's Travels*, ed. Christopher Fox (New York: Bedford/St. Martin's, 1995), 39. Subsequent citations given in the text.

14. Carole Fabricant, "Swift the Irishman," in Chris Fox, ed., *The Cambridge Companion to Swift* (Cambridge: Cambridge University Press, 2003), 68.

15. Fabricant, "Swift the Irishman," 56.

16. Jonathan Swift, *Jonathan Swift: The Drapier's Letters and Other Works, 1724–1725*, ed. Herbert Davis (Oxford: Basil Blackwell, 1966), 59. Subsequent citations given in the text as *DL*.

17. Christopher Fox, "Introduction," *Gulliver's Travels*, 5.

18. Claude Rawson, "The Injured Lady and the Drapier: A Reading of Swift's Irish Tracts," in *Prose Studies* 3 (1980): 21.

19. Louis Landa, "The Dismal Science in Houyhnhnmland," *Novel* 13 (1979): 49.

20. Landa, "The Dismal Science in Houyhnhnmland," 38.

21. "I have often taken notice," he remarks in *A Proposal that the Ladies and Women of Ireland should appear constantly in Irish Manufactures* (1729), "that there is no topic so fallacious . . . as to argue how we ought to act in Ireland from the example of England, Holland, [or] France" (21).

22. "The Irish School of Economic Development" in *The Manchester School of Economic Thought* 56 (1988): 348.

23. Jonathan Swift, *The Prose Works of Jonathan Swift*, ed. Herbert Davis (Oxford: Shakespeare Head Press, 1948), 3:8.

24. Ibid., 3:5–6.

25. Ibid., 3:134.

26. Swift frequently ridiculed Irish proposals to alleviate Ireland's shortage of coin with substitutes for money. However, in *A Letter on Maculla's Project about Half-Pence and a New One Proposed* (1729), Swift suggests alleviating the coinage woes by minting copper coins. Unlike Wood's tokens, the intrinsic value of these coins would be guaranteed by a "club" of lenders who would agree to exchange the copper half-pence for gold or silver on demand for a period of seven to ten years. This proposal offers another example of Swift's belief that frugality, coupled with an understanding of the relation between public and private interest, could enable the Irish to solve their economic problems without reliance on or interference from England.

27. Swift, *Prose Works*, 3:9.

28. Oliver Ferguson, "The Last Proposals," in *Jonathan Swift: A Collection of Critical Essays*, ed. Claude Rawson (Upper Saddle River, N.J.: Prentice Hall, 1995), 280.

29. Jonathan Swift, *Jonathan Swift: Irish Tracts, 1728–1733* ed. Herbert Davis (Oxford: Basil Blackwell, 1955), 177.

30. Ferguson, "The Last Proposals," 283.

31. Fabricant, "Swift the Irishman," 67; Reilly, "The Displaced Person: Swift and Ireland," in *Swift Studies* 8 (1993): 68.

32. Swift, *Irish Tracts*, 89.

33. Ibid, 65.

Anglo-Irish Antiquarianism and the Transformation of Irish Identity, 1750–1800

Lesa Ní Mhunghaile

FROM A RELIGIOUS, POLITICAL, AND CULTURAL PERSPECTIVE, EIGHTEENTH-century Ireland was a diverse society with various confessions and ethnic groupings living side by side in a state of "tense co-existence."[1] These groups consisted of a Catholic majority, a dominant Anglican minority, Presbyterians, and a number of other nonconformists such as Huguenots, Quakers, and Palatines. The ethnic background of these diverse communities included native Gael and Old English, as well as post-Reformation settlers consisting primarily of the New English and Ulster-Scots. During the course of the eighteenth century the descendants of New English settlers came to view themselves as "Irish" and this new sense of identity found its expression in antiquarian literature. Protestant antiquarians and historians, many of whom were directly or indirectly involved in the establishment of the Royal Irish Academy in 1785, played a significant role in the forging of an Anglo-Irish identity, although even within the antiquarian circle, contesting notions existed.

Although an ever-increasing body of work in the field of Irish antiquarianism and identities has appeared in recent years, notably the work of Colin Kidd, Joep Leerssen, and Clare O'Halloran, research has focused primarily on Protestant antiquarians. The important contribution of native scholars and scribes to the process of identity formation, taking place in the transfer of traditional Gaelic learning to nonnative scholars, has remained relatively unexplored. These native men of learning, termed "shadowy figures" by Diarmaid Ó Catháin, occupied a gray area between both cultures, belonging fully to neither one nor the other.[2] Although often dependant on Protestant patrons for a living, they were also motivated by other reasons to assist antiquarian research, not least by the wish to explicate and defend their own culture. Through the provision of manuscript material, translations, and advice, they served as mediators between both cultures and facilitated the appropriation of Gaelic heritage by Protestant antiquarians, who otherwise would have been unable to utilize Gaelic culture for ideological purposes.

Antiquarianism was very much the pursuit of the gentry who possessed the financial means to indulge in it, as well as the leisure time that was necessary for a pastime of this nature. Scholars covered a wide range of topics, including history, genealogy, description of ancient monuments, and the development of language and literature. They collected artifacts, coins, and ancient manuscripts in the Irish language. In contrast with England, there was less emphasis on topographical antiquarianism.[3] Ann de Valera has suggested that antiquarian investigations in Ireland during the course of the eighteenth century may be divided into three chronological periods.[4] The first, at the beginning of the century, focused on the collection of material relating to Ireland's past. Investigations were of an isolated and sporadic nature. The second period lasted from 1738 to 1760 and included the efforts of the Physico-Historical Society. It was dominated by the endeavors of Charles O'Conor, the recognized authority on all matters relating to Irish history and language, and Walter Harris, both of whom based their studies on authentic documents. In the third period, which lasted from around 1760 to the end of the century, one can speak of an antiquarian movement. A widening of interest in Ireland's past can be discerned during this period, in addition to an increase in the number of related publications. Antiquarians began corresponding and cooperating with one another and a number of antiquarian societies were founded. Gaelic scribes were employed as amanuenses or to provide translations of Gaelic texts and the 1780s in particular witnessed a shared interest in Gaelic culture by native custodians and the descendants of those who had once sought to denigrate it. Antiquarianism was closely linked to the patriot movement in the final decades of the century, as the latter took on a cultural dimension.

Throughout the early modern period, the relationship between settler and mother country was at best ambiguous. Although many within the Anglo-Irish ruling class considered Ireland a separate kingdom, they were still politically, economically, culturally, and militarily dependent on England. Despite retaining their allegiance to the English crown, they nevertheless aspired to a certain degree of political independence. On both a political and an economic level, a divergence between Anglo-Irish and English interests helped to foster an increasing sense of a distinct Irish identity. As R. F. Foster notes, "those who in the 1690s called themselves 'the Protestants of Ireland' or even 'the English of this kingdom' could see themselves as 'Irish gentlemen' by the 1720s."[5] A further example may be found in an anonymous open letter, addressed to the new Lord Lieutenant, Lord Halifax in 1762: "Of this be assured, that now we are thoroughly naturalized we are as warmly attached and bigoted to this little island as the best of yourselves are to old England."[6] Such claims serve to demonstrate the extent to which members of the ruling class began to consider Ireland their home.

By the 1760s the Anglo-Irish were increasingly confident in their political dominance. Once the threat of another uprising had receded in the aftermath of the Williamite war and the failure of the native Gael to rise in support of the Pretender during the Scottish insurrections of 1715 and 1745, Catholics were no longer perceived as a threat. Anglo-Irish antiquarians could thus view native culture, in decline from the beginning of the seventeenth century, in a more favorable light. By now, they had also begun to appreciate the necessity of validating the legitimacy of their community in Ireland and differentiating themselves from the English. Appropriation of Gaelic heritage came to be perceived as a means for achieving this.[7] Joep Leerssen terms this development, taking place during the period 1760–1845, an act of "total political self-invention, a collective psychological de-Anglicization."[8] As a result, the Gaelic past, both ecclesiastical as well as secular, was appropriated with the assistance of native scholars and scribes. Indeed, the practice of appropriation already had its precedents in early modern Ireland, featuring in expressions of identity by the Old Irish, and Old English, as well as by the New English.[9]

For centuries, the denigration of Irish culture and society had formed the basis of English colonial discourse on Ireland and claims for the necessity of anglicizing the "barbaric Irish" and converting them to the Protestant faith were utilized as justification for the subjugation of the Gaelic population.[10] This situation was by no means unique to Ireland and as Edward Said has suggested, "almost all colonial schemes begin with an assumption of native backwardness and general inadequacy to be independent, 'equal,' and 'fit.'"[11] Allegations of Gaelic barbarity came to prominence particularly in the sixteenth and seventeenth centuries with the arrival of the New English settlers. This assumption was reinforced by works such as John Derricke's *Image of Ireland* (1581), Sir John Davies's *A Discovery of the True Causes why Ireland was never Entirely Subdued* (1612), and Edmund Spenser's *A View of the Present State of Ireland* (1633).[12] According to the newcomers, the Old English had become "Hiberniores Hibernis ipsis," or in other words more Irish than the Irish themselves, and were therefore considered no better than, or even worse than, the natives. By the eighteenth century, however, the older classification of "native Irish," "Old English," and "New English" had begun to disappear and the distinction made by the English between the native Irish and descendants of the erstwhile settlers was no longer as clear as it had once been. As the Anglo-Irish community became increasingly aware that the term "barbarous Irish," once reserved for the Gaelic Irish only, now also referred to them, it became imperative to challenge this slur. Strategies employed by writers to contest this negative image included constructing an alternative identity by rewriting their history and subverting the identity imposed by England.[13]

Arguably, origin myths may be considered "invented traditions" and as Anthony Smith has demonstrated, a shared sense of history and myths of origin or descent are key elements in the identity formation process.[14] In the case of the Anglo-Irish, a new identity was achieved either "by the creation of new origin legends or the manipulation of the Milesian myth."[15] Apart from providing their community with a continuous historical past, the purpose of such myths was to promote the notion of a glorious ancient Gaelic past or to support the argument that held that native Gaels were savage barbarians. Essentially, Protestant antiquarians adopted two types of origins myth—the Milesian/Phoenician and the Scytho-Celtic/Gothic—for their own political and cultural purposes. In the process, ideas from primitivism, Celticism, Gothicism, and Orientalism, in vogue across Europe at the time, were also adapted.

In the first model, the Celts were descendants of the Phoenicians and had migrated from the East through Carthage and Spain to Ireland. This coincided with the native Gaelic myth of Milesian origins, as recounted in the eleventh-century manuscript *Leabhar Gabhála Éirin.* Geoffry Keating's *Foras Feasa ar Éirinn*, completed in 1634, held that the Milesians had migrated to Ireland from Egypt through Spain around 1000 BCE. According to this tradition, ancient Gaelic civilization had been highly sophisticated and at the forefront in Europe in scholarship and the arts, but was destroyed as a consequence of the twelfth-century Norman invasion. This formed the basis of a golden-age myth of pre-Christian Gaelic cultural sophistication, which was utilized by a number of Protestant antiquarians and Catholic native scholars as a means of refuting allegations of Gaelic barbarity. The antiquarian and cartographer Charles Vallancey, who was also an officer in the British army, adopted orientalist theories to transform the Milesian conquest myth in his *Essay on the Antiquity of the Irish Language* (1772) and *Grammar of the Iberno-Celtic or Irish Language* (1773). Vallancey was particularly influenced by the works of Sir William Jones on the relationship between the Celtic language and the

Persian and Sanskrit languages. Vallancey also drew on Francis Wilford, who argued that the "White Island" referred to in ancient Indian manuscripts known as the Puranas was England, and that the British Isles were in fact the "Sacred Isles of the Hindus."

The Phoenician origin myth was very much to the fore in the works of two Protestant antiquarians, Joseph Cooper Walker's *Historical Memoirs of the Irish Bards* (1786) and Charlotte Brooke's *Reliques of Irish Poetry* (1789).[16] Walker's *Historical Memoirs* was the first attempt in the English language to provide a history of Irish poetry and music from the earliest times down to the eighteenth century, while Brooke's *Reliques* was the first substantial anthology of Irish poetry translated into English. Both works provide important examples of how native culture was appropriated in the formation of Anglo-Irish identity. They also demonstrate how the Phoenician myth was employed as a means of challenging the negative image of the Anglo-Irish held by the English.[17] Walker based his work on the premise that Ireland had been invaded by the Milesians, the earliest period "in which history wears the semblance of truth."[18] In an attempt to refute accusations that learning was not respected by the ancient Gaels, he argued that it was as highly regarded in ancient Ireland as military skill: "Can that nation be deemed barbarous, in which learning shared the honours next to royalty? Warlike as the Irish were in those days, even arms were less respected amongst them than letters,—Read this, ye polished nations of the earth, and blush!"[19]

Brooke claimed that the hero Cucullin in the Ulster Cycle of Gaelic tales would have had knowledge of ancient Greece, Persia, or indeed India due to the Phoenician origin of the Gael: "had our early ancestors been really such as modern writers represent them: Barbarians, descended from barbarians, and ever continuing the same; but their Phoenician origin of itself sufficiently accounts for their knowledge of the situation, inhabitants, manners, &c. of the various nations of the earth."[20] Furthermore, she argued that the ancient Irish were civilized while the rest of Europe was still in a state of barbarism: "The productions of our Irish Bards exhibit a glow of cultivated genius,—a spirit of elevated heroism,—sentiments of pure honor,—instances of disinterested patriotism, and manners of a degree of refinement, totally astonishing, at a period when the rest of Europe was nearly sunk in barbarism!" This provided her with an opportunity of demonstrating to her fellow Anglo-Irish that they had reason to be proud of their ancestors, the Irish Bards. She asks, "and is not all this very honorable to our countrymen? Will they not be benefited,—will they not be gratified, at the lustre reflected on them by ancestors so very different from what modern prejudice has been studious to represent them?"[21] Drawing attention to the poem *Magnus the Great* as proof of the civility of the ancient Gaels, Brooke argues that although the poem was most likely written in the Middle Ages, it provides evidence that the Irish remained a civilized people despite suffering invasion and civil unrest: "The ancient Irish have been repeatedly stigmatised with the name of Barbarians. Their souls, their manners, and their language, were thought alike incapable of any degree of refinement . . . and were we less barbarians, when torn with civil broils, and foreign invasions, than when we were a conquering and flourishing people?"[22] The Catholic antiquarians Charles O'Conor and Sylvester O'Halloran, to whom both Walker and Brooke were indebted for the provision of transcripts and translations from manuscripts, also promoted the Milesian myth of origin in their respective works: *Dissertations: An Account of the Ancient Government, Letters, Sciences, Religion, Manners and Customs of Ireland* (1753), *An Introduction to the Study of the History and Antiquities of Ireland* (1772), and *General History of Ireland* (1774).[23] As their primary aim was the vindication of Gaelic civility, rather than adopting ideas from primitivism popular throughout Europe at that time, the highly literate and sophisticated Gaelic past constructed by Joseph Cooper Walker, Charlotte Brooke, Charles Vallancey, Charles O'Conor, and Sylvester O'Halloran resembled modern English society in its refinement and sophistication.[24]

The opposing Scytho-Celtic model, in use for generations to promote and confirm the barbarity of the Celts, held that the Celts had descended from the biblical Scythians and had migrated across Northern and Eastern Europe. Its most prominent advocates, Church of Ireland rectors Edward Ledwich and Thomas Campbell, and the schoolmaster William Beauford, argued that the Norman and English invasion had been a civilizing influence on the country. These antiquarians were influenced by the Gothic model of early British history, promoted by the Scottish historian John Pinkerton, which claimed that Germanic or Teutonic barbarian tribes had settled Britain and subsequently Ireland.[25] Its adherents argued, therefore, for a common origin for the people of Britain and Ireland and saw the Norman conquest as part of the long series of Nordic settlements in the country. These theories are present in works such as Campbell's *Strictures on the Ecclesiastical and Literary History of Ireland* (1789), which cast doubts on the existence of a great pre-Christian Celtic civilization, and Ledwich's influential *Antiquities of Ireland* (1790). The latter tried to "Gothicize" most of early Irish history, thereby eliminating all ethnic distinctions between the Irish and British, and as a consequence arguing for a continuous process of colonization from Britain since ancient times.[26] Antiquarian debates in the late eighteenth century therefore became highly politicized, and according to Oliver MacDonagh, as subsequent controversies about Ledwich's work revealed, signaled that the Irish past had become an additional arena for political conflict.[27] Indeed, both origin models proved to be so contentious within the Anglo-Irish antiquarian circle that they split its members into two opposing camps. Heated exchanges took place between the various parties on the pages of Charles Vallancey's *Collectanea de Rebus Hibernicis,* with Edward Ledwich and schoolmaster William Beauford on one side, and Vallancey and Charles O'Conor on the other. The issue proved to be so divisive that it ultimately led to the dissolution of the Hibernian Antiquarian Society in 1783.[28]

Ledwich was particularly vocal in defending the Protestant Anglo-Irish community against accusations of barbarity, re-attributing it solely to the native Gaels. An adversary of O'Conor, who he suspected of combining agitation for Catholic relief with claims of a highly sophisticated pre-Christian Gaelic past, Ledwich upheld the conservative opinion that the English had exerted a civilizing influence on the country. His comment to Joseph Cooper Walker, reminding the latter of his duty to be polite to the English, is a case in point: "You are bound personally, politically & patriotically to be polite to the English; & it is historically true that they under providence, humanized the Irish. Who otherwise at this day would be perfect barbarians even as it is they are half civilized."[29] This notion is further expanded upon in the preface to his *Antiquities of Ireland* where he contrasts native barbarism with English civility: "When Hibernians compare their present with their former condition; their just and equal laws, with those that were uncertain and capricious; the happy security of peace with the miseries of barbarous manners, their hearts must overflow to the Author of such blessings, nor will they deny their obligations to the fostering care of Britain, the happy instrument for conferring them."[30]

In contrast to Ledwich, however, other Protestants within the antiquarian circle were of a more conciliatory disposition toward the native Gael. The 1780s thus may be considered a key phase in the development of a shared Protestant and Catholic Irish identity. MacDonagh has suggested that the study of Gaelic antiquities provided common ground for a "new Catholic intelligentsia" and "Anglo-Irish liberals" in the 1770s and 1780s.[31] In particular, the foundation of the Royal Irish Academy in 1785 with the purpose of promoting the study of Gaelic antiquities proved to be a landmark in the cooperation of Protestant and Catholic scholars. Catholics such as Sylvester O'Halloran, Charles O'Conor and Theophilus O'Flanagan were welcomed into the elite circle of Protestant antiquarians, although only O'Conor was admitted to the Royal Irish Academy as an honorary member.[32] O'Halloran and Charlotte Brooke expressed the aspiration in their respective works that the study of antiquities would unite the various ethnic groupings in Ireland. In an attempt to find common ground between the various warring factions, the pre-Christian era proved to be the most suitable area of study for both groups as it was less politically sensitive. Consequently, both Catholic scholars and liberal Anglo-Irish antiquarians were active in promoting the early Irish church's independence from Rome, arguing instead that Roman influence had first been introduced with the coming of the Anglo-Normans. Catholics, such as O'Conor, who were involved in the campaign for the amelioration of the penal laws employed this strategy in order "to detach the question of Gaelic civility from aggressive Counter-Reformation ideology."[33]

The controversy sparked by the publication of James Macpherson's *Fragments of Ancient Poetry* in 1760, *Fingal* in 1761/62 and *Introduction to the History of Great Britain and Ireland* (1771) provided an important context where both native and nonnative, Catholic and Protestant scholars could cooperate. It also provided a further stimulus for Anglo-Irish antiquarians to begin expressing an interest in the remote Gaelic past.[34] Their aims were twofold. First, they wished to challenge Macpherson's version of Irish and Scottish history, which claimed that Ireland had been colonized by the Scots rather than vice versa, as hitherto had been accepted. Second, they attempted to disprove his claims regarding the Scottish provenance of Ossian. In their endeavors to disprove Macpherson, liberal Protestant antiquarians relied on native scholars and scribes to provide them with the necessary documentary evidence to support their arguments. Brooke's *Reliques* may be viewed not only as a vindication of Gaelic civility and an expression of Anglo-Irish identity, but also as a direct challenge to Macpherson, and the ballads contained in her collection appear to have been carefully selected for this purpose.[35] Her criticism of the Scotsman is implicit, however, as the work does not contain a single reference to either Macpherson or his publications. It seems likely that Charles O'-Conor, Sylvester O'Halloran, and Theophilus O'Flanagan, all of whom she acknowledged in her introduction, carefully guided her choice of Gaelic manuscript material with a particular political agenda in mind. Their aim was the promotion of a remote Gaelic past that was sophisticated and literate in order to support Catholic claims for social and political equality with the Protestant ruling class. It may be argued, therefore, that these native scholars were active in setting the agenda for the kind of Gaelic language material studied by a number of Anglo-Irish antiquarians.

It is noteworthy that only certain areas of Gaelic heritage were investigated by Protestant antiquarianism. Jacobite verse, which championed the cause of the Stuarts, was notably absent from such inquiries. This is hardly surprising, however, given the fact that references to land and religion were prominent in such poems and it is likely that native scholars who were financially dependent on their Protestant patrons would have avoided providing them with seditious material. Furthermore, as their primary interest lay in romantic and heroic tales, the subject matter of Jacobite verse would not have suited Anglo-Irish antiquarian purposes. Instead, the mythology of the Fionn and Ulster Cycles, both ideologically neutral, formed the basis of Joseph Cooper Walker and Charlotte Brooke's works and provided a more suitable area for study as it was less politically charged.[36] It would be another half a century before a collection of Jacobite poetry was published under the title *Reliques of Irish Jacobite Poetry* (1844) by Edward Walsh and John O'Daly.[37]

Until recent times, modern scholars have tended to underestimate the extent and nature of contact between both the Gaelic and Anglo-Irish traditions. The concept of a divided society comprising two separate nations that had no common interest or purpose was advanced by Daniel Corkery in the early twentieth century in reaction to William E. H. Lecky's *History of Ireland in the Eighteenth Century* (1892). He coined the term "hidden Ireland" to describe a Gaelic society and cultural heritage that was inaccessible to the Anglo-Irish.[38] This primarily nationalist model of an oppressive Protestant minority and a repressed Catholic peasant majority with little or no contact between either class has since been discounted as it was too simplistic and failed to take into account a sizable Catholic and Protestant middle class, in addition to the various groups of dissenters throughout the country.[39] It also ignored the fact that a certain degree of interaction necessarily occurred between both cultures, particularly in the houses of the gentry as well as in trade and services. Declan Kiberd has questioned what he terms a "schematic distinction between an Irish-speaking peasantry and an English speaking gentry" and has contended instead that a "confluence of cultures" occurred.[40] As evidence of this, he emphasizes the spread of bilingualism throughout the country and argues that it was more widespread in both traditions than has hitherto been recognized. The Irish language was still widely spoken throughout the country at this time, but by the 1770s, it had begun to decline. Although a large number of the emerging Catholic middle class spoke English, members of the gentry would still have needed a certain amount of Irish to enable them to buy goods, to request services and to give orders to the Gael employed as servants and nannies in their houses.[41]

Based on available evidence, Protestant attitudes towards the Irish language during the eighteenth century varied considerably from attempts to eradicate it completely, to use of the language for proselytizing purposes, to a romantic love for it.[42] Most Protestant antiquarians never succeeded in learning the written language and appeared to have had little interest in the modern spoken language either.[43] Charles Vallancey, for example, refered to the spoken language as "jargon yet spoken by the unlettered vulgar."[44] Although a number of antiquarians possessed substantial collections of manuscripts, most were unable to interpret them and completely reliant on the assistance of native scholars and scribes. As is evident from Joseph Cooper Walker's comments in a letter to Lady Moira from Co. Down, who acted as a patron to the Gaelic scribe Muiris Ó Gormáin, the Irish language was viewed almost as an obstacle that prevented them from reaching their ultimate goal, the "hidden treasures" of Gaelic literature: "What a hoard of literary treasure is locked up in the Irish language."[45] Brooke, on the other hand, argued in favor of the beauty of the language, claiming that it was almost impossible to translate, as its beauty could not be carried over into the English language:

> It is really astonishing of what various and comprehensive powers this neglected language is possessed. In the pathetic, it breathes the most beautiful and affecting simplicity; and in the bolder species of composition, it is distinguished by a force of expression, a sublime dignity, and rapid energy, which it is scarcely possible for any translation fully to convey; as it sometimes fills the mind with ideas altogether new, and which, perhaps, no modern language is entirely prepared to express.[46]

As may be inferred from the above example, a more sympathetic attitude toward the Gaelic heritage is evident particularly in the closing decades of the century among Protestant antiquarians. Commenting on this change in attitude, Seamus Deane has noted that many came to respect it, particularly after the 1800 Act of Union when it was "clothed in nostalgic associations, having become the symbol of a lost culture rather than the reminder of a rebellious one."[47] By the latter half of the eighteenth century increasing numbers of Anglo-Irish began to act as patrons to Gaelic scribes, many of whom were heavily dependent on employment of this nature in order to earn a living. It may be argued, then, that a reciprocal relationship existed between scribe and patron.

The foundation had already been laid in the seventeenth century for cooperation between native and nonnative scholars, leading to a situation where traditional bardic learning was passed on to nonnative scholars. An early example is provided by the antiquarian work of Sir James Ware who employed the Gaelic scholar Dubhaltach Mac Fhirbhisigh as both translator and amanuensis.[48] But cooperation of this nature was the exception rather than the rule, and it was not until the beginning of the eighteenth century that the number of Anglo-Irish patrons increased. Among the most significant of these in the first quarter of the eighteenth century was Anthony Raymond, Vicar of Trim.[49] A close friend of Jonathan Swift, he learned to speak Irish and conducted church services in it. His interest in Irish language manuscripts was sparked by his desire to write a history of Ireland from earliest times down to the eighteenth century as well as writing a history of the Gaelic language. Because he was unable to read such manuscripts, he came into contact with members of the Ó Neachtain circle of scholars in Dublin who provided him with transcripts and translations.[50] Indeed, these scholar-scribes, men such as Seán Ó Neachtain, Tadhg Ó Neachtain, and Aodh Buí Mac Cruitín played an important role as intermediaries between both cultures. As a result of this cooperation, members of the Ó Neachtain group contributed to the intellectual life of the Anglo-Irish.[51] Other significant patrons during the second quarter of the century included Professor of Laws at Trinity College Dublin, Francis Stoughton Sullivan, and the College librarian, Tomas Leland.

One of the most prolific scribes of the eighteenth century, Muiris Ó Gormáin, Irish teacher and minor poet, provides an important link between the Ó Neachtain and the Anglo-Irish antiquarian circles of the 1780s. Employed for a time as an amanuensis by the Catholic historian Charles O'-Conor, he also copied Gaelic manuscripts for a number of prominent Anglo-Irish antiquarians. Like O'Conor, Ó Gormáin's scribal career spanned more than half of the century and he interacted with the most important and influential antiquarians of the day. William O'Sullivan referred to him as "the fashionable scribe of his day" and his services appears to have been in considerable demand by both Protestants and Catholic scholars.[52] The manuscripts Ó Gormáin transcribed for his patrons consist mainly of Ossianic poems, romantic tales, grammatical tracts, genealogies, medical tracts, legal tracts, religious tracts, extracts from the Annals such as *The Annals of Connaught*, *The Annals of Innisfallen,* and excerpts from the *Book of Ballymote*. Lady Moira had a particular interest in romantic tales, and posessed a large collection of Gaelic manuscripts with literal translations, including one entitled *The Adventures of Farbhlaidhe, Daughter of the King of Scotland, and Cearbhaill, son of Donnchaid Mhoir Uí Daluigh of Finebheara* (now) in Ó Gormáin's handwriting.[53] Joseph Cooper Walker also possessed an English version of this manuscript, written in his own hand. Since Walker's knowledge of the language was very limited, it is probable that Ó Gormáin provided him with a rough translation, which Walker then "dressed up" in his own florid style.[54] The manuscript Ms. G. 141 (An English-Irish Phrasebook) in the National Library of Ireland, compiled by Ó Gormáin, is of particular interest because it was written for members of the Anglo-Irish gentry.[55] For example, section 22 contains phrases relating to "A dialogue between a Lady and her waiting Woman / Comhradh eidir bean uasal agus a bean coimhidheachta."[56] The manuscript gives important insight into the vocabulary and phrases necessary for the Anglo-Irish to be able to communicate effectively with their servants. Phrasebooks such as this are also an important example of the "confluence of cultures" suggested by Kiberd.

Ó Gormáin also supplemented his scribal work with teaching Irish. Among his pupils were distinguished scholars such as Matthew Young, a clergyman and Fellow of Trinity College Dublin, and Charles Vallancey, although his success in teaching the latter is debatable. Desmond Ryan notes that Vallancey did everything for the Irish language except learn it and claimed that Ó Gormáin "ghosted" the Irish passages of his writings.[57] It is evident from the Walker/Vallancy correspondence that both men relied heavily on Ó Gormáin for manuscript material, advice, and assistance. For example, Ó Gormáin assisted Vallancey's research for *Grammar of the Iberno-Celtic or Irish Language* (1773), a work intended as an instrument for Anglican proselytization in Ireland. It also provided a vindication of Gaelic culture, however, by arguing for the antiquity of the Irish language which Vallancey portrayed as "masculine" and therefore "nervous" and capable of complex articulation and abstract subtlety.[58] Vallancey and Ó Gormáin's partnership seems to have been troubled in some respects. In an intriguing letter from Vallancey to O'Conor dated March 1772, regarding the Irish grammar he was working on with Ó Gormáin's assistance, Vallancey writes, "In all this poor Gorman is rather a stumbling block than an assistance, rather a check than a spur."[59] As a postscript to the letter, he noted: "I am now in treaty with the Printer. I have also wrote to the Dublin Booksellers—if I can throw 20 pounds in poor Gorman's pocket and be no loser myself is all I wish by this Grammar."[60] It is impossible to establish with certainty why Vallancey called Ó Gormáin a "check," but one could speculate that Ó Gormáin may have attempted to tone down Vallancey's efforts to prove that the Irish language had originated from the Punic language.

Both Walker's *Historical Memoirs of the Irish Bards* and Brooke's *Reliques of Irish Poetry* were pioneering Anglo-Irish attempts to not only explicate Gaelic culture to English readers but also to vindicate the civility of the pre-Christian era. They may also be viewed as an attempt to reassess the ambiguity of the Anglo-Irish position and to come to a better understanding of Ireland's position within Britain. Both authors clearly express a sense of Anglo-Irish identity in the prefaces to their respective works. Walker opens with, "I trust I am offering to my countrymen an acceptable present: the gift has novelty, at least to recommend it;"[61] while Brooke writes, "I trust I am doing an acceptable service to my country, while I endeavour to rescue from oblivion a few of the invaluable reliques of her ancient genius."[62] The use of the first-person plural pronoun in describing their relationship with Ireland in the works of Brooke and others writing before the 1801 Union provides a further indication of identification with Ireland. At this time, Anglo-Irish authors were writing for a local audience. The focus was to change after the union, however, when Anglo-Irish authors began to write for an English audience. As Leerssen notes, "a paradoxical dissociation of the Irish author from his/her subject matter" occurred resulting in a change from "we the Irish" to "they the Irish."[63] In effect, rather than identifying with the country they were representing, these authors acted as detached observers instead.[64] Walker, for instance, lost enthusiasm for Gaelic antiquities post-Union and he turned instead toward Italian literature and antiquities.

In a direct appeal to her fellow Anglo-Irish, Brooke called on those who considered themselves to be Irishmen to join the attempts to preserve whatever remained of the Gaelic literary heritage, and clearly saw herself as providing a public service: "But *Irishmen*—all of them at least who would be thought to pride themselves in the name, or to reflect back on any part of the honour they derive from it; *they* are *particularly* called upon, in favour of their country, to rescue these little sparks from the ashes of her former glory." For Brooke, the rescue of such remnants of Gaelic heritage was an act of patriotism and she urged her fellow scholars to collect poetry composed by the Gaelic bards, as examples of "disinterested patriotism."[65] It should be noted, however, that her notion of patriotism was not synonymous with "nationalism" or "national pride" as it is today. Leerssen has argued that among the meanings linked to the term "patriotism" in that age was a libertarian notion where the patriot was a defender of the rights of parliament against the crown.[66] It also included the depoliticized notion of the patriot as one who promoted the common good of society. Brooke believed that by contributing to the preservation of Gaelic heritage, she was carrying out a public service: "to throw some light on the antiquities of this country, to vindicate, in part, its history, and prove its claim to scientific as well as to military fame." Furthermore, she wished to awaken "a just and useful curiosity, on the subject of our poetical compositions."[67]

Brooke also considered her work a vehicle for bringing about mutual respect, and understanding, and better relations between the Irish, the Anglo-Irish and the English, which would result in political stability. In the preface, she likens the muses of both countries to sisters, the Irish muse being the elder, and calls for a "cordial union" between both countries: "The British muse is not yet informed that she has an elder sister in this isle; let us then introduce them to each other! Together let them walk abroad from their bowers, sweet ambassadresses of cordial union between two countries that seem formed by nature to be joined by every bond of interest, and of amity." The type of union Brooke means here is unclear but it is likely that her wish is to improve relations between both countries by making the Gael less "exotic" and portraying the English and Irish as equals. She continues: "Let them tell her, that the portion of her blood which flows in our veins is rather ennobled than disgraced by the mingling tides that descend from our heroic ancestors."[68] This call may be viewed as a form of "cultural unionism."[69] Brooke's literary endeavors were not of a secessionist nature, however, but situated within the framework of a continued union with Britain.

During the final two decades of the century, agrarian protests, the deteriorating political climate of the 1780s, and, ultimately, the 1798 insurrection had a detrimental effect on antiquarian pursuits among the Anglo-Irish. Such research became politicized and as Luke Gibbons notes, turned into a battleground between warring factions.[70] This can be seen in the change of attitude toward Gaelic culture in the writings of people such as Rev. Edward Ledwich and the Rev. Thomas Campbell. Particularly in the aftermath of the 1798 Uprising and the 1801 Act of Union, interest in Irish antiquarian matters rapidly went into decline for a further two decades as it came to be equated with pro-Gaelic sympathy and therefore anti-British sentiment. Many of the Anglo-Irish antiquarians who had been such enthusiastic advocates of Gaelic antiquities prior to the insurrection became disenchanted and avoided the field altogether.

A salient feature of Anglo-Irish interest in Gaelic antiquity during the final decades of the eighteenth century is that it provided common ground for a number of deeply divided groups, in the neutral area of the distant Gaelic past. One immediate consequence of the Anglo-Irish appropriation of Gaelic culture was the preservation and copying of numerous Irish language manuscripts, which might otherwise have perished. The Macpherson controversy provided an impetus to both native and nonnative scholars to undertake the collecting and preservation of Gaelic material in defense of their country's reputation. Gradually, traditional native learning, along with manuscripts, passed from Gaelic custodians into the hands of Protestant antiquarians. This, in turn, opened up the wealth of the Gaelic literary tradition to those who had been unaware of it before and helped to instill a sense of Irish identity in the Anglo-Irish. This could only have been achieved with the assistance of Gaelic scholars and scribes. Investigations into the distant Celtic past brought the Gaelic and English languages into contact with one another, preserved the richness of the Gaelic tradition, and paved the way for the emergence of Anglo-Irish literature. Finally, and possibly most importantly, the investigation of Gaelic antiquities by Anglo-Irish antiquarians led "ultimately to a separatist politics and the reversal of the political and cultural hierarchies that governed eighteenth-century Irish life."[71]

Notes

1. This term is borrowed from Norman Vance, *Irish Literature: A Social History. Tradition, Identity and Difference,* 2nd ed. (Dublin: Four Courts Press, 1999), 65.

2. Diarmaid Ó Catháin, "Dermot O'Connor, Translator of Keating," *Eighteenth Century Ireland: Iris an dá chultúr* 2 (1987): 87.

3. Rosemary Sweet's study of antiquarianism in eighteenth-century Britain argues that antiquarian activity was directed by the imperative of establishing a national past. See *Antiquaries: The Discovery of the Past in Eighteenth-Century Britain* (New York: Hambledon and London, 2004). Influenced to a certain extent by the Celtic revival, antiquarianism in Wales was utilized by the new elite class as a means for appropriating the native traditions of hospitality, bards, and music in order to legitimize their position after 1760. See Philip Jenkins, *The Making of a Ruling Class: The Glamorgan Gentry, 1640–1790* (Cambridge: Cambridge University Press, 1983), 235–39; Philip Jenkins, "The Creation of an 'Ancient Gentry': Glamorgan, 1760–1840," *Welsh History Review* 12 (1984): 24–49.

4. Ann de Valera, *Antiquarian and Historical Investigations in Ireland in the Eighteenth Century* (master's thesis, University College Dublin, 1972), 9–10.

5. R. F. Foster, *Modern Ireland 1600–1972* (London: Penguin, 1989), 178.

6. *Ways to Mend and Grow Better or Thoughts on the Present Posture of Affairs in a Letter to His E——y, the Lord L——t* (Dublin, 1963), 11–12. Quoted in Thomas Bartlett, " 'A People Made rather for Copies than Originals': The Anglo-Irish, 1760–1800," *International History Review* 12 (1990): 12.

7. Parallels may be drawn with the rise of Creole nationalism in South America toward the end of the eighteenth century, where a Creole identity had begun to emerge among the "Españoles americanos" who appropriated the pre-Hispanic past of the Aztecs and Incas. See Benedict Anderson, *Imagined Communities: Reflections on the Origin and Spread of Nationalism* (New York: Verso, 1991), 47–66.

8. Joep Leerssen, *Hidden Ireland, Public Sphere* (Galway: Arlen House, 2002), 24.

9. Colin Kidd, *British Identities before Nationalism: Ethnicity and Nationhood in the Atlantic world, 1600–1800* (Cambridge: Cambridge University Press, 1999), 147.

10. Giraldus Cambrensis's twelfth century *Topographia Hibernicae* (1188) may be considered the foundational text of this discourse. Clare Carroll, "Barbarous Slaves and Civil Cannibals. Translating Civility in Early Modern Ireland," *Ireland and Postcolonial Theory*, ed. Clare Carroll and Patricia King (Cork: Cork University Press, 2003), 63–80.

11. Edward Said, *Culture and Imperialism* (London: Chatto and Windus, 1993), 96.

12. Spenser's text had circulated in manuscript form from the late 1590s onward.

13. Thomas McLoughlin, *Contesting Ireland: Irish Voices against England in the Eighteenth Century* (Dublin: Four Courts, 1999), 36.

14. The term "invented traditions" was coined by Eric Hobsbawm to define "a set of practices, normally governed by overtly or tacitly accepted rules and of a ritual or symbolic nature, which seek to inculcate certain values and norms of behaviour by repetition, which automatically implies continuity with the past." *The Invention of Tradition*, ed. Eric Hobsbawm and Terence Ranger (Cambridge: Cambridge University Press, 1984), 1; Anthony Smith, *The Ethnic Origins of Nations* (Oxford: Basil Blackwell, 1987), 24–25.

15. Clare O'Halloran, *Golden Ages and Barbarous Nations: Antiquarian Debate and Cultural Politics in Ireland, c. 1750–1800* (Cork: Cork University Press, 2004), 69.

16. See Lesa Uí Fhathaigh (Ní Mhunghaile), "Joseph Cooper Walker (1760–1810). Beatha agus Saothar Historical Memoirs of the Irish Bards (1786)" (Ph.D. diss., National University of Ireland, Galway, 2001); Lesa Ní Mhunghaile, ed., *Charlotte Brooke's Reliques of Irish Poetry* (forthcoming).

17. David Hayton, "From Barbarians to Burlesque: English Images of the Irish c. 1660–1750," *Irish Economic and Social History* 15 (1988): 5–31; "Anglo-Irish Attitudes: Changing Perceptions of National Identity among the Protestant Ascendancy in Ireland, ca. 1690–1750," *Studies in Eighteenth-Century Culture* 17 (1987): 145–57.

18. Joseph Cooper Walker, *Historical Memoirs of the Irish Bards, interspersed with anecdotes of, and occasional observations on, the music of Ireland* (Dublin, 1786), 2.

19. Ibid., 5.

20. Charlotte Brooke, *Reliques of Irish Poetry: Consisting of Heroic Poems, Odes, Elegies, and Songs, translated into English verse* (Dublin, 1789), 27.

21. Ibid., vii.

22. Ibid., 62.

23. O'Conor, a linear descendant of Ruaidhrí Ó Conchubhair, the last High King of Ireland, played a central role in promoting Gaelic literature amongst Anglo-Irish antiquarians who sought his advice and assistance. Sylvester O'Halloran was an antiquarian, eye surgeon, and prolific letter writer from Limerick.

24. Clare O'Halloran, "Irish Re-Creations of the Gaelic Past: The Challenge of Macpherson's Ossian," *Past and Present: A Journal of Historical Studies* 124 (1989): 73.

25. John Pinkerton, *A Dissertation on the Origin and Progress of the Scythians or Goths: Being an Introduction to the Ancient and Modern History of Europe* (London, 1787).

26. O'Halloran, "Irish Re-Creations," 60.

27. Oliver MacDonagh, *States of Mind: A Study of Anglo-Irish Conflict, 1780–1980* (Boston: Allen and Unwin, 1985), 1.

28. Walter D. Love, "The Hibernian Antiquarian Society: A Forgotten Predecessor to the Royal Irish Academy," *Studies* 51 (1962): 419–31.

29. Trinity College Dublin, Ms 1461/2.

30. Edward Ledwich, *Antiquities of Ireland,* 2nd ed. (London, 1804), iv.

31. MacDonagh, *States of Mind*, 1–9.

32. Theophilus O'Flanagan, a native Irish speaker from Co. Clare who titled himself "Professor of the Irish language," was employed by the Royal Irish Academy to translate the Brehon Laws.

33. Colin Kidd, "Gaelic Antiquity and National Identity in Enlightenment Ireland and Scotland," *The English Historical Review* 109, no. 434 (1994): 1201.

34. For a discussion of the Ossian controversy in an Irish context, see Mícheál Mac Craith, "The Forging of Ossian," *Celticism*, ed. Terence Brown (Atlanta: Rodopi, 1996), 125–42.

35. Mícheál Mac Craith, "Charlotte Brooke and James Macpherson," *Litteraria Pragensia* 10 (2000): 5–17.

36. The Ulster cycle consists of a group of heroic tales relating to the Ulaid tribe in the north of Ireland and deal with the conflict between the Ulaid and the Connachta. The famous *Táin Bó Cuailnge* group of tales belongs to this cycle. The Fionn or Ossianic Cycle of tales consists of stories, in both prose and ballad form, involving the exploits of a band of warriors known as the Fianna under the leadership of Fionn mac Cumhaill.

37. Proinsias Ó Drisceoil, "Lámhscríbhinní agus an léitheoir coitianta sa 19u haois: John O'Daly agus foinsí *Reliques of Irish Jacobite Poetry,*" *Léachtaí Cholm Cille* 34 (2004): 257–315.

38. Daniel Corkery, *The Hidden Ireland* (Dublin: M. H. Gill, 1925).

39. L. M. Cullen, "The Hidden Ireland: Re-assessment of a Concept," *Studia Hibernica* 9 (1969): 7–48; Declan Kiberd, *Idir Dhá Chultúr* (Dublin: Coiscéim, 1993).

40. Declan Kiberd, "Irish Literature and Irish History," *The Oxford Illustrated History of Ireland*, ed. R. F. Foster (Oxford: Oxford University Press, 1989), 252–53.

41. Kiberd, *Idir Dhá Chultúr,* 1–2.

42. Alan Harrison, "Scéal na Gaeilge agus an Protastúnachas san ochtú haois déag," *Lá,* February 2, 1995, 10.

43. Charlotte Brooke was an exception in that she learned the language within two years. Joseph Cooper Walker, however, acknowledged that his knowledge of Irish was "very limited."

44. Charles Vallancey, *A Grammar of the Iberno-Celtic, or Irish Language* (Dublin, 1773), ii.

45. National Archive of Scotland Ms. GD297/18.

46. Brooke, *Reliques*, vi.

47. Seamus Deane, *A Short History of Irish Literature* (London: Hutchinson, 1986), 63.

48. Nollaig Ó Muraíle, *The Celebrated Antiquary Dubhaltach Mac Fhirbhisigh (c. 1600–1671): his Lineage, Life and Learning* (Maynooth: An Sagart, 1996), 99–101.

49. Alan Harrison, *Ag Cruinniú Meala: Anthony Raymond (1675–1726), ministéir Protastúnach agus léann na Gaeilge i mBaile Átha Cliath* (Dublin: An Clóchomhar, 1988).

50. T. F. O'Rahilly, "Irish Scholars in Dublin in the early eighteenth century," *Gadelica* (1912): 156–62; Nessa Ní Shéaghdha, "Irish Scholars and Scribes in Eighteenth-Century Dublin," *Eighteenth Century Ireland/Iris an dá chultúr* 4 (1989): 41–54.

51. Harrison, *Cruinniú Meala*, 28.

52. William O'Sullivan, "The Irish Manuscripts in Case H in Trinity College Dublin cataloged by Matthew Young in 1781," *Celtica* 11 (1976): 231–32.

53. National Library of Ireland Ms. G 144.

54. Lesa Ní Mhunghaile, "Murris Ó Gormáin (†1793): scoláire idir dhá chultúr," in *Aistí in Omós do Mháirtín Ó Briain*, ed. Pádraig Ó Héalaí and Micheál Mac Craith (forthcoming).

55. Terence P. McCaughey, "Muiris Ó Gormáin's English-Irish Phrasebook," *Éigse* 12 (1968): 203–27.

56. National Library of Ireland, Ms. G. 141 (An English-Irish Phrasebook), 84–90.

57. Desmond Ryan, *The Sword of Light*: *From the Four Masters to Douglas Hyde* (London: Barker, 1938), 74–76. British Library Ms. Eg. 87 is a copy of John O'Brien's *Irish-English Dictionary* printed in Paris in 1768 and may have been used as an instruction book when Ó Gormáin was teaching Vallancey Irish, as it contains notes in the handwriting of both men.

58. Robert Welch, *The Companion to Irish Literature* (Oxford: Clarendon, 1996), 585.

59. Royal Irish Academy Ms B. I. 4.

60. Ibid.

61. Walker, *Historical Memoirs*, 1.

62. Brooke, *Reliques*, vii.

63. Joep Leerssen, *Remembrance and Imagination. Patterns in the Historical and Literary Representation of Ireland in the Nineteenth Century* (Cork: Cork University Press, 1996), 34.

64. Ibid., 34.

65. Brooke, *Reliques*, vii.

66. Joep Leerssen, "Anglo-Irish Patriotism and its European Context: Notes towards a Reassessment," *Eighteenth Century Ireland/Iris an dá chultúr* 3 (1988): 7–24. Leerssen calls for a reassessment of the traditional view that "the Anglo-Irish Patriots were caught in the dilemma between their privileged, indeed colonial, Ascendancy position, and their national solidarity with 'the causes of Ireland.'" See also Stephen Small, "The Twisted roots of Irish Patriotism: Anglo-Irish Political Thought in the Late Eighteenth Century," *Éire-Ireland* 35 (2000–2001): 187–216.

67. Brooke, *Reliques*, v.

68. Ibid., vii–viii.

69. The term is borrowed from Cathal G. Ó Háinle, "Towards the Revival. Some translations of Irish Poetry: 1789–1897," *Literature and the Changing Ireland*, ed. Peter Connolly (Gerrards Cross: Smythe, 1982), 37–57.

70. Luke Gibbons, "From Ossian to O'Carolan: The Bard as Separatist Symbol," *From Gaelic to Romantic: Ossianic Translations*, ed. Fiona Stafford and Howard Gaskill (Atlanta: Rodopi, 1998), 242.

71. Gregory A. Schirmer, *Out of What Began: A History of Irish Poetry in English* (Ithaca: Cornell University Press, 1998), 65–66.

From Owenson to Morgan: History, Sensibility, and the Vagaries of Reception in *The Wild Irish Girl*

Christopher Nagle

DESPITE HER ONCE CONSIDERABLE POPULARITY, SYDNEY OWENSON, LADY Morgan seems for many readers to be a difficult writer to like. Though she certainly has had her admirers, especially in her own era, she has always had an abundance of detractors at the same time. What is more striking, perhaps, is that the line between praise and damnation is often substantially blurred in the reception of Owenson's writing, almost as though critics cannot resist a kind of attraction-repulsion dynamic in their responses to her work. This dynamic does not merely point to inconsistency or a change in the response of an individual reader over time. It often can be found in the mixed feelings of readers at the very heart of their responses. I will attempt to untangle this distinct characteristic of Owenson criticism and to account for the critic's desire for distance from her work, particularly as these manifestations emerge in engagements with her third and most well-known novel, *The Wild Irish Girl* (1806).

Coming on the heels of the 1800 Act of Union between Ireland and Great Britain, it is not altogether surprising that this novel serves as a politically vexed fiction, styling itself on the title page as "A National Tale." Indeed, most scholarly responses to the novel foreground this aspect of the work and the degree to which it inaugurates something new in the history of the genre, stimulating a striking increase in the number of novels with Irish themes.[1] Addressing contemporary political issues relevant to the Union while drawing on antiquarian themes that are virtually foregrounded by the rich paratextual features in the novel—especially its vast proliferation of footnotes—Owenson arguably contributes to something new in the genre of history as well. Following the earlier surplus of Gothic novels such as Ann Radcliffe's, which provide their own distinct sense of history—often significantly distanced in both time and place from the author's environment—and preceding the celebrated historical romances of later novelists such as Sir Walter Scott, *The Wild Irish Girl* departs from its predecessors and proves unmatched by the fiction that follows in its wake. In a certain sense, the novel seems to exist "out of time" as it shuttles between a timeless love story and its very specific historical context, the years immediately following the 1798 Rising.

If the novel is still largely unfamiliar, its plot is immediately recognizable: an Anglo-Irish spin on the boy-meets-girl, boy-loses-girl, boy-gets-girl-back theme, with the attendant complication of cross-cultural conflict for this pair of star-crossed lovers. Horatio M——, the dissolute son of an English lord, is punished by exile to his father's estate in the western wilds of Ireland, where he discovers a rich but atavistic Gaelic culture within the Gothic-Romantic environment of Connaught. In addition to the wild landscape, this setting includes the moldering castle and estate of the now aging and deposed Prince of Inismore, his stunningly beautiful, learned, passionate, and virtuous daughter, Glorvina, and a kindly, intellectual Catholic priest, Father John. All these elements are directly tied to the hero's own family history, unbeknownst to him, and they transform his previous Anglocentric bias into deep respect for and love of Gaelic cultural traditions in general, and Glorvina and her circle in particular. The allegorical dimensions of the love story are fairly obvious, especially given the invocation of "national unity" (250/241) in the context of the impending marriage, but they are additionally complicated by a triangulated competition for Glorvina's affection between father and son, part of which is framed by the father's implied involvement in the 1798 Rising and the family's inheritance of an estate from the era of Cromwellian plantation.[2] Clearly, this national tale is thoroughly suffused with history, which surely accounts for much of the attention paid to it by scholars and general readers attuned to issues of Irish cultural nationalism.

One might even suggest that the novel incorporates an excess of history, including varying degrees of anachronism, as scholars have charged. But if so, it is only one of the many forms of excess in which the novel indulges, the combined force of which helps to explain the mixed reception I will examine in more detail below. At the very least, one could identify five categories of overlapping but nominally distinct excess: theme, sentiment, typography, plot, and footnotes. One of the primary preoccupations of the novel, for instance, is established thematically in the opening pages, the "Introductory Letters" between the Earl of M—— and his son, Horatio, which include an attack on the son for seeking "the destructive atmosphere of pleasure" and for "idly presiding as the high priest of libertinism at the nocturnal orgies of vitiated dissipation" (4/4). Eventually the young Englishman's excessive enthusiasm for the implied indulgences of the flesh will be met with the Wild Irish Girl's equally excessive enthusiasm for Gaelic cultural forms and the convergence of the two will produce a special kind of Anglo-Irish sublimation uneasily contained by the forms of union invoked by the novel's conclusion.

Excesses of sentiment abound, especially surrounding the courtship of Glorvina by Horatio, both of whom are moved to astonishing effusions. For Glorvina, engaging in traditional Irish dance, "every thing swims gayly before me; and I feel as if swiftly borne away in a vortex of pleasurable sensation" (148/142); while desperately wooing her, Horatio responds in a similar register: "—to time, therefore, I commit my fate; but while thus led by the hand of virtue, I enebriate at the living spring of bliss" (166/160). Clearly, the thematic preoccupation with pleasure is foregrounded by the main characters' sentiments, and these in turn are heightened through the deployment of excessive typographical features. One example should suffice: "Oh! Had not her celestial confidence, her angelic purity, sublimed every thought, restrained every wish—at that moment—that too fortunate—too dangerous moment!!!—Yet even as it was, in the delicious agony of my soul, I secretly exclaimed, with the legislator of Lesbos—*'It is too difficult to be always virtuous!'*" (159/153). In Horatio's epistolary confession to his friend and confidant, "J.D. Esq. M.P.," Owenson's contemporary readers would recognize the hallmarks of the earlier literature of Sensibility: apostrophe, ejaculation, heightened rhetoric, the trope of pleasing pain, and the literal multiplication of punctuation to excess—all reflecting the excited emotional state of the speaker or writer and generally presumed to incite a similar response in the reader.[3]

Naturally, incorporating these elements within an epistolary structure, itself a central feature of sentimental narrative, calls further attention to Owenson's purposes. All these features serve as a perfect fit to a plot that is sentimental in its dramatic effect as well. The climactic discovery scene near the novel's conclusion provides the most excessive moment, when the wedding of Glorvina and the Earl is interrupted at the last moment by his son, Horatio, leading to a fainting bride and her swiftly expiring father, the Gaelic patriarch. Though all is resolved to the relative satisfaction of the surviving parties—the Earl gives way to his more age-appropriate son—this climax is extreme and ultimately unsettling to many readers, with the correspondent gesture toward narrative closure providing a source of ongoing critical debate. The major source of this contention surrounds

Owenson's putative politics, a vexed matter that cannot be resolved without recourse to the last category of excess I have identified.

One of the principal features that immediately stands out to any reader is the remarkable superfluity of footnotes interwoven throughout the novel, providing both a supplement and a distraction from the conventional elements of the fictional narrative. These notes provide the means by which much additional antiquarian history is adduced to supplement the more contemporary history evoked by the plot, and to establish the rich heritage of Gaelic culture, as well as its primacy in age and influence over the traditions of the English and other nationalities. The excess of notes functions both quantitatively and qualitatively, spanning multifarious disciplines while at times overwhelming the pages themselves, literally pushing the primary narrative to the margins of the printed page. One of the best examples of this feature comes through the nearly two thousand-word digression regarding "the mon wi the twa heads." This amateur ethnographic excursion tells the tale of the Bard of the Magilligans, Dennis Hampson of Co. Derry, a blind harpist with a wen on his neck so large that he came to be known as having "two heads." The note allegedly reproduces a firsthand account passed on to the author by a third party, to which is appended a lyrical "addenda," followed by an additional authenticating anecdote from the author herself, who was offered the famous performer's harp for sale (199–202/193–96). Like other footnotes in the text, one of the purposes of this illustrative anecdote is to provide an opportunity for Owenson to establish her own direct, authentic connections to Gaelic culture, but it also provides a historical figure so eccentric and intriguing that his tale cannot avoid displacing the reader's interest, at least momentarily, in the novel's primary characters. In effect, "historical" narratives embedded within other (fictional) narratives consistently compete for readerly attention, and the composite effect troubles the distinction between genres.

Taken together, these categories of excess present a formidable challenge—or even perhaps a provocation—to readers expecting a more conventional romance or travel narrative, or a mix of the two, and especially for those who expected an early nineteenth-century woman novelist to more suitably reflect feminine domestic propriety in the wake of the scandalous earlier work by writers such as Mary Wollstonecraft, Mary Hays, Elizabeth Inchbald, and others who mixed sex and politics during the volatile decade of the 1790s. Still later readers who bring the expectation of realist conventions to their encounter with Owenson are likely to be similarly unsettled, as we will see in a moment. Providing her critics with so much ammunition, Owenson's novel experiment ventures into uncharted terrain, and in doing so, it sets in motion a critical debate about the style of politics, which masks an implicit conflict over the politics of style.

To be sure, some figures fought her charms more successfully than others and maintained a fairly consistent posture of denigration. The most splendidly vitriolic of her contemporaries was a figure who is notorious in the circles of Romantic scholarship, especially for his predictable responses to women writers, and indeed any writers who threatened to raise the specter of radical politics—John Wilson Croker. The vicious attacks to which he subjected Owenson after the publication of *The Wild Irish Girl* are typically Crokerian, direct, wide-ranging, hyperbolic, and guided by a clear moral urgency: "I accuse Miss Owenson of having written bad novels and worse poetry—volumes without number and verses without end. Nor does my accusation rest upon her want of literary excellence. I accuse her of attempting to vitiate mankind, of attempting to undermine morality by sophistry, and that under the insidious mask of virtue, sensibility, and truth . . . such are the charges."[4] Regardless of the genre, Croker finds her writing consistently offensive and a threat to society, not only because it lacks both literary and moral "excellence," as she "masks" the degenerate character of her work with the veneer of goodness, but also because she refuses to stop producing it. These "volumes without number and verses without end" pose an additional threat, at least in Croker's imagination, because Owenson seems poised to spread her influence through a veritable glut in the literary marketplace; about this much he was prescient. If quantitative concerns seem less considerable to twenty-first-century readers, we would do well to remember that, from at least Pope to Wordsworth, the sheer proliferation of print is one of the primary issues at the heart of critical objections to the taste of the day's readership. For Croker, the only thing worse than having to read *The Wild Irish Girl* is to imagine its successor novels and volumes of poetry—both Owenson's own as well as those of her rivals and imitators—expressing similar sentiments. The intensity of his concern is made clear in his own responses, seemingly "without end"; policing her future literary endeavors while writing under the pseudonym, "M.T.," Croker devoted at least six energetic pieces to the denigration of the author and her work. This commitment spurred an ongoing public debate between Croker and Owenson's defenders—Claire Connolly styles this a significant "media event"—which was only interrupted by Croker's sudden departure from Dublin to serve in the English parliament for Downpatrick.[5]

Croker's atrabilious abuse did not end here, however, it simply came from another source, the new Tory periodical, the *Monthly Review*, rather than the *Freeman's Journal* as before. This change offered the additional benefit of preventing dialogue in the journal itself, since the *Review* did not follow the *Journal*'s practice of publishing letters of protest.[6] And since Owenson's novel, by her estimation, had been far more successful in England than in Ireland, this change of environment might have seemed like a double victory for Croker. Perhaps more surprisingly, the publication of Owenson's novel also brought a kinder, gentler prodding by the well-known education reformer, Richard Lovell Edgeworth, and by extension, his famous daughter:

> As a sincere and warm friend of Ireland, I return you my thanks for the just character which you have given to the lower Irish, and for the sound and judicious observations which you have attributed to the priest. The notices of Irish history are ingeniously introduced and are related in such a manner as to induce belief among the infidels . . . Maria, who reads (it is said) as well as she writes has entertained us with several passages from *The Wild Irish Girl* which I thought superior to any other book I had read. Upon looking over her shoulder I found she had omitted some superfluous epithets. Dare she had done this if you have been by? I think she would have dared, because your good taste and good sense would have been instantly her defender.[7]

Rather than reading this passage simply as a form of backhanded praise or as a passive-aggressive corrective gesture, I would suggest that this judiciously measured critical response demands a more nuanced reading. Beginning with specific praise for Owenson's characterizations of "the lower orders" and the sound moral guidance espoused by Father John, Edgeworth approves of her use of Irish history, which is "related in such a manner as to induce belief among the infidels." The latter quote seems a bit cryptic. Given the play of the 1798 Rebellion in the back-story of the novel, as well as the unionist reconciliation seemingly underwritten by the novel's resolution, one might imagine Edgeworth in accord with such representations, and willing to label those still opposed to such political ideals as "infidels."

But most important to this particular piece of criticism, I would argue, is its own blend of voices. Rather than speaking alone on his own authority—itself surely considerable—Edgeworth chooses to include Maria, Owenson's novelist colleague and competitor. But he does so slyly, at second-hand, almost in the guise of a "ghost editor" rather than ghostwriter. It is Maria, of course, who "edits" while she reads *The Wild Irish Girl* to her father, as he later discovers, and it is in part thanks to this collaborative effort of Sydney and Maria that he ultimately finds Owenson's novel "superior to any other book I had read." If such a selective reading of the author's work might come as an offense to her, Edgeworth cleverly suggests otherwise, playing on Owenson's own better judgment while at the same time reinforcing the superior judgment of his daughter, and of course, implicitly, of himself.

Rather than claiming that he knows better, or deferring to Maria and her better judgment, or even simply appealing to that of Owenson herself, who might think better of her excessive and eccentric "epithets" in retrospective moments of more sober reflection, Edgeworth does something more clever and perhaps more radical. By placing all three readers on ostensibly equal footing, and building the rhetorical force of his argument by subtle, incremental steps, he ultimately imagines all three "judges" drawn into the same circle of reasonable "good taste and good sense." He creates, in other words, a feeling community of readers out of their small, virtual "circle," and in doing so gives full credit back to Owenson for what he and his daughter have done in her absence.[8] Without the corrosive condescension of other, more politically opposed critics, Edgeworth engages in a paternalist correction of Owenson's excesses and defuses it by crediting both Maria and Sydney for a judgment which he seems merely to articulate, serving as the mouthpiece for what he already knows them to think and feel.

If Croker's response lacks ambiguity or nuance, the Edgeworths' collaborative venture is more in line with the typical attraction-repulsion dynamic evident in most modern critical assessments, especially those of academic scholars. In addition to corrective editorial urges, both outright dismissal and damning with faint praise are characteristics of reception past and present. While the past decade or so has seen a minor efflorescence of scholarship, especially on *The Wild Irish Girl*, there are few critics who are able to fight the temptation to distance themselves through some measure of disavowal as they approach Owenson's aesthetic. In this gesture of repudiation, such critics (and biographers as well) follow directly in the line of nineteenth-century critics like Croker and Edgeworth, and this propensity merits further examination.

Beginning with the treatment of Owenson's "sentimental patriotism" in his classic 1959 study, *The Irish Novelists, 1800–1850*, Thomas Flanagan is one of the first critics to take the time to pay attention to Owenson within the context of a literary tradition, or indeed to attend to her at all. He begins on a note picked up by most critics who follow, as he generously acknowledges "the unhappy fact—*The Wild Irish Girl* is a bad novel."[9] To Flanagan, the reason for this judgment is self-evident: despite her laudable ability to represent "many Irelands," she is ultimately damned for the mode in which she captures them. In an interesting logical step he makes an assertion meant to invoke a commonsense equation: "Because the image was sentimental it was false."[10] Thus, both Ireland and England suffer "an unpleasant disillusionment" from Owenson's significant influence on the tradition of Irish fiction that follows her bold experiment with the Anglo-Irish national tale. Even her patriotism is ultimately vitiated by the more sober judgment of the critic, who sees it as "a nebulous pastel over which some Ossianic coloring has been daubed."[11]

Here Owenson is cast as an artist, but only one of the sloppiest (and implicitly derivative) sort. If she provides local color, it is only in feminized "pastels" with hints, perhaps, of a deeper, more masculine "coloring" borrowed from James Macpherson's infamous "translations." The reader might be forgiven for suspecting that this literary connection is also meant as an unkind cut: if Ossianic poetry was a fad of the moment and Owenson's writing style derives from it, this makes her even less significant than an elaborate literary forgery by Macpherson.[12] In addition to the explicitly gendered paternalism reflected in this commentary—less remarkable, perhaps, in a critical work from the 1950s—we are also left with a subtle suggestion that Owenson's and Macpherson's works share not only a pervasive sentimentalism but also a corrupt and compromised scholarly attempt at cultural recovery. Sentimentalism, as the sign of inauthentic feeling, here signals a correspondent inauthenticity in antiquarian reconstructions of cultural history (in Owenson) or poetic translation (in Macpherson). Feeling and history, in other words, do not mix—at least, not in this explicitly feminized mode.

Lest this judgment appear a formative aberration, Seamus Deane follows nearly thirty years later (1986) with an even more thorough dismissal: *The Wild Irish Girl*, Deane quips, is "a work deficient in almost everything a novel should have, except success."[13] In general, as one often finds in critical writing on the early nineteenth century, Owenson pales in his comparison to the artistry of Edgeworth. This disdain for Owenson is clearly due in large part to what Deane labels "the anachronistic nature of her political convictions." Unlike the Edgeworths, Deane has little time for "the unreality of her Whig dream of reconciliation," so the fate of "exile and bitterness" she earns late in life sounds in his assessment like fitting punishment for a writer who could never get her politics quite right.[14] If for Flanagan, patriotic politics are largely undermined by sentimental style, for Deane, matters of style are completely subsumed by political considerations; they are beneath the critic's notice altogether. Owenson becomes little more than an annoying historical curiosity.

In an article from the following year (1987), Elmer Andrews is far more extreme as well as comprehensive, hitting on all the major objections previously articulated by critics of the novel. Sounding like Croker's legitimate heir in his dismissals of both style and politics, Andrews insists that "*The Wild Irish Girl* is a poor novel . . . [filled with] fulsome extravagance," "the most extravagant hyperbole," "pompous pedantry . . . [and] pseudo-facts . . . clumsily incorporated," "inherent chauvinism, the glamorization of ineffectualness and impracticality . . . [and] preoccupation with the past"; it is "overtly propagandistic, pedantic, false . . . easily and perhaps mercifully forgotten," as well as "wearisomely repetitive, laboured, and pompous." Then, in a moment approaching analytic judgment, he claims that "[t]he writing lacks coherence for it does not spring from any deep centre of emotional involvement." Finally, perhaps worst of all, he concludes that "[t]he novel is inadequate to its epoch because of its ethical reduction of history."[15] Without a doubt, this excessive criticism attempts to match its excessive subject.

But rather than succumb to the temptation to dismiss the critic on the same basis for which he would do so with the author, I want to suggest that there is something suggestive and important to be learned from taking both Owenson and Andrews seriously. What could it mean for a literary work to be "inadequate to its epoch," and on what grounds could one make such an assessment? One might just as easily make an analogous claim about Jane Austen's fiction in relation to Sir Walter Scott's, and nineteenth-century critics—led in part by Scott himself—certainly did. But measuring "adequacy" here begs a multitude of potentially useful questions, as does an unarticulated notion of history or ethics. In what ways does Owenson fall short, in comparison to what more adequate works, and with what implications for the epoch, or for its critic? What kind of history is being reinforced here, and what others undermined or occluded? These questions are related directly to matters of politics and ethics; as David Lloyd has argued so persuasively, the frames of historical narrative have a way of detaching "pasts that envisaged different futures," and thus "furnishing only debris, remnants, whose excavation proves only the inevitability of their passing."[16]

Thus, if Andrews's last statement seems puzzling in the midst of so much rebarbative reductionism, it is nonetheless important to examine as an indicator of persistent cultural assumptions that require unmasking. In order to clarify these issues in relation to literary history in particular, I would like to interrupt the strict chronology established thus far in order to help make sense of this extraordinary response from one of our own contemporaries by comparing it to a response by a contemporary of Owenson. One might, for instance, compare Andrews's rhetoric to a well-known piece of commentary that precedes Owenson's novel by four years:

> a multitude of causes unknown to former times are now acting with a combined force to blunt the discriminating powers of the mind, and unfitting it for all voluntary exertion to reduce it to a state of almost savage torpor . . . The invaluable works of our elder writers . . . are driven into neglect by frantic novels, sickly and stupid German Tragedies, and deluges of idle and extravagant stories in verse.—When I think upon this degrading thirst after outrageous stimulation I am almost ashamed to have spoken of the feeble effort with which I have endeavored to counteract it.[17]

In this uncharacteristically overwrought prose, William Wordsworth identifies the literary and cultural enemies against which he will distinguish himself and his work for an audience contemporary with Owenson's first literary efforts. Given the canonical stature of this quintessential Romantic poet and his polemical "Preface" to the famous collection of *Lyrical Ballads*, it is clear that he succeeded in creating the taste by which he would be judged. What is less clear is whether his success was inevitable, as literary histories also tend to assume. Like Horatio, berated by his father at the outset of Owenson's novel, we might say that Wordsworth has been schooled in "the destructive atmosphere of pleasure." In fact, Wordsworth's own (post–*Lyrical Ballads*) trajectory begins much less auspiciously in the eighteenth century with a classic poetic address of Sensibility to Helen Maria Williams, radical firsthand chronicler of French Revolutionary events and a fellow "feeling poet" who translated the sentimental blockbuster, *Paul et Virginie*.

This debut effort proves embarrassing enough to Wordsworth that, instead of merely moving on in a fresh vein, he inveighs against the very forms of literary expression in which his own are so fully steeped. For his mature writings are part of a Romantic project that is realized through the construction of a powerful developmental narrative of individual growth —still predicated on pleasure, though pleasure properly tempered and constrained—a bold new narrative that is erected over the stylistic and ideological infrastructure provided by these offending varieties of excessive writing he now decries. Returning to our Owenson parallel, it would be more accurate to say that Wordsworth occupies both positions, errant son and moralizing father at the same time; in his own well-known formulation: "the child is father of the man." Thus, when literary historians search for a moment when the death knell of Sensibility and sentimentalism was sounded, this document must serve as one of the principal pieces of evidence. It should scarcely be necessary to note that the bulk of this writing was done by women writers, most of whom wrote in a sentimental mode of stylistic "extravagance," and many of whom broached the unladylike territory of politics (even in the form of genuine radicals), and some of whom also managed to do one or both successfully enough to give a literary innovator like Wordsworth a significant measure of market competition. Owenson, naturally, committed all three sins, and she did so during Wordsworth's heyday.[18]

In addition to the Ossianic poetry of Macpherson, Owenson evidently was influenced by the Germanic excesses of Goethe's *Sorrows of Young Werther*, if not by the "sickly and stupid German Tragedies" mentioned in the "Preface." And there is little doubt that from Wordsworth's perspective *The Wild Irish Girl* would be considered, among other things, a "frantic novel" further exacerbated by the inclusion of some "idle and extravagant stories in verse"—one of Owenson's other specialties, as Croker noted. Both Wordsworth's and Andrews's responses show that throughout the critical history of responses to Owenson, the intense crescendo of rhetoric conveys a disturbed response bordering on moral panic. Critical excess is called in to stamp out literary excess because the stakes are much higher than mere "taste." In both instances, distaste for the sentimental excesses of women writers such as Owenson signals a deeper, unacknowledged distaste for a specific flavor of cultural politics, as well as the politics of style. The more biting the invective, the more likely we are to find these two concerns of style and politics conflated, here and elsewhere, with fears of an "ethical reduction" clearly spanning from the late-eighteenth to the late twentieth century.

Another decade after Deane and Andrews, Terry Eagleton discusses "the problem of Morgan's texts" as an "imagination at odds with their ideology" and refers to her "saccharine confection" generated from a "vein of vacuously sublimated desire," which works against what is to him a far more laudable element of "adroit satirical intelligence."[19] A mixed review, perhaps, and one might expect to find the usual unfavorable comparison to a rival novelist, given his appreciation of a "satirical intelligence" more commonly associated with Edgeworth. Instead, Eagleton finds Owenson's political intentions—if not their execution—to be ideologically exculpatory. In rather extravagant fashion himself, he claims that "[i]n *The Wild Irish Girl*, she manufactured a whole new symbolic matrix for Irish female identity"; this celebration is merited by a politics which he places "considerably to the left of any other major 19th-century Irish writer."[20] But Owenson is indeed more complex than this judgment suggests, as Eagleton himself acknowledges in allowing for her passionate contraries: she is "a passionate feminist . . . an admirer of radical republicanism, an advocate of Catholic Emancipation, and a dedicated antagonist of the Tory Ascendancy"; yet all of these characterizations are counterbalanced by her seeming "ease in the bosom of the Establishment," her dislike of Catholics and well-documented distrust of O'Connell, her putative nature as a "spiritual aristocrat and Gaelic traditionalist," and her claim "to a friend that she was 'every inch a wife.' "[21] As Owenson criticism goes, this is considerably generous, far closer than most of her previous critics come to establishing a balance between perceived limitations and acknowledged accomplishments.

Of course, this assessment also succeeds in foregrounding the critic's own political commitments. If for Croker, Owenson was too radical in her anti-Tory politics, for Eagleton she is clearly not radical enough. Indeed, the latter perspective is not a new one; Deane makes similar claims for the limits of Owenson's Whiggish conciliatory nationalism, as he sees it. But neither Croker nor Eagleton are interested in taking seriously the "extravagances" that nearly every critic of Owenson has duly noted and then decried, or at best, for which they have felt the need to apologize. The problem with this blind spot, shared in equal measure by both critics, is that to read Owenson's novel for what it is one needs to understand the degree to which her style is in fact central to her politics. Style is not a superficial dressing garment, culled from the theatrical wardrobe so often called to mind by her father's profession, or mere "coloring" to be daubed on the artistic canvas of the novel. Owenson is working within a specific kind of aesthetic which makes assumptions of its early nineteenth-century readers that simply are not shared by most readers two centuries later. This aesthetic practice, already presumed dead in Owenson's day and preferred in this state by today's critics, is still an actively shaping force that betrays a specific politics of its own in 1806 and beyond: the politics of Sensibility.

The ongoing investment in Sensibility by writers of the era commonly labeled Romantic emerges as a significant literary historical problem in part as a result of the general assumption that this tradition was confined to the cultural landscape of the eighteenth century. Since the period dating roughly from 1780 to 1830 is dominated by the more celebrated aesthetic movement of Romanticism and its most traditionally visible (mostly male) figures, this inheritance and its continued presence are often obscured in conventional narratives of nineteenth-century literary history. With rare exceptions, when attention is paid to earlier influences, they are relegated to precursors who throw into comparatively stark relief the bold, visionary, even revolutionary change initiated by the later writers. Through the dialectical machinery of literary history, they are set up in order to be absorbed and transcended, if not merely knocked down. When this narrative is accepted, major features of writing like Owenson's—in this case, her excesses or so-called stylistic eccentricities—seem both exceptional and exceptionable to most readers: imagination at odds with its own ideology.

I would insist, however, that what they really are is unreadable, at least to the critic who presumes their inevitable and fortuitous passing.

The problem is far more wide-ranging than my brief summary has suggested to this point, especially when one considers not just the presence of active antagonism or apologetics, but also the startling absence of critical attention to the source of the excesses considered so offensive by the critics mentioned. One might expect fewer commonalities between early nineteenth- and late twentieth-century critical opinions, especially from those in the latter group who profess an investment in history. In fact, this absence of attention to specific issues of style is all the more surprising because there has been outstanding recent work on Owenson that is far more in tune with the subtleties of her project and the context in which she wrote—particularly the immediate historical context of the early nineteenth century—some of which has rich implications for a wide range of central issues addressed by current literary and cultural theorists. But even when scholars are more friendly to Owenson's perceived political agenda, an explanation for the nagging question of *why* she indulges in such stylistic excesses is simply not sought. Better, it would seem, to pass over this matter in silence, despite its admitted centrality to the text, than to appear to condone (or worse, even to enjoy) such writing. No one, of course, wants to publicly embrace "bad taste."[22] So if recent critics can reclaim her ethics from the realms of the reductive, and her politics from anachronism, it should be possible now to reframe her aesthetic commitments as well.

As I have suggested, a politics of taste is exactly what is at stake here, in addition to a taste for politics. Regardless of one's feelings about ideological positioning, everyone is willing to agree that sentimental stylistic excesses are beyond the pale, especially in the early nineteenth century, when such features are supposed to be a thing of the past. Viewed in the context of the Wordsworthian prescriptions mentioned earlier, these kinds of once-pleasurable excesses are now simply tasteless. Small wonder that with such critical unanimity no one wants to touch Owenson without inoculation from this contagion. The primary concern I have is to make a strong case against such literary hygienics. The reason for this commitment is at least twofold. Firstly, it will help us to account for the still unaccountable style of Owenson—occluded largely because it remains divorced from its earlier, eighteenth-century context—and to examine its significance to her own era rather than presuming it has none beyond marking the limits of her talent. Secondly, such attention also can provide a means of assessing how useful the mode of Sensibility is in enabling the nationalist cultural work she undertakes with *The Wild Irish Girl*. Tracing the play of Sensibility in Owenson's work will also allow us to see her as less anomalous in other ways, for instance, as an Anglo-Irish writer with mixed loyalties and a complex politics that need not be explained away as simply inconsistent or ambiguous or anachronistic—features that characterize what Joep Leerssen refers to as "Morganatic Ireland."[23] The tradition of Sensibility in fact draws her into the well-established company of a large group of Irish and Scottish writers—Eagleton dubs them "Good-Natured Gaels"—whose names are readily associated with Sensibility.[24]

Since Janet Todd's influential primer on Sensibility, the reigning assumption has been that, wildly popular as it was, writing in this vein was virtually stamped out during the repressive 1790s, when all forms of excess became too threatening for British tastes to entertain.[25] But it is vital to note that this narrative is not only incomplete, failing as it does to account for exceptions to the rule; it also establishes a rule that is plainly inaccurate: consider Wordsworth's oft-cited "Preface" and his first published poem, the weeping sonnet written to Helen Maria Williams, Mary Wollstonecraft's short fiction from roughly the same time, the novels of both William Godwin and Ann Radcliffe, later writing in prose and verse by Mary and Percy Shelley, the poetry of John Keats, the fiction of Frances Burney and Jane Austen, as well as the less canonical work of figures such as Ann Batten Cristall, Mary Robinson, Charlotte Dacre, Isabella Lickbarrow, Mary Tighe, and Owenson herself. This short list is representative but far from exhaustive and, with these writers privileging pleasure and feeling communities at the center of their work, it attests that Sensibility was alive and well in the late eighteenth and early nineteenth century.

What still obscures its full recognition by most readers today is the development of a new aesthetic revolution called Romanticism, a literary mode with explicit ties to major historical events that conventionally serve to demarcate its period dates (while begging questions about the inspiration and influence of these events on the literary works): the American and French Revolutions on one end and the Reform Act and accession of Victoria on the other. Owenson's own career extends further into the nineteenth century, but the principal historical events with which critics presume her to be concerned—the 1798 Rising, the 1800 Act of Union, Emmet's abortive rising in 1803, Waterloo (1815), and Catholic Emancipation in 1829—all fall within the confines of the same period and encourage the commonsense view of her as another Romantic writer.[26] This is all the more reason to note that these influential historical events are themselves embedded within a discursive network that depends on imaginative forms of representation for their own emergence. To be made visible at all, in other words, both literary and historical tales must be crafted, they must have "recourse to figuration," and the boundaries between the two are seldom likely to be clean or clear, especially in an Irish context.[27] Additionally, the forms of Owenson's early work are not merely "Romantic," but first and foremost sentimental, products of the culture of Sensibility, which imagined the blurring of boundaries between individuals and nations through acts of sympathetic benevolence in all of its key texts that follow Laurence Sterne. One of the great losses to literary history of this period is not just our difficulty in understanding why such works of excessive feeling continued to be popular, that is, of appreciating the work as its original audience was able to do.[28] Even more importantly, perhaps, is our inability to recognize Sensibility even when it is—a favorite spot of Sterne's—right under our noses.

To return us to this spot, then, I want to return to the puzzle of Owenson reception by considering the perspective of one other key nineteenth-century critic. This individual took Owenson to task on the occasion of the reissuing of *The Wild Irish Girl* in 1846. The critic regards the now forty-year-old work as "a juvenile indiscretion"—misattributing the novel in the process as "a first book"—characterized by "*incorrigible* errors of style," "exaggerated and very youthful opinions," and "early ignorance."[29] Credit is due, in other words, for maturity, and Owenson (now Lady Morgan, following her marriage) is acknowledged as the author of her more recent and perhaps more ambitious work, *Woman and her Master*, and credited with writing now from "*a more enlarged experience*" (246). In the process, she is also placed within the company of those considered to be the most illustrious living examples of Irish writers (including "Miss Edgeworth"), and given retrospective credit for writing a book of this sort at a time when "it was dangerous to write on Ireland, hazardous to praise her, and difficult to find a publisher for an Irish tale which had a political tendency"; for all of these reasons, it was an act of "no small *publishing moral courage*" (254–55). Ultimately, this critic means not to bury the author, despite her numerous and well enumerated failings, but to justify Owenson's ways to men and women who might still read her in 1846, in a new and substantially altered political climate. In this particular instance, critic and author are the same.

Thus the current Lady Morgan will enter her contribution to the vexed reception of Sydney Owenson. And this distinction takes on an added significance since the critical assessment cited above comes from the author's new "Prefatory Address" to the 1846 edition of the novel, a work which is now advertised as written by Sydney Owenson, but "edited by" Lady Morgan. Such a textual peculiarity might seem to suggest an identity crisis, but this curious bifurcation of identity is arguably fitting in a number of ways, not the least of which is the shift in emphasis—mirrored throughout the

"Address"—that both calls attention to her 'hyphenated' identity as an Anglo-Irish writer and makes clear that her perspective increasingly reflects an Anglo perspective on Irish affairs. Between its initial publication in 1806 and its reissue a generation later, four turbulent decades of change had shaped Owenson's perspective on Ireland and on life more generally. Enough had changed, apparently, to make Owenson's original work seem almost unrecognizable even to the author herself. Or to be more accurate, her work has become altogether too recognizable, the product of an early identity of which she is now "a *little* ashamed" (245). In a virtual echo of her old detractors, the satisfaction with which Owenson can enjoy "[becoming] her own posterity," as she sees her first major work back into print, must be counterbalanced by a gesture of distance bordering on disavowal.

Does this explain the choice to label the book's editor as "Lady Morgan"? Surely the gesture to establish a component of "juvenile indiscretion" in the original work enables the emergence of an older, wiser persona, one who will temper "its *incorrigible* errors of style" with the maturity and judgment of one who has studied both her craft and her place in society more fully over the years. But interestingly, not only do we find a surprisingly self-deprecatory preface which performs a standard kind of gendered apologia, but we also encounter an array of corrective footnotes, often criticizing, but also embellishing the original novel of "Sydney Owenson." In other words, the shift from Owenson to Morgan is not merely a matter of registering distance; it is also an acknowledgment of intimate connection and a measure of almost treasured recognition. The attraction-repulsion dynamic is not the reserved province of other critics of Owenson. In the end, she is drawn in as fully as they are.

Unlike the typical apologetics of so many women writers of the first half of the nineteenth century, Owenson does not shirk at the outset from her intrusion into the public arena of publishing. Rather, having boldly intervened in an extraordinarily significant cultural debate over the politics of Anglo-Irish relations at the turn of the century, she now chooses to revisit her earlier success and call it into question. In some ways this move might seem utterly conventional and expected: the comfortably pensioned and established writer looking back wistfully to her more naïve days and wishing to disavow the flights of fancy many might see as her juvenilia. But Owenson is certainly also aware that in many circles this novel was taken terribly seriously, and it is not merely with its politics that she now quibbles. Here is where the 1846 footnotes are particularly telling. Amid omissions and additions there are clear political statements meant to contrast her earlier, more heated ideals. In general they tend to be highly animated but mostly middle-of-the-road perspectives like the following note to volume 3: "If liberty means the enjoyment of natural rights, the Irish never enjoyed it;—neither under the tyranny of their own barbarous despots, nor under the sway of the ungrateful Stuarts, the enemies of Ireland and paid slaves of France. It was an act of the Imperial Parliament of Great Britain that bestowed on them the rights of men through that of conscience—Catholic Emancipation" (323, n. 185.4). Both the presumably Gaelic "despots" and the francophile English of the Stuart line are long gone by now, and so too, apparently, is that most tempestuous debate over the Union of the two nations; astonishingly, she passes over it in silence on the way to celebrating the great Emancipation at the hands of the generous British Parliament. To drive the moral home more clearly, a footnote in the preface notes that "Ireland, who is made so well acquainted with her Saxon foes, should also know something of her English friends" (262). One imagines that Owensen now numbers herself, implicitly, among the latter.

Amid the multitude of additional textual notes there are also outright attacks on extravagances of style—"What a bathos!" she adds at one point in the narrative—including those where she is clearly laughing at her own expense (324, n.200.9). But there are also quite a number of sentimental embellishments in this curious mix, usually introduced to establish her continued proximity to Irish culture. These intimate moments function much like the famously copious footnotes of the original edition of the novel, performing a running testimony to the authenticity of Owenson's firsthand experiences in Ireland. Since most readers would acknowledge the original footnotes as one of the novel's primary forms of excess, one might reasonably wonder why she would elect to add still more rather than simply to omit or emend. One reason is suggested in Owenson's prefatory claim that "her early ignorance has been corrected, by a more extensive reading" than previously was available to her (246). But establishing proof of an editor more learned than the original author is only part of the picture, especially in instances where the character of the note is profoundly sentimental. How else can we explain a seemingly random reminiscence like that in which "The Editor" claims her ability "at this moment [to] *hum* the air with which the women of Connaught call in their cow, when they have one"? Or when another scene in the novel is described as "a portrait," for which "[t]he original is impressed in memory in indelible characters"?[30]

Again we can make sense of this decision by returning to the tradition of Sensibility. One year before Tennyson's "Tears, Idle Tears" will commemorate "the days that are no more" Owenson takes a similar stylistic path. Maintaining and even reinforcing her sentimental connection to an imagined community and a cultural identity that is now increasingly distant from her current life and career in London—after Catholic Emancipation and after the production of her Irish novels—is Owenson's best means of reestablishing a feeling connection to the people and times with which she has lost touch. As Eagleton cannily notes, contrasting Owenson with her competition again, "For Edgeworth, the past is mainly loss, to be relinquished for a reforming future; for Morgan, it is the present which is void, and the past a dangerously two-sided instrument for renewing it."[31] This pithy summation is at least partly true. With a touch like that of Sterne, an attempt to engage in what the earlier writer called "sentimental commerce," Owenson can try to navigate this difficult and increasingly attenuated landscape, selectively renewing the past in the present so it is not "void" at all.

In other words, the feeling testimony provided by Owenson's reminiscences is not merely an escape into the past, it is a reactivation of it, both Ireland's and her own—from genuine glory to regrettable bathos, warts and all—for herself and for her audience, present and future. In this sense, "becom[ing] her own posterity" is a gesture more radical than retrograde, opening up the possibility that she has not only inadvertently bequeathed this youthful work to an older, wiser self, but also suggesting that the cultural work done so ably in an earlier time might, in its renovated state, be of new use in future eras. The degree to which emotion is foundational in animating her narrative enables her to put history in motion, assuring that the past will never really be past, but ready to come alive for new generations. If others follow her model—from Owenson to Morgan, and back again—similar narratives might be written. This endless circuit provides a kind of feedback loop of sentimental and historical pleasure, comfortably shuttling back and forth between nations, perspectives, and personae. It seems the perfect model for the writer who is now perhaps most famous for her claim that she was born on the Irish Sea, between the nations that both made their claims on her, two nations on which she left her own troubling and enduring mark.

Notes

1. Jacqueline Belanger, "Some Preliminary Remarks on the Production and Reception of Fiction Relating to Ireland, 1800-1829," *Cardiff Corvey: Reading the Romantic Text* 4.2 (2000), http://www.cf.ac.uk/encap/corvey/articles/cc04_n02.html.

2. See Kathryn Kirkpatrick's trade edition of Sydney Owenson, Lady Morgan, *The Wild Irish Girl: A National Tale* (New York: Oxford University Press, 1999) and the scholarly edition edited by Claire Connolly and Stephen Copley (London: Pickering & Chatto, 2000). For ease of reference I cite both editions in this order; all subsequent citations appear within the text above.

3. I use capitalization here to distinguish the broader cultural movement and stylistic mode of Sensibility from its merely local manifestations in texts from the era. This choice also is made in part to reinforce the fact that Sensibility, like Romanticism, refers not just to a discrete body of literary texts—or still less, the transitory fashion of a "cult"—but rather to a wide body of ideas, attitudes, and practices that were central to various forms of cultural production from approximately 1740 to 1840. Throughout the essay I follow John Mullan's useful distinction between Sensibility and "sentimental," using the latter to describe a representation; as he puts it, "a person possessed 'sensibility'; a text was 'sentimental.'" See "Sentimental Novels," in *The Cambridge Companion to the Eighteenth Century Novel*, ed. John Richetti (Cambridge: Cambridge University Press, 1996), 238. For a slightly different and more expansive treatment of this subject see my *Sexuality and the Culture of Sensibility in the British Romantic Era* (New York: Palgrave, 2007).

4. Mary Campbell, *Lady Morgan: The Life and Times of Sydney Owenson* (London: Pandora, 1988), 72. For those who are familiar, these remarks are reminiscent of the extreme vitriol of the moralizing critic Vicesimus Knox in his attacks on Laurence Sterne and other "immoral" writers of excessive sentiment in the 1780s and 1790s.

5. Claire Connolly, "'I accuse Miss Owenson': *The Wild Irish Girl* as Media Event," *Colby Quarterly* 36.2 (June 2000): 98–115. Connolly is borrowing this label from William Warner's *Licensing Entertainment: The Elevation of Novel Reading in Britain, 1684–1750* (Berkeley and Los Angeles: University of California Press, 1998).

6. Campbell, *Lady Morgan*, 96.

7. Quoted in Ibid., 73–74.

8. It is a moment worthy, in fact, of an Edgeworth novel such as *Belinda*: through the proper moral influence of a healthy and respectable family (the Percivals), the ingénue is saved from the errors into which she might be seduced by the darker but flashier example of a morally dubious parent-mentor (Lady Delacour) or such a figure's flamboyant and flattering consorts (Clarence Hervey and Harriet Freke).

9. Thomas Flanagan, *The Irish Novelists, 1800–1850* (New York: Columbia University Press, 1959), 119.

10. Ibid., 119–20.

11. Ibid., 125.

12. For a good, brief synopsis of the controversy and the ongoing (not merely faddish) influence of Ossian, see Fiona Stafford's introduction to Howard Gaskill's edition of *The Poems of Ossian and Related Works* (Edinburgh: Edinburgh University Press, 1996). See also Joep Leerssen, *Remembrance and Imagination: Patterns in the Historical and Literary Representation of Ireland in the Nineteenth Century* (Notre Dame: University of Notre Dame Press, 1997), 40.

13. Seamus Deane, *A Short History of Irish Literature* (Notre Dame: University of Notre Dame Press, 1986), 97–98.

14. Ibid., 99.

15. Elmer Andrews, "Aesthetics, Politics and Identity: Lady Morgan's *The Wild Irish Girl*," *Canadian Journal of Irish Studies* 12.2 (December 1987): 7–19. Quoted citations, respectively, from pages 7, 14, 15, 18, 7, 13, 13, 16.

16. David Lloyd, *Ireland After History* (Notre Dame: University of Notre Dame Press, 1999), 1.

17. William Wordsworth, "Preface to *Lyrical Ballads*," in Anne K. Mellor and Richard Matlak, eds., *British Literature 1780–1830* (New York: Harcourt Brace, 1996), 575–76.

18. Though Wordsworth never mentions Owenson by name, Duncan Wu notes the family's purchase of at least six volumes of her works, *The Book of the Boudoir* (2 vols., 1829)

and *The O'Briens and the O'Flaherty's* (4 vols., 1827). See *Wordsworth's Reading, 1800–1815* (New York: Cambridge University Press, 1995), 267–68. It is fair to assume that he knew her work. On Wordsworth's relationship to women writers and the Sensibility tradition, see *Sexuality and the Culture of Sensibility*.

19. Terry Eagleton, *Heathcliff and the Great Hunger* (New York: Verso, 1995), 178, 179.

20. Ibid., 184; 185.

21. Ibid., 185; 185–86.

22. Thus, we find even a fairly recent edition of the novel introduced by Brigid Brophy: "Many novels are deplorably bad. *The Wild Irish Girl* is one of a few to be delightfully so." *The Wild Irish Girl*, ed. Brigid Brophy (London: Pandora, 1986), vii. A familiar paradox returns here: the novel might be bad, but it still brings a kind of guilty pleasure nonetheless. Mary Campbell's biography of Owenson remarks that the novel "seems now a light-weight piece of confection," with "flimsy" plots and "fit-up scenery . . . straight out of the property basket" on stage (*Lady Morgan*, 71). Though Campbell at least addresses the novel's cultural influence, there seems little reason now to revisit a novel that she suggests would have made a better play.

23. Leerssen, *Remembrance and Imagination*, 53–57.

24. Terry Eagleton, *Crazy John and the Bishop* (Notre Dame: University of Notre Dame Press, 1998), 68–139. These figures include: Richard Steele, David Hume, Adam Ferguson, Robert Burns, Oliver Goldsmith, Adam Smith, Henry Mackenzie, Hugh Blair, Frances Sheridan, Laurence Sterne, Charlotte Brooke, Henry Brooke, Frances Hutcheson, James Macpherson, Edmund Burke, Charles Macklin, Hugh Kelly, and David Fordyce. The virtual absence of women writers and thinkers from this list deserves separate consideration. Good starting points that address women's central contribution to this tradition can be found in G. J. Barker-Benfield, *The Culture of Sensibility: Sex and Society in Eighteenth-Century Britain* (Chicago: University of Chicago Press, 1992); Jerome McGann, *The Poetics of Sensibility: A Revolution in Literary Style* (New York: Oxford University Press, 1996); and Patricia Spacks, *Privacy: Concealing the Eighteenth-Century Self* (Chicago: University of Chicago Press, 2003). Ina Ferris's *The Romantic National Tale and the Question of Ireland* (New York: Cambridge University Press, 2002) brilliantly illuminates the dynamics of Humean "sympathy" in Owenson's work, but does not explore the significant literary tradition of Sensibility.

25. Janet Todd, *Sensibility: An Introduction* (London: Methuen, 1986).

26. As biographies such as Campbell's make clear, there are good reasons for seeing Owenson's public persona as Romantic, in all senses, particularly thanks to her self-display through sartorial excesses and performance on the harp. Natasha Tessone explicitly connects this facet of performance with the antiquarianism of the novel, arguing that Owenson plays Glorvina to great effect in her public life. See "Displaying Ireland: Sydney Owenson and the Politics of Spectacular Antiquarianism," *Eire-Ireland* 37.3–4 (2002): 169–86.

27. Luke Gibbons, *Transformations in Irish Culture* (Notre Dame: University of Notre Dame Press, 1996), 142. See also Gibbons's "Narratives of the Nation: Fact, Fiction and Irish Cinema" in Luke Dodd, ed., *Nationalisms: Visions and Revisions* (Dublin: Film Institute of Ireland, 1999), 66–73.

28. Indeed, the success of *The Wild Irish Girl* itself provides some testimony to this fact, racing through seven editions by 1813, including three American editions, as well as additional translations into German and French, followed by later English editions in 1822, 1846, 1850, 1855, 1857, 1867, 1879, and 1883.

29. *The Wild Irish Girl*, ed. Claire Connolly and Stephen Copley (London: Pickering & Chatto, 2000), 245, 246. Hereafter cited in the text.

30. Owenson 313 (n.26.42; n.22.36). In a recent analysis that does not examine the 1846 preface, Lisa L. Moore reads the use of a fictional "editor" of the original 1806 tale along with the novel's characters as betraying a "slippage between two equally fictional interpretations of history . . . between romance and history," but her reading ignores both the conventions of Sensibility and the possibilities of irony within a work she sees as marked by a standard mode of (Romantic) "sincerity." See "Acts of Union: Sexuality and Nationalism, Romance and Realism in the Irish National Tale," *Cultural Critique* 44 (Winter 2000): 131.

31. Eagleton, *Heathcliff*, 186.

"So near to us as a Sister": Incestuous Unions in Sydney Owenson's *The Wild Irish Girl* and Maria Edgeworth's *The Absentee*

Susan M. Kroeg

IN 1799, ONE YEAR AFTER THE VIOLENT REBELLION THAT PROMPTED BRITAIN to put an end to Irish independence, English law student George Cooper toured through Ireland to see for himself with what and whom Britain was about to unite.[1] He published his account, *Letters on the Irish Nation*, in 1800, the year of the Act of Union. Despite his less-than-flattering portrayal of the Irish people, Cooper favored the Act of Union as a means of returning Ireland to the imperial fold and strengthening Britain's position vis-à-vis France. Cooper draws on a number of tropes then current to describe the relationship between Great Britain and Ireland, most reflecting a Burkean notion of the state as a patriarchal family: "Men form the rudiments of families; families constitute the elements of states; and in every system the parts will be found by their respective excellencies to promote the perfection and harmony of the whole."[2] Ireland is repeatedly described by Cooper (and others) as the "sister kingdom," a familial term indicative of the intimate bond between Britain and Ireland. "Sisterhood," however, placed Britain and Ireland on relatively equal footing, so Cooper repeatedly reconfigures the "family" of the new United Kingdom to reflect his perception of their sharply differentiated roles within it.[3] In several places, Ireland is described as the wayward child of an indulgent parent: "The mother country opens out her arms to embrace and relieve the child which had deserted her."[4] Elsewhere, Cooper invokes the metaphor which came to dominate contemporary discourse about the Union, a marriage in which a "wealthy suitor offers his hand" to an impoverished wild Irish girl.[5] Child or bride, after the Union "the (then no longer) sister kingdom" must occupy a "dependant and subordinate" position in the family-state.[6]

Writers and artists in many genres and on all sides of the issue gravitated toward the metaphor of marriage to describe the Union, as one that stressed the potential for a contractual and therefore more reciprocal (albeit hierarchical) partnership. Ireland is figured as Hibernia to England's John Bull, or more rarely, a cautious "Pat" succumbing to the charms of Britannia.[7] While, as Mary Jean Corbett notes, it is dangerous to assume the naturalness of any metaphor that relies on gendered notions of power,[8] marriage seems to have worked well as a vehicle for characterizing many aspects of the relationship between Britain and Ireland: an awkward and belated courtship, Ireland's reluctance, Britain's "coersive kindness," and later, the desire for a legal separation to end what many saw as a failed marriage.[9] Novels, too, participated readily in this nuptial discourse. Numerous scholars have read the impending marriages of the "English" heroes and "Irish" heroines at the conclusions of Sydney Owenson's *The Wild Irish Girl* (1806) and Maria Edgeworth's *The Absentee* (1812) as figurative, even allegorical, "acts of union."[10]

Although the novels' marriage plots are not, as some have claimed, "unproblematic,"[11] the centrality, and seeming fitness, of the marriage metaphor has obviated other interpretive possibilities. Cooper's *Letters*, however, remind us that, despite its prominence, marriage had not yet been fixed as the "natural" metaphor for the relationship between Great Britain and Ireland at the time of the Act of Union; other possibilities were actively in play, and some threatened to undermine the appropriateness of the "marriage" bond. In particular, the metaphor of Ireland as child or sister to Britain reflects a long-standing, turbulent, yet intimate relationship between Britain and Ireland.[12] A shared history, combined with physical proximity, fosters a powerful bond—between countries, no less than between parent and child, or between siblings—but under what circumstances, if any, could a child or sister become a wife? As Ireland and Britain debated the desirability of a union between the two kingdoms, another "marriage" debate raged in English society among those who sough to prohibit certain relationships, once and for all, on the grounds of incest.[13]

Ellen Pollak has argued in *Incest and the English Novel* that "incest narratives of the long eighteenth century work both to articulate and to obscure the ideological contradictions occasioned by the shift from patriarchal to 'egalitarian' models of familial order."[14] Within an Irish context, when more patriarchal metaphors of consanguinity (i.e., Ireland as "sister kingdom") fail to give way completely to supposedly more egalitarian metaphors of affinity (Union as "marriage" or partnership), incest signals the incomplete paradigm shift. Incest was a contested concept throughout the long eighteenth century, one that at various times included sexual relations between not only siblings or parent and child, but also guardian and ward or first cousins. By Union-era standards, the proposed marriages in both *The Wild Irish Girl* and *The Absentee* bear some taint of incest. In suggesting the potentially incestuous nature of Anglo-Irish union, Edgeworth and Owenson expose the troubling collapse of boundaries and conflation of identities inherent in it.

Although they did not see eye-to-eye politically (Owenson was a separatist, while Edgeworth supported the Union),[15] both women recognized the need to negotiate and carefully construct their own "Irishness." Edgeworth was born in 1767 or 1768 in England to a prominent Anglo-Irish family; she first went to Ireland in 1773 and subsequently spent much of her adult life there. Owenson is believed to have been born in 1776; she "liked to claim that she was born while her English mother was crossing the Irish Channel to meet her Irish father."[16] As Owenson's apocryphal tale of her birth suggests, she saw herself as a border crosser, someone who did not fit neatly in a purely "Irish" or purely "English" identity, although she was intensely patriotic about issues of Irish nationalism. Similarly, Maria Edgeworth saw herself as a "friend" to Ireland, but not necessarily "Irish," and her work repeatedly reveals her ambivalence about the ability of the Anglo-Irish colonizers to speak for the native Irish people. As both authors' lives and works indicate, identity can be learned, performed, and denied, but the ability to do so depends on an awareness, even an acceptance, of difference. Union, no less than incest, transgresses boundaries, breaks down distinctions, and erases difference. Terry Eagleton has argued that "The Act of Union between Great Britain and Ireland . . . is a peculiarly incestuous form of congress, in which the border between difference and identity, alienness and intimacy, is constantly transgressed."[17] In both *The Wild Irish Girl* and *The Absentee*, the union-as-marriage must first be freed of its incestuous implications. In the process, Edgeworth and Owenson emphasize that, in being recast from sister to wife, Ireland has been denied "the liberty of choice" necessary for an effective companionate "marriage."[18]

In brief, *The Wild Irish Girl* is an epistolary novel that relates the adventures of an English nobleman and younger son, Horatio M——, whose dissipated lifestyle in London has caused his father to banish him to the family estate in Ireland. Although initially dismissive of Irish culture, Horatio soon discovers an ancient ruin on his father's property, inhabited by a poor Irishman who identifies himself as "The Prince of Inismore," his daughter Glorvina, and a priest. Captivated by Glorvina, Horatio assumes the identity of a traveling artist, calling himself Henry Mortimer. A minor accident enables "Henry" to stay with the family as he recuperates, and as he grows closer to Glorvina, he develops a sympathetic appreciation for Irish culture and for the Irish people his own ancestors had dispossessed. When he receives a letter from his father, informing him that his father is coming to Ireland and bringing a bride for his son, Horatio realizes that he wants only to marry Glorvina, who is betrothed to a mysterious stranger. The climax of the novel comes when Horatio interrupts Glorvina's marriage to the stranger, only to discover that the stranger is his father. When Horatio's father sees his son's genuine affection for Glorvina and her family, he releases Glorvina to marry his son and turns his Irish estate over to his son's management.

The Wild Irish Girl demonstrates that both legislative and marital unions are means of affirming social and economic status, legitimating existing patterns of ownership and patrilineal inheritance. When Horatio arrives at his father's Irish estate, he is reminded that "the estate fell into our family in the civil wars of Cromwell, and in the world's language, was the well-earned meed of my progenitors' valour," but an acquaintance with descendants of the Irish family who had been robbed of the estate makes Horatio reflect on the related, but more troubling, proposition that he is also the "descendant of a murderer."[19] Determined to heal old rifts and rectify old wrongs, Horatio plots to "unite in bonds of friendship these two worthy men, but *unknown* enemies," the Prince of Inismore and the Earl of M—— (122). The Prince, for his part, comes to think of Horatio (in his assumed identity of Henry Mortimer) as a son (220).

Lord M—— knows, however, that the most secure alliance will be formed through a marriage between the two families. Because his elder son is engaged and Horatio requires a bride with a fortune for his economic well-being (247), Lord M—— plans, unbeknownst to Horatio, to marry Glorvina himself. As Mary Jean Corbett explains, "the heterosexual relations of the marriage plot are primarily mobilized to resolve homosocial relations of property and power between men, in keeping with the dictates of the imperial family romance."[20] Horatio's mocking observation, that "The Prince fancies . . . he is at once the 'Law and Prophet' to his family; never suspecting that he is all the time governed by a girl of nineteen," registers the importance of the daughter's place in the patriarchal structure of the "domestic government" (87). Marriage to Glorvina will provide Lord M—— with the means "of confirming my amity with her father . . . and retributing the parent through the medium of the child" (247).

Marriage as a means of solidifying the homosocial bond is echoed in the plan to marry Horatio to the fifteen-year-old daughter of Lord M——'s "old sporting friend," who may "purchase" Horatio's name for a hundred thousand pounds (166). Horatio's "brilliant establishment," Lord M——'s primary concern, is secured by the exchange of one form of property (money, land) for another (Mr. D——'s daughter), and the bond between the two fathers is strengthened in the course of planning the property exchange (226–27). The girl's innocence and immaturity belie her father's claim that the marriage to Horatio was solely her choice (166); such an important decision cannot be left to a daughter, of course, but Horatio will have the consolation of "form[ing] this young and ductile mind" to suit his tastes, à la Rousseau (226). As both Glorvina's and Miss D——'s marriage settlements demonstrate, daughters play a key role in mediating the legitimate transfer of power and property.

Glorvina's body becomes the means of securing a debt and reaffirming an already established pattern of inheritance. Lord M—— has maneuvered his way into the Prince's affections first, by pretending to be a United Irish rebel,[21] and second, by paying a debt for which the Prince and his family have been imprisoned. For this last service, Lord M—— asks the Prince, who is near death, for "a legal claim to become the protector of your daughter" (248); the Prince unknowingly gives his daughter to his sworn enemy, and an "obedient" Glorvina accedes to her father's wishes against her personal inclination (249). Lord M—— later insists that he felt only "parental affection" for Glorvina and considers her "a child of my adoption"; despite her beauty and charms, "the gratification of any selfish wish, the compliance with any passionate impulse, held no influence over the determination" to marry her (243, 246–47). However, Horatio's previous descriptions of his father's youthful vigor, such that "a Platonic passion" might yet "terminate *in the old way*" (131), combined with Lord M——'s admission that he had not planned to reveal his marriage to his sons until "the final issue of my adventure" (the birth of a child?) necessitated it (247), suggest that Lord M—— intended to function both as Glorvina's father-substitute and her lover.

The two male figures of father and lover are not as distinct in Glorvina's mind as Horatio, in particular, would like. As the Prince's health declines, Glorvina devotes countless hours to his care, and Horatio fears that "her heart was more occupied by her father than her lover" (180). Later, seeing a young woman crying over a grave, Horatio assumes from her behavior that the deceased is the woman's lover, but Glorvina knowingly corrects him: " . . . *her Father*!" (185). Glorvina's devotion to her father, to the exclusion of any lover, reflects her acceptance of her father's power over her: only he can decide whether she is to be given to another or kept for himself. Furthermore, Lord M—— is "old enough to be [Glorvina's] father" (237); he is forty-five, she nineteen. When her father hands her to the earl, Glorvina's affections, as well as her land, are poised to be transferred from one father figure to another.

Taken in isolation, a relationship between Glorvina and Lord M—— would not be incestuous; they are not related through blood or marriage, and he is not her legal guardian. However, the tenor of his marriage proposal (he asks the dying Prince for a "legal claim" to be his daughter's "protector") invokes the discourse of guardianship and gives the relationship an incestuous charge. Because guardians came to be seen, during and after the reign of Charles II, as "temporary parent[s]," in the words of Justice William Blackstone, guardian-ward relationships were regarded as potentially incestuous.[22] In his 1756 tract, *The Case of Marriages Between Near Kindred Particularly Considered, With Respect to the Doctrine of Scripture, the Law of Nature, and the Laws of England*, John Fry argued that "by the *Relation* Parents and Children bear to each other, there are such *relative Duties* which they owe one another, as makes it *unfit* for them to be joined together in Marriage . . . [A]s Marriage in the right ascending and descending Line, is thus prohibited by the Law of Nature; so, *proportionably* all such as stand in the Place, or are the Representatives of such; as all Fathers and Mothers-in-law [stepparents], and all those that are appointed Guardians, with those that are left under their Care . . . are to be looked on as *effectually* barred from marrying one another."[23] Because daughters functioned as a medium of exchange between men, their sexual purity (as the principal sign of their value) required careful guardianship. An unscrupulous guardian might desecrate his trust in order to secure the property the ward represents. Like the marriage bond, which first and foremost represented a link between powerful men, "incestuous heterosexual relations between guardians and wards double . . . as sites of homosocial struggle in which guardians violate paternal trust by usurping the posthumous rights of fathers over daughters."[24] The Prince's animosity toward the M—— name is an impediment to a union between the two families, but in his more palatable role as a United Irishman, Lord M—— can "protect" Glorvina from involvement with another man, hold his place until the Prince's death, and legitimate an Englishman's inheritance and ownership of Irishland through marriage to an Irish "princess."

At the conclusion of the novel, Glorvina finds herself pulled not only between fathers, but also between father and son. Conscious of the need to usurp the Prince's place in Glorvina's heart, Horatio has urged "a closer kindred . . . than even parental affinity can assert," a "sacred union" (186).

In vying for Glorvina's affection, he has also positioned himself as the mystery lover's (i.e., his own father's) "substitute" (225) and "rival" (37, 227). The latter conflict is not merely intergenerational, but potentially Oedipal, given Lord M——'s plan to keep his marriage a secret from his sons. Glorvina is unknowingly moments away from becoming the stepsister *and* stepmother of her beloved, Horatio. To borrow Eagleton's description of Britain and Ireland under the Union, the characters' identities are "incestuously garbled," and "subject-positions (strangers, siblings, parents, spouses, partners) become dizzyingly interchangeable."[25] When the revelation of her suitors' identities precipitates her father's death, Glorvina shrieks and faints, later asking the priest, another father substitute, to choose for her between the men Glorvina now knows to be "murderers" (242). Lord M—— bows out of the triangle, leaving Horatio and Glorvina to form a "family alliance" that he describes as "prophetically typical of a national unity of interests and affections," a union in which "the names of Inismore and M—— [will] be inseparably blended, and the distinctions of English and Irish, of protestant and catholic, for ever buried" (250).

What the marriage plot of Owenson's novel reveals, however, is that distinctions are necessary for legitimate unions. Identities may be assumed—a young nobleman may be an artist, an impoverished elder can act the part of a prince, an earl can play at being a rebel—but a lack of fixity, a lack of awareness of another's true identity, may result in the inadvertent violation of cultural taboos. The fluidity of the characters' relationships to one another demonstrates the dangerous instabilities inherent in a union between two parties with different understandings of a shared history. The earl acknowledges that a marriage between Glorvina and himself would be a "disproportioned union" (228). Differences in age and wealth come first to mind, but the union would also be "disproportioned" in terms of knowledge: Lord M—— assumes he knows Glorvina, and through her, Ireland, but a similar knowledge of his (national) identity and character are denied Glorvina, such that the fitness of their union cannot fairly be assessed and true choice is impossible.[26]

The impact of past relationships on future ones is again felt in *The Absentee*. Edgeworth's novel, as one might guess from the title, has the persistent problem of absenteeism at its center. Lord and Lady Clonbrony, their son Lord Colambre, and Lady Clonbrony's niece, Grace Nugent, have taken up residence in London, at prodigious expense and with devastating results for the tenants of their Irish estates, largely because Lady Clonbrony fears the loss of metropolitan cultural identity inherent in life on the periphery. Although Lord Colambre (who is secretly in love with his cousin) has not lived in Ireland since he was six years old, he believes that his family will be happier in Ireland, so he sets out on a tour through Ireland, incognito. There he observes firsthand the horrors of absenteeism and the importance of an honest agent. When he returns to London, he learns that a financial crisis has placed his family in unfortunate circumstances, a situation that enables him to persuade them that they are needed on their Irish estates. Meanwhile, Colambre also discovers the real identity of Grace's parents and reveals that she is in fact an Englishwoman of considerable wealth, and not his poor cousin, freeing the way for their marriage. The novel ends on a note of anticipation—the family has just returned to their Irish estate, and the proposed marriage between Lord Colambre and Grace Nugent has not yet taken place, but the future appears to be bright, both for the family and for Ireland.

Like *The Wild Irish Girl*, *The Absentee* presents its readers with a marriage that can be read as a figure of the Act of Union: Lord Colambre, a self-described "British" nobleman, will marry Grace Nugent, whose name, mirroring the title of the Irish ballad by Carolan, marks her as Irish.[27] The repeated invocation in the novel of an "invincible obstacle" to their union refers to Colambre's uncertainty regarding Grace's parentage and legitimacy. While in Ireland Colambre learns, much to his dismay, that Grace's mother was a St. Omar, a family of whom "none of the women [were] *sans reproche*."[28] No marriage between Grace's mother and her father, an army officer by the name of Reynolds, has been proved, and thus "her friends were obliged to hush up" the relationship, despite Grace's birth. Colambre's uncle (Lady Clonbrony's brother) was willing to ignore Grace's mother's tainted past and married her, adopted her daughter, and "after some years, the whole story was forgotten" (123). It resurfaces now only because the deceitful Lady Dashfort hopes to turn Colambre's attention away from his cousin and toward her own daughter. Colambre spends the better portion of the novel unraveling the mystery of Grace Nugent's parentage, ultimately uncovering a marriage certificate for Miss St. Omar and Mr. Reynolds and a family fortune for Grace, now "Miss Reynolds" and an English heiress (240, 259).

The critical focus in understanding Edgeworth's use of the marriage metaphor in this novel has been on Grace's mother's supposed misconduct. Julia Anne Miller argues that "Grace Nugent's mother, suspected of sexual impropriety and revolutionary French Catholic origins, fits in with the archetypal presentation of revolution as a sexually depraved woman." Edgeworth must recuperate this revolutionary energy into more positive channels, and once the "French Catholic St. Omar blood is diluted and purified with English blood . . . Grace 'Reynolds' can take her rightful place by Colambre's side." Ultimately, "Edgeworth's allegorical marriage reveals that colonial union is accomplished only through the violent suppression of the insurgent heroine."[29] While I do not disagree with this interpretation of Grace's narrative "ethnic cleansing," I would like to return to what the novel says about marriage, and cousin marriage in particular, to consider other implications for reading the marriage between Grace and Colambre as an allegory for union.

Two views of marriage are juxtaposed in the novel: marriage for love and marriage for money. Colambre is urged by his parents to marry an heiress, but declines: "marry for money, that I cannot do" (19). Although his models for this type of pecuniary union are doubtless legion, he need look no further than his parents; Lady Clonbrony, we are told, "had not . . . the slightest notion . . . how any body out of Bedlam could prefer, to a good house, a decent equipage, and proper establishment, what is called love in a cottage" (42). She brought to her marriage a large fortune, now spent (26), and no affection is evident between Lord and Lady Clonbrony. Colambre is their only child. The Clonbronys move in circles where rank and even birth may be bought, but not hearts (31–32). This economically oriented view of marriage has particular implications for women, "who have not always the liberty of choice, and therefore . . . can't be expected to have always the power of refusal" (247). In a marriage for money, women are merely markers of value, exchanged between men, as also shown in Owenson's novel.

In contrast, *The Absentee* offers several depictions of marriage for love, including Sir Arthur Berryl and Miss Broadhurst, Grace Nugent and Colambre, and even Grace and Brian O'Neil's "love in a cottage." Rather than a sentimentalized notion of love at first sight, however, Edgeworth shows that love is the product of esteem, affection, and friendship, developed over time. "Propinquity"—proximity that provides opportunities for frequent and honest communication—is presented as the key to securing both a loving and financially beneficial marriage (45). The parallels with national union are not far to seek. The type of "esteem and affection" necessary for a successful union between Britain and Ireland, already near neighbors, may be achieved through habits of familiarity and friendship, "discovering more of each other's good qualities, and interchanging little good offices in common life," argues Count O'Halloran, the most dominant Irish voice in the novel (116–17). Ireland can and does inspire affection: Grace and Colambre love one another for their shared love of Ireland (106, 209), and Lady Clonbrony's willingness to return to Ireland prompts Lord Clonbrony to kiss his wife more passionately than he has since leaving that country (203). Those who, like Lady Dashfort, treat Ireland as a "market" in which economic resources—in her case, a nobleman for her daughter—may be acquired, and who believe that "absence might be as effectual as too much propinquity," must settle in the end for a loveless union or no union at all (92, 113, 246–47).

Too much propinquity can pose difficulties, however. Britain had long regarded Ireland's proximity as a problem; as one scholar has explained it, "the sea between the countries was too wide for union and too narrow for independence—or so England thought."[30] Ireland was simply too close, both physically and culturally, to be part of the Empire, and too alien and remote to be considered "home." Britain's positional superiority could only be maintained by emphasizing the differences between Englishness and Irishness, differences "founded upon maintaining the distance which separated the English from the Irish."[31] At the turn of the century, however, increased travel and communication, combined with the Act of Union, threatened to collapse the distance, and thus the difference, between the two countries.

The dangers of "too much propinquity" are explored in the initial objection to an attachment between Colambre and Grace: their family tie. Lady Clonbrony specifically focuses on their relationship as cousins: "first cousins should never marry, because they form no new connexions to strengthen the family interest, or raise its consequence. This doctrine her ladyship had repeated for years so often and so dogmatically, that she conceived it to be incontrovertible, and of as full force as any law of the land, or as any moral or religious obligation" (42–43). The specific elements of Lady Clonbrony's objections must be noted. "Although its respectability was much debated," Ellen Pollak reminds us, "cousin marriage in and of itself was not illegal," and had not been since Henry VIII's statute of 1540, which legitimated his marriage to Catherine Howard, Anne Boleyn's first cousin.[32] In fact, the aristocracy tended to support cousin marriage as "an act of incorporation that *maintained* a family's standing, since cousin marriage . . . prevented the loss of a family's name or land."[33] The middle classes, however, preferred to think of marriage in terms of an alliance which "could be used to improve social standing" and tended to frown on cousin marriages.[34] Thus, no "law of the land" or "any moral or religious obligation" specifically denied cousin marriage, but it tended, in the eighteenth century at least, to be seen as a class peculiarity. Lady Clonbrony's sentiments against it, and in favor of a marriage that will form "new connexions to strengthen the family interest," align her with the upwardly mobile middle classes, to a degree with which she would likely be uncomfortable.

Of course, Lady Clonbrony knows, as Grace, Colambre, and the reader initially do not, that Grace and Colambre are not related by blood. Despite his mother's objections, Colambre finds himself falling in love with his demure cousin, and prior to leaving on his Irish tour announces to his family that his "affections are engaged," although he tells no one, not even Grace, to whom (71). His aristocratic leanings and male prerogative see no obstacle to a union with Grace Nugent, and so another obstacle must be discovered to sustain the drama of the courtship plot for the remaining two-thirds of the novel: the mystery of Grace's legitimacy.

However, the stigma of cousin marriage has not yet been removed for Grace. A further charge against cousin marriage was related to the cousin's status within the kinship network; cousins (like Grace and Colambre) might be raised within the same household and form bonds more typically associated with siblings. In fact, it is a cousin's "*representative* status as a . . . sibling that renders the idea of cousin-love incestuous."[35] Lawyer John Alleyne, in his 1775 contribution to the marriage prohibitions debate, quotes from Montesquieu's *Spirit of Laws* on the legitimacy of cousin marriage: "There are nations . . . amongst whom cousin-germans [first cousins] are considered as brothers, because they commonly dwell in the same house: there are others, where this custom is not known. Among the first, the marriage of cousin-germans ought to be regarded as contrary to nature; not so among the others."[36] Lord Clonbrony is Grace's guardian, giving Colambre the familial status of her brother, and Grace thinks and behaves toward Colambre "exactly as if he was her brother," and not, the narrator assures us, "in the equivocating sentimental romance style in which ladies talk of treating men as their brothers, whom they are all the time secretly thinking of . . . as lovers" (43).

Grace's awkward position with respect to her brother-lover is also evoked by the account of her Irish namesake, Grace O'Neil, who lives with a young man whom Colambre initially assumes to be her brother and who is, in fact, her "bachelor" or "sweetheart." The Widow O'Neil, the woman both Grace and her intended call "mother," explains the relationship in a lowered voice, as if it, like Grace Nugent's mother's affair, must be "hushed up." In fact, they are simply "too poor" to legitimate their union before a priest (150). In depicting this ambiguous intimacy between the agrarian laboring poor, Edgeworth calls to mind repeated accusation of impropriety within the Irish cabin made by numerous observers, since the days of Giraldis Cambrensis: "From the promiscuous way these people lie together, a suspicion naturally arises in a stranger's mind, that incest is unavoidable amongst them," claimed one traveler in 1777.[37] However, in 1805, Sir John Carr insisted that "every degree of decency prevails within" the Irish cabin, and that "instinctive delicacy which exists between the sexes, in every thing which is the subject of it in higher life, is not banished from the poor cabin."[38] Edgeworth and her father reviewed Carr's *Stranger in Ireland* and took issue with it for various reasons,[39] but she here seems to confirm his belief that the incest taboo and other sexual mores were not violated in rural Ireland: when the O'Neils acquire enough money to renew the lease on their cabin, freeing the way economically for their marriage, Brian and Grace kiss for the first time, which Mrs. O'Neil excuses because "he's as good as your husband now, Grace" (164). "Brothers" may become lovers only when all obstacles to a union have been removed.

However, when Colambre declares his love for Grace Nugent, her protests demonstrate her proper resistance to thinking of her cousin-brother as lover: " 'O, let me not hear it!' said she; 'I must not—ought not. Never till this moment did such a thought cross my mind—I thought it impossible—O, make me think so still' " (214). Grace has long been accustomed to think of her cousin as ineligible, and, we are told, the "barriers of habit, the ideas of duty, cannot, ought not, to be thrown down, or suddenly changed, in a well-regulated female mind" (249). To betray a sudden affection for Colambre would make Grace other than she is—pure, innocent, desexualized—and further align her with her mother's putative sexual impropriety. She must learn who she is, and who others believed her to be, before she can freely choose Colambre as her partner.

The revelation of Grace's true parentage not only relieves the lingering anxiety over her legitimacy but also removes the suspicion of incest. Both Lord and Lady Clonbrony immediately seize on the changed relationship between the two: Grace is "a very great heiress—and no more Colambre's cousin" (256). Grace's changed status as an heiress and not Colambre's cousin is proclaimed as if the two characteristics are equally reassuring. In fact, her inheritance, her ability to "raise [the family's] consequence," has removed any remaining doubt about the moral or legal validity of cousin marriage. In combining "love," "esteem," and economic considerations, Grace and Colambre prove that couples can marry for love *and* money.

The objections to Grace and Colambre's marriage, based not only on Grace's mother, but also on Grace and Colambre's close affinity, reflect Edgeworth's uncertainty about the legitimacy of a union between Great Britain and Ireland. Ireland is Britain's "sister," Edgeworth reminds us more than once (6, 92). And as *The Absentee* insists, even if the obstacle of kinship can be overcome, a true marriage values esteem over economic gain. But most important, Edgeworth questions the nature of the new "national" identity that has been called into being by the Act of Union. Will it, as Lord M—— prophesies in *The Wild Irish Girl*, create a new generation in whom ancient distinctions of nation, culture, and religion are "inseparably blended, and . . . for ever buried" (250)? Is such an outcome even desirable?

In *The Absentee*, at least, the answer seems to be, no. By the end of the novel, the hero and heroine's identities have been questioned and qualified to such a degree that it becomes problematic to claim that their marriage figures the Union between Britain and Ireland. As a "British nobleman" (21), Lord Colambre exemplifies the ideal melding of (admittedly stereotyped) English and Irish character traits:

> The sobriety of English good sense mixed most advantageously with Irish vivacity: English prudence governed, but did not extinguish, his Irish enthusiasm. But, in fact, English and Irish had not been invidiously contrasted in his mind: he had been so long resident in England, and so intimately connected with Englishmen, that he was not obvious to any of the commonplace ridicule thrown upon Hibernians; and he had lived with men who were too well informed and liberal to misjudge or depreciate a sister country. (6)

Ultimately, he sees very little difference between Englishness and Irishness. He claims that he does not know that prejudice against the Irish exists, at least "not among well-informed, well-bred people" (16), but he has been educated and resident in England since his early childhood. Colambre's exposure to his mother's acquaintances' cruelty, and his own reluctance to be identified as an absentee, inspire him to travel to Ireland and to discover the country and the people for himself.

Colambre's decision to travel to Ireland is primarily actuated by a search for self-identity. Colambre travels to Ireland essentially as an Englishman, an unknowing outsider, much like *The Wild Irish Girl*'s Horatio M——. He assumes the identity of a Welshman and travels incognito, wearing shabby clothing, although his voice soon reveals him to be a gentleman (129, 139). He describes himself and is described by the Irish people variously as English and Welsh (but never Irish) —a conflation of identities that does not bode well for Ireland's ability to maintain an individuated national identity under the Union. A similar loss of identity has already befallen the Clonbronys. As Liz Bellamy argues, "[t]he Anglo-Irish exist in a cultural no-man's land, rejected by the English for their Irishness, and by the Irish for their Englishness . . . in relation to the peasantry, the Anglo-Irish might be seen to constitute a class of colonial exploiters, in relation to the English they could be seen as the colonized—an alien other sharing much of the culture and assumptions of their tenantry."[40] Lord Clonbrony is described by his wife's English acquaintances as "nothing, nobody," and Lady Clonbrony openly fears the loss of identity inherent in the ambiguity of the Anglo-Irish position: "one gets . . . a notion, one's nobody out of Lon'on" (2, 202).

Only Lord Colambre, for all intents and purposes an Englishman, and Grace Nugent, who, like Colambre, combines the best of English and Irish characteristics, escape the social abrogation that results from the marginalized position occupied by most Anglo-Irish. Despite the traditional associations with her name (the blind harper still plays "Gracey Nugent" when she arrives in Ireland) and her own avowals, by the end of the novel, Grace Nugent too has become English. She, like Maria Edgeworth, describes herself as a "friend" to Ireland (73), and we see her Irish ties confirmed even in her material possessions—her Limerick gloves, for example (106). But in order for the relationship between Grace and Colambre not to be incestuous, then Grace must not be who she seems, that is, she must not be Irish, and so she inherits both an English identity and an English fortune.[41] However, as Robert Tracy has argued, "her English legitimacy removes her apparent ability to reconcile two traditions."[42] As Grace's Irishness is erased, Ireland loses its voice, and therefore its choice, in the Union her marriage to Colambre represents.

Notes and references in their novels demonstrate Sydney Owenson and Maria Edgeworth's familiarity with many layers of contemporary debate about the Union between Britain and Ireland, including travel accounts such as George Cooper's *Letters on the Irish Nation*. In Cooper's concluding claim that, after the Union, "[n]ational and local distinctions, prejudices and grievances will be removed . . . all will be melted and blended into one great people," we hear the Earl of M——'s call for a marriage that will blend names and bury distinctions.[43] However, just as Owenson doubtless would have distanced herself from Cooper's pro-Union position, her readers are not encouraged to align themselves with Lord M——'s perspective, even though his authoritative voice concludes the novel. Readers have already invested too much in the education of the sentimental hero, whose growing and genuine affection for both Glorvina and Ireland stands in sharp contrast to his father, an absentee landowner whose interest in Ireland appears primarily to be an economic one. The union of "the names of M—— and Inismore" remains merely symbolic for Lord M—— as it did not for Owenson's readers. The line reads as Owenson's ironic commentary on the lack of openness and real understanding between the two families, in that Horatio's name is literally a blank and Glorvina's has been effaced throughout the novel. *Glorvina*, Gaelic for "sweet voice" we learn in one of Owenson's many footnotes, is a descriptive nickname, and upon learning her surname, Horatio says he can "never endure to hear my Glorvina called Miss O'Melville" (75, 196). Identity—not only who one is, but also who one is in relation to another—is more difficult to pin down than a mere name, or even a genealogy, but such work must be done for the union to be legitimate or successful, Owenson urges.

Similarly, George Cooper's belief that residence and education in England "sometimes almost melts down the Irish gentleman into an English one" comes to fruition in Edgeworth's creation of Lord Colambre, the man whose name is an Irish place, but whose national identity is disturbingly indeterminate. Cooper's note of hesitancy—"sometimes almost" —voices his belief in the continued existence of tangible differences between English and Irish and reflects a common, if contradictory, desire for continued separation after the Union, for the maintenance of necessary distinctions between Great Britain and Ireland. Despite his arguments in favor of the Union, Cooper's descriptions of Ireland doubtless contributed to English ambivalence: these "illiterate and uncivilized people," who "approximate to the degraded state of a horde of Hottentots," are "hasty and impetuous, rash and choleric, and subject to the most violent attacks of anger and passion," he reports. Small wonder that the English are "naturally . . . cautious of indulging too great a degree of intimacy with them." Ireland, particularly in travel accounts, could be made to seem reassuringly remote, "as if the Atlantic . . . flowed between us, instead of dividing them from the new world." But the Union will overcome this perceived distance and "raise a powerful colossus, . . . resting one foot upon the Irish shore, and the other upon British soil," joining two kingdoms and granting a people previously regarded as colonized dependents at least some of the rights of British citizenship.[44] As David Cairns and Shaun Richards observe, "writing by Englishmen about Ireland and the Irish . . . [may have served] to define the qualities of 'Englishness,' by simultaneously defining 'not-Englishness' or 'otherness.'"[45] English readers of Cooper's *Letters* would have been forced to imagine "Hottentots" in Parliament and left to wonder about the impact of Ireland's changing status on their own cultural identity.

The images of dissolution—burying, blending, melting—that accompany the marriage metaphor highlight Britain's greatest fears for the Union, that in the process of erasing Ireland's colonial status and making it part of Britain, essential differences would be destroyed. Slippage is already evident in the uneven shift between metaphors of sisterhood and metaphors of marriage. Edgeworth and Owenson lay bare this imperial anxiety in their depiction of Ireland as a vulnerable young woman with an ambiguous familial connection to the wealthy and powerful Englishman who intends to marry her. According to Ellen Pollak, women writers "use incest narratives to expose women's purely intermediary role in dramas of masculine desire and privilege."[46] In orchestrating the Act of Union, Britain demonstrated its willingness to dismiss the bonds of siblinghood with Ireland in order to assert its dominance as "Hibernia's husband." In *The Wild Irish Girl* and *The Absentee*, Owenson and Edgeworth quietly remind their English readers that behind the violence of the Union lies the crime of incest.

Notes

1. Maria Edgeworth's suggestive but rather idiosyncratic use of "British" in *The Absentee* as a term describing the combined national identity created by the union of Great Britain and Ireland, and thus inclusive of the Anglo-Irish, requires some deviation from standard usage. In an effort to maintain consistency and clarity, and following the majority of my sources and most scholars working on these texts, I have used "English" (rather than "British") throughout to designate citizens of Great Britain (particularly England).

2. George Cooper, *Letters on the Irish Nation. Written During a Visit to that Kingdom, in the Autumn of the Year 1799* (London, 1800), 51–52.

3. The premises of a 1751 tract entitled *A Proposal for Uniting the Kingdoms of Great Britain and Ireland*, by Lord Hillsborough, were rejected by one Irish MP "on the grounds that since Ireland was a 'sister' kingdom to England . . . 'it ought not to be deemed or treated as a branch or colony of another kingdom.' " Nevertheless, in the 1770s, English unionists were reluctant "to accept Ireland as an equal within the empire," as Irish patriots demanded, "because they perceived no difference between equality and loss of control. Control of Ireland, they believed, could only be assured through subordination." James Kelly, "The Origins of the Act of Union: An Examination of Unionist Opinion in Britain and Ireland, 1650–1800," *Irish Historical Studies* 25 (1987): 246, 253.

4. Cooper, *Letters on the Irish Nation*, 170.

5. Ibid., 183.

6. Ibid., 177, 151.

7. On artistic renderings of the Union as marriage, see Nicholas Robinson, "Marriage Against Inclination: The Union and Caricature," in *Acts of Union: The Causes, Context and Consequences of the Act of Union*, ed. Daire Keogh and Kevin Whelan (Dublin: Four Courts Press, 2001), 140–58.

8. Mary Jean Corbett, *Allegories of Union in Irish and English Writing, 1790–1870: Politics, History, and the Family from Edgeworth to Arnold* (Cambridge: Cambridge University Press, 2000), 1–3.

9. On the suitability and use of the metaphor, see Jane Elizabeth Dougherty, "Mr. and Mrs. England: The Act of Union as National Marriage," in *Acts of Union* (see n. 7), 202–15. The phrase "coersive kindness" is Willa Murphy's in "A Queen of Hearts or an Old Maid? Maria Edgeworth's Fictions of Union," also in *Acts of Union*, 187.

10. Mary Jean Corbett and Julia Anne Miller describe the marriages in Owenson and Edgeworth's novels as "allegories," but allegory seems to me to imply a stability of reference that the characters' shifting identities belie.

11. Liz Bellamy, "Regionalism and Nationalism: Maria Edgeworth, Walter Scott and the Definition of Britishness," in *The Regional Novel in Britain and Ireland, 1800–1990*, ed. K. D. M. Snell (Cambridge: Cambridge University Press, 1998), 63.

12. According to Lawrence Stone, "there is evidence of the frequent development of very close ties indeed" among siblings in the early modern period. *The Family, Sex, and Marriage in England, 1500–1800*, abridged ed. (New York: Harper, 1979), 87. If one were to regard Britain and Ireland's long history as a shared childhood, then the sibling metaphor seems particularly appropriate. The other dominant sibling image in Romantic-period literature—that of rivalry, particularly rival sisters—might call to mind economic tensions and cultural differences between the two countries, such that the Union could be perceived as a means of containing Britain's competitor (on this point, see Kelly, "Origins of Union," 249–50) and Englishness came to be defined in opposition to Irishness. See David Cairns and Shaun Richards, *Writing Ireland: Colonialism, Nationalism and Culture* (England: Manchester University Pres, 1988). The staying power of the sibling metaphor is demonstrated by the quotation in the title of this essay, from the preface to English novelist Anne Plumptre's 1817 travel account, *Narrative of a Residence in Ireland*.

13. On the controversy over the prohibited degrees of marriage, see *The Marriage Prohibitions Controversy: Five Tracts*, ed. Randolph Trumbach (New York: Garland, 1985), and Ellen Pollak, *Incest and the English Novel, 1684–1814* (Baltimore: Johns Hopkins University Press, 2003), 28–45, 55–58.

14. Pollak, *Incest and the English Novel*, 17.

15. For brief comparative analyses of Owenson and Edgeworth's political views, see Julia Anne Miller, "Acts of Union: Family Violence and National Courtship in Maria Edgeworth's *The Absentee* and Sydney Owenson's *The Wild Irish Girl*," in *Border Crossings: Irish Women Writers and National Identities*, ed. Kathryn Kirkpatrick (Tuscaloosa: University of Alabama Press, 2000), 14–15, and Terry Eagleton, *Heathcliff and the Great Hunger: Studies in Irish Culture* (London: Verso, 1995), 185–86.

16. Joseph W. Lew, "Sidney Owenson and the Fate of Empire," *Keats-Shelley Journal* 39 (1990): 39.

17. Eagleton, *Heathcliff and the Great Hunger*, 128; on incest and difference, see Pollak, *Incest and the English Novel*, 9.

18. Maria Edgeworth, *The Absentee*, ed. W. J. McCormack and Kim Walker (Oxford: Oxford University Press, 1988), 247.

19. Sydney Owenson [Lady Morgan], *The Wild Irish Girl: A National Tale*, ed. Kathryn Kirkpatrick (Oxford: Oxford University Press: 1999), 42. Subsequent references will appear parenthetically in the text.

20. Corbett, *Allegories of Union*, 66.

21. The mysterious stranger's arrival at Inismore is recounted on pages 213–15. Mary Jean Corbett offers a compelling analysis of the earl's choice to masquerade as a United Irishman, a political ideology he doubtless does not support (ibid., 65–67).

22. Pollak, *Incest and the English Novel*, 87–88.

23. John Fry, *The Case of Marriages Between Near Kindred Particularly Considered . . .* (London, 1756), facsimile reprint in *The Marriage Prohibitions Controversy* (see n.13), 66–67.

24. Pollak, *Incest and the English Novel*, 92.

25. Eagleton, *Heathcliff and the Great Hunger*, 128.

26. In the eighteenth century, relationships were considered incestuous only if committed with foreknowledge of a partner's close affinity or consanguinity. Contemporaries believed that "marriages which have once been contracted, *ex ignorantia*, between close relatives need neither be punished nor annulled, and if the partners wish, can even be continued *salva conscientia*." Johann Jakob Cella, *Über Verbrechen und Strafe in Un-*

zuchtsfällen (1787), quoted in W. Daniel Wilson, "Science, Natural Law, and Unwitting Sibling Incest in Eighteenth-Century Literature," *Studies in Eighteenth-Century Culture* 13 (1984): 256. Glorvina, and by implication Ireland, remains innocent in her ignorance, but Lord M— knowingly transgresses.

27. W. J. McCormack traces the Irish associations of both "Nugent" and "St. Omar" in *Ascendancy and Tradition in Anglo-Irish Literary History from 1789–1939* (Oxford: Clarendon Press, 1985), 139–47. See also Appendix II, "The Tradition of Grace Nugent," in McCormack's edition of *The Absentee*.

28. Edgeworth, *The Absentee*, 110. Subsequent references will appear parenthetically in the text.

29. Miller, "Acts of Union," 22, 23.

30. John McVeagh, ed., *All Before Them: 1660–1780* (London: Ashfield Press, 1990), 44.

31. Cairns and Richards, *Writing Ireland*, 4.

32. Pollak, *Incest and the English Novel*, 165, 13; see also Randolph Trumbach, *The Rise of the Egalitarian Family: Aristocratic Kinship and Domestic Relations in Eighteenth-Century England* (New York: Academic Press, 1979), 18–22. In his 1673 defense of cousin marriage, Simon Dugard describes the practice as "severely censur'd" and answers its "many enemies" point by point. *The Marriages of Cousin Germans, Vindicated from the Censures of Unlawfullnesse, and Inexpediency* (Oxford, 1673; facsimile reprint in *The Marriage Prohibitions Controversy*, see n. 13), 5.

33. Trumbach, *Rise of the Egalitarian Family*, 18–19.

34. Ibid., 32.

35. Pollak, *Incest and the English Novel*, 165.

36. John Alleyne, *The Legal Degrees of Marriage Stated and Considered, in a Series of Letters to a Friend*, 2d ed. (London, 1775; facsimile reprint in *The Marriage Prohibitions Controversy*, see n. 13), appendix, 43.

37. Thomas Campbell, *A Philosophical Survey of the South of Ireland, in a Series of Letters to John Watkinson, M.D.* (London, 1777), 148.

38. John Carr, *The Stranger in Ireland; or a Tour in the Southern and Western Parts of that Country in 1805* (1806; facsimile reprint, Shannon: Irish University Press, 1970), 268.

39. *Edinburgh Review* 10 (1807), cited in Marilyn Butler, *Maria Edgeworth: A Literary Biography* (Oxford: Clarendon Press, 1972), 372 n1.

40. Bellamy, "Regionalism and Nationalism," 61, 62.

41. On the Irish associations of the Reynolds name, see Robert Tracy, "Maria Edgeworth and Lady Morgon: Legality versus Legitimacy," *Nineteenth-Century Fiction* 40.1 (1985); reprint, Robert Tracy, *The Unappeasable Host: Studies in Irish Identities* (Dublin: University College Dublin Press, 1998), 34.

42. Ibid., 33.

43. Cooper, *Letters on the Irish Nation*, 201.

44. In order of citation in the text, Cooper, 26, 35, 40, 19, ix.

45. Cairns and Richards, *Writing Ireland*, 2.

46. Pollak, *Incest and the English Novel*, 20.

Economic Identity and the Irish Peasantry on the Eve of the Great Hunger

David A. Valone

VARIOUS CIRCUMSTANCES DURING THE PAST TWO DECADES HAVE LED TO AN explosion in scholarly interest in the catastrophic events in Ireland during the Great Hunger. Widespread observance of the sesquicentennial in the late 1990s created a worldwide torrent of famine commemoration. In addition, movement toward a resolution of the political situation in Northern Ireland seemingly opened up space for historical perspectives hitherto stifled by the conflict. Finally, research from economic, social, and cultural historians—many of whom were trained in Ireland or the United States—has shed new light on many dimensions of the Great Hunger and deepened our understanding of the event beyond the traditional political and administrative considerations. All these factors have led to what can only be characterized as a revolutionary transformation in Famine historiography.[1]

This paper seeks to contribute further to this process through a consideration of the ideological underpinnings of the crisis in Ireland during the 1840s. In particular, it examines the construction of an Irish economic identity in a series of debates during the eighteenth and early nineteenth centuries. My argument develops along two lines. First, I hope to show that there has been a considerable misreading of the Famine in relation to the work of pioneering political economist and demographer, T. Robert Malthus. My goal in this regard is to rescue Malthus himself from the Malthusian specter that haunts him and his views of Ireland. Second, this paper proposes that although the dominant ideological discourse concerning Irish economic identity imagined Ireland as ripe for disaster, nonetheless considerable dissent concerning the condition of the Irish economy during the era prior to the Famine did exist. These alternative ideological constructions can tell us something significant about the power of imagined identity in creating the very realities they posit to exist. Here, my argument follows the work of Peter Gray by embedding the economic dimensions of the Famine into a broader historical context: that of the developing field of political economy during the first half of the nineteenth century. While Gray has convincingly explored the diversity of viewpoints *within* classical economics just before and during the Famine years, I show that viewpoints *outside* of the classical tradition also existed. These brought strikingly different views to bear on the Irish economy, especially with regard to the peasantry.[2] It is my contention that many of the perceived economic realities of the Famine period in Ireland were in important ways reflections of an ideological system that had imagined Ireland as on the brink for decades, indeed even centuries, before the Great Hunger. Hence, the response to the Famine was deeply conditioned by sets of ideas that had been constructed about Ireland and the Irish economy over a long period of time. In so arguing, I do not mean to downplay the impact that other ideas, specific political circumstances, or the actual situation on the ground during the 1840s made in determining the course of the crisis; instead, I suggest that all these contemporary circumstances were fundamentally colored by a set of deeply rooted ideological frameworks that served to constrain thinking about Ireland along very narrow lines.

One such framework is the intellectual tradition represented by Edmund Spenser's *A View of the Present State of Ireland.* While much less frequently mentioned than Malthus by historians of the Famine, Spenser's sixteenth-century colonialist proposals for dealing with the insurgent Gaelic population of Ireland through a scorched earth policy of occupation and starvation would seem to have much to say about the historical experience of the Great Hunger. Spenser vividly presents an image of the broken, defeated, and famished Irish:

> Out of every corner of the woods and glens they came creeping forth upon their hands, for their legs could not bear them. They looked like anatomies of death, they spake like ghosts crying out from their graves, they did eat of the dead carrions, happy where they could find them . . . [so] that in short space there were none almost left and a most populous and plentiful country suddenly left void of man or beast. Yet sure in all that war there perished not many by the sword, but all by the extremity of famine.[3]

Spenser's *View* was reprinted twice in the century preceding the Famine, in 1763 and again in 1809.[4] The timing of these reprintings suggests that there was at least some market for Spenserian solutions to "the Irish problem" in the century leading up to the Famine. As Rachid Khalifa has suggested, thinking about the degree to which a Spenserian "politics of depopulation had seeped into the metropolitan mind" during the late eighteenth and early nineteenth century warrants deeper consideration.[5]

Another powerful ideological context that clearly played a role in coloring the discussion of the Irish economy in the pre-Famine era is the contentious religious situation in Great Britain during the early nineteenth century. Certainly, much has been written about the Protestant/Catholic divide and its influence on attitudes toward the Irish during the decades leading up to and through the Famine. Still, the degree to which this divide impacted economic debates in particular has been largely overlooked. Similarly, although the role of Protestant Providentialism has received some attention in shaping the response of powerful political figures such as Charles Trevelyan and Sir Robert Peel during the crisis years, the deeper influence of not only Providentialism but also High Church Anglicanism and even millenarianism on thinking about Ireland and the Irish economy during the era preceding the Famine deserves greater attention.[6]

While I cannot discuss all these varied ideological contexts in detail here, I do want to suggest that many different ideologies had impact on what have been viewed primarily as economic debates. My point here is to give voice to some of the disagreements among political economists about the state of the Irish economy as a way to understand the power of the dominant economic identity foisted upon the Irish. This projected identity had long imagined the Irish as a people on the verge of a cataclysm. This created economic identity contributed, I would argue, to the British reaction when the blight struck in 1845, since they were already ideological preconditioned to expect starvation, disease, death, and all the other attendant horrors that were experienced in Ireland during the time. Interestingly, this ideological preconditioning has been remarkably well replicated in modern historiography, which in spite of recent reevaluations of the course of the Great Hunger has not significantly challenged the underlying Malthusian assumptions about "overpopulation" and "the fragility of the potato as a stable food" in Ireland.[7] My work, in contrast, argues that alternative economic philosophies concerning the Irish existed, and there were other ways to imagine the Irish economy that did not posit catastrophe for Ireland.

The "dismal science" of political economy clearly had an important impact on shaping the policies and beliefs of the British government when the potato blight struck in 1845. There is no question that one of the great folk villains of the Famine, Sir Charles Trevelyan, was heavily influenced by classical economics.[8] Political economy and laissez-faire ideology similarly dominated debates over the establishment of the new Irish Poor Law, the repeal of the Corn Laws, and the administration of relief measures which impacted Ireland before and during the Famine. Viewing the Famine solely through the lens of classical economic ideology, however, misses the considerable development and debate that had gone on in the nascent field of political economy during the years between the 1770s and the 1840s. It also fails to take into consideration important discussions about the Irish economy that had preoccupied both Anglo-Irish and British intellectuals during the eighteenth century and the larger ideological context of English colonialism dating back to the time of Spenser. My aim is to give a voice to some of this complexity of economic thought in the early nineteenth century as it relates to Ireland, and to propose some ways that a deeper understanding of the complexities of political economy during the period can shed new light on the experiences of the Famine years.

To begin this discussion, I want to critique the widely accepted interpretation of the Famine within classical economic theory as a "Malthusian" catastrophe. The connection of the Famine with Malthus himself or Malthusian principles occurs in numerous writings on the Great Hunger. Cormac Ó Gráda begins *Ireland Before and After the Famine,* his classic economic investigation of nineteenth-century Ireland, with the simple statement "Pre-Famine Ireland has become the classic 'Malthusian country.'" However, as Ó Gráda himself points out, Malthus himself was rather curiously uninterested in Ireland. Nonetheless, the Famine in Ireland and Malthus have become inextricably linked. Almost no account of the Great Hunger fails to mention the Malthusian context. To again quote Ó Gráda: "Pre-Famine Ireland has thus become 'a case study in Malthusian economics,' a 'rabbit warren' where poverty and a 'vortex of subdivision' led to the 'ultimate Malthusian catastrophe.'"[9]

This connection of Malthus with the Famine does a considerable injustice to both Malthus and the larger political, economic, social, and demographic situation in Ireland during the early nineteenth century. As far as Malthus himself is concerned, he seems to have had little interest in using Ireland as a case study for his *Principle of Population*. He wrote very sparingly on Ireland, and what he did write did not portend any great catastrophe looming. Nonetheless, many commentators on the Great Hunger have commonly misconstrued Malthus in order to fit him into the Malthusian reading of the Famine. The most prominent example of this is a frequently cited excerpt of a letter that Malthus wrote to David Ricardo upon his return from his only trip to Ireland in 1817. In his discussion of the demographic situation in pre-Famine Ireland, for example, Joel Mokyr uses this letter to argue for the generally Malthusian view of British political economists at the time. Mokyr asserts: "Many contemporaries firmly adhered to the overpopulation thesis and as a result advocated various measures encouraging emigration to relieve the pressure. In a widely cited letter to Ricardo, Malthus wrote in 1817 that 'The *Land* in Ireland is infinitely more peopled than in England; and to give full effect to the natural resources of the country, a great part of this population should be swept from the soil.' "[10] Mokyr and others, such as Christine Kinealy in her sweeping treatment of the Famine, *This Great Calamity*, use this quotation from Malthus seemingly to imply a degree of culpability for Malthus concerning the subsequent events of the 1840s.

An examination of the full text of this letter finds Malthus's intent to be far different that the one implied by the truncated wording commonly used by Mokyr and others. As a reading of the whole letter makes clear, in this correspondence Malthus was conveying his surprise that the Irish economy was not as bad as he had been led to expect. He commented earlier in the letter that "[t]hough the distress was certainly great, it was I think on the whole less than I expected." Referring particularly to the south, where he had toured through Tipperary, Waterford, Kerry, and Limerick, Malthus noted that "great marks of improvement were observable." It is in this context that Malthus undertook his observation on the Irish population that Mokyr cites. In this section of the letter, Malthus was reflecting not on overpopulation and hunger, but rather on employment and wages. He noted that Ireland possesses "a population greatly in excess above the demand for labor." In this context, Malthus went on to make an economic argument concerning the distribution of labor "[t]he *Land* in Ireland is infinitely more peopled than in England; and to give full effect to the natural resources of the country, a great part of this population should be swept from the soil *into large manufacturing and commercial Towns*."[11] In examining the unedited quotation, it is clearer why Malthus emphasized the word *Land* in his letter, to very explicitly contrast it to the towns mentioned in the frequently elided ending phase. The central issue here for Malthus was not the absolute scale of the population of Ireland, but rather its concentration in agriculture rather than industry. As this example well illustrates, the tendency to misread Malthus as a Malthusian is strong, especially in the wake of the Great Hunger.[12]

Let me now move to a consideration of the manner in which the Irish economy was represented in the late eighteenth and early nineteenth century. I will not say much about dominant mode of representation of the Irish economy, which rested heavily on laissez-faire ideology, outside of a brief discussion of the work of David Ricardo. Instead, I will primarily consider few figures including Malthus himself and several less well known political thinkers, particularly Thomas Newenham and Richard

Jones, who presented alternative visions of Ireland. Neither of these latter two thinkers attracts much attention in traditional histories of political economy, and neither has received any notice from historians of nineteenth century Ireland or the Famine.[13] In their own day, though, both were reasonably well-known. Neither was nearly as prominent as Malthus, of course, who after the publication of his *Essay on the Principle of Population* became a major touchstone in economics.

Both Jones and Newenham in many ways shared Malthus's economic viewpoint with regard to Ireland; their perspectives were far less catastrophic than the representations of Ireland from others who undertook a political or economic assessment of the Irish situation. They each analyzed the Irish economy in terms that were strikingly different from the generally gloomy analysis characteristic of much of the economic literature of the eighteenth and early nineteenth century. Views of Irish economic deprivation can be traced at least as far back as the spate of economic writings on Ireland that emerged in the early eighteenth century around the time of Jonathan Swift's *Drapier's Letters*. While as James Kelly has argued these debates were "an important step in the ideological evolution of a Patriot nationalism," with regard to the fundamental condition of the Irish economy they reinforced a view of Ireland as economically distressed and ripe for disaster.[14] As Swift himself complained in a letter to Knightly Chetwode, Ireland was a land where "we expect nothing but plague, poverty, and famine."[15] While Swift certainly blamed government policy for much of the problem, he was equally critical of the native Gaelic population, and advocated banning the Irish language. This, he asserted, would "in time, abolish that part of barbarity and ignorance for which our natives are so despised by all foreigners: this would bring them to think and act according to the rules of reason, by which a spirit of industry and thrift, and honesty would be introduced among them."[16] Such attitudes became characteristic of the dominant mode of economic thought about Ireland during the rest of the century, and are well represented in various economic thinkers of the period like David Ricardo.

Ricardo became the main voice of utilitarian and laissez-faire economic philosophy in Britain during the first half of the nineteenth century. Ricardo's work, while abstract in its foundations and thus discussed by a fairly limited and specialized group, effectively redefined the foundations of economic science. His political economy, he claimed, would begin with an attempt to "elucidate principles," and to reason correctly from them.[17] Modeling his science on the mathematical physics of Newton, Ricardo proposed to make political economy a rigorously deductive scientific enterprise. Aided by his entry into parliament in 1819, Ricardo rapidly became the leading representative of political economy in England.[18] Central to Ricardo's economics was the notion that the interests of the landlord and those of the farm master and laborer were continually and unavoidably in conflict. These theories, of course, had a special poignancy for Ireland based on its heavy dependence on an agricultural economy. Ricardo's conclusions in many ways naturalized the system of economic exploitation that had long been a feature of the Irish economy. If the interests of landlords and peasants were inherently in opposition to one another, then no amount of hand wringing or legislation would be sufficient to correct the problem.

In contrast, Malthus, Newenham, and Jones had more inductive and historical approaches to economics that also produced more sanguine views of the Irish economy. As mentioned before, Malthus wrote very little on Ireland specifically, outside of two articles that appeared in the *Edinburgh Review* in 1808 and 1809. In these essays, Malthus forcefully argued that in the wake of the Act of Union a greater understanding of Irish issues was critical to the future of Britain. He was outraged in particular by the continued denial of civil privileges to Irish Catholics, a position that he presaged risked the "dismemberment of the empire."[19] With regard to economic issues, Malthus was not surprisingly interested primarily in the rapid increase in population that had been occurring there during the previous century, when the Irish population had according to some estimate quadrupled. The cause of this increase, Malthus argued, must necessarily be different from the causes of population growth cited by eighteenth-century economic speculators such as Adam Smith and David Hume, who suggested that populations increase under "wise institutions" and "increased demand for labor," respectively. In contrast, Malthus saw the population growth in Ireland as a representation of the population expanding in response to a plentiful supply of food that had been the by-product of the introduction of the potato to Ireland. For him, "the means of subsistence practically regulate the increase of population in civilized societies."[20]

For Malthus, though, this increase in population was hardly a cause for alarm, at least demographically. He speculated that should the current rate of increase continue, Ireland would hold twenty million people by the end of the century. Malthus made no suggestion that this would create the potential for a disastrous famine, but only that it would be a politically untenable situation for Britain to keep such a huge population in submission without "sharing, in every respect, the full benefits of its constitution." For him, then, the population issue in Ireland had more striking political than demographic or economic implications. Indeed, Malthus felt that the rapid increase in population was likely to moderate based largely on internal economic factors like the increase in the price of land and of rents, and the eventually the rise in price of potatoes which would transform the Irish system of agriculture. Malthus did admit that in the meantime the population would be "much more exposed to the pressure of scarcity," but in general he saw many benefits to the expansion of a potato economy to Britain as well as Ireland.[21]

Newenham, similarly, had a very optimistic view of the Irish economy and of Ireland's economic, political, and social destiny. He was no nationalist, publicly calling the 1798 rebellion "deplorable." On the other hand, he did not see any great benefits accruing to Ireland as a result of the Union. He was a staunch opponent of the act in the Irish parliament before its approval. Having lost that battle, Newenham left Ireland for England and began a campaign to promote the interests of Ireland in Britain. He argued that "[f]rom that event [the Act of Union] there has evidently arisen an obligation on every Irishman who has endeavored to make himself acquainted with any of the circumstances of his county, to rescue himself from the trammels of faction, and extend to this part of the United Kingdom whatever authentic information he may happen to possess."[22] Newenham's greatest concern was with raising awareness in England concerning the true state of the Irish economy. In his view, the Irish economy, particularly its growing population, presented both a problem and an opportunity for Britain. The growing population in Ireland was not a situation for Newenham that spelled disaster. The increase in population, he felt, was a natural outgrowth of the economic and social conditions in Ireland, particularly the spread in cultivation of the potato and the continual subdivision of the land. Newenham asserted that even "[t]his comparatively small quantity of land (one acre) has hitherto, throughout most parts of Ireland, been easily obtainable, in lieu of wages, by almost all descriptions of operative people resident in the country: the cultivation of the potato being in most cases serviceable, in none injurious, to the land." Indeed, Newenham was generally optimistic about the state of the Irish peasantry: "The poorest cottiers have generally raised, over and above an ample supply for their families, enough to fatten two or three pigs, besides poultry; and always enough to enable them to exercise their characteristic hospitality to the vagrant stranger or more indigent neighbor. Thus a redundancy of that simple but wholesome food, to the growth of which the climate of Ireland is particularly favorable, has almost uniformly been secured."[23] Newenham painted a fairly cheerful picture of the economic prospects of the Irish peasantry. For him, their economic identity was not that of destitution and desperation, but rather of generosity and plenty.

Jones is in many ways the most significant of the three, since he consciously fought to combat the dominant economic philosophy of the era. Throughout the decade of the 1820s, Jones worked to refine his economic views and to seek the most appropriate way to enter the growing debate over both the theory of political economy and some of its practical applications. Eventually, Jones settled into writing what he envisioned as a complete study of political economy's three major branches: rents, wages, and taxation. Through these studies Jones planned to address the entire spectrum of economic activity, making a complete inquiry into "the causes of the varying wealth and poverty of nations."[24] Due to a combination of personal and professional distractions, Jones completed only the first volume on rent. Still, in the years that followed the publication of this book, Jones became a leading figure in the economic debates that developed in the wake of Catholic Emancipation and the Reform Act of 1832. During the middle of the 1830s, Jones became active in the commission to reform the tithes of the Anglican Church. He had little sympathy for Whig reformers or for Daniel O'Connell. Jones warned a friend that "while their close connection with Irish agitators lasted, they must not count on me as a political follower."[25] Based in part on the reputation he earned through the book on rent, Jones drew closer to Malthus, who was still active in his position at Haileybury College. Jones, who himself had accepted a position at King's College, began a more intimate acquaintance with Malthus. As he later described in a letter to his good friend, the renowned astronomer John Herschel: "I had just taken King's College when you left [on Herschel's observational journey to South Africa in 1831]. This led to a more intimate acquaintance with Malthus. He communicated to me in confidence an intension of retiring from Haileybury that he might instigate me to secure his chair—his death hastened matters and after a short struggle . . . I was appointed."[26]

Jones's work on rent holds the most interest for my purpose. In this volume, he focused on the origin and development of the economic principle of rent. Jones defined rent in the broadest sense possible as any form of payment made for the occupancy of land. This definition was in explicit opposition to the narrow version of rent as payments in cash or in kind used by Ricardo. Ricardo had erred, Jones insisted, by "overlooking altogether the limited extent of the field to which [his] principles were really applicable, undertook from them alone to deduce the laws which regulate the nature and amount of the revenue derived from land at all places, and under all circumstances; and not content with this, proceeded from the same narrow and limited data, to construct a general system of the distribution of wealth, and to explain the causes of variations which take place in the rate of profits, or amount of wages over the surface of the globe."[27] Jones sought both to correct Ricardo's erroneous conclusions, which had generalized his system of rents to apply across time and space, and to demonstrate the errors inherent in Ricardo's method of deductive reasoning from limited experience.

The central focus of Jones's book was to analyze economic exchanges in the form of rents across the world and throughout time. His central questions addressed the manner in which this exchange was conducted and according to what rules it operated. Further, he wished to determine whether these principles were universal, or if they were contingent on local circumstances. From this, Jones hoped to be able to better understand both the historical origins of various economic systems and to prognosticate future development. Jones surmised that the nature of property holding and the forms of land tenure would "furnish to the people the most influential elements of their national character."[28] Thus for Jones it was the case that economics fundamentally shaped a nation's identity. The influence ran directly counter to that proposed by the followers of Ricardo. Rather than assuming people's inner motivations and creating an economics based upon that assumption, Jones worked to discover the manner in which economic systems formed people's lives and sense of self. Examining various agricultural systems across the world, Jones attempted to work out systematically the connections among economic conditions, historical development, and national identity.

Jones's analysis of cottier rents, and hence the condition of Ireland, is of course of particular interest. As Jones well understood, it was precisely the proximity of Ireland to its colonial dominator, England, that created and entrenched the system of cottier rents there. It was "highly probably," he argued, that "were Ireland placed in a remoter part of the world, surrounded by nations not more advanced than herself, and were her cultivators dependant for their means of getting cash on her own internal opportunities of exchange . . . landlords would soon be driven by necessity to adopt a system of either labor or produce-rents, similar to those that prevail over the large portion of the globe cultivated by the other classes peasant tenantry."[29] Given his inductive and historical approach to economics, Jones argued that the establishment and longevity of the system of cottier rents in Ireland had a tremendous impact on the economic identity of the Irish peasantry. First, and most importantly, the cottier system of rents and the subdivision of the land that it encouraged provided no check to population growth, as he termed it "beyond the bounds of easy subsistence." Second, the system of cash payments gave a tremendous power to the landowner, who could set the rate of payment without limits. Hence, the system of cottier rents provided little protection to the tenant laborer. In Jones's words, the tenants were in a precarious situation due to the "want of any protection to their interests, from the influence of usage and prescription in determining the amounts of their payments." Finally, and again significantly, the cottier system created a disconnection between the interests of the landowner and the tenant. Here, Jones analyzed the dangers of this system with near prescience of the Famine: the "absence of . . . common interest, between the owners and occupiers of the soil, which under the other systems of peasant rents, serve to the tenants the forbearance and assistant of their landlords when calamity overtakes them."[30]

Jones's views of Ireland, then, at least as they are contained in his more general assessment of peasant rents, demonstrate his rather unique appreciation of the relationship between the political, economic, and social structures of Ireland as they had developed under English rule. In 1833, as he assumed the Chair of Political Economy at Haileybury, Jones delivered a series of lectures. In these lectures, Jones discussed the general economic structure of Ireland and its relationship to Britain as well as the issues of absentee landlords, compulsory provisions for the poor, the policy of creating artificial employment, and various means of combating some of the economic evils of Ireland.[31] Based upon his published introductory lecture we can get a good sense of the way in which Jones's alternative vision of political economy could have had important ramifications for a consideration of the economic, demographic, and political crisis that broke across Ireland in the 1840s. With regard to Ireland, Jones urged a cautious approach: "while we pronounce the gunpowder name, dismiss for a moment, if we can, political feelings from our mind."[32] To begin with, Jones was very explicit in this lecture to once again point out the deep errors the existed in the accepted models of political economy drawn from the tradition of Ricardo. In particular, Jones lamented the degree to which political economy had been reduced by many authors to seem "a study connected exclusively with trade and finance."[33] Jones's alternative understanding of political economy considered a much broader range of views. It had as its subject "*the wealth of nations*. Knowledge on such a subject is, of course, desirable only so far as it may enable us to understand the circumstances which affect the happiness and well being of ourselves, our fellow men. We have to consider public wealth, therefore, in all the points of view in which it can affect the interest and happiness of mankind; and to observe men, under all the points of view in which, either as individuals or communities, they can affect, or be affected by, the progress of public wealth."[34] This larger view of political economy, Jones hoped, would be useful to more than just the "financier or politician." Instead, Jones, reasoned, the scholar (interested in "the deep-seated causes of long chains of events in the history of nations"), the philosopher ("who might understand the physical constitution of our world and the moral government and character of the inhabitants of our earth"), the statesmen, and every individual of the state would take notice of this pursuit.[35]

Jones's system, and his consideration of the situation among the Irish peasantry, created a very different set of assumptions about the nature of Ireland and its economic problems than did classical economics. By focusing on the local nature of economic activity, and by seeing the economy as part of wider cultural and historical patterns, Jones's economics provided a view of Ireland that took into account the complex and often explosive history of interaction between the ruling class and the Irish peasants. Further, Jones's economic principles were much less based on the notion of the inevitability of scarcity than the views of classical economists. Instead, Jones's economic schema was thoroughly embedded in a web of Christian historical and social assumptions. He never questioned his principle that a wise and benevolent Creator had established certain laws of economic activity and moral development. While some of these laws might still be unknown, he assumed them to be wise and ultimately beneficent; without question, the abundance and productivity of the earth was more central to his concern than the possibility—which Jones did not deny—of shortages and hunger. The overall effect of Jones's political economy was to severely limit the inevitability of conflict and tension within societies. Even when these conflicts would arise, Jones was much more confident that all such tensions must have a beneficent outcome. Perhaps as a result, Jones was not so focused on the problem of scarcity, but instead on the web of connections among individuals within an environment that could produce amply.

Jones would not have denied the possibility of extreme economic and social dislocations, such as the Great Hunger. But his political economy, at least, provided a very different approach to its understanding and the relief measures that might have been undertaken. Jones's confidence in the ultimately progressive character of economics was well demonstrated in his 1833 "Introductory Lecture":

> We can trace the bondman, the serf, and all the most degraded vassals of harsh power, gradually changing the economical position and while the sources and modes of gaining their substance alter, enlarging at the same time their rights, and approaching nearer to the level of the higher class of society. We display this progress, always in connection with a truth, not less beautiful as a moral, than valuable as a political lesson; namely, that with increased civil privileges and capacities, increased intellectual and

> moral elevation must go hand in hand; or the progress of improvement must be stayed, and advances in it rendered nugatory or worse.[36]

Despite Jones's prescience about the course of Ireland's economic and political development, he was in many ways not particularly sympathetic to the Irish people. He was no friend of the Irish Catholics or of their political leader Daniel O'Connell. He lamented to his friend John Herschel that Catholic Emancipation and O'Connell would bring "a slow but gradual approach to democracy of the worst kind."[37] So although Jones had a more sympathetic view of the Irish economy, he was not confident about Ireland's political future. Despite these views, Jones's economic identity for Ireland was much more hopeful that those produced by the dominant school of economic thought during the first half of the nineteenth century.

So what are we to make of these varied economic identities that were available within the ideological constructs of the early nineteenth century? On the one hand, there can be no question that in many ways economic realities trump economic ideologies. No matter how optimistic one's view of the Irish economic condition, the extreme dislocation caused by the potato blight could not be entirely erased by cheerful assessments of the state of Irish peasants. On the other hand, there can be little doubt that economic ideologies help to shape both the expectations that overhang economic realities, and the reactions of individual, organizations, and governments to economic conditions and crises. In the case of nineteenth century Ireland, despite the various assessments of the economy discussed above, the ideological preconditioning represented by classical economics clearly was the dominant strain of thought. Such preconditioning unquestionably had a tremendous, and tragic, impact on the lives of the Irish peasantry during the 1840s.

Notes

1. An excellent summary of recent Famine historiography is Christine Kinealy, " 'The Famine Killed Everything': Living with the Memory of the Great Hunger," in *Ireland's Great Hunger: Silence, Memory, and Commemoration,* edited by David A. Valone and Christine Kinealy (Lanham, Md.: University Press of America, 2002), 3–14.

2. The various stripes of classical economics that existed around the time of the Famine are delineated in Peter Gray, "Ideology and the Famine," in *The Great Irish Famine*, ed. Cathal Póirtéir (Chester Springs, Pa.: Dufour Editions, 1995), 88–91. Gray embeds a similar discussion in the larger political and economic context of the early nineteenth century in his *Famine, Land and Politics: British Government and Irish Society 1843–1850* (Dublin: Irish Academic Press, 1999), 7–26. Robert Haines's magisterial work on Charles Trevelyan has challenged Gray's somewhat schematic formulization of the various religious and po-

litical positions within the Whig-liberal cabinet, see Robert Haines, *Charles Trevelyan and the Great Irish Famine* (Dublin: Four Courts Press, 2004), 45–48.

3. Edmund Spenser, *A View of the Present State of Ireland,* ed. W. L. Renwick (Oxford: Clarendon Press, 1970), 104.

4. I am indebted to Ciaran Brady for insight into the republication history of Spenser's *View* and its ideological ramifications in the pre-famine period.

5. Rachid Khalifa, "W. B. Yeats's Politics of Proximity: or The Famine's Absence in Yeats's Poetry," in *Ireland's Great Hunger: Silence, Memory and Commemoration*, Christine Kinealy and David A. Valone, eds. (Lanham, Md.: University Press of America, 2002), 123. It is interesting to note that Khalifa also cites the edited version of the Malthus quote I discuss below in note 11.

6. For a fine-grained discussion of the influence of religion on policy in the era immediately preceding the Famine, see Peter Gray's analysis of the differing religious perspectives of Robert Peel and James Graham in Gray, *Famine, Land and Politics,* 98. On millenarianism see F. C. Mather, *High Church Prophet: Bishop Samuel Horsley (1733–1806) and the Caroline Tradition in the Later Georgian Church* (Oxford: Oxford University Press, 1992); debates over political economy within High Church Anglicanism are thoroughly examined in Pietro Corsi, *Science and Religion: Baden Powell and the Anglican debate, 1800–1860* (Cambridge: Cambridge University Press, 1988); a more general analysis of the connections between religion and political economy is A. M. C. Waterman, "The Ideological Alliance of Political Economy and Christian Theology, 1798–1833," *Journal of Ecclesiastical History* 34 (1983): 231–44.

7. Haines, *Charles Trevelyan*, 93.

8. Christine Kinealy, *A Death Dealing Famine: The Great Hunger in Ireland* (Chicago: Pluto Press, 1997), 10. Haines paints a much more complicated picture of Trevelyan, but concludes that "Trevelyan adopted as his own . . . the tenets of economic liberalism and laissez-faire (scorning both enthusiasm and false modesty), and a reverence for quantification and data gathering." Haines, *Charles Trevelyan,* 546.

9. Cormac Ó Gráda, *Ireland Before and After the Famine* (New York: Manchester University Press, 1988), 1–2. Ó Gráda's previous work challenged many of these assumptions along lines similar to those I present here, and includes Malthus hypothetically replying "je ne suis pas malthusian" to those who would misinterpret him. Ó Gráda is without doubt more interested in actual economic realities than the ideological contexts discussed here, and comes around to concluding that " 'Population Malthus' will continue to provide a context for, and spur further research on, the prefamine economy." See Comac Ó Gráda, "Malthus and the pre-famine economy," in *Economists and the Irish Economy,* edited by Antoin E. Murphy (Dublin: Irish Academic Press, 1984), 80, 92.

10. Joel Mokyr, *Why Ireland Starved* (London: Allen & Unwin, 1983), 38. Emphasis in original.

11. Letter from T. R. Malthus to David Ricardo, August 17, 1817, reprinted in David Ricardo, *Works and Correspondence,* ed. Piero Sraffa (Cambridge: Cambridge University Press, 1952), 7:175. Emphasis in original.

12. I imply here a distinction between the views of Malthus himself and those who used his ideas as part of a broader system of ideological justifications. For similar arguments see Ó Gráda, "Malthus and the pre-famine economy," 80.

13. James P. Henderson, *Early Mathematical Economics* (Lanham, Md.: Roman & Littlefield, 1996), 29–33; S. F. Cannon, *Science in Culture* (New York: Science History Publications, 1978), 242; Lawrence Goldman, "The Origins of British 'Social Science': Politi-

cal Economy, Natural Science and Statistics 1830–1835," *The Historical Journal* 26, no. 3 (1983): 591.

14. James Kelly, "Jonathan Swift and the Irish Economy in the 1720s," *Eighteenth Century Ireland* 6 (1991): 36.

15. Quoted in Kelly, "Jonathan Swift," 12.

16. Kelly, "Jonathan Swift," 23.

17. Ricardo to Malthus, May 4, 1820, reprinted in James Bonar, ed., *Letters of David Ricardo to Thomas Robert Malthus, 1810–1823* (Oxford: Clarendon Press, 1987), 167.

18. Contemporary accounts made frequent reference to the "fashion" or "rage" for political economy during the late 1810s and early 1820s. For a listing of such references see Gary Langer, *The Coming of Age of Political Economy* (Westport, Conn.: Greenwood Press, 1987), 3–33.

19. T. Robert Malthus, *Occasional Papers of T. R. Malthus on Ireland, Population, and Political Economy,* ed. Bernard Semmel (New York: Burt Franklin, 1963), 33.

20. Malthus, *Occasional Papers,* 36.

21. Ibid., 40–41.

22. Thomas Newenham, *A Statistical and Historical Inquiry into the Progress and Magnitude of the Population of Ireland* (London: R. Baldwin, 1805), ii–iii.

23. Newenham, *A Statistical and Historical Inquiry*, 15–16.

24. Richard Jones, "Preface," to *An Essay on the Distribution of Wealth* (London: J. Murray, 1831), i.

25. Richard Jones to John Herschel, undated [c. 1837], Herschel Papers, Royal Society of London, 10.410.

26. Ibid.

27. Jones, "Preface," to *An Essay on the Distribution of Wealth,* vii.

28. Jones, *An Essay on the Distribution of Wealth,* 4.

29. Richard Jones, "A Short Tract on Political Economy," in William Whewell, ed., *Literary Remains of the Late Richard Jones* (London: J. Murray, 1859), 209.

30. Jones, *An Essay on the Distribution of Wealth*, 145.

31. Unfortunately, only Jones's introductory lecture, and an outline of the remaining topics is apparently extant. Richard Jones, *An Introductory Lecture of Political Economy* (London: J. Murray, 1833), 63.

32. Ibid., 30.

33. Ibid., 1.

34. Ibid., 2.

35. Ibid., 4.

36. Ibid., 573.

37. Jones to John Herschel, undated [c. 1837], Herschel Papers, Royal Society of London, 10.410.

Bibliography

"A Covent-Garden Eclogue." *Universal Spectator and Weekly Journal*. April 26, 1735, unpaginated.

"A Pastoral Poem on the Union." *The Observator*. March 12, 1707, unpaginated.

"A Pastoral Suited to the Times." *Berwick Museum* 1 (1785): 261–63.

"A Wapping Eclogue." *Universal Spectator and Weekly Journal*. November 10, 1739, unpaginated.

Aitken, George A., ed. *The Life and Works of John Arbuthnot*. New York: Russell & Russell, 1892.

Anderson, Benedict. *Imagined Communities: Reflections on the Origin and Spread of Nationalism*. London: Verso Editions, 1983.

Andrews, Elmer. "Aesthetics, Politics and Identity: Lady Morgan's *The Wild Irish Girl*." *Canadian Journal of Irish Studies* 12 (1987): 7–19.

Anon. *The Present State of Ireland Consider'd*. London, 1730.

Anon. *Ways to Mend and Grow Better or Thoughts on the Present Posture of Affairs in a Letter to His E——y, the Lord L——t*. Dublin, 1763.

Aquilo. "A Pastoral, Suited to the Times. In the Caledonian Dialect, with a Glossary." *Weekly Magazine or Edinburgh Amusement*, January 25, 1776, 145–46.

Arbuthnot, John. *A Sermon Preach'd to the People at the Mercat-Cross of Edinburgh; on the Subject of the Union*. London: Reprinted for Andrew Bell at the Cross-Keys and Bible in Cornhill, 1707.

Armitage, David. *The Ideological Origins of the British Empire*. Cambridge: Cambridge University Press, 2000.

Atkinson, Thomas. *Hibernian Eclogues. To Which Are Added, Miscellaneous Poems*. Dublin: For the author, 1791.

Ball, John. *Odes, Elegies, Ballads, Pictures, Inscriptions, Sonnets*. Dublin: Thomas Ewing, [1775].

Barbon, Nicholas. *A Discourse of Trade*. London: Tho. Milbourn, 1690.

Barker-Benfield, G. J. *The Culture of Sensibility: Sex and Society in Eighteenth-Century Britain*. Chicago: University of Chicago Press, 1992.

Barnard, T. C. "Protestants and the Irish Language, c. 1675–1725." *Journal of Ecclesiastical History* 44 (1993): 243–72.

Barnard, Toby. *A New Anatomy of Ireland. The Irish Protestants, 1649–1770*. New Haven: Yale University Press, 2003.

———. *Irish Protestant Ascents and Descents, 1641–1770*. Dublin: Four Courts Press, 2004.

Bartlett, Thomas. " 'A People Made rather for Copies than Originals': The Anglo–Irish, 1760–1800." *International History Review* 12 (1990): 11–25.

———. *The Fall and Rise of the Irish Nation: The Catholic Question, 1690–1630*. Savage, Md.: Barnes & Noble Books, 1992

Beattie, Lester M. "John Arbuthnot: Mathematician and Satirist." In *Harvard Studies in English*, vol. 16. Cambridge: Harvard University Press, 1935.

Beckett, J. C. *The Making of Modern Ireland, 1603–1923*. London: Faber and Faber, 1966.

Belanger, Jacqueline. "Some Preliminary Remarks on the Production and Reception of Fiction Relating to Ireland, 1800–1829." *Cardiff Corvey: Reading the Romantic Text* 4 (May 2000), http://www.cf.ac.uk/encap/corvey/articles/cc04_n02.html.

Belhaven, John Hamilton. "Lord Beilhaven's Speech in Parliament, the Second Day of November 1706." *On the Subject-Matter of an Union Betwixt the Two Kingdoms of Scotland and England*. Edinburgh, 1706.

Bellamy, Liz. "Regionalism and Nationalism: Maria Edgeworth, Walter Scott and the Definition of Britishness." In *The Regional Novel in Britain and Ireland, 1800–1990*, edited by K. D. M. Snell, 54–77. Cambridge: Cambridge University Press, 1998.

Berkeley, George. *The Works of George Berkeley, Bishop of Cloyne*. 9 vols. Edited by A. A. Luce and T. E. Jessop. Edinburgh: Thomas Nelson, 1948–57.

———. *The Alciphron* (1732), in *Works*.

———. *An Essay toward Preventing the Ruin of Great Britain* (1721), in *Works*.

———. *An Essay towards a New Theory of Vision* (1709), in *Works*.

———. *Maxims Concerning Patriotism* (1750), in *Works*.

———. *Philosophical Commentaries* (1706–9), in *Works*.

———. *The Querist* (1735–37), in *Works*.

———. *Word to the Wise* (1749), in *Works*.

Berman, David."The Culmination and Causation of Irish Philosophy." *Archiv für Geschichte der Philosophie* 64 (1982): 257–79.

———. "Disclaimers and Offence Mechanisms in Charles Blount and John Toland." In *Atheism from the Reformation to the Enlightenment*, edited by Michael Hunter and David Wootton, 255–72. Oxford: Clarendon Press, 1992.

———. "Enlightenment and Counter-Enlightenment in Irish Philosophy." *Archiv für Geschichte der Philosophie* 64 (1982): 148–65.

———. *George Berkeley: Idealism and the Man*. Oxford: Clarendon Press, 1994.

———. "The Irish Counter-Enlightenment." In *The Irish Mind: Exploring Intellectual Traditions*, edited by Richard Kearney, 229–40. Dublin: Wolfhound Press, 1985.

———. "The Irish Freethinker." In *John Toland's Christianity not Mysterious: Text, Associated Works, and Critical Essays*, edited by Philip McGuinness, Alan Harrison, and Richard Kearny, 223–30. Dublin: Lilliput Press, 1997.

Bhabha, Homi. *The Location of Culture*. London: Routledge, 1994.

Blácam, Aodh de. *Gaelic Literature Surveyed*. Dublin: Talbot Press, 1933.

Bogel, Frederick. *The Difference Satire Makes: Rhetoric and Reading from Jonson to Byron*. Ithaca: Cornell University Press, 2001.

Bonar, James, ed. *Letters of David Ricardo to Thomas Robert Malthus, 1810–1823*. Oxford: Clarendon Press, 1987

Bond, Donald, ed. *The Spectator*. 5 vols. Oxford: Clarendon Press, 1965.

Bottigheimer, Karl S. "The Failure of the Reformation in Ireland: *Un Question Bien Posée*." *Journal of Ecclesiastical History* 36 (1985): 196–207.

———. "Kingdom and Colony: Ireland in the Westward Enterprise, 1536–1660." In *The Westward Enterprise*, edited by K. R. Andrews, N. P. Canny, and P. E. H. Hair, 45–65. Detroit: Wayne State University Press, 1979.

Brooke, Charlotte. *Reliques of Irish Poetry: Consisting of Heroic Poems, Odes, Elegies, and Songs*, translated into English verse. Dublin: George Bonham, 1789.

Boyce, D. George. *Nationalism in Ireland*. 3rd ed. London: Routledge, 1995.

Bracken, Harry. "George Berkeley: The Irish Cartesian." In *The Irish Mind: Exploring Intellectual Traditions*, edited by Richard Kearney, 107–18. Dublin: Wolfhound Press, 1985.

Bradford, Ernle Dusgate Selby. *Three Centuries of Sailing*. London: Country Life, 1964.

Bradshaw, Brendan, and Peter Roberts, eds. *British Consciousness and Identity: The Making of Britain 1533–1707*. New York: Cambridge University Press, 1998.

Brady, Ciaran. *The Chief Governors: The Rise and Fall of Reform Government in Tudor Ireland 1536–1588*. Cambridge: Cambridge University Press, 1994.

Brady, Ciaran, ed. *A Viceroy's Vindication? Sir Henry Sidney's Memoir of Service in Ireland, 1556–78*. Cork: Cork University Press, 2002.

Brown, Nicholas. *The North-Country-Wedding, and the Fire, Two Poems in Blank Verse*. Dublin: J. Hyde, 1722.

Burgess, Glenn, ed. *The New British History: Founding a Modern State 1603–1715*. London: I. B. Tauris, 1999.

Burke, Tim. " 'Yet Tho' I'm Irish All Without, I'm Every Item Scotch Within': Poetry and Self-Fashioning in 1790s Ulster." *John Clare Society Journal* 22 (2003): 35-49.

Burkhead, Henry. *A Tragedy of Cola's Furie, or Lirenda's Miserie*. Kilkenny: n.p., 1646.

Burns, Robert. *Poems Chiefly in the Scottish Dialect*. Kilmarnock: John Wilson, 1786.

Butler, Marilyn. *Maria Edgeworth: A Literary Biography*. Oxford: Clarendon Press, 1972.

Byrne, Matthew J., ed. *The Irish War of Defence, 1598–1600: Extracts from the* De Hibernia Insula Commentarius *of Peter Lombard*. Trans. Matthew J. Byrne. Cork: Cork University Press, 1930.

Caball, Marc. *Poets and Politics: Reaction and Continuity in Irish Poetry*. Cork: Cork University Press, 1998.

Caffentzis, C. George. *Exciting the Industry of Mankind: George Berkeley's Philosophy of Money*. Boston: Kluwer Academic Publishers, 2000.

———. "Why Did Berkeley's Bank Fail? Money and Libertinism in Eighteenth-Century Ireland." *Eighteenth Century Ireland* 12 (1997): 100–115.

Cairns, David, and Shaun Richards. *Writing Ireland: Colonialism, Nationalism and Culture*. Manchester: Manchester University Press, 1988.

Calendar of State Papers for Ireland. 4 vols. Nendeln, Liechtenstein: Kraus Reprint, 1974.

Campbell, Mary. *Lady Morgan: The Life and Times of Sydney Owenson*. London: Pandora, 1988.

Campbell, Thomas. *A Philosophical Survey of the South of Ireland, in a Series of Letters to John Watkinson, M.D.* London: W. Stahan and T. Cadell, 1777.

Canning, Rick G. " 'Ignorant, Illiterate Creatures': Gender and Colonial Justification in Swift's Injured Lady and the Answer to the Injured Lady." *ELH* 64 (1997): 77–97.

Cannon, S. F. *Science in Culture*. New York: Science History Publications, 1978.

Canny, Nicholas. "Early Modern Ireland, c. 1500–1700." In *The Oxford History of Ireland*, edited by R. F. Foster, 104–60. New York: Oxford University Press, 2001.

———. "Identity Formation in Ireland." In *Colonial Identity in the Atlantic World, 1600–1800,* edited by Nicholas Canny and Anthony Pagden, 159–212. Princeton: Princeton University Press, 1987.

———. *Making Ireland British, 1580–1650.* New York: Oxford University Press, 2001.

Carpenter, Andrew. *Verse in English from Eighteenth-Century Ireland*. Cork: Cork University Press, 1998.

Carr, John. *The Stranger in Ireland; or a Tour in the Southern and Western Parts of that Country in 1805*. Facsimile reprint. Shannon: Irish University Press, 1970.

Carroll, Clare. "Barbarous Slaves and Civil Cannibals. Translating Civility in Early Modern Ireland." In *Ireland and Postcolonial Theory*, edited by Clare Carroll and Patricia King, 63–80. Cork: Cork University Press, 2003

Carroll, Clare, and Patricia King, eds. *Ireland and Postcolonial Theory*. Cork: Cork University Press, 2003.

Cassirer, Ernst. *Philosophy of the Enlightenment*. Princeton: Princeton University Press, 1950.

Champion, Justin. "Enlightened Erudition and the Politics of Reading in John Toland's Circle." *The Historical Journal* 49 (2006): 111–41.

———. "John Toland, the Druids, and the Politics of Celtic Scholarship." *Irish Historical Studies* 32 (2001): 321–42.

———. *Republican Learning: John Toland and the Crisis of Christian Culture, 1696–1722.* Manchester: Manchester University Press, 2003.

Churchill, Charles. *The Prophecy of Famine. A Scots Pastoral*. London: G. Kearsly, 1763.

Clark, J. C. D. *English Society 1660–1832: Religion, Ideology and Politics During the Ancien Regime*, 2nd ed. Cambridge: Cambridge University Press, 2000.

Claydon, Tony, and Ian McBride, eds. *Protestantism and National Identity: Britain and Ireland c. 1650–1850*. New York: Cambridge University Press, 1998.

Colley, Linda. *Britons: Forging the Nation, 1707–1837*. New Haven: Yale University Press, 1992.

Coombe, Thomas. *Edwin: Or the Emigrant. An Eclogue. To Which Are Added Three Other Poetical Sketches*. Philadelphia: John Dunlap, 1775.

Cooper, George. *Letters on the Irish Nation. Written During a Visit to that Kingdom, in the Autumn of the Year 1799*. London: J. White, 1800.

Congleton, James Edmund. *Theories of Pastoral Poetry in England 1684–1798*. Gainesville: University of Florida Press, 1952.

Connolly, Claire. " 'I accuse Miss Owenson': *The Wild Irish Girl* as Media Event." *Colby Quarterly* 36 (2000): 98–115.

Connolly, S. J. *Allegories of Union in Irish and English Writing, 1790–1870: Politics, History, and the Family from Edgeworth to Arnold*. Cambridge: Cambridge University Press, 2000.

———. "The Glorious Revolution in Irish Protestant political thinking." In *Political Ideas in Eighteenth-Century Ireland*, edited by S. J. Connolly, 27–63. Dublin: Four Courts Press, 2000.

———, ed. *Political Ideas in Eighteenth-Century Ireland*. Dublin: Four Courts Press, 2002.

———. *Religion, Law and Power, the Making of Protestant Ireland, 1660–1760*. Oxford: Clarendon Press, 1992.

———. "Swift and Protestant Ireland: Images and Reality." In *Locating Swift: Essays from Dublin on the 250th Anniversary of the Death of Jonathan Swift, 1667–1745*, edited by Aileen Douglas, Patrick Kelly, and Ian Campbell Ross, 28–46. Dublin: Four Courts Press, 1998.

Corbett, Mary Jean. "Allegories of Prescription: Engendering Union in *The Wild Irish Girl*." *Eighteenth-Century Life* 22 (1998): 92–102.

Corkery, Daniel. *The Hidden Ireland*. Dublin: M. H. Gill, 1925.

Corish, Patrick J. "The Origins of Irish Nationalism." In *A History of Irish Catholicism*, edited by John Brady and Patrick J. Corish, 3:1–64. Dublin: Gill & Son, 1968.

Corsi, Pietro. *Science and Religion: Baden Powell and the Anglican Debate, 1800–1860*. Cambridge: Cambridge University Press, 1988.

Costello, Julie. "Maria Edgeworth and the Politics of Consumption: Eating, Breastfeeding, and the Irish Wet Nurse in *Ennui*." In *Inventing Maternity: Politics, Science, and Literature, 1650–1865,* edited by Susan C. Greenfield and Carol Barash, 173–92. Lexington: University of Kentucky Press, 1999.

Cowan, Brian. "Mr Spectator and the Coffeehouse Public Sphere." *Eighteenth-Century Studies* 37 (2004): 345–66.

Cronin, Mike. *A History of Ireland*. New York: Palgrave, 2001.

Cullen, L. M. *An Economic History of Ireland since 1660*. London: B. T. Batsford, 1972.

———. "The Hidden Ireland: Re-Assessment of a Concept." *Studia Hibernica* 9 (1969): 7–48.

———. "Landlords, Bankers, and Merchants: The Early Irish Banking World, 1700–1820." In *Economists and the Irish Economy from the Eighteenth Century to the Present Day*, edited by A. E. Murphy, 25–44. Dublin: Irish Academic Press, 1984.

Cunningham, John. "Corydon: A Pastoral. To the Memory of William Shenstone, Esq." *St. James's Chronicle or British Evening Post*, March 12, 1763, unpaginated.

Curtis, Edmund. *A History of Ireland*. Routledge: London, 1988.

Daniel, Stephen H. *John Toland: His Methods, Manners, and Mind.* Montreal: McGill-Queen's University Press, 1984

Deane, Seamus. *A Short History of Irish Literature*. London: Hutchinson, 1986.

Defoe, Daniel. *An Argument Proving that the Design of Employing and Enobling Foreigners, is a Treasonable Conspiracy . . . With an Appendix; Wherein an insolent Pamphlet, Entitled, The Anatomy of Great Britain in Anatomiz'd.* London, 1717

———. *An Essay at Removing National Prejudice against a Union with England*. 1706.

Dennis, Ian. *Nationalism and Desire in Early Historical Fiction*. New York: St. Martin's Press, 1997.

Dermody, Thomas. *Poems: Consisting of Essays, Lyric, Elegiac, & C.* Dublin: J. Jones, 1792.

De Valera, Ann. *Antiquarian and Historical Investigations in Ireland in the Eighteenth Century.* Master's thesis, University College Dublin, 1972.

Dickson, David. *New Foundations: Ireland 1660–1800*. Dublin: Irish Academic Press, 2000.

Dilworth, W. H. *The Life of Dr. Jonathan Swift.* [London, 1758.] Reprinted in *Three Biographical Pamphlets, 1745–1758.* New York: Garland Publishers, 1975.

Dobbs, Arthur. *An Essay on the Trade and Improvement of Ireland.* Dublin: J. Smith, 1729.

Dobbs, Francis. *A History of Irish Affairs.* Dublin: M. Mills, 1782.

Dougherty, Jane Elizabeth. "Mr. and Mrs. England: The Act of Union as National Marriage." In *Acts of Union: The Causes, Contexts and Consequences of the Act of Union*, edited by Daire Keogh and Kevin Whelan, 202–15. Dublin: Four Courts Press, 2001.

Douglas, Eileen, et. al. "Introduction." In *Locating Swift: Essays from Dublin on the 250th Anniversary of the Death of Jonathan Swift.* New York: Four Courts Press, 1984.

Douglas, Mary. *Risk and Blame: Essays in Cultural Theory.* London: Routledge, 1992.

Downie, J. A. *Robert Harley and the Press: Propaganda and Public Opinion in the Age of Swift and Defoe.* Cambridge: Cambridge University Press, 1979.

Doyne, Philip. *The Triumph of Parnassus, a Poem. On the Birth of His Royal Highness the Prince of Wales.* Dublin: W. Ross, 1763.

Duddy, Thomas. *A History of Irish Thought.* London: Routledge, 2002.

Dunne, Tom. "Fiction as 'the best history of nations': Lady Morgan's Irish Novels." In *The Writer as Witness: Literature as Historical Evidence*, edited by Tom Dunne, 133–59. Cork: Cork University Press, 1987.

Eagleton, Terry. *Crazy John and the Bishop.* South Bend: University of Notre Dame Press, 1998.

———. *Heathcliff and the Great Hunger.* New York: Verso, 1995.

Eccleshall, Robert. "Anglican political thought in the century after the Revolution of 1688." In *Political Thought in Ireland since the Seventeenth Century*, edited by D. George Boyce, Robert Eccleshall, and Vincent Geoghegan, 36–72. London: Routledge, 1993.

Edgeworth, Maria. *The Absentee.* Edited by W. J. McCormack and Kim Walker. Oxford: Oxford University Press, 1988.

Ehrenpris, Irvin. *Acts of Implication.* Berkeley: University of California Press, 1980.

———. *Swift: The Man, His Works, and the Age.* Cambridge: Harvard University Press, 1962.

Elliott, Marianne. *Partners in Revolution: The United Irishmen and France.* New Haven: Yale University Press, 1982.

Ellis, Steven. *Tudor Ireland: Crown, Community and the Conflict of Cultures 1470–1603.* London: Longman, 1985.

Erskine, Andrew. "The Chairmen: A Town-Eclogue." In *A Collection of Original Poems. By the Rev. Mr. Blacklock, and Other Scotch Gentlemen,* 180–83. Edinburgh: A. Donaldson, 1760.

"Esthonian Poetry." *The Port Folio* 1 (1801): 16.

Evans, Robert Rees. *Pantheisticon: The Career of John Toland.* New York: Peter Lang, 1991.

Fabricant, Carole. "Speaking for the Irish Nation: The Drapier, the Bishop, and the Problems of Colonial Representation." *ELH* 66 (1999): 337–72.

———. "Swift the Irishman." In *The Cambridge Companion to Swift,* edited by Chris Fox, 48–72. Cambridge: Cambridge University Press, 2003.

———. *Swift's Landscape.* Baltimore: Johns Hopkins University Press, 1982.

Ferguson, Oliver Watkins. *Jonathan Swift and Ireland*. Urbana: University of Illinois Press, 1962.

———. "The Last Proposals." In *Jonathan Swift: A Collection of Critical Essays*, edited by Claude Rawson. Upper Saddle River, N.J.: Prentice Hall, 1995

Fergusson, Robert. "A Drink Eclogue." *Weekly Magazine or Edinburgh Amusement*, November 11, 1773, 209–10.

———. "Mutual Complaint of Plainstanes and Causey, in Their Mother-Tongue." *Weekly Magazine or Edinburgh Amusement* March 4, 1773, 306–7.

———. "To Dr. Samuel Johnson: Food for a New Edition of His Dictionary." *Weekly Magazine or Edinburgh Amusement*, October 21, 1773, 114.

Ferris, Ina. *The Romantic National Tale and the Question of Ireland.* New York: Cambridge University Press, 2002.

Fichant, Michel. "Leibniz et Toland: philosophie pour Princesses?" *Revue de Synthèse* 116 (1995): 421–39.

Finkelstein, Andrea. *Harmony and the Balance: An Intellectual History of Seventeenth-Century English Economic Thought*. Ann Arbor: University of Michigan Press, 2000.

Flanagan, Thomas. *The Irish Novelists, 1800–1850*. New York: Columbia University Press, 1959.

Fontana, Biancamaria. *Rethinking the Politics of Commercial Society: The* Edinburgh Review *1802–1832*. Cambridge: Cambridge University Press, 1985.

Foster, R. F. *Modern Ireland 1600–1972*. London: Penguin, 1989.

Fox, Christopher. "Swift's Scotophobia." *Bullan*: *An Irish Studies Journal* 6 (2002): 43–65.

———, ed. *The Cambridge Companion to Jonathan Swift.* Cambridge: Cambridge University Press, 2003.

Gaustad, Edwin S. *George Berkeley in America*. New Haven: Yale University Press, 1979.

Gauti, Kristmannsson. *Literary Diplomacy: The Role of Translation in the Construction of National Literatures in Britain and Germany, 1750–1830.* New York: Peter Lang, 2005.

Gay, John. *The Shepherd's Week. In Six Pastorals*. London: Ferd. Burleigh, 1714.

Gibbons, Luke. "From Ossian to O'Carolan: The Bard as Separatist Symbol." In *From Gaelic to Romantic. Ossianic Translations*, edited by Fiona Stafford and Howard Gaskill, 226–51. Amsterdam and Atlanta: Rodopi, 1998.

———. "Narratives of the Nation: Fact, Fiction and Irish Cinema." In *Nationalisms: Visions and Revisions*, edited by Luke Dodd, 66–73. Dublin: Film Institute of Ireland, 1999.

———. *Transformations in Irish Culture*. South Bend: University of Notre Dame Press, 1996.

Goldie, Mark. "Divergence and Union: Scotland and England 1660–1707." In *The British Problem, c. 1534–1707*, edited by Brenden Bradshaw and John Morrill, 220–45. London: Palgrave Macmillan, 1996.

Goldman, Lawrence. "The Origins of British 'Social Science:' Political Economy, Natural Science and Statistics 1830–1835." *The Historical Journal* 26 (1983): 587–616.

Goldsmith, Oliver. *The Deserted Village, a Poem*. London: W. Griffin, 1770.

Gray, Peter. *Famine, Land and Politics: British Government and Irish Society 1843–1850.* Dublin: Irish Academic Press, 1999.

———. "Ideology and the Famine." In *The Great Irish Famine*, edited by Cathal Póirtéir, 86–103. Chester Springs, Pa.: Dufour Editions, 1995.

Gregory, George. "American Eclogues. Eclogue I. Morning; or the Complaint." *Gentleman's Magazine* 53 (1783): 1043–44.

———. "American Eclogues. Eclogue Ii. Evening; or the Fugitive." *Gentleman's Magazine* 54 (1784): 45–46.

Grotius, Hugo. *The Law of War and Peace: A Documentary History*. Edited by Leon Friedman. New York: Random House, 1972.

Haines, Robert. *Charles Trevelyan and the Great Irish Famine.* Dublin: Four Courts Press, 2004.

Halévy, Elie. *The Growth of Philosophic Radicalism.* London: Faber & Faber, 1927.

Hall, Stuart. "Who Needs 'Identity'?" In *Identity: A Reader*, edited by Paul du Gay, Jessica Evans, and Peter Redman, 1–17. London: Sage Publications, 2000

Harris, Tim. *Politics under the Later Stuarts: Party Conflict in a Divided Society 1600–1715.* London: Longman, 1993.

Harrison, Alan. *Ag Cruinniú Meala: Anthony Raymond (1675–1726), ministéir Protastúnach agus léann na Gaeilge i mBaile Átha Cliath*. Dublin: An Clóchomhar, 1988.

———. "John Toland's Celtic Background." In *John Toland's Christianity Not Mysterious: Text, Associated Works and Critical Essays*, edited by Philip McGuinness, Alan Harrison, and Richard Kearney, 243–60. Dublin: The Lilliput Press, 1997

———. "Scéal na Gaeilge agus an Protastúnachas san ochtú haois déag." *Lá*, February 2, 1995.

Hawkesworth. John. *An Account of the Life of the Revd. Jonathan Swift.* [London, 1755.] Reprinted in *Three Biographical Pamphlets, 1745–1758.* New York: Garland Publishers, 1975.

Hayes-McCoy, G. A. "The Completion of the Tudor Conquest, and the Advance of the Counter-Reformation, 1571–1603." In *A New History of Ireland,* edited by T. W. Moody, 3:94–141. Oxford: Clarendon Press, 1976

Hayton, David. "Anglo-Irish Attitudes: Changing Perceptions of National Identity among the Protestant Ascendancy in Ireland, ca. 1690–1750." *Studies in Eighteenth-Century Culture* 17 (1987): 145–57.

———."From Barbarians to Burlesque: English Images of the Irish c. 1660–1750." *Irish Economic and Social History* 15 (1988): 5–31.

———. "Ideas of Union in Anglo-Irish Political Discourse, 1692–1720: Meaning and Use." In *Political Discourse in Seventeenth- and Eighteenth-Century Ireland*, edited by D. G. Boyce, Robert Eccleshall, and Vincent Geoghegen, 142–68. New York: Palgrave, 2001.

Hayton, D., and D. Szechni. "John Bull's Other Kingdoms: The English Government of Scotland and Ireland." In *Britain in the First Age of Party, 1680–1750: Essays Presented to Geoffrey Holmes*, edited by C. Jones, 241–80 London: Hambledon Press, 1987.

Hearne, Thomas. *The Remains of Thomas Hearne*. Edited by John Buchanan-Brown. London: Centaur Press Ltd., 1966.

Henderson, James P. *Early Mathematical Economics*. Lanham, Md.: Roman & Littlefield, 1996.

Hershbell, Jackson. "Berkeley and the Problem of Evil." *Journal of the History of Ideas* 31 (1970): 543–54.

Hill, Brian W. *Robert Harley: Speaker, Secretary of State and Premier Minister.* New Haven: Yale University Press, 1988.

Hill, Jacqueline. "The meaning and significance of 'Protestant ascendancy,' 1787–1840." In *Ireland After the Union*, edited by Lord Blake, 1–22. Oxford: Oxford University Press, 1989.

Hobsbawm, Eric, and Terence Ranger, eds. *The Invention of Tradition*. Cambridge: Cambridge University Press, 1984.

Hoppen, K. Theodore. *The Common Scientist in the Seventeenth Century: A Study of the Dublin Philosophical Society, 1683–1708*. Charlottesville: University of Virginia Press, 1970.

Hull, Eleanor. *A Text Book of Irish Literature*. 2 vols. New York: AMS Press, 1974.

Hutchison, Terence. *Before Adam Smith: The Emergence of Political Economy 1662–1776.* Cambridge: Basil Blackwell, 1988.

Jacob, Margaret C. *The Radical Enlightenment: Pantheists, Freemasons and Republicans*. Rev. 2nd ed. Morristown, N.J.: Temple Publishers, 2003.

Jenkins, Philip. "The Creation of an 'Ancient Gentry': Glamorgan, 1760–1840." *Welsh History Review* 12 (1984): 24–49.

———. *The Making of a Ruling Class: The Glamorgan Gentry, 1640–1790*. Cambridge: Cambridge University Press, 1983.

Johnston, Joseph. *Bishop Berkeley's Querist in Historical Perspective*. Dundalk: Dundalgan Press, 1970.

Jones, Clyve, and Geoffrey Holmes, eds. *The London Diaries of William Nicolson Bishop of Carlisle 1702–1718.* Oxford: Clarendon Press, 1985.

Jones, Richard. *An Essay on the Distribution of Wealth*. London: J. Murray, 1831.

Justice, George. *The Production of Literature in Eighteenth-Century Britain*. Ph.D. diss., University of Pennsylvania, 1994.

Kearney, Richard. *Postnationalist Ireland: Politics, Culture, Philosophy*. London: Routledge, 1997.

Kelly, James. "Eighteenth-Century Ascendancy: A Commentary." *Eighteenth Century Ireland* 5 (1990): 173–87.

———. "The Genesis of 'Protestant Ascendancy': The Rightboy Disturbances of the 1780s and their Impact upon Protestant Opinion." In *Parliament, Politics and People: Essays in Eighteenth Century Irish History*, edited by G. O'Brien, 93–127. Dublin: Irish Academic Press, 1989.

———. "Jonathan Swift and the Irish Economy in the 1720s." *Eighteenth Century Ireland* 6 (1991): 7–36.

———. "The Origins of the Act of Union: An Examination of Unionist Opinion in Britain and Ireland, 1650–1800." *Irish Historical Studies* 25 (1987): 236–63.

———. " 'We Were All to have been Massacred': Irish Protestants and the Experience of Rebellion." In *1798: A Bicentenary Perspective*, edited by Thomas Bartlett, David Dickson, Dáire Keough, and Kevin Whelan, 312–30. Dublin: Four Courts Press, 2003.

Kelly, Patrick. " 'Industry and Virtue versus Luxury and Corruption': Berkeley, Walpole, and the South Sea Bubble Crisis." *Eighteenth Century Ireland* 7 (1992): 57–74.

———. "Ireland and the critique of Mercantilism in Berkeley's *Querist*." In *George Berkeley: Essays and Replies*, edited by David Berman, 101–16. Dublin: Irish Academic Press, 1985.

———. "Recasting a Tradition: William Molyneux and the Sources of *The Case of Ireland Stated* (1689)." In *Political Thought in Seventeenth-Century Ireland*, edited by Jane H. Ohlmeyer, 83–106. Cambridge: Cambridge University Press, 2000.

Kemble, John M., ed. *State Papers and Correspondence Illustrative of the Social and Political State of Europe from the Revolution to the Accession of the House of Hanover*. London: John W. Parker and Son, 1857.

Kennedy, Liam. *Colonialism, Religion and Nationalism in Ireland*. Belfast: Institute of Irish Studies, 1996.

Khalifa, Rachid. "W. B. Yeats's Politics of Proximity: or The Famine's Absence in Yeats's Poetry." In *Ireland's Great Hunger: Silence, Memory and Commemoration*, edited by David A. Valone and Christine Kinealy, 121–41. Lanham, Md.: University Press of America, 2002.

Kiberd, Declan. *Idir Dhá Chultúr*. Dublin: Coiscéim, 1993.

———. "Irish Literature and Irish History." In *The Oxford Illustrated History of Ireland*, edited by R. F. Foster, 252–53. Oxford: Oxford University Press, 1989.

Kidd, Colin. *British Identities before Nationalism: Ethnicity and Nationhood in the Atlantic World, 1600–1800*. Cambridge: Cambridge University Press, 1999.

———. *Subverting Scotland's Past: Scottish Whig Historians and the Creation of an Anglo-British Identity, 1689–1830*. Cambridge: Cambridge University Press, 1993.

Kinealy, Christine. *A Death Dealing Famine: The Great Hunger in Ireland*. Chicago: Pluto Press, 1997.

———. " 'The Famine Killed Everything': Living with the Memory of the Great Hunger." In *Ireland's Great Hunger: Silence, Memory and Commemoration*, edited by David A. Valone and Christine Kinealy, 1–37. Lanham, Md.: University Press of America, 2002.

Kishlansky, Mark. *A Monarchy Transformed: Britain 1603–1714*. London: Penguin Books, 1996.

Klein, Lawrence E. *Shaftesbury and the Culture of Politeness: Moral Discourse and Cultural Politics in Early Eighteenth-Century England.* Cambridge: Cambridge University Press, 1994.

Landa, Louis. "The Dismal Science in Houyhnhnmland." *Novel* 13 (1979): 38–49.

Langer, Gary. *The Coming of Age of Political Economy*. Westport, Conn.: Greenwood Press, 1987.

Learmont, John. *Poems Pastoral, Satirical, Tragic, and Comic*. Edinburgh: for the author, 1791.

Ledwich, Edward. *Antiquities of Ireland*. 2nd ed. Dublin: John Jones, 1804.

Leerssen, Joep. "Anglo-Irish Patriotism and its European Context: Notes towards a Reassessment," *Eighteenth Century Ireland/Iris an dá chultúr* 3 (1988): 7–24.

———. *Hidden Ireland, Public Sphere*. Galway: Arlen House, 2002.

———. *Mere Irish and Fíor-Ghael: Studies in the Idea of Irish Nationality, its Development and Literary Expression Prior to the Nineteenth Century*. South Bend: University of Notre Dame Press, 1986.

———. *Remembrance and Imagination: Patterns in the Historical and Literary Representation of Ireland in the Nineteenth Century*. South Bend: University of Notre Dame Press, 1997.

Lennon, Joseph. *Irish Orientalism. A Literary and Intellectual History*. Syracuse: Syracuse University Press, 2004.

Lew, Joseph W. "Sidney Owenson and the Fate of Empire." *Keats-Shelley Journal* 39 (1990): 39–65.

Livesey, James. "The Dublin Society in Eighteenth-Century Irish Political Thought." *The Historical Journal* 47 (2004): 615–40.

Lloyd, David. *Ireland After History*. South Bend: University of Notre Dame Press, 1999.

Love, Walter D. "The Hibernian Antiquarian Society. A forgotten predecessor to the Royal Irish Academy." *Studies* 51 (1962): 419–31.

Luce, A. A. *The Life of George Berkeley, Bishop of Cloyne*. New York: Thomas Nelson and Sons, 1949.

"Lunny, Lightwit, and Common Sense. A Stage Eclogue, in Imitation of Virgil's 3d Pastoral." *The Prompter*, February 13, 1736, unpaginated.

Maalouf, Amin. *In the Name of Identity: Violence and the Need to Belong*. Translated by Barbara Bray. New York: Penguin, 2000

Mac Craith, Mícheál. "Charlotte Brooke and James Macpherson." *Litteraria Pragensia* 10 (2000): 5–17.

———. "The Forging of Ossian." In *Celticism*, edited by Terence Brown, 125–42. Amsterdam and Atlanta: Rodopi, 1996.

MacDonagh, Oliver. *States of Mind: A Study of Anglo-Irish Conflict, 1780–1980*. London: Allen and Unwin, 1985.

Macinnes, Allan. "Union Failed, Union Accomplished: The Irish Union of 1703 and the Scottish Union of 1707." In *Acts of Union: The Causes, Contexts and Consequences of the Act of Union*, edited by Daire Keogh and Kevin Whelan, 67–94. Dublin: Four Courts Press, 2001.

MacNeill, Hector. *The Pastoral, or Lyric Muse of Scotland; in Three Cantos*. Edinburgh: Constable, 1808.

Macpherson, James. *The Poems of Ossian and Related Works*. Edinburgh: Edinburgh University Press, 1996.

Mahony, Robert. "Swift, Postcolonialism, and Irish Studies: The Valence of Ambivalence." In *Representations of Swift*, edited by Brian Connery, 217–35. Newark: University of Delaware Press, 2002.

Malcomson, A. P. W. *John Foster. The Politics of the Anglo-Irish Ascendancy*. Oxford: Oxford University Press, 1978.

Mansergh, Daniel. "The Union and the Importance of Public Opinion." In *Acts of Union: The Causes, Contexts, and Consequences of the Act of Union*, edited by Kevin Whelan and Daire Keogh, 126–39. Dublin: Four Courts Press, 2001.

Martin, Martin. *A Description of the Western Islands of Scotland.* London, 1716.

Mather, F. C. *High Church Prophet: Bishop Samuel Horsley (1733–1806) and the Caroline Tradition in the Later Georgian Church*. Oxford: Oxford University Press, 1992.

Maxwell, Constantia, ed. *Irish History from Contemporary Sources, 1509–1610*. London: Allen and Unwin, 1923.

McCaughey, Terence P. "Muiris Ó Gormáin's English-Irish Phrasebook." *Éigse* 12 (1968): 203–27.

McCormack, W. J. *Ascendancy and Tradition in Anglo-Irish Literary History from 1789–1939*. Oxford: Clarendon Press, 1985.

McGann, Jerome. *The Poetics of Sensibility: A Revolution in Literary Style*. New York: Oxford University Press, 1996.

McGuirk, Carol. "Augustan Influences on Allan Ramsay." *Studies in Scottish Literature* 16 (1981): 97–109.

McGuire, J. I. "The Church of Ireland and the 'Glorious Revolution' of 1688." In *Studies in Irish History, Presented to R. Dudley Edwards*, edited by Art Cosgrove and Donal McCartney, 137–49. Dublin: University College, 1979.

McInnes, Angus. *Robert Harley, Puritan Politician.* London: Victor Gollancz, 1970.

McLoughlin, Thomas. *Contesting Ireland. Irish Voices against England in the Eighteenth Century*. Dublin: Four Courts Press, 1999.

McMinn, Joseph. "A Weary Patriot: Swift and the Formation of an Anglo-Irish Identity." *Eighteenth Century Ireland* 2 (1987): 103–13.

McVeagh, John, ed. *All Before Them: 1660–1780. English Literature and the Wider World*, no. 1. London: Ashfield Press, 1990.

Mears, William. *An Historical Account of the Life of Mr. John Toland* in *The Theological and Philological Works of the Late Mr. John Toland*. London, 1732.

Mendyk, Stan A. E. *'Speculum Britanniae': Religional Study, Antiquarianism, and Science in Britain to 1700.* Toronto: University of Toronto Press, 1989.

Miller, Julia Anne. "Acts of Union: Family Violence and National Courtship in Maria Edgeworth's *The Absentee* and Sydney Owenson's *The Wild Irish Girl*." In *Border Crossings: Irish Women Writers and National Identities*, edited by Kathryn Kirkpatrick, 13–37. Tuscaloosa: University of Alabama Press, 2000.

Miller, Liam, and Eileen Power. "Introduction" in *Holinshed's Irish Chronicle.* Dublin: Dolemen Editions, 1979.

Mitchell, Joseph. *The Doleful Swains: A Pastoral Poem. Written Originally in the Scotch Dialect, with an English Version.* London: T. Jauncy, 1720.

Mokyr, Joel. *Why Ireland Starved*. London: Allen and Unwin, 1983.

Molyneux, William. *The Case of Ireland's being bound by acts of parliament in England, stated*. Dublin: Joseph Ray, 1698.

Moore, Dafydd. *Enlightenment and Romance in James Macpherson's The Poems of Ossian*. Aldershot: Ashgate, 2003.

Moore, Lisa L. "Acts of Union: Sexuality and Nationalism, Romance and Realism in the Irish National Tale." *Cultural Critique* 44 (Winter 2000): 113–44.

Moore, Sean. " 'Our Irish Copper-Farthen Dean': Swift's Drapier's Letters, the 'Forging' of a Modernist Anglo-Irish Literature, and the Atlantic World of Paper Credit." *Atlantic Studies* 2 (2005): 65–92

Monod, Paul Kleber. *The Power of Kings: Monarchy and Religion in Europe, 1589–1715.* New Haven: Yale University Press, 1999.

Morgan, Hiram. *Tyrone's Rebellion*. Bury St Edmunds: Boydell Press for the Royal Historical Society, 1993.

Morissey, Thomas J. *James Archer of Kilkenny: An Elizabethan Jesuit*. Dublin: Grenville Printing, 1979.

Moroney, Maryclaire. "Apocalypse, Ethnography, and Empire in John Derrike's *Image of Irelande* (1581) and Spenser's *View of the Present State of Ireland* (1596)." *English Literary Renaissance* 29 (1999): 355–74.

Mullan, John. "Sentimental Novels." In *The Cambridge Companion to the Eighteenth Century Novel*, edited by John Richetti, 236–54. Cambridge: Cambridge University Press, 1996.

Mulligan, Hugh. *Poems Chiefly on Slavery and Oppression, with Notes and Illustrations*. London: W. Lowndes, 1788.

Murphy, Andrew. *But the Irish Sea Betwixt Us: Ireland, Colonialism, and Renaissance Literature.* Lexington: University of Kentucky Press, 1999

Murphy, Willa. "A Queen of Hearts or an Old Maid? Maria Edgeworth's Fictions of Union." In *Acts of Union: The Causes, Contexts and Consequences of the Act of Union*, edited by Daire Keogh and Kevin Whelan, 187–201. Dublin: Four Courts Press, 2001.

Myers, James P. *Elizabethan Ireland: A Selection of Writings by Elizabethan Writers on Ireland.* Hamden, Conn.: Archon Books, 1983.

N., J. "Evening; or, the Politicians: An Eclogue." *Dublin Mercury*, October 8, 1771, unpaginated.

———. "Midnight; or, the Wake. An Eclogue." *Dublin Mercury*, August 22, 1771, unpaginated.

———. "Morning; or the Discovery. An Eclogue." *Dublin Mercury*, August 15, 1771, unpaginated.

———. "Night, or the Charm: An Eclogue." *Dublin Mercury*, September 7, 1771, unpaginated.

Nagle, Christopher. *The Culture of Sensibility in the British Romantic Era.* New York: Palgrave, 2007.

Newenham, Thomas. *A Statistical and Historical Inquiry into the Progress and Magnitude of the Population of Ireland.* London: R. Baldwin, 1805.

Ní Mhunghaile, Lesa. "Muiris Ó Gormáin: Scoláire idir dhá chultúr," In *Aistí in Omós do Mháirtín Ó Briain*, edited by Pádraig Ó hÉalaí and Mícheál Mac Craith. Indreabhán: Cló Iarchonnachta, 2006.

Ní Shéaghdha, Nessa. "Irish Scholars and Scribes in Eighteenth-century Dublin." *Eighteenth Century Ireland/ Iris an dá chultúr* 4 (1989): 41–54.

Nisbet, W. "The Exile." In *Poems; Chiefly Composed from Recent Events*, 95–106. Edinburgh, 1780.

Ní Úrdail, Meidhbhín. *The Scribe in Eighteenth– and Nineteenth-Century Ireland.* Münster: Nodus Publikationen, 2000.

North, Dudley. *Discourses on Trade.* London, 1691.

Norton, David Fate. "The myth of 'British Empiricism.' " *History of European Ideas* 1 (1981): 331–44.

Novak, Maximillian E. *Daniel Defoe Master of Fictions: His Life and Ideas.* Oxford: Clarendon Press, 2001.

Ó Buachalla, Breandán. "The Gaelic Response to Conquest." In *New Perspectives on Ireland*, edited by Daltún Ó Ceallaigh, 51–97. Dublin: Elo Press, 1998.

Ó Catháin, Diarmaid. "Dermot O'Connor, Translator of Keating." *Eighteenth Century Ireland: Iris an dá chultúr* 2 (1987): 68–87.

Ó Ciardha, Éamonn *Ireland and the Jacobite Cause, 1685–1766.* Dublin: Four Courts Press, 2002

Ó Conchubhair, Breandán. *Scríobhaithe Chorcaí 1700–1850.* Dublin: An Clóchomhar, 1982.

O Connor, Murroghoh. *A Pastoral in Imitation of the First Eclogue of Virgil: Inscrib'd to the Provost, Fellows, and Scholars, of Trinity College, Dublin.* [Dublin: James Carson, 1719.] Reprint, *Miscellaneous Poems . . .* published by Mr. Concanen. Dublin: Peele, 1724.

Ó Drisceoil, Proinsias. "Lámhscríbhinní agus na léitheoir coitinata sa 19u haois: John O'-Daly agus foinsí Reliques of Irish Jacobite Poetry." *Léachtaí Cholm Cille* 34 (2004): 257–315.

Ó Gráda, Cormac. *Ireland Before and After the Famine*. New York: Manchester University Press, 1988.

———. "Malthus and the pre-famine economy." In *Economists and the Irish Economy,* edited by Antoin E. Murphy, 75–95. Dublin: Irish Academic Press, 1984.

Ó Háinle, Cathal G. "Towards the Revival. Some Translations of Irish Poetry: 1789–1897." In *Literature and the Changing Ireland*, edited by Peter Connolly, 37–57. Gerrards Cross: Smythe, 1982.

O'Halloran, Clare. *Golden Ages and Barbarous Nations. Antiquarian Debate and Cultural Politics in Ireland, c. 1750–1800*. Cork: Cork University Press, 2004.

———. "Irish Re-Creations of the Gaelic Past: The Challenge of Macpherson's Ossian." *Past and Present. A Journal of Historical Studies* 124 (1989): 69–95.

Ó Laidhin, Tomás, ed. *The Sidney State Papers 1565–70*. Dublin: Dublin Stationery Office for the Irish Manuscripts Commission, 1962.

Ó Muraíle, Nollaig. *The Celebrated Antiquary Dubhaltach Mac Fhirbhisigh (c. 1600–1671): His Lineage, Life and Learning*. Maynooth: An Sagart, 1996.

O'Rahilly, T. F. "Irish scholars in Dublin in the early eighteenth century." *Gadelica* (1912): 156–62.

O'Sullivan, William. "The Irish Manuscripts in Case H in Trinity College Dublin catalogued by Matthew Young in 1781." *Celtica* 11 (1976): 231–32.

Owenson, Sydney (Lady Morgan). *The Wild Irish Girl*. Edited by Brigid Brophy. London: Pandora, 1986.

———. *The Wild Irish Girl: A National Tale*. Edited by Claire Connolly and Stephen Copley. London: Pickering & Chatto, 2000.

———. *The Wild Irish Girl: A National Tale*. Edited by Kathryn Kirkpatrick. New York: Oxford University Press, 1999.

"Pat's Query on the Union." *The Morning Herald*, February 2, 1799.

Peart, Shirley Adawy. *English Images of the Irish, 1570–1620*. Lewiston: Edwin Mellen Press, 2002.

Pinkerton, John. *A Dissertation on the Origin and Progress of the Scythians or Goths: Being an Introduction to the Ancient and Modern History of Europe*. London, 1787.

Pittock, Murray G. H. *Inventing and Resisting Britain: Cultural Identities in Britain and Ireland, 1685–1789*. New York: St. Martin's Press, 1997.

———. *Poetry and Jacobite Politics in Eighteenth-Century Britain and Ireland, Cambridge Studies in Eighteenth-Century English Literature and Thought*. New York: Cambridge University Press, 1994.

Plumb, J. H. *The Growth of Political Stability in England 1675–1725*. London: Macmillan, 1967.

Plumptre, Anne. *Narrative of a Residence in Ireland during the Summer of 1814, and that of 1815*. London, 1817.

Pocock, J. G. A. "British History: A Plea for a New Subject." *Journal of Modern History* 47 (1975): 601–28.

———. "The Limits and Divisions of British History: In Search of the Unknown Subject." *The American Historical Review* 87 (1982): 311–36.

———. "The New British History in Atlantic Perspective: An Antipodean Commentary." *The American Historical Review* 104 (1999): 490–500.

———. *Politics, Language and Time: Essays on Political Thought and History.* New York: Atheneum, 1971.

Pollak, Ellen. *Incest and the English Novel, 1684–1814*. Baltimore: Johns Hopkins University Press, 2003.

Pope, Alexander. *Correspondence of Alexander Pope.* Edited by George Sherburn. 5 vols. Oxford: Clarendon Press, 1956.

Prior, Thomas. *A List of the Absentees of Ireland, and the Yearly Value of their Estates and Incomes Spent Abroad. With Observations on the Present State and Condition of that Kingdom.* 2nd edition. With appendix. Dublin: R. Gunne, 1729.

Radcliffe, David Hill. "Ancient Poetry and British Pastoral." In *From Gaelic to Romantic: Ossianic Translations*, edited by Fiona J. Stafford and Howard Gaskill, 27–40. Amsterdam: Rodopi, 1998.

Ramsay, Allan. *The Ever Green, Being a Collection of Scots Poems*. 2 vols. Edinburgh: Thomas Ruddiman, 1724.

———. *Patie and Roger: A Pastoral Inscribed to Josiah Burchet Esq. Secretary of the Admiralty*. [Edinburgh], 1720.

———. *Poems by Allan Ramsay*. Edinburgh: Ruddiman, 1721. Reprinted in *Works*, edited by Burns Martin and John W. Oliver. Edinburgh: W. Blackwood, 1974.

———. *Richy and Sandy, a Pastoral on the Death of Mr. Joseph Addison*. Edinburgh, 1719.

———. *Robert, Richy and Sandy. A Pastoral on the Death of Matthew Prior, Esq; Dedicated to the Right Honourable Person Design'd by the Old Shepherd.* London: Bernard Lintot and J. Roberts, 1721. Reprinted in, *Works*, edited by Burns Martin and John W. Oliver. Edinburgh: W. Blackwood, 1974.

Rashid, Salim. "The Irish School of Economic Development: 1720–1750." *Manchester School of Economic and Social Studies* 56 (1988): 345–69.

Rawson, Claude. "The Injured Lady and the Drapier: A Reading of Swift's Irish Tracts." *Prose Studies* 3 (1980): 15–43.

Raymond, James Grant. *The Life of Thomas Dermody: Interspersed with Pieces of Original Poetry, Many Exhibiting Unexampled Prematurity of Genuine Poetical Talent: And Containing a Series of Correspondence with Several Eminent Characters*. 2 vols. London: Printed for William Miller . . . and J. Archer and M. Mahon, Dublin, 1806.

Reilly, Patrick. "The Displaced Person: Swift and Ireland." *Swift Studies: The Annual of the Ehrenpreis Center* 8 (1993): 68–82.

Ricardo, David. *Works and Correspondence*. Edited by Piero Sraffa. Cambridge: Cambridge University Press, 1952.

Ritson, Joseph. *The Letters of Joseph Ritson Edited Chiefly from Originals in the Possession of His Nephew*. 2 vols. London: Pickering, 1833.

Robertson, John. "An Elusive Sovereignty: The Course of the Union Debate in Scotland, 1698–1707." In *A Union for Empire,* edited by John Robertson, 198–227. Cambridge: Cambridge University Press, 1995.

Robinson, Nicholas. "Marriage Against Inclination: The Union and Caricature." In *Acts of Union: The Causes, Contexts and Consequences of the Act of Union*, edited by Daire Keogh and Kevin Whelan, 140–58. Dublin: Four Courts Press, 2001.

Rosenheim, Edward E. *Swift and the Satirist's Art*. Chicago: University of Chicago Press, 1963.

Rowley, Hercules. *An Answer to a Book entitled "Reasons offered for erecting a bank in Ireland*." Dublin, 1721.

Ryan, Desmond. *The Sword of Light: From the Four Masters to Douglas Hyde*. London: Barker, 1938.

Sage, John, Thomas Morer and Alexander Monro. *An Account of the Present Persecution of the Church in Scotland, in Several Letters*. London: Printed for S. Cook, 1690.

Said, Edward. *Culture and Imperialism*. London: Chatto and Windus, 1993.

Schirmer, Gregory A. *Out of What Began. A History of Irish Poetry in English*. Ithaca and London: Cornell University Press, 1998.

Schwoerer, Lois G. "The Role of King William III of England in the Standing Army Controversy 1697–1699," *Journal of British Studies* 5 (1966): 74–88.

Semmel, Bernard, ed. *Occasional Papers of T. R. Malthus on Ireland, Population, and Political Economy*. New York: Burt Franklin, 1963.

Shapin, Steven. *A Social History of Truth: Civility and Science in Seventeenth-Century England*. Chicago: University of Chicago Press, 1994.

Sheehan, Anthony. "Irish Towns in a Period of Change, 1558–1625." In *Natives and Newcomers: Essays on the making of English colonial Society, 1534–1641*, edited by Ciaran Brady and Raymond Gillespie, 93–119. Dublin: Irish Academic Press, 1986.

Simms, J. G. "John Toland (1670–1722), a Donegal Heretic." *Irish Historical Studies* 16 (1969): 304–20.

Siskin, *The Work of Writing: Literature and Social Change 1700–1830*. Baltimore: Johns Hopkins University Press, 1998.

Small, Stephen. "The Twisted Roots of Irish Patriotism: Anglo-Irish Political Thought in the Late Eighteenth Century." *Éire-Ireland* 35 (2000–2001): 187–216.

Smith, Anthony. *The Ethnic Origins of Nations*. Oxford: Basil Blackwell, 1987.

Smyth, Jim. *The Making of the United Kingdom, 1660–1800*. London: Longman, 2001.

———. " 'No Remedy More Proper': Anglo-Irish Unionism before 1707." In *British Consciousness and Identity: The Making of Britain 1533–1707*, edited by B. Bradshaw and P. Roberts, 301–20. Cambridge: Cambridge University Press, 1998.

Southam, B. C., ed. *Jane Austen: The Critical Heritage*. London: Routledge, 1968.

Spacks, Patricia. *Privacy: Concealing the Eighteenth-Century Self*. Chicago: University of Chicago Press, 2003.

Spenser, Edmund. *A View of the Present State of Ireland*. Edited by W. L. Renwick. Oxford: Clarendon Press, 1970.

Stafford, Fiona. *The Noble Savage James Macpherson and the Poems of Ossian*. Edinburgh: Edinburgh University Press, 1988.

Stephens, John Calhoun, ed. *The Guardian*. Lexington: University Press of Kentucky, 1982.

Stets, Jan E., and Peter J. Burke, "Identity Theory and Social Identity Theory." *Social Psychology Quarterly* 63 (2000): 224–37.

Stone, Lawrence. *The Family, Sex, and Marriage in England, 1500–1800*. Abridged edition. New York: Harper, 1979.

Stratford, Thomas. "Four Pastoral Essays." *Dublin Mercury*, March 18, July 1, 4, 1769, March 29, April 5, 1770, 1769–70, unpaginated.

Sullivan, Robert E. *John Toland and the Deist Controversy: A Study in Adaptations.* Cambridge: Harvard University Press, 1982

Sweet, Rosemary. *Antiquaries, The Discovery of the Past in Eighteenth Century Britain.* London and New York: Hambledon and London, 2004.

Swift, Jonathan. "Advice to the Free-Men of the City of *Dublin* in the Choice of a Member to Represent them in Parliament." *Irish Tracts 1728–1733.* Edited by Herbert Davis. Oxford: Basil Blackwell, 1979.

———. *Contributions to "The Tatler," "The Examiner," "The Spectator," and "The Intelligencer."* London: George Bell, 1900–1914.

———. *The Correspondence of Jonathan Swift.* Edited by Harold Williams. 5 vols. Oxford: Clarendon Press, 1963–65.

———. *The Correspondence of Jonathan Swift, D.D.* Edited by F. Elrington Ball. 6 vols. London: G. Bell & Sons, 1910–14.

———. *The Examiner. Prose Works.* Edited by Temple Scott. 12 vols.

———. *Irish Tracts 1728–1733.* Edited by Herbert Davis. Oxford: Basil Blackwell, 1964.

———. *Jonathan Swift: Irish Tracts, 1728–1733.* Edited by Herbert Davis. Oxford: Basil Blackwell, 1955.

———. *Jonathan Swift: The Drapier's Letters and Other Works, 1724–1725.* Edited by Herbert Davis. Oxford: Basil Blackwell, 1966.

———. *The Journal to Stella, Vol I.* Edited by Harold Williams. Oxford: Clarendon Press, 1948. New York: Harper, 1975.

———. "Letter IV: To the whole People of Ireland." *Swift's Irish Pamphlets.* Edited by Joseph McMinn, 71–85. Gerrards Cross: Colin Smythe, 1991.

———. *Miscellanies. The Third Volume.* London: Benjamin Motte and Lawton Gilliver, 1733. Reprint, *Poems,* edited by Harold Williams. 3 vols. Oxford: Clarendon Press, 1937/ 66.

———. *Poems of Jonathan Swift.* Edited by Harold Williams. 3 vols. Oxford: Clarendon Press, 1938.

———. "A Proposal for the Universal Use of Irish Manufacture in Cloaths, and Furniture of Houses, &c.," *Swift's Irish Pamphlets.* Edited by Joseph McMinn, 49–55. Gerrards Cross: Colin Smythe, 1991.

———. *The Prose Works of Jonathan Swift.* Edited by Herbert Davis. 9 vols. Oxford: Shakespeare Head Press, 1948.

———. *Prose Works of Jonathan Swift.* Edited by Herbert Davis. 2 vols. Oxford: Shakespeare Head Press, 1948.

———. *Prose Writings, Miscellaneous and Autobiographical Pieces Fragments and Marginalia.* Edited by Herbert Davis. 5 vols. Oxford: Blackwell, 1962.

———. "A Short View of the State of Ireland." *Swift's Irish Pamphlets.* Edited by Joseph McMinn, 107–13. Gerrards Cross: Colin Smythe, 1991.

———. "The Story of the Injured Lady. Written by Herself. In a letter to her Friend, with his Answer." In *Swift's Irish Pamphlet.* Edited by Joseph McMinn, 22–28. Gerrards Cross: Colin Smythe, 1991.

———. *Swift's Irish Pamphlets.* Edited by Joseph McMinn. New York: Barnes and Noble Books, 1991.

Swift, Jonathan, and Thomas Sheridan. *The Intelligencer.* Edited by James Woolley. Oxford: Clarendon Press, 1992.

Tacitus. *The Life of Cnaeus Julius Agricola*. In *Complete Works*. Translated by Alfred John Church and William Jackson Brodribb. Edited by Moses Hadas, 677–706. New York: Random House, 1942.

Tessone, Natasha. "Displaying Ireland: Sydney Owenson and the Politics of Spectacular Antiquarianism." *Èire-Ireland* 37 (2002): 169–86.

"The Billingsgate Contest. A Piscatory London Eclogue." *Universal Spectator and Weekly Journal*, May 25, 1734, unpaginated.

The Drivers: A Dialogue. Cambridge: J. Dodsley, 1770.

Thompson, Paul and Dorothy. *The Account Books of Jonathan Swift*. Newark: University of Delaware Press, 1984

Thomson, Samuel. *Poems, on Different Subjects, Partly in the Scottish Dialec*. Belfast: for the author, 1793.

Todd, Janet. *Sensibility: An Introduction*. London: Methuen, 1986.

Toland, John. *Anglia Libera: or the Limitation and Succession of the Crown of England Explain'd and Asserted*. London, 1701.

———. *An Apology for Mr. Toland, In a Letter from Himself to a Member of the House of Commons in Ireland; written the day before his Book was resolv'd to be burnt by the Committee of Religion*. London, 1697.

———. *The Art of Restoring. Or, the Piety and Probity of General Monk In bringing about the Last Restoration*. London, 1714.

———. *Christianity not Mysterious, or a Treatise Shewing That There is Nothing in the Gospel Contrary to Reason, Nor above it that no Christian Doctrine can be Properly Call'd A Mystery*. London, 1696.

———. *The Danger of Mercenary Parliaments*. London, 1698.

———. *A Defence of Mr. Toland, In a Letter to Himself*. London, 1697.

———. *A Letter to a Member of Parliament, Shewing, that a Restraint on the Press Is Inconsistent with Protestant Religion, and dangerous to the Liberty of Nation*. London, 1698.

———. *Nazarenus, or, Jewish, Gentile, and Mahometan Christianity*, edited by Justin Champion. [1718]. Oxford: The Voltaire Foundation, 1999

———, ed., *The Oceana and Other Works of James Harrington Esq*, 3rd ed. London, 1747.

———. *The Second Part of the State Anatomy, &c.* London, 1717.

———. *The State Anatomy of Great Britain. Containing a particular account of its several interests and parties, their bent and genius*, 4th ed. London, 1717.

———. *Vindicius Liberius: or, M. Toland's Defence of himself, Against the late Lower House of Convocation*. London, 1702.

Topliss, Iain. "Maria Edgeworth: The Novelist and the Union." In *Ireland and Irish-Australia: Studies in Cultural and Political History*, edited by Oliver MacDonagh and W. F. Mandle, 270–84. London: Croom Helm, 1986.

Tracy, Robert. "Maria Edgeworth and Lady Morgan: Legality versus Legitimacy." *Nineteenth-Century Fiction* 40 (1985): 1–22. Reprinted in *The Unappeasable Host: Studies in Irish Identities*, 25–40. Dublin: University College Dublin Press, 1998.

Tracy, Thomas. "The Mild Irish Girl: Domesticating the National Tale." *Èire-Ireland* 39 (2004): 81–109.

Trumbach, Randolph. *The Rise of the Egalitarian Family: Aristocratic Kinship and Domestic Relations in Eighteenth-Century England*. New York: Academic Press, 1978.

Trumpener, Katie. *Bardic Nationalism: The Romantic Novel and the British Empire*. Princeton: Princeton University Press, 1997.

Vallancey, Charles. *A Grammar of the Iberno-Celtic, or Irish Language*. Dublin, 1773.

Vance, Norman. *Irish Literature: A Social History. Tradition, Identity and Difference*. 2nd ed. Dublin: Four Courts Press, 1999.

Vickers, Douglas. *Studies in the Theory of Money, 1690–1776*. London: Peter Owen, 1960.

Victory, Isolde. "The Making of the Declaratory Act of 1720." In *Parliament, Politics and People: Essays in Eighteenth-Century Irish History*, edited by Gerard O'Brien, 9–29. Dublin: Irish Academic Press, 1989.

Walker, Joseph Cooper. *Historical Memoirs of the Irish Bards, interspersed with anecdotes of, and occasional observations on, the music of Ireland*. Dublin: Luke White, 1786.

Walsh, Micheline Kerney. *"Destruction by Peace": Hugh O'Neill after Kinsale*. Monaghan, Ireland: R. & S. Printers, 1986.

"Warbletta: A Suburban Eclogue." *The Grub-Street Journal*, July 19, 1733, unpaginated.

Ward, James. *The Smock-Race, at Finglas: With Some Other Poems and Translations*. Dublin: George Grierson, 1716. Reprint, *Miscellaneous Poems* . . . published by Mr. Concanen. Dublin: Peele, 1724.

Warner, William B. *Licensing Entertainment: The Elevation of Novel Reading in Britain, 1684–1750*. Berkeley and Los Angeles: University of California Press, 1998.

Waterman, A. M. C. "The Ideological Alliance of Political Economy and Christian Theology, 1798–1833," *Journal of Ecclesiastical History* 34 (1983): 231–44

Weinbrot, Howard D. *Britannia's Issue: The Rise of British Literature from Dryden to Ossian*. Cambridge: Cambridge University Press, 1993.

Welch, Robert. *The Companion to Irish Literature*. Oxford: Clarendon Press, 1996.

Whelan, Kevin. *The Tree of Liberty*. South Bend: University of Notre Dame Press, 1996.

White, Terence De Vere. *The Anglo-Irish*. London: Victor Gollancz, 1972.

Wilson, W. Daniel. "Science, Natural Law, and Unwitting Sibling Incest in Eighteenth-Century Literature." *Studies in Eighteenth-Century Culture* 13 (1984): 249–70.

Wordsworth, William. "Preface to *Lyrical Ballads*." In *British Literature 1780–1830*, edited by Anne K. Mellor and Richard Matlak. New York: Harcourt Brace, 1996.

Woolley, James. "Thomas Sheridan and Swift." *Journal of Irish Literature* 16 (1987): 3–32.

Wu, Duncan. *Wordsworth's Reading, 1800–1815*. New York: Cambridge University Press, 1995.

Yeats, W. B. "Introduction" to J. M. Hone and H. M. Rossi's *Bishop Berkeley*. London: Faber & Faber, 1931. Reprinted in W. B. Yeats, *Essays and Introductions*. London: Macmillian, 1969.

York, Neil Longley. *Neither Kingdom Nor Colony: The Irish Quest for Constitutional Rights, 1698–1800*. Washington, D.C.: Catholic University Press, 1994.

Contributors

JILL MARIE BRADBURY is an assistant professor of English at Gallaudet University. She has published articles on the history of prose genres and eighteenth-century economic writings. She is currently working on a comparative study of Restoration and early eighteenth-century Irish and English economic tracts. Bradbury received her PhD from Brown University and holds undergraduate degrees in both English and Economics.

SCOTT C. BREUNINGER is currently an assistant professor of British and Irish History at the University of South Dakota. His research interests focus on early eighteenth-century Irish intellectual history, particularly the political and economic thought of George Berkeley. He has published articles examining Atlantic theories of empire and Berkeley's political sermons and is currently finishing a manuscript that locates Berkeley's non-philosophical work within its specifically Irish context.

EVAN R. DAVIS is associate professor of English at Hampden-Sydney College. He has published articles on castaway narratives, eighteenth-century publishing, and pedagogy and technology, and he is currently working on a study of eighteenth-century collaboration, especially in the works of the Scriblerus Club.

SUSAN B. IWANISZIW, who earned a PhD in English from the University of Pennsylvania, is an independent scholar currently researching modes of forced labor in the Atlantic arena and the interaction of Native Americans, Africans, and European settlers in northern Pennsylvania. She has numerous publications, including reference articles, book chapters, and journal essays, and has edited two books with Ashgate Publishing: *Troping Oroonoko from Behn to Bandeli* (2004); and *Oroonoko: Adaptations and Offshoots* (2006).

SUSAN M. KROEG is associate professor of English at Eastern Kentucky University. She has completed extensive research on Irish travel literature of the late eighteenth and early nineteenth centuries, and her work has appeared in journals such as *Eighteenth-Century Ireland* and *Women's Writing*. Her current projects include a book about British women and domestic tourism in the Romantic period, tentatively entitled *Home Travels and Lady Travellers*.

VIRGINIA LA GRAND is associate professor of English at Trinity Christian College in Palos Heights, Illinois. Her publications include "Brave New Performance Space: Castaway Pedagogy in the Age of Caliban," in *Christian Scholar's Review* 35 (Summer 2006), and "Castaway Detectives and Companionate Marriage: Patterns of Social Engagement in the Post-Colonial Whodunit" in *Christianity and Literature* 65 (Summer 2007), both with the collaboration of Dr. Craig Mattson.

MARGARET MC PEAKE is core faculty in the Humanities BA Program at New College of California where she co-directs an emphasis in Irish Studies. In addition, she is a director of the Crossroads Irish-American Festival, an annual event in San Francisco. Her research focuses on women's roles in constructing community/nation in Irish and Irish American literatures. She is currently at work on a project focused on Irish American women in *Noir* fiction.

LESA NÍ MHUNGHAILE lectures on eighteenth-century Irish literature in the Irish Department of Mary Immaculage College, Limerick, Ireland. She is also Irish language editor of the journal *Eighteenth Century Ireland/ Iris an dá chultúr*. She has published in the Irish, English, and German languages on various aspects of Anglo-Irish antiquarianism and Gaelic scholars and scribes in the eighteenth century, including Charles O'Conor of Belanagare and Muiris Ó Gormáin, and is currently editing a new edition of Charlotte Brooke's *Reliques of Irish Poetry* (1789).

CHRISTOPHER NAGLE is associate professor of English at Western Michigan University. He is the author of *Sexuality and the Culture of Sensibility in the British Romantic Era* (Palgrave, 2007) as well as essays appearing in *ELH*, *Comparative Drama*, and *Persuasions: The Jane Austen Journal*. His current research projects include a book-length study of women writers' political engagement in Anglo-Irish cultural conflict after 1798 and *INISMORE*, a grant-sponsored electronic media resource project for teaching Sydney Owenson's *The Wild Irish Girl*.

DAVID HILL RADCLIFFE is professor of English at Virginia Tech. He has published *Forms of Reflection: Genre and Culture in Meditational Writing* (1993) and *Edmund Spenser: A Reception History* (1996) and scholarly articles on British literature of the early modern era. A principal research interest is the development of modern ideas about culture as developed in eighteenth-century poetry. In 2007 he published *English Poetry 1579–1830: Spenser and the Tradition,* an online database of poetry, commentary, and biography (Englishpoetry.org) that contains texts and commentary for most of the poems discussed in his essay on Irish and Scottish pastorals. He is presently director of the Center for Advanced Technology in the Humanities at Virginia Tech.

DAVID A. VALONE is associate professor of History at Quinnipiac University in Hamden, Connecticut. His primary research focus is on the history of ideas of population control and eugenics in the nineteenth and twentieth centuries. He is the coeditor of three books: *Ireland's Great Hunger: Silence, Memory and Commemoration* with Christine Kinealy; *Philanthropic Foundations and the Globalization of Scientific Medicine and Public Health* with Benjamin B. Page; and *Reverence for Life Revisited: Albert Schweitzer's Relevence Today* with David Ives.

JEFFREY R. WIGELSWORTH is a Social Sciences and Humanities Research Council of Canada Postdoctoral Fellow in the Department of History, Dalhousie University. Dr. Wigelsworth researches the intellectual climate of seventeeth- and eighteenth-century England, specifically studies of the popularization of science and studies of English deism. He is the author of three previous articles on John Toland, which appeared in the *Canadian Journal of History*, *Journal of the Printing Historical Society*, and *History of European Ideas*. He most recent book, *Deism in Enlightenment England: Theology, Politics, and Newtonian Public Science,* is forthcoming from Manchester University Press.

Index